Understanding
SYBASE SQL SERVER 11

A Hands-on Approach

SRIDHARAN KOTTA • GOPINATH CHANDRA • TANYA KNOOP

International Thomson Computer Press

I(T)P ™ An International Thomson Publishing Company

London • Bonn • Boston • Johannesburg • Madrid • Melbourne • Mexico City • New York • Paris
Singapore • Tokyo • Toronto • Albany, NY • Belmont, CA • Cincinnati, OH • Detroit, MI

Copyright © 1997 International Thomson Computer Press

International Thomson Computer Press is
A division of International Thomson Publishing Inc.
The ITP Logo is a trademark under license.

Library Congress Catalog Card Number

ISBN: 1-85032-852-8

For more information, contact:

International Thomson Computer Press
20 Park Plaza, 13th Floor
Boston, MA 02116
USA

International Thomson Publishing GmbH
Königswinterer Strasse 418
53227 Bonn
Germany

International Thomson Publishing Europe
Berkshire House
168–173 High Holborn
London WCIV 7AA
England

International Thomson Publishing Asia
221 Henderson Road #05-10
Henderson Building
Singapore 0315

Thomas Nelson Australia
102 Dodds Street
South Melbourne, 3205
Victoria, Australia
Australia

International Thomson Publishing Japan
Hirakawacho Kyowa Building, 3F
2-2-1 Hirakawacho
Chiyoda-ku, 102 Tokyo
Japan

Nelson Canada
1120 Birchmount Road
Scarborough, Ontario
Canada M1K 5G4

International Thomson Editores
Campos Eliseos 385, Piso 7
Col. Polanco
11560 Mexico D.F. Mexico

International Thomson Publishing Southern Africa
Bldg. 19, Constantia Park
239 Old Pretoria Road, P.O. Box 2459
Halfway House, 1685 South Africa

International Thomson Publishing France
1, rue st. Georges
75 009 Paris France

QEBFF 16 15 14 13 12 11 10 9 8 7 6 5 4 3 2

Library of Congress Cataloging-in-Publication Data

(available upon request)

Publisher/Vice President: Jim DeWolf, ITCP/Boston
Project Director: Chris Grisonich, ITCP/Boston
Manufacturing Supervisor: Sandra Sabathy Carr, ITCP/Boston
Marketing Manager: Kathleen Raftery, ITCP/Boston
Project Manager: Trudy Neuhaus

Editor: J. W. Olsen
Technical Editor: Sethu Meenakshisundaram

Production: mle design • 562 Milford Point Road • Milford, CT 06460

Table of Contents

Acknowledgments

First, I thank God for blessing me with the knowledge to share with you. Special thanks to Sandy Emerson for encouraging us to write this book, for her suggestions, and for her best wishes. I thank many of my friends, especially Gopinath, for his persistence and encouragement to undertake a project of this kind, and his development of Chapters 8, 9, 10, 13, and 14. Though Tanya joined our team after we began the project, she was very helpful in many ways, developing Chapters 1, 2, 3, 5, 17, the section introductions, the "Foundation Topics," and graphics throughout the book.

Special thanks to Sethu Meenakshisundaram for his patience and dedication in reviewing the entire book for technical accuracy in record time. Many thanks to Jim DeWolf and Jose Cartagena for their assistance and coordination. I acknowledge many friends in the Sybase engineering group and in professional consulting and technical support, especially Bob Gallagher.

I acknowledge Trudy Neuhaus and Jerry Olsen for their excellent support reviewing our entire book. I thank the entire production staff. This book evolved in less than eight months because of the sincere contributions of many people. Thanks to all.

Finally, this book was made possible only by extraordinary support received from my family, which words cannot describe. Special thanks to my mom, my wife, Lakshmi, and my children, Guruganesh and Gurubala, for never-ending support and love. I thank my wife for her extraordinary patience.

Sridharan Kotta

I would like to thank Sandy Emerson for accepting our book proposal and for her constant encouragement and advice throughout the project. I would also like to thank Sridharan Kotta for initiating the project and for his invaluable review and feedback for all of the chapters. I would like to thank Tanya Knoop for her outstanding contribution to the style, contents, and graphics for all of the chapters. Sethu Meenakshisundaram did a marvelous job in reviewing our book for technical accuracy. I thank him for his timely and invaluable feedback. Jerry Olsen and Trudy Neuhaus did a splendid job reviewing our book for style and flow. Many thanks to them. Finally, I would like to thank my parents, my wife Sridevi, son Dhiraj, and daughter Deepthi for their cooperation and patience during the many long hours and weekends it took to write this book.

Gopinath Chandra

The close of this project marks the realization of a long-held personal goal, and so it is with deep respect and appreciation that I express my gratitude to both Sri and Gopi for initiating this project, and for their confidence in making me an equal partner. In addition, I want to thank Sandy Emerson of Sybase Press, and International Thomson Computer Press, especially Trudy Neuhaus, for her exceptional management skills and dependable composure; Jerry Olsen, for his superior editing capabilities; and Jo-Ann Campbell, for accommodating the graphics during production. I want to acknowledge the efforts of our technical editor, Sethu Meenakshisundaram. I also appreciate the time F. M. Honsal donated in helping with miscellaneous preproduction tasks. I want to thank Frances Thomas and Dee Elling for being models of competence and for giving me their essential support. Thanks also to Karen Paulsell and Kathy Shelton Saunders for their willingness to share their great knowledge of Sybase systems and for their awesome inspiration. I thank the SQL Server Publications Group for developing the excellent set of documents upon which all books about Sybase are fundamentally based. Thanks too to the SQL Server development team for creating an RDBMS well worth writing about. Thanks to Becky Petersen for her mentorship so long ago. And much heartful appreciation to my family, Judith, Michelle, Geoffrey, and John. Most of all, thanks to my Freddy and Amanda for their enduring patience and support.

Tanya Knoop

Preface

Before we started this project, we observed two things. First, although the Sybase SQL Server product documentation is very good, it is enormous. It includes more than 15 manuals, many of which individually run 300 to 500 pages. The second thing we noticed is that, although bookstores carry several books about Sybase products, there simply aren't any resources for the newcomer to Sybase technology. If you don't already have some background, where do you start?

This book starts at the beginning and explains the full range of SQL Server topics. It distills the information contained in the Sybase documentation set for you so that you know what the essential concepts, commands, and procedures are. It also presents this information in the order you need it so that you can avoid trying to piece together fragments of information you gather by searching in one source after another, with each answer leading to another question.

This book describes SQL Server's technological origins in client/server computing and where SQL Server fits with respect to other Sybase products. The book doesn't just fling around acronyms such as OLTP, DSS, and SMP. Instead, you'll actually learn about on-line transaction processing (OLTP), decision support systems (DSS), data warehousing, and mass deployment. You'll also find much more information on System 11 architecture than exists in any other public source. This book explains SQL Server's engine and client implementation, and breaks down the concepts of symmetric multiprocessor (SMP) systems step by step.

Armed with a solid understanding of the technological context within which SQL Server fits, you'll be ready for a comprehensive discussion of practical topics. Concepts and procedures build on each other as you progress through the book. You'll learn about database devices and how to create and manage them. Then, you'll find out how to populate database devices with databases and data objects, and manage them in such a way as to ensure recoverability, a topic you'll also find right when you need it. You'll learn how to manage users and maintain a secure system.

We also start at the beginning with performance issues, an understanding of which is based on the information given in the first three sections of this book. The fourth, final section introduces a spectrum of performance topics.

This book contains the information you need to integrate quickly and confidently into the pool of knowledgeable Sybase users.

A Comprehensive Approach to Presenting System 11

This book is a comprehensive description of SQL Server that starts with the product's position in today's database computing technology and continues the discussion through the advanced topics of performance and tuning. This book is divided into four sections, which cover topics in the following four categories.

- Technological context
- SQL Server fundamentals
- Installation, configuration, and control
- Performance and tuning

Layout and Style

We present the material in this book in a concise and to-the-point manner to make it as easy as possible to find the information you need when you refer back to it. We do this by using many brief sections that clearly label their topics. We understand that different people learn in different ways: Some learn by doing, some learn by watching, some learn through graphics, some learn through words, but most of us learn best using a combination of these learning tools. So we use a variety of methods to convey the information in this book.

- **Graphics** We provide numerous illustrations to help you understand concepts.

- **Examples** These straightforward, realistic examples illustrate the concepts.

- **Exercises** At the end of Chapters 6 through 15, we provide exercises so that you can test what you've learned and reinforce it. Each chapter also includes answers to all exercises.

- **Tips** The Tips sprinkled throughout this book give extra bits of helpful information that we've garnered through our combined years of experience in the field.

- **Points to Note** Points to Note are blocks of text that call attention to information that you need to keep in mind to successfully perform the task being described.

- **What Happens in the Server** These sections within chapters describe the SQL Server internal behavior associated with the current topic.

Additional Resources

We've made every effort to give you all of the resources that you need to gain a thorough knowledge of SQL Server. We also include extra resources—the SQL Server 11 product documentation set on your *SyBooks* CD and the appendices—which are described in the next sections.

Your SyBooks Companion CD

The CD that accompanies this book contains *SyBooks*, an on-line documentation interface that gives you access to the entire SQL Server documentation set. This documentation is a rich source for reference designed to satisfy both the inexperienced user's preference for simplicity and the experienced user's need for convenience and comprehensiveness. The user's guide and the reference documents address the various needs of users, database and security administrators, application developers, and programmers.

The *SyBooks* CD contains documentation for every product we mention in this book. We hope that you'll make a point of looking at the following SQL Server documentation.

- *Transact-SQL User's Guide* documents Transact-SQL, Sybase's enhanced version of the relational database language. This guide is the most introductory material of the product documentation set.

- *SQL Server System Administration Guide* provides in-depth information about administering servers and databases. It includes instructions and guidelines for managing physical resources, user databases, and system databases, and for specifying character conversion, international language, and sort order settings.

- *SQL Server Performance and Tuning Guide* explains how to tune SQL Server for maximum performance. It includes information about database design issues that affect performance, about query optimization, about how to tune SQL Server for very large databases, about disk and cache issues, and about the effects of locking and cursors on performance.

- *SQL Server Reference Manual* contains detailed information on all of the commands and system procedures discussed in this *Understanding System 11* book.

- *SQL Server Reference Supplement* contains a list of the Transact-SQL reserved words, definitions of system tables, a description of the *pubs2* sample database, a list of SQL Server error messages, and other reference information that is common to all of the manuals.

- SQL Server utility program manuals document the Sybase utility programs, such as **isql** and **bcp**.

You will find instructions for installing the SyBooks CD-ROM in Appendix D.

The Appendixes

This book provides a variety of reference material in three appendices.

- Appendix A: System Tables

- Appendix B: Global Variables

- Appendix C: Transact-SQL Quick Reference, which contains a list of system datatypes, Transact-SQL commands, built-in functions, and system procedures

- Appendix D: SyBooks Installation Guide

A Book for All Platforms

This book devotes roughly equal attention to both concepts and practice. Most of the concepts are consistent on all of the software and hardware platforms that Sybase supports, such as PCs with Microsoft Windows or Windows NT, Sun, HP, and DEC UNIX. However, SQL Server is much easier to install, configure, and manage on desktop platforms, such as Windows NT, because you can use automatic management tools. These tools have sophisticated interfaces through which you can accomplish tasks by point-and-click and drag-and-drop methods. Because administration in nondesktop platforms is less intuitive, we often illustrate the administration tasks using UNIX examples. If you keep in mind that the commands used in SQL Server desktop tools translate into the appropriate SQL Server commands (like the ones you see in the UNIX examples), you'll find it instructive to understand these no matter which administration interface you use.

Style Conventions

The style conventions used in this guide are mostly consistent with those used in the Sybase documentation. The style conventions are shown in the following table.

Sybase style conventions

Key	Definition
command	Command names, utility names, utility flags, and other keywords are in **bold** in syntax statements and in parag graph text.
variable, database object	Parameter variables (words that stand for placeholders that you replace with actual values) and database objects are in *italic*.
{ }	Braces indicate that you choose at least one of the enclosed options. Do not include the braces themselves.
[ ]	Brackets mean choosing one or more of the enclosed options is optional. Do not include the brackets themselves.
( )	Parentheses are to be typed as part of the command.
|	A vertical bar means you may select only one of the options shown.
,	A comma means you may choose as many of the options shown as you like, separating your choices with commas that are typed as part of the command.
" "	Quotation marks in commands are part of the command.

The following example illustrates each of the conventions defined in the accompanying table.

```
sp_addtype typename,
    phystype[(length) | (precision [, scale]) |
        [, "identity" | {"null" | "not null"}]
```

Your Background

This book will be of value to anyone who wants to learn about Sybase SQL Server. However, the following background will help you to get the most from the book.

- Some knowledge of SQL

- A basic understanding of relational database concepts

- A working knowledge of your UNIX or NT operating system

- Access to Sybase SQL Server (preferably version 11.x)

Regardless of your background as you begin reading this book, we believe that by the time you have read through the following pages and the accompanying resources, you will have a solid grounding in the intricacies of Sybase SQL Server System 11. As we turn now to Section I, Technological Context, we will serve as your tour guides, carefully leading you during each step of our journey together.

As you move forward through this book, you may want to refer back to this preface to refresh your memory on the layout and style conventions that you encounter as well as to identify the most appropriate resources that we have provided to further explore the topics that are of most importance and interest to you. Let the journey begin...

Technological Context

This section provides a foundation for the rest of the book by establishing the technological context within which the Sybase SQL Server product resides. It also provides the background that you need to develop a deep understanding of SQL Server from all levels—from the most general big picture to some of the smallest details.

In Chapter 1, Introduction to Database Computing with Sybase SQL Server, you learn about SQL Server's technological origins in client/server computing. You learn about the Sybase family of products and how those products fit together to form an integrated solution for the most common computing requirements, including on-line transaction processing (OLTP), decision support systems (DSS), data warehousing, and mass deployment.

Chapter 2, System 11 Architecture, presents the SQL Server architecture in much more detail than you've seen anywhere else. It explains SQL Server's engine and client implementation, and how it uses operating system threads to handle tasks far more efficiently than a process implementation could. This chapter breaks down the concepts of symmetric multiprocessor systems step by step so you can visualize how SQL Server fulfills client requests. Finally, this chapter gives you a conceptual understanding of transaction management and logging, describes Sybase APIs (Open Server, Open Client, and OmniCONNECT), and explains two- and three-tier system models.

Chapter 3, The SQL Server Engine, describes the components that SQL Server uses to create storage for data and to manage that data. This chapter is an overview of SQL Server's data definition—the characteristics, attributes, and relationships for all SQL Server database objects. Chapter 3 also introduces the system databases and defines SQL Server objects: tables, databases, rules, defaults, indexes, stored and system stored procedures, triggers, and views. Finally, this chapter describes how SQL Server manages database storage and gives an overview of page allocation and row updates.

Chapter 4, System 11.0 Features Provide New Solutions, offers a tour of System 11 features through example solutions to a variety of scenarios. You'll see an approach to Sybase computing solutions from an application developer's perspective—an approach that takes advantage of System 11's unique feature set to solve a wide range of everyday business requirements.

Chapter 5, Interacting with SQL Server, prepares you for practical tasks by introducing the interactive SQL interface that you can use to perform all SQL Server operations at any level of sophistication.

When you finish Section I, you'll have a more sophisticated understanding of what Sybase and System 11 are all about. You'll be well prepared to delve into the practical concepts and procedures of Sections II and III, and you'll have much of the background information you'll need to understand the performance tuning discussion in Section IV.

1

Introduction to Database Computing with Sybase SQL Server

Sybase has one of the most popular database product lines in the industry because, with it, you can create, develop, and maintain an enormous range of computer applications. Sybase SQL Server—at the heart of the Sybase product line—is a high-performance relational database management system (RDBMS) that features an advanced multithreaded architecture, server-enforced integrity, and high transaction throughput for multiple users.

This chapter provides a technological context for understanding SQL Server by covering the following topics.

- Relational database management basics

- Distributed client/server relational database computing

- The core of the Sybase product line

- The most common uses for distributed database computing: on-line transaction processing and decision support

Relevance of Database Systems

Our relatively new ability to create, store, access, and transmit information cheaply and quickly affects so many aspects of modern life that it's easy to take practical computer applications for granted. Here are some examples of how science, education, business, and government use database systems.

- Schools and universities maintain student and course records, and provide reference material for students using database systems.

- Law enforcement agencies prevent and solve crimes using techniques that would be impossible without database systems. For example, they make quick work of matching crimes to criminal records and of analyzing complex physical evidence.

- Banks, stock markets, and investment firms worldwide maintain accounts and associate the accounts with their owners through database transactions.

- Businesses use database systems to track inventories, and to manage employee and customer records.

- Hospitals use databases to maintain patient records, menus, and home care instructions for thousands of conditions.

- Scientists in most fields store and analyze research results with the help of databases. For example, physicists proved the existence of quarks using databases to store voluminous experimental results. They also used computers to help analyze and interpret the data.

- Doctors, chemists, psychologists, financial analysts, lawyers, and engineers are among the many professionals and business people who use database information services to keep up with the latest publications in their fields.

More and more people who work in the computer industry find that their livelihood either already depends in some way on database computing, or it is progressing in that direction.

RDBMS Overview

The Sybase approach to database computing is founded on client/server computing. We discuss that approach in the following sections.

The fundamental characteristic of a database is that it stores data independently of the computer application that uses the data. This characteristic offers many advantages: Applications can share data, reducing the need for redundancy; applications are less affected by data changes; and data access can be controlled for security.

A database organizes a collection of data into a two-dimensional matrix, or table. A database management system (DBMS) maintains the database and allows data users and applications to work with their specific data requirements.

The Relational Model

A *relational database* is one that can link data among multiple tables. There are other types of models, such as the flat-file model, which allow you to manipulate data one table at a time. The relational database depicted in Figure 1-1 holds several tables, with related data indicated by lines leading from one table to the next.

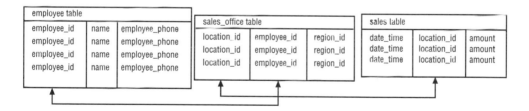

Figure 1-1. *A database with related tables*

Data relationships are classified in the following two ways.

- **One-to-one relationships** For example, one *employee_id* in a *sales_office* table relates to one name in an *employee* table.

- **One-to-many relationships** For example, one *location_id* in a *sales_office* table might relate to many *date_times* in a *sales* table.

Interacting with an RDBMS

Many client interfaces are available that allow you to interact with an RDBMS. Four general categories of RDBMS user interfaces are indicated here.

- Interactive command interfaces such as **isql** (*Interactive* SQL) let you make ad hoc queries and see the results immediately

- Forms-based interfaces that users fill out just as they would a paper form

- Graphical user interfaces (GUIs) present the user with menus and point-and-click options

- Application programming interfaces (APIs) give programmers access to database functions

Mainframe Computing

Mainframe computing was the popular computing model before the client/server model became the widespread standard. In mainframe computing, the mainframe computer performs all processing and uses a "dumb" terminal (one with no processing power of its own) as a display and input unit. The following steps take place to retrieve and display employee information on a dumb terminal.

1. Display a form on the terminal into which a user can specify an employee ID

2. Accept employee ID information

3. Validate the format of the information

4. Check the availability of the employee information

5. Get the employee information from a database

6. Format the data for display on the user's terminal

7. Display the employee information on the terminal

We can categorize these tasks as those related to data presentation (steps 1, 6, and 7), those related to data validation (steps 2 and 3), and those related to data access (steps 4 and 5). In the mainframe model, the mainframe performs all of the steps, because the terminal has no processing capability. In this model, the mainframe does a lot of work to process each client request.

In the client/server computing model, the server and client share the processing. The client machine is often a smart terminal—one that can perform some of the routine processing, such as data presentation and some data validation. This improves performance because the client and server perform the types of processing that each does best. Typically, the client is specialized to handle a range of client-specific tasks so the server has more time for processing requests.

Client/Server Computing in a Database Environment

In just the last few years, the client/server model has gone from being a new trend in distributed (networked) computing to being the standard model for implementing distributed computing. Client/server computing divides processing into *client applications* and *server applications* that cooperate to accomplish tasks for an application as a whole.

Overview of Client/Server Concepts

Under the client/server model, client applications make requests for service. Server applications receive these requests and respond by returning data or other information to the client applications or by taking some action.

Figure 1-2 depicts a common client/server interaction. In this example, the client application makes a request and delivers it to the server. The server application receives the request and processes it (that is, determines what the request means). The server then takes action or returns a result to the client. If the server returns a result, the client receives it and uses it to continue the task it was performing.

Assume that Client A makes a request to print a file named *chapter.doc*. Server A retrieves *chapter.doc* from the file system and becomes a client to the print server. Server A remains a client until the print job is done. If the print server could not print *chapter.doc*, Server A might return an error message to Client A to let it know that its request could not be granted. We say that the server *might* return an error message because that depends on how the server application designer decided to handle print errors.

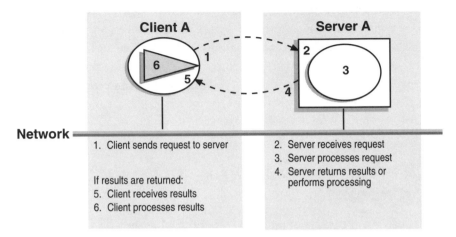

Figure 1-2. Basic client/server interaction

Benefits of Client/Server Computing

Client/server computing offers many advantages over the computing models that preceded it. It allows desktop workstations to present graphical user interfaces (GUIs) and multimedia applications, which simplify computer interactions for the user. The cost of developing applications that use these types of interfaces for desktop workstations is less expensive than it is for mainframe computing.

The client/server computing model also reduces network traffic, thus improving performance. Consider the example given previously in the section titled Mainframe Computing. The mainframe model requires three network events: in step 1 when the mainframe must display the form on the screen, in step 2 when the client sends the employee ID back to the mainframe, and in step 6 when the mainframe sends the employee information back to the terminal. The same example using the client/server model requires only two network events: for step 4 when the client sends the employee ID to the server and in step 6 when the server returns the employee information to the client.

Another advantage of the client/server model is that it allows an organization to use a variety of equipment to meet the needs of different applications and users; that is, it supports a heterogeneous environment. Programmers can get the processing power they need from workstations, and managers can easily work with computers that are best for creating schedules and other spreadsheets using desktop computers. The organization can save money by giving each employee the right amount of computing power to do their jobs.

Finally, the client/server model facilitates implementation of open systems, because it is built around the International Standards Organization's Reference Model for networked systems. This model specifies an application programming interface layer that hides the intricacies of lower level software, making it easier to add new hardware and applications.

Client/Server Nodes and Implementation

Client and server applications can reside on the same computer, or *node*; however, in a distributed computing environment, they are usually on different nodes. We classify nodes as *client nodes* and *server nodes*, depending on their role in a computing environment.

Client nodes tend to be generalized. Computers that run client applications may include many types of clients, such as a directory client, a file client, and a print client. Many nodes often are running the same client applications so that a single server node, such as a print server, serves several client nodes. Although a single server node can accommodate more than one server application, system designers often implement server applications on dedicated server nodes, because servers tend to be more specialized and require more processing and system resources than clients.

A server is typically a continuous process, or *daemon*, while a client is more often a standard application program. During normal processing, a client calls routines to send requests to a server. When the client has finished its work, it stops execution. As a dedicated process, the server runs continuously: It waits for requests, processes them, returns the results, then waits for the next request.

Figure 1-3 shows a typical relationship between client and server nodes on a network. Each client accesses all servers: database server, file server, and print server. The print server might be a client to the file server, and the file server could be a client to the database server.

Relative Roles of Clients and Servers

The terms *client* and *server* characterize relative rather than absolute roles. For example, in executing a print request the print server becomes a client if it asks a file server to send it a copy of a file it wants to print.

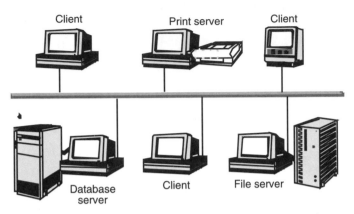

Figure 1-3. *Client and server nodes on a network*

Architecture is fully functional when it allows clients to act as servers and servers to act as clients when necessary. For example, Sybase implements this capability with its Open Client and Open Server products. Sybase applications that have both client and server functionality incorporate both Open Client and Open Server libraries.

Figure 1-4 shows an application that acts as both a client and a server. As a server, it responds to requests from, and returns results to, the Open Client application. As a client, it makes requests of SQL Server and processes the results of those requests.

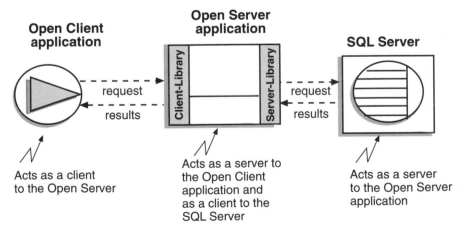

Figure 1-4. *An application can act as both client and server*

Sybase Client/Server Database Environment

In the Sybase client/server database environment, SQL Server runs all of the actual database management system; it does all of the processing associated with database access. The database client does the rest; that is, it does all of the processing *not* associated with database access.

A database server carries out the tasks initiated by client requests directed to the database. It is built on a multithreaded architecture and ensures data integrity, concurrency control, and the ability to recover from failures. The database server also maintains the *data dictionary,* which defines the structure and contents of the database. (If you are not already familiar with these terms, you will be by the time you finish this book.)

In the Sybase environment, the server is SQL Server and the client is any client software that can interact with SQL Server. The **isql** program, for example, is a client application that you use with SQL Server on an ad hoc basis, submitting queries and receiving results on the screen or redirected to a file.

In general, a database client contains application-specific functionality and the processing related to interactions with the user's terminal. These interactions include, among others, keyboard input, display of cursor motions, and mapping of keystrokes.

It is more common for users to work with a program's graphical user interface than to interact directly with a program. GUIs are often forms into which the user types. For example, when a patient checks into a hospital, an intake nurse types registration information into a form managed by a client application. The client application might check the input to make sure that the entered information is consistent with the proper type of data. For example, the application might check that entered dates are valid. The client application might also take the entered information to access the server for related data.

Client/Server Advantage in Sybase

SQL Server's client/server architecture allows applications to reside on separate client workstations or computer-supported terminals, which off-load their tasks from the database server. This allows cooperative processing between an application on one processor and the server on another processor or processors, and is one of the major reasons that SQL Server can handle the workload of hundreds to thousands of users.

Migrating to Client/Server Technology

Typically, an organization evolves toward client/server computing from some other model, such as a mainframe or minicomputer system. It might start by implementing a new client/server model in one department, then gradually extend the model to the entire organization.

An essential consideration in choosing a client/server infrastructure to support the organization is how well the infrastructure can integrate or migrate legacy data—that is, existing applications and data sources. A client/server infrastructure might support data migration from a legacy source to the client/server environment in an acceptable way.

Sybase products can integrate many legacy data sources into distributed systems that are otherwise based on cutting edge technology. Sybase designed its product line to facilitate interoperability between a multitude of data and equipment types.

The Sybase Family of Products

Sybase has developed a clear vision about technology needs for now and for the future. This vision has produced flexible product offerings with customizable options for the three major classes of distributed applications: on-line transaction processing (OLTP), data warehousing, and mass deployment.

Organizations implement these applications using three categories of technology layers: database, middleware, and tools. Table 1-1 summarizes Sybase's strategic product direction, which represents an adaptive and open architecture.

Table 1-1. Sybase's open and adaptive architecture strategy

	OLTP	**Data Warehouse**	**Mass Deployment**
Database	Sybase SQL Server Sybase MPP Sybase IQ	Sybase SQL Server	SQL Anywhere
Middleware	Replication Server DB Gateways Open Server	OmniCONNECT InfoPump	Enterprise Messaging Services
Tools	PowerBuilder S-Designor Watcom Compilers Optima++	PowerBuilder InfoMaker Optima++	PowerBuilder Desktop Optima++

The strategy is adaptive because you can customize the components to meet your organization's distributed computing needs at every level. The strategy is open because each cell in the matrix is independent of the others, so you can use Sybase products with third-party products. For example, you can use a Sybase database server with third-party middleware and tools, or you can use Sybase middleware and tools with third-party database engines.

Table 1-2 gives a quick overview of some of Sybase's most popular products.

Table 1-2. *Sybase database, middleware, and tools products*

Sybase	Product	Description
Database	SQL Server	A high-performance relational database that features an advanced multithreaded architecture, server-enforced integrity, and high transaction and query throughput for multiple users.
	Sybase MP	Lets you distribute processing across multiple SQL Servers while providing a consistent interface for users of very large databases on different platforms. Supports Massively Parallel Processing (MPP).
	Sybase IQ	Uses patented advanced data access technology and query processing techniques to help users navigate through massive amounts data to quickly find what they need. Sybase IQ is built on bitwise indexing technology, which is unique in that it accesses only the minimum amount of data needed to resolve each query, whether it is planned or ad hoc (interactive).
	SQL Anywhere	A PC-based, full-function SQL database management system. You can develop applications on SQL Anywhere and later implement them on larger SQL Server systems without modification. SQL Anywhere also supports message-based communication and mobile operations.

(continued)

Table 1-2. *(continued)*

Sybase	Product	Description
Middleware	Replication Server	Replication Server allows you to create and maintain a copy of the original data at distributed sites. The alternative to Replication Server is typically to access data at a central location from remote locations. Remote database access can be slow and, when long distance networks are down, remote databases are inaccessible.
	Open Client	Open Client Client-Library is a versatile interface for tools and applications that permits access to SQL Server data and other Sybase servers.
	Open Server	Many companies offer the developer a client-side application programming interface, but Sybase's Open Server uniquely offers a server-side API. The implication is that you can develop a custom server for any application or data source.
	OmniCONNECT	OmniCONNECT provides platform independence for users by letting them access and view data from different sources in a single, consistent manner. It also performs cross-platform table joins; for example, between DB, Sybase SQL Server, VSAM, and Oracle.
Tools	PowerBuilder	PowerBuilder is Powersoft's comprehensive development tool for client/server development and deployment. It allows developers to create fast applications with compiled code technology on many different platforms.
	Third-party tools	Sybase Open Partners offer hundreds of compatible applications.

The next three sections describe typical on-line transaction processing, data warehousing, and mass deployment applications.

OLTP Applications

On-line transaction processing typically involves accessing and updating data, and is characterized by a large number of users that need fast on-line access to results. For example, a manager for a large tool store chain wants to look up all the outstanding invoices for customer *Amandala*. Figure 1-5 shows that this query involves a simple join between the *purchase* and *customer* tables that returns three records.

Purchase Table

Cust_id	Purch_date	Invoice_no	Amount
11189	4/20/96	1025	356.02
33060	3/2/90	8001	1585.76
11189	5/11/96	1152	400.32
17623	5/23/96	8991	75.37
14524	9/24/96	1732	1990.22
11189	7/14/96	1002	9035.05

Customer Table

Custo_name	Cust_id	Bill_address	City
Elise & Co.	17623	2001 College Ave	Providence
L. Rico	33060	11 23rd St. #7	San Francisco
Amandala	11189	549 Higher Plc	Hilltown

Outstanding Invoices for Customer Amandala:

Invoice Number	Date	Amount
1025	4/20/96	$356.02
1152	5/11/96	$400.32
1002	7/14/96	$9,035.05

Figure 1-5. *A simple join returning a small result set*

Before Sybase introduced SQL Server, no databases were designed to respond quickly enough for OLTP requirements; now, database OLTP applications are everywhere. Here are some examples.

- A bookstore price scanner scans a bar code, which a bookstore application uses to query a database and retrieve the book's name and price. The application prints this information on your receipt and updates an inventory database.

- A customer at a gas station inserts a credit card into a card reader on the gas pump. After an application checks a central database to ensure that the account is valid, the application writes a message to the pump's display instructing the customer to lift the lever, insert the nozzle into the gas tank, and start filling.

- A customer calls a mail-order nursery to order Iris bulbs from a catalog. The call establishes a connection to the nursery's call-center application program. The application uses the customer's telephone number as input to a caller identification service, which returns the customer's name. The application uses the name to retrieve the customer's past purchase records from the central database. By the time the call-center employee greets the customer, all of the information is on the employee's terminal screen. The employee might begin a conversation with, "Hello, Ms. Leaf, we just received a shipment of those rare Iris bulbs you purchased in 1992. Would you like to order more of them?"

Decision Support and Data Warehousing Applications

In contrast to OLTP, it is common for *decision support system* (DSS) queries to access entire tables or large portions of tables, involve joins among many tables, and return summaries of large result sets. Decision support queries generally answer specific *what?* and *which?* kinds of questions. For example, an airline marketing agent might ask, "What were the most common New York departure times for female business travelers between the ages of 35 and 45 on Fridays during the last seven weeks?" It is usually acceptable for a query to take several minutes or even several hours to complete, because the information is scheduled as part of routine marketing research.

In data warehousing, data may come from different sources and be converted to a format that the database server can use to make queries. Typical data warehouse users include managers, strategic marketers, and merchandisers looking for information to help them understand and predict market trends. A special branch of decision support involves users who apply the results of data warehouse queries to help them make crucial business decisions. Often, users need to make several adjustments to a query before it gives them the most valuable information. A user typically constructs ad hoc queries, then follows up by issuing further queries based on the information they receive. Therefore, the user expects faster results than he or she would accept with a normal DSS query.

Data Replication

Data replication is now one of the most common ways to distribute data to remote sites. If a large number of remote users and remote applications need to perform ad hoc queries, customized batch reports, and transaction processing, the network can bog down. Users and applications must wait unacceptable lengths of time for results. Instead, if you replicate the data to local servers, users can access replicated data locally.

For example, during peak banking hours, many tellers simultaneously use forms on their terminals to enter queries. This can generate a large amount of network traffic, which translates to slow data access for the teller and bank patron if they are waiting for remote transactions that involve a central database at headquarters.

Replication Server

Sybase Replication Server lets you maintain a copy of original data at distributed sites. As Figure 1-6 illustrates, Replication Server transmits data from the primary database server (where data originates) to secondary sites (replicate database servers) on users' local area networks (LANs). Rather than requiring each user to access the remote database server over a long-distance network, Sybase Replication Server handles data transmission and ensures that each local server has an up-to-date copy of the data.

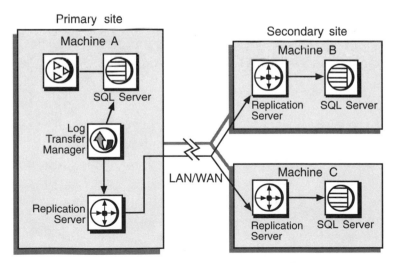

Figure 1-6. *Data replication with Sybase Replication Server*

This approach is a remedy for the problems associated with the direct access method described earlier. Using Replication Server is efficient, because Replication Server only replicates original data that is added, modified, or deleted. It also is fast, because Replication Server copies all of the data to the local server, so users can access it over the LAN. Replication Server provides a third important advantage. If the local data server or the local network is down and transactions need to be replicated, Replication Server performs all of the necessary synchronization when the local network is available to each user.

Here's how Replication Server works. The Log Transfer Manager tracks what data needs to be replicated and puts that data in a queue for replication. Replication Server at the primary site reads the queue and determines where to send the replicated data. The Replication Servers at secondary sites (machines B and C in Figure 1-6) receive the data and store it in a local queue. Finally, the local Replication Servers read their queues and apply the transactions or changes to the replicate database.

MPP: Massively Parallel Processing

When queries involve massive amounts of data, you can speed up processing by dividing the work among several processors rather than waiting for a single processor to do all of the work. This is called *parallel processing*, which can greatly enhance performance for tasks such as sorts, aggregates, report generation, list management, and data maintenance. Parallel processing helps keep performance consistent as you add processors to handle increasing amounts of data, users, or both. Massively Parallel Processing (MPP) is parallel processing on a very large scale. Sybase MPP addresses these needs.

Sybase MPP Server

Sybase MPP (previously known as Navigation Server) distributes processing by linking multiple SQL Servers into what appears to users to be a single, very large database server. The many machines work in parallel to accommodate a much larger database than is possible with any individual database server. All applications and users in the MPP environment communicate with the MPP Server rather than with the individual SQL Servers that are performing the work. MPP Server breaks up the queries, manages processing on the multiple SQL Servers, and consolidates results while providing a consistent interface to users.

The SQL Servers can be single CPU machines, or symmetric multiprocessing machines (SMP) to improve performance even more. Figure 1-7 shows an example in which a service provider for marketing firms stores a national telephone directory database on an MPP system with three SMP machines. In this example, names are stored in alphabetical order such that each of the three SMP machines contains one-third of the database: one for last names starting with letters A to I, one for J to R, and one for S to Z.

If a customer wants to send marketing mail to all people who live in zip code 94114, Sybase MPP Server divides the work among the SMP machines and manages the processing. The SMP machines work simultaneously to deliver all of the addressing information for records in the database with a zip code equal to 94114, and the results are available in roughly one-third of the time.

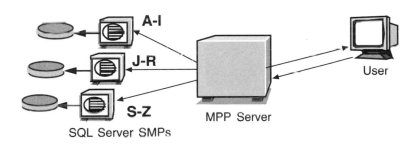

Figure 1-7. *MPP Server divides work and processes it in parallel*

Sybase IQ

Sybase IQ facilitates decision support and data warehousing. Other database environments look up data in the database using an indexing method based on columns. The index stores the column identifier and a pointer to the indexed data. This method occupies more space and takes longer than Sybase IQ's bitwise indexing scheme, a new technology introduced with SQL Server 11. Bitwise indexing is much more efficient than traditional indexing schemes for data sets that have a small range of values (low cardinality) in a large number of rows; for example, five million rows that accept values of *male* and *female*.

Sybase IQ's index technology compresses data so that it uses as little as 40 percent as much disk space as uncompressed data. Compressing data also reduces the number of times that the server gets data from its storage location on a disk, which is another big performance advantage. That's because operations associated with data transmission are more time consuming than any other operation.

Mass Deployment Applications

Mass deployment is a Sybase term that describes applications that run both as independent (standalone) databases on small systems and as connected nodes in a distributed-computing environment. Sybase SQL Anywhere is a Sybase product that supports mass deployment. It is a PC-based, full-function SQL database management system. It supports mobile options, such as remote networks, mobile computers, and other nomadic devices. This "anywhere" idea for sharing data extends the data replication model. SQL Anywhere uses a new replication feature that permits two-way, message-based (like e-mail) replication of data between nodes; for example, between a central database and a laptop in the field.

Future Trends

Computer technology changes so fast that it seems as though we just begin to fully understand the implications of the current industry model, then it changes. Some of the latest changes include trends toward distributed computing using the Internet, including the World Wide Web, and stringent, built-in data security and authenticity methods.

The Internet and the World Wide Web

Widespread Internet use has resulted in an information revolution for those who have a computer, a modem, and a telephone line. Our capability to access information of all types is rapidly changing the way we do so many things—including the way we interact with each other.

The Internet, including the World Wide Web, offers opportunities for computer-based organizations to provide and access information, and supports services in new ways. For instance, research services can return lists of custom-tailored publications in response to a query for specific information.

It almost goes without saying these days that businesses of all descriptions have Web sites that you can browse for product information, marketing collateral, and job postings. Many businesses optimistically view the Internet as a mechanism for improving customer service and interacting with anyone who is interested.

Challenges of the New Paradigm

Database system architects and developers face challenges proportional to opportunities when designing applications for the Internet. Two of these challenges are reconciling Internet paradigms with existing client/server models and security.

The paradigm for developing technology that is well suited for the Internet is different from the client/server paradigm. Protecting an investment in the systems on which we currently depend is as important as keeping up with industry trends. Sybase tools don't make you choose between traditional client/server architectures and Internet-based innovations; some of these tools are PowerBuilder 5.0, web.works, web.sql, and media.splash.

Security is the other issue that we raised. A large number of businesses want to distribute their services over the World Wide Web. These businesses run the gamut from financial institutions, such as banks and brokerage firms, to merchants of food, clothes, music, and vacations. All of them have an issue in common—how to keep information about their customers safe from people who would abuse it. Businesses need ways to keep account numbers, credit card numbers, addresses, and other information reliably secure. Sybase is developing methods for enforcing data security for Internet and Web-based applications.

Built-in Data Security

Integrity and security are critical requirements of on-line applications that involve data access by dozens, hundreds, or thousands of users. Security refers to authorizing and controlling access to data, from requesting a password to ensuring that users and applications don't corrupt or destroy data through improper operations in data sources.

SQL Server has built-in security enforcement and meets the Class C2 standard defined by the Department of Energy. This means that SQL Server does much of the checking and patrolling so that applications don't have to do so. Without this type of central security support, application developers would have to incorporate security measures in every application that accesses the data. Sybase Secure SQL Server offers class B1 security—a more stringent security standard for segments of the US government that include defense and intelligence, and for some civilian organizations.

Higher Security in an RDBMS

Developers of civilian applications would like to see several of these more stringent security features more readily available. For example, consider a personnel database containing information about employees that includes their name, address, marital status, salary, work history, and performance record. Currently, without special security features, a system administrator with permissions to insert or delete a new employee record could also browse the employee database, even if the organization had written rules against doing so. If you want to make sure this kind of thing can't happen, you need mechanisms to prevent and patrol it. Here are two examples.

- To prevent a user who is authorized to access a table but not to freely inspect its contents from browsing, you can encrypt the data. That is, you can render the data incomprehensible to anyone who is not strictly authorized to decode it.

- To patrol a database, you need a mechanism for auditing. That is, you need an after-the-fact way to track who has read, written, or updated something.

In the future, SQL Server will incorporate these and other useful security features.

Summary

This chapter put the Sybase computing environment into perspective by providing a technological context in terms of client/server computing, by describing business and organizational application requirements, and by offering an overview of Sybase solutions that meet these requirements. The next few chapters further set the stage for a more practical look at SQL Server by presenting its architecture and data structure, and by discussing the **isql** interface that you use to communicate with it.

2

System 11 Architecture

Sybase SQL Server 11 architecture is on the cutting edge of relational database technology for its scalability, for its ability to integrate with numerous third-party products, and for its sophisticated multithreaded and multiprocessor implementation. System 11 uses a component approach, which results in an open architecture that offers the freedom to choose the Sybase or third-party components that best suit your application.

This chapter gives you an overview of SQL Server architecture for both single-processor and multiprocessor systems by covering the following topics from an architectural point of view.

- A process model based on multithreading

- The multiple engine concept and client implementation

- Symmetric multiprocessing in System 11

- Low-memory requirements in shared memory

- The kernel and DBMS

- Information about how SQL Server performs disk and network I/O

- Data and procedure cache management

- An examination of Sybase components as part of enterprise architecture by looking at two-tier and three-tier architecture configurations, and Sybase APIs

SQL Server's Multithreaded Process Model

SQL Server is a multithreaded, single-process server. That is, no matter how many users access SQL Server, it consumes only a single operating system process for each server. Each connection consumes only about 65KB of memory. The following sections cover some of the underlying technology on which SQL Server architecture is based. These topics include a discussion of SQL Server's process model, how clients are implemented using threads, and what SQL Server tasks are.

Process and Client Implementation

In systems supported by a single CPU, SQL Server runs as a single operating system process, sharing CPU time with other processes as scheduled by the operating system. Figure 2-1 shows a run queue for a single CPU architecture in which the process with a process identifier (PID) of 8 is running on the CPU, while PIDs 4, 7, 1, and 6 are waiting their turn in the run queue for CPU time. PID 7 in the figure is a SQL Server process; the others can be any other operating system process.

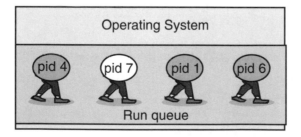

Figure 2-1. *Processes wait their turn in the run queue for a single CPU*

Client Tasks and Threads

SQL Server *clients* are programs that open connections to SQL Server. Examples are **isql**, Open Client Client-Library, and Optima++. A single client can open multiple connections to SQL Server, which launches a new *client task* (thread) for every new connection. SQL Server uses a dedicated stack to track each client task's state during processing. This ensures that only one task at a time accesses a common, modifiable resource such as memory by using *spinlocks*. A spinlock is a special type of resource lock that helps synchronize access to code and memory areas that need to be accessed as though the environment were only single threaded.

The Advantage of Threads over OS Processes

Threads are called *lightweight processes* because they use only a small fraction of the operating system resources that a process uses. Processes require operating system resources to accomplish anything and *switch context* (time-share) from one to the next.

For conventional database management systems with a one-process-per-user architecture, the overhead of paging, context switching, and page or table locking, in addition to other operating system functions, has the potential to reduce throughput. These systems experience reduced performance as the number of users increases, or they require significantly more hardware to perform well. Threads, on the other hand, do not need any operating system resources after they are launched and they can share memory space with each other. SQL Server's multithreaded kernel architecture, running as a single process for each CPU, handles scheduling, context switching, disk caching, locking, and transaction processing without any operating system overhead.

Figure 2-2 illustrates the difference in system resources required by client connections implemented as processes and client connections implemented as threads. Threads exist and operate within a single instance of the executing program and its address space.

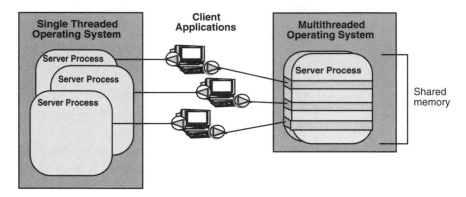

Figure 2-2. *Single-threaded versus multithreaded architecture*

SQL Server Engines and Sybase SMP

Sybase *Virtual Server Architecture* (VSA) extends the performance benefits of Sybase's multithreaded kernel architecture and SQL Server engines to multiprocessor systems. VSA is Sybase's implementation of symmetric multiprocessing (SMP), an environment in which multiple CPUs work together to perform work more quickly than a single processor. What makes it symmetric is the lack of affinity between processes and CPUs. Processes are not attached to a specific CPU.

These sections describe the Sybase multiprocessing system. They introduce the concept of engines, how engines communicate, and SMP processing in general.

Scheduling Engines to CPUs

With multiple CPUs, you can enhance performance by configuring SQL Server to run using multiple server instances called *engines*. All engines are peers that communicate through shared memory. The engines perform all database functions, including updates and logging.

Figure 2-3 represents SQL Server engines as the unshaded ovals awaiting their turn in the run queue for processing time on one of three CPUs. It shows two SQL Server engines, PID 3 and PID 8, being processed simultaneously. If a multiprocessing system had only a single SQL Server engine, SQL Server could not take advantage of multiple CPUs, because it could never run more than one engine at a time. In a system with multiple CPUs, multiple processes can run concurrently.

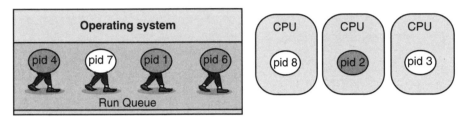

Figure 2-3. *Processes queue for multiple CPUs*

There is no affinity of engines to particular CPUs. The operating system schedules engines to CPUs as CPUs become available in the same way it schedules non-SQL Server processes to CPUs. So it makes sense to run a minimum number of other processes on the database machine.

Scheduling Tasks to Engines

Figure 2-4 shows tasks queued for a SQL Server engine. So tasks are queued for engines, and engines are queued for CPUs. SQL Server, not the operating system, dynamically schedules client tasks onto available engines from its run queue.

When an engine becomes available, it executes any runnable task. The SQL Server kernel schedules a task onto an engine for processing by a CPU for a configurable length of time called a *timeslice*. At the end of the timeslice, the engine yields to the CPU, and the next process in the queue starts. Figure 2-4 also shows a *sleep* queue with two sleeping tasks. Tasks are put to sleep when they are waiting for resources or the result of a disk I/O operation. The kernel uses the task's stack to track its state from one execution cycle to the next.

Engines are numbered sequentially, starting with engine 0. With one exception, all engines do the same work. The exception is this: When a new user logs into SQL Server, engine 0 handles the login to establish packet size, language, character set, and other login settings. After the login is complete, engine 0 determines which engine is managing the fewest user connections and passes the file handle for the new client task to that engine, which then becomes the task's *network engine*.

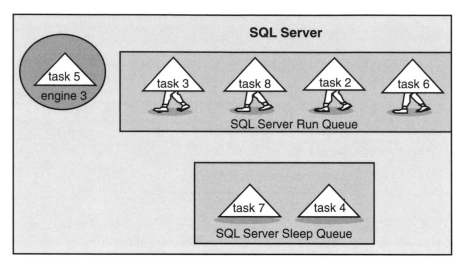

Figure 2-4. *Tasks queue for SQL Server engines*

Communication Among Multiple Engines

In a multiple CPU configuration, multiple SQL Server engines perform operations that affect data. There must be some way to ensure that the objects don't act completely independently. Otherwise, data would quickly become corrupt. Multiple engines share memory to communicate and use spinlocks to coordinate data access. Figure 2-5 illustrates how all of the mutual resources that engines use exist in shared memory, allowing all engines equal access to the following resources.

- SQL Server executable

- Kernel and server structures

- Procedure cache, where stored procedures are kept in cache

- Data cache and overhead, where data and transaction logs are kept in cache

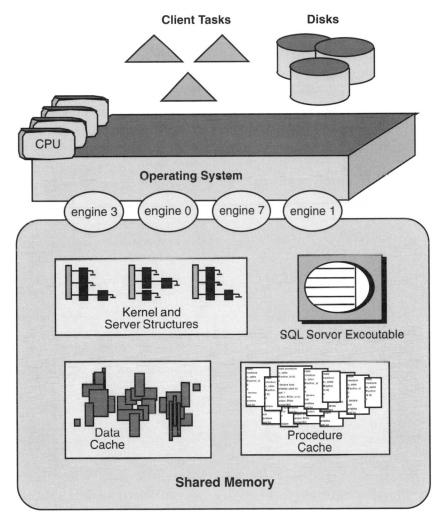

Figure 2-5. *Equal access to shared resources in an SMP environment*

The following sections describe the kernel and server structures, procedure cache, and data cache.

SMP Processing

Figure 2-5 also illustrates the SMP subsystems, consisting of clients, disks, the operating system, multiple CPUs, and the SQL Server executable. In addition, it represents the resources in shared memory, which include data caches and procedure cache; queues for network and disk I/O (not shown); and structures that perform resource management. As shown in Figure 2-4, there is also a sleep queue for processes that are awaiting a resource or that are idle, and there is a run queue for processes that are ready to begin or continue execution.

After a client connection is made, a new task is put to sleep on the run queue, and its network engine checks for incoming client requests every clock tick. When the network engine receives a request, it awakens the task and places it on the end of the run queue.

When the task becomes first in the queue, any available engine can begin execution. The engine parses, compiles, and begins execution. If the task needs to perform disk I/O, the disk I/O request is issued and the task sleeps again. Once each clock tick, the pending I/O queue is checked to see if the task's I/O has completed. If it has, the task is moved to the run queue and the next available engine resumes execution.

When the task needs to return results to a user, it performs a network write using its network engine. The task sleeps again while the network engine begins the network operation and continues with other processing, periodically checking to determine if the network operation is pending. When it is, the network engine loads the network I/O from the network I/O queue. When the write completes, the task is awoken and placed in the run queue. Processing continues in this way.

A single-processor system handles task switching, putting tasks to sleep while they wait for disk or network I/O, and checking queues in the same way.

SQL Server Layout in Memory

SQL Server can handle approximately 16 users for each megabyte of RAM. This low user-memory requirement means that SQL Server can use more of the available memory for data caching, so performance improves because there are fewer disk I/Os. When SQL Server starts, it allocates memory for the executable and other static memory needs. What remains after all other memory needs have been met is available for the procedure cache and data cache. Figure 2-6 shows the SQL Server components that occupy space in shared memory.

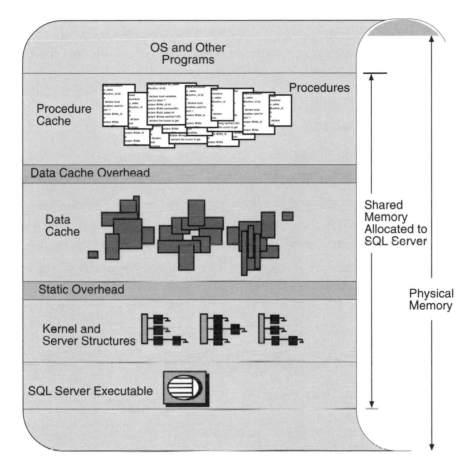

Figure 2-6. *SQL Server layout in memory*

The Kernel and DBMS

When Sybase created its first relational database management system in the early 1980s, one of the principal design goals was efficient use of operating system and hardware resources. Use of a threaded operating system would be a big step toward realizing that goal, but few operating systems supported threading at that time. So Sybase designed its own kernel.

A SQL Server process consists of the kernel and the DBMS. Both perform work associated with tasks. The kernel manages work associated with SQL Server's clients. For example, it tracks the task's state, which is necessary in a multithreaded environment because of context switching. The other component, the DBMS, includes query processing, resource management, and data access. The SQL Server kernel takes care of the following tasks that the DBMS would otherwise require from the operating system.

- Managing scheduling

- Performing task switching

- Handling multiple engines

- Overseeing network and disk I/O

- Performing low-level memory management

- Handling query optimization

Performing this work in the database kernel eliminates nearly all the inefficient operating system overhead typically associated with many relational database management systems. It also results in low memory requirements (as shown in the last section), achieving the goal of efficient use of hardware.

The kernel provides a running environment for the DBMS. As illustrated in Figure 2-7, the kernel creates and manages DBMS tasks, handles disk and network I/O, provides time of day, obtains memory resources from the operating system, and insulates the DBMS, providing operating system and hardware independence.

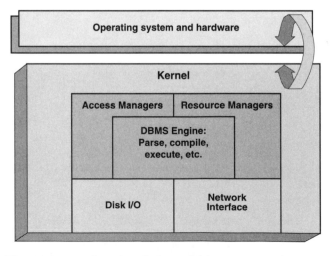

Figure 2-7. *A functional view of SQL Server architecture*

SQL Server requires operating system services for the following tasks.

- Creating and managing processes

- Managing interprocess communication

- Handling device and file requests

- Creating and managing space for objects in shared memory

Server Structures

The kernel manages server structures, which are programming language structures that hold the constructs that SQL Servers uses for system management. These constructs include all services needed for user connections, such as stacks and status structures; lock structures; and many of the configurable aspects of SQL Server behavior. They also include structures that track database object states and those that track devices.

Network Components

SQL Server's network architecture is based on the ISO OSI Reference Model for the network protocol stack. SQL Server supports most common network protocols, and you can install additional protocols if necessary. Application software interacts directly with the Sybase APIs (discussed in a later section in this chapter called APIs), so application developers need not be bogged down by the intricacies of network-level protocols.

Transact-SQL and Tabular Data Stream (TDS)

Tabular Data Stream is Sybase's application-level protocol. TDS implements the key components of presentation, session, and application layers of the OSI Reference Model. It handles the following tasks.

- Establishing connections to servers

- Requesting data and server status

- Receiving data, status, error information, and other SQL Server results

- Requesting stored procedures

- Providing orderly shut down for connections

Application developers need not consider specifics about target data, because TDS provides protocol independence for client applications. TDS handles field types and the number of values returned, as well as other information. The practical result of TDS for the application programmer is that clients can also use remote procedure calls, package commands, bulk copy commands, and message commands, to name a few of the alternatives to Transact-SQL. Sybase's competitors do not offer this advantage.

Disk I/O

The disk I/O operations that take place when SQL Server writes data to, or reads data from, disk have a much bigger impact on SQL Server system performance than any other operation because disk I/O performance includes the time that the CPU and operating system need to process the data packet. So disk I/O is a potential bottleneck in relational database management systems running on-line applications.

The database management system should minimize the number of actual physical reads and writes, and amortize the cost of disk I/O over many users. SQL Server architecture is designed to maximize disk I/O performance. It has several ways to do that, including minimizing the number of I/O operations and performing overlapping disk I/O.

The Data Cache

The data cache contains pages from recently accessed objects, such as tables, log pages, and indexes. The Logical Memory Manager (LMM), which also is referred to as the Buffer Cache Manager in some documents, lets you carve the global data cache into independent caches that you name. You can then bind database objects or entire databases to your named caches.

Without named caches, data access goes something like this. When a query needs to access a table on disk, SQL Server brings the data into the server's data cache. If the cache doesn't have enough room, older data in the cache is written to disk to make room. However, if the data that was just written is needed again, it must be read back into cache. Performance degrades if this happens repeatedly.

You can avoid this problem by using named caches. If you know in advance that certain tables are heavily used, you can create a named cache and associate one or more tables with it so that SQL Server only needs to read that data into cache once; the data does not get flushed. These user-defined caches tailor SQL Server's use of the data cache to meet the system's current work-load requirements. Figure 2-8 illustrates how you might divide the global cache in a hypothetical production environment. If you have a small, very frequently accessed *Customer_List* table, you might want to devote a buffer cache to it that contains enough buffers to keep the entire table in memory. Because no other table shares that cache, its pages remain in memory for quick access. If, on the other hand, you have a large *Payment_History* table that is only used for low priority batch processing, you can allocate a small cache and assign the *Payment_History* table to it. Only old *Payment_History* pages are read, because queries on this table use buffers from the small cache and no other. These reads will not cause valuable pages (such as those in the frequently accessed *Customer_List* table) to be removed from cache.

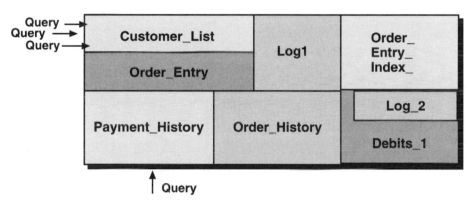

Figure 2-8. *SQL Server 11's named caches*

The Off-Peak Disk Writer

SQL Server *checkpoint* operations write modified pages from cache to disk. In a high-transaction environment, the need to perform frequent checkpoints can become expensive in terms of CPU and disk I/O resources. System 11's *housekeeper* task automatically begins writing changed pages from cache to disk whenever there is an idle cycle. Because of this, they are called *free writes*. The housekeeper provides huge benefits for smoothing system response in transaction-intensive environments. In addition, the housekeeper can improve CPU utilization to reduce recovery time.

Procedure Cache

The *procedure cache* is used for query plans, stored procedures, and triggers. SQL Server offers the capability to store procedures written by the user, and stores hundreds of built-in system procedures that you can use to manage SQL Server and your database objects.

Figure 2-9 shows a client invoking a stored procedure. A copy of the procedure is still in the procedure cache when the next client needs it if it already has been called. If a copy isn't already in the procedure cache, SQL Server creates a compiled query plan from the partially compiled procedure tree on disk. Stored procedures give a three-part performance gain. First, because the procedure is stored as a precompiled tree on disk, it takes less time to prepare for execution. Second, there is a network benefit because the precompiled procedure is less data to transmit then the uncompiled version. Last, after the procedure is in procedure cache, no disk I/O time is associated with running it.

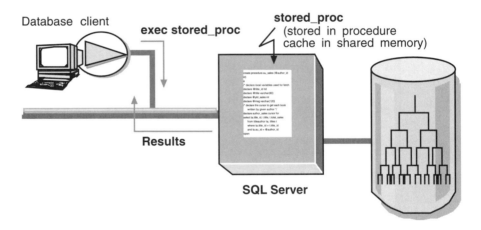

Figure 2-9. SQL Server's use of stored procedures

Overview of Transaction Management and Logging

A DBMS must have a mechanism for tracking all transactions. The SQL Server RDBMS does this by keeping a transaction log for each Sybase database. The transaction log records any changes a user makes to that database. Figure 2-10 shows the data cache during a transaction. The data cache holds the data pages that the transaction is using as well as all other log pages and data pages that currently reside in the data cache.

The transaction log is a write-ahead log. When a user issues a SQL statement that modifies any data in the database, SQL Server automatically writes the change to the log before it writes the change to the actual data page in cache. This strategy ensures that SQL Server can reverse all changes made by a transaction if any part of the transaction fails.

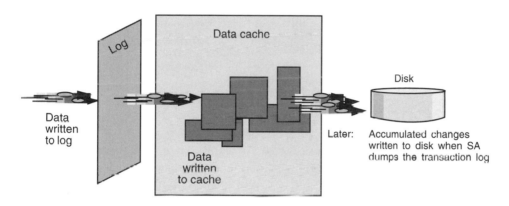

Figure 2-10. *SQL Server writes changes to the log first*

Efficiency and the User Log Cache

Because every transaction involves logging, logging efficiency is very important for good transaction throughput. System 11 uses a logging mechanism called *user log caches* (ULCs) to improve I/O and scalability on multiprocessor systems. These special caches acquire locks in such a way that they dramatically reduce contention.

APIs

The Open Client and Open Server application programming interfaces let you satisfy your unique software requirements by integrating your choice of third-party tools and services into the Sybase environment. The next two sections describe the Open Client and Open Server interfaces, which are based on ISO's Remote Database Access Protocol.

Open Client

Open Client's Client-Library is a versatile interface for tools and applications that lets them access SQL Server data, other Sybase servers, and (when used with Open Server) non-Sybase data and services. Client-Library is an extension of an earlier Sybase client API, Sybase DB-Library. Client-Library incorporates cursors, ANSI SQL syntax, and the initiation of multiple actions on a single connection.

Open Client architecture makes it easy to integrate your non-Sybase applications and tools without the need for porting. For example, you can continue to use the SQL Access Group Call Level Interface or Microsoft's Open Database Connectivity (ODBC) API without the need to modify the applications first.

Open Server

Many companies offer the developer a client-side API, but Sybase's Open Server uniquely opens the door to the client/server communication path through a server-side API. The implication is that you can develop a custom server for *any* application or data source. Sybase offers Open Server as an integrated component in its distributed client/server product line, which you can use to access any client tool or application. The functional diagram in Figure 2-11 illustrates this concept.

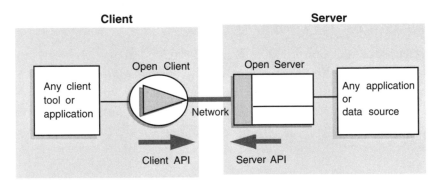

Figure 2-11. Open Server is a server-side API

Open Server In Enterprise-Wide Computing

Open Server's ability to be any kind of server in any kind of client/server topology obviously is extremely valuable in and of itself. In addition to its ability to solve an enormous variety of server problems, Open Server can be the key component in making enterprise-wide client/server implementation possible. In addition, Open Server allows you to reuse the enterprise client/server infrastructure. For example, consider an enterprise with tens of thousands of workstations, each equipped with Sybase Open Client and a connection to the enterprise network. It is highly advantageous to reuse the communication path for every service that each workstation requires rather than to create new communication paths as each new service is added.

Open Server provides a mechanism for making all workstations as standard and efficient as possible, and delivers the ability to reuse the communication path in an enterprise client/server computing environment. Most Open Server applications are based on the following five configurations.

 Standalone server A two-tier topology in which a client connects directly to a standalone Open Server application

 **Gateway server** A topology in which Open Server acts as a translator between an Open Client application and a foreign data source

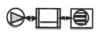 **Application server** A three-tier topology in which the Open Server application resides in a middle tier, independent of the client component and the data server

 **Auxiliary server** A topology in which Open Server extends the functionality of the primary server from the back end

 **Pass-through server** A topology in which Open Server transparently relays client requests and database responses

OmniCONNECT

Sybase OmniCONNECT allows the distributed Sybase system to include databases and data from other vendors. It is an interface that makes cross-vendor combinations invisible to the user. You can even process combinations of data from these different sources in a single query.

Enterprise Architecture

The Sybase architecture and product family provide a wide range of options and configurations with which you can create an infinite number of solutions for enterprises with distributed database requirements. Two versatile examples are the two-tier and three-tier configurations that we discuss next.

Two-Tier Architecture

In a two-tier configuration, client applications connect directly to server applications and submit requests using RPCs and other client commands. The SQL Server application programmer can write custom event handlers to process client requests.

The first tier consists of presentation and application logic. Examples of applications at this level are SQL access tools and application development tools (code generators).

The second tier offers direct service management and handles connections. It can include database servers and general-purpose servers, such as e-mail and print servers. Examples of these applications are SQL Server applications that do not require global distributed transaction support; print, mail, or compute servers built with Open Server; and client-messaging services built on event notification. Figure 2-12 shows SQL Server and Open Server applications in a two-tier configuration.

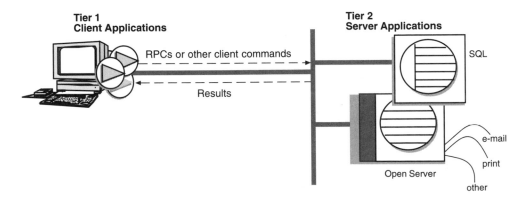

Figure 2-12. *An Open Server two-tier architecture*

Three-Tier Architecture

When developers design and implement software using a component model, they create self-contained software blocks or *components*, each with a specific function. One component can be replaced by another that has the same specifications without rewriting or changing surrounding components. This component model for software design also results in the ability to reuse components.

Three-tier architecture, based on the component model, is a popular design solution for large or complex server applications that run under some type of middleware, such as a transaction processing monitor or an object-oriented environment. Because it is based on the component model, the three-tier architecture allows the flexibility and freedom to replace components without affecting the rest of the system. Figure 2-13 illustrates the three-tier topology using Sybase products.

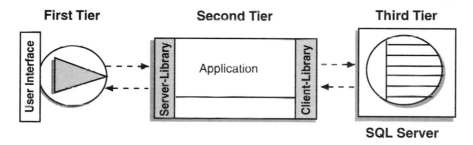

Figure 2-13. *An Open Server three-tier architecture*

The functionality of each tier is as follows.

- The first tier supports presentation services on the client system. Minimally, this tier helps windowing systems display and manipulate data. This tier might also validate user input.

- The second (or middle) tier can support distributed query optimization, it can enforce business rules and referential integrity across all components of the third tier, and it can service mapping similar to a gateway application. This tier is implemented as an intermediate server.

- The third tier is a back-end server that handles data integrity and local transaction branches. It has local responsibility for controlled resources, which are often database systems.

Three-tier architecture gives an application complete independence with respect to both the front-end tool and the back-end datastore, and makes it easy to extend database functionality. Many MIS developers find the three-tier construct imperative.

An example of a three-tier configuration is a pass-through (or transparent) configuration in which servers reside between the client application and the server that contains the datastore. The pass-through server invisibly relays client requests and database responses. Figure 2-13 shows the pass-through server configuration.

In environments that do not support a three-tier topology, developers must integrate business rules, for example, either in the front-end tool or the back-end datastore. Business rules can be integrated with the back-end datastore by programming them in stored procedures or in a *trigger,* a special kind of stored procedure that automatically executes whenever data is inserted, updated, or deleted in the columns with which the trigger is associated. Programming business rules in triggers results in dependence on the datastore. Triggers are discussed in detail in Chapter 8, Database Objects: Tables and Data Integrity, and in Chapter 9, Transact-SQL and Its Extensions.

Summary

This chapter gave you an overview of all the major topics and issues associated with System 11 architecture. Although there is a lot more involved with System 11 architecture, this chapter provided a foundation for understanding why you need to perform many of the commands and procedures presented in Sections II and III. In addition, what you've learned in this chapter is essential for comprehending the performance-tuning topics that Section IV discusses.

3

The SQL Server Engine

SQL Server's *engine* consists of the components that SQL Server uses to create storage for data and to manage (or process) that data. This chapter describes those components. It also introduces SQL Server's data dictionary, or *data definition*—the characteristics, attributes, and relationships for all SQL Server database objects. We begin by discussing the engine's components, including an overview of the relationships among SQL Server's objects. We then go into more detail about the components by discussing the following topics.

- System databases, including the *master*, *model*, *tempdb*, *sybsystemprocs*, and *sybsecurity* system databases

- SQL Server objects, which include tables, databases, rules, defaults, indexes, stored and system-stored procedures, triggers, and views

- How SQL Server manages database storage, including an overview of pages allocation and row updates

Many of the topics in this chapter are more fully discussed in other parts of the book. In such cases, we provide cross references.

Overview of Engine Components

A relational database stores information in database tables, which are composed of a collection of rows and columns containing individual data items. Tables in a relational database are related to one another by one or two like columns that act as links between the tables. Figure 3-1 shows a functional model for SQL Server that illustrates the complexity of the interactions among the objects within it. Starting from the top-left corner of the figure, we take a look inside SQL Server and see two collections of databases.

- A collection of *system databases* that contain system tables in which all of the administrative information about the database system is stored.

- A collection of *user databases* created to do work for the applications that they serve. These user databases also contain some of their own system tables.

Figure 3-1 expands toward the right to show a simplified conceptual depiction of the inside of a user database. Within the database, you see the transaction log and many data tables. Following the figure downward, it zooms into the objects around the table, which we introduce in the "SQL Server Objects" section of this chapter.

This oversimplified representation of the SQL Server system gives only a small view of the number of objects and the interactions that take place among them within a SQL Server system. The SQL Server *engine* is the mechanism for coordinating and managing all of the database system's objects and interactions.

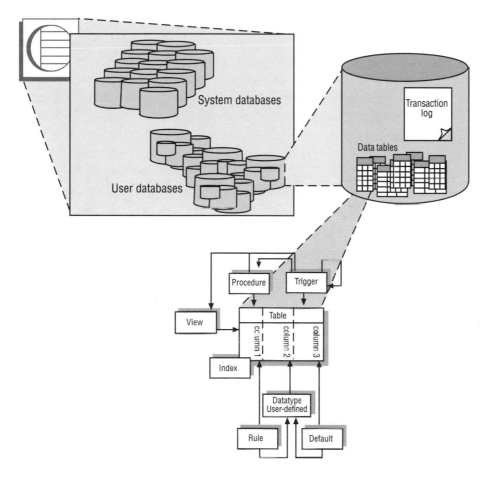

Figure 3-1. *SQL Server object management is complicated*

Databases

SQL Server has two general categories of databases, system databases and user databases. SQL Server uses system databases to manage the entire SQL Server system. User databases are for user data. The following sections give background on system and user databases.

System Databases

The SQL Server installation program installs the system databases that SQL Server uses to manage the entire system. But first, the installation program must create the *master database device* as a storage location for the system databases. A database device is the physical location, such as a disk or operating system file, on which one or more databases reside. (Chapter 6, Database Devices and Fault Tolerance, covers the database device in detail.)

Figure 3-2 shows the system databases—*master*, *model* and *tempdb*—on the *master* database device, and the *sybsystemproc* on the *sybprocdev* database device. The figure also shows an optional database, the *sybsecurity* database, which—if you choose to install it—resides on the *sybsecurity* database device.

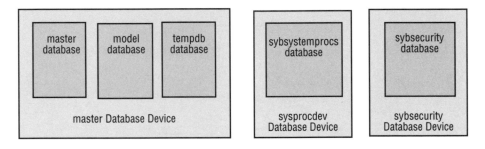

Figure 3-2. *System databases on their database devices*

The master *Database*

All tables in the *master* database are system tables. If you create a new user database, SQL Server automatically establishes some system tables in your new database as well to track database-specific activities. The system tables store control information and have names starting with the prefix *sys*.

The *master* database stores all control information that SQL Server needs to manage the system. For example, SQL Server manages the allocation of disk space to databases using the system tables *sysdevices* and *sysusages*, which store all device and database information, respectively. Another example is the *syslogins* table, which SQL Server uses to control user access. Because of the *master* database's vital role in system status and management, it is important to keep up-to-date backups of this database. Table 3-1 lists the most important system tables.

Table 3-1. *System tables in the master database*

System table name	Information that the table holds
syslogins	Local user accounts
sysremotelogins	Remote user accounts
sysservers	Remote servers with which this server can interact
sysprocesses	Ongoing processes
sysconfigures	Configurable environment variables
sysmessages	System error messages
sysdatabases	Databases on SQL Server
sysusages	Storage space allocated to each database
sysdevices	Tapes and disks mounted on the system
syslocks	Active locks
syscharsets	Character sets
syslanguages	Languages
sysloginroles	Users who hold server-wide roles
syssrvroles	Server roles
sysengines	SQL Server engines that are on-line
sysconfigures	SQL Server's configuration parameters

The model *Database*

SQL Server uses the *model* database as a template for new databases. When you use the **create database** command, SQL Server copies the *model* database to the new database name. If you want to apply custom requirements to every database you create (such as a rule, procedure, or datatype), you can modify the *model* database. Every database you create after that automatically incorporates your requirements; however, this should be done only after careful consideration.

The tempdb *Database*

SQL Server uses the *tempdb* database as a scratch pad to store temporary results while it processes requests. For example, if you issue a SQL command that includes a *group by* clause, SQL Server requires at least two steps to process the command. Here's a simplified synopsis of the process: First, SQL Server processes the command as it would without the *group by* clause and stores the results in *tempdb*; then, it performs the *group by* aspect of the command on the stored results and delivers the final results to you.

The sybsystemprocs *Database*

The *sybsystemprocs* database holds all of SQL Server's system stored procedures. When you execute a system procedure (a stored procedure that starts with the *sp_* preface), SQL Server looks for the procedure in the *sysprocedures* table stored in the current database. If it does not find it there, it looks in the *sybsystemprocs* database. If it still does not find it, it looks in the *master* database. Finally, SQL Server issues an error message if it could not find the system procedure in the *master* database.

The sybsecurity *Database*

The *sybsecurity* database stores auditing information when you use SQL Server's auditing feature. You need to install *sybsecurity* if you use the auditing feature. The *sysauditoptions* system table resides only in the *sybsecurity* database. This table contains one row for each global audit option.

The sybsyntax *Database*

The *sybsyntax* database stores information about Transact-SQL commands, system procedures, utilities, and Open Client DB-Library routines. This database is not automatically installed; if you want to use it, you need to install it using the scripts *ins_syn_sql* and *ins_syn_dblib*.

When you need information about syntax, you can type the following command, replacing the *item* parameter with the command, procedure, utility, or DB-Library routine for which you need a syntax definition.

```
sp_syntax "item"
go
```

The pubs2 *Database*

The optional *pubs2* database is useful as a test database on which you can try commands as you learn them. Almost all of the examples in the Sybase product documentation that show output were performed on or within the *pubs2* database. Consult the SQL Server documentation set on your SyBooks CD for more information.

User Databases

User databases are created to contain and manage data for users. They are created on a database, normally separate from the *master* database. (For details, see Chapter 6, Database Devices and Fault Tolerance, and Chapter 7, Creating and Managing Databases.)

When a user database is created, it contains a set of system tables with entries that describe the system tables themselves. The *sysusers* table contains at least one entry—the user name of the database creator. By default, the database creator is also its owner, though the database creator can transfer ownership to another user. The database owner is granted many privileges and responsibilities for controlling system tables and the rest of the database.

SQL Server Objects

A database is a container for all of the objects that are needed to orchestrate the secure handling of an enormous range of information. Physically, the database is disk storage space made usable by the **create database** command. Logically, a database is composed of a data area and a transaction log area. The data area stores the database objects, which include tables, databases, rules, defaults, indexes, stored procedures, triggers, and views. Figure 3-3 illustrates a user database and its objects.

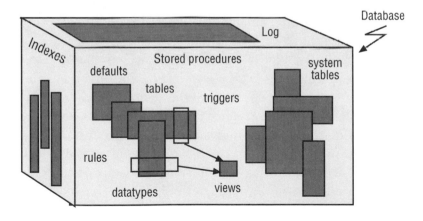

Figure 3-3. *A user database and its objects*

All of the objects covered in the "SQL Server Objects" section of this chapter are discussed in detail in Chapter 8, Database Objects: Tables and Data Integrity, and Chapter 9, Transact SQL and Its Extensions.

Tables

Tables are the storage mechanism for all data in a database. A database table is a collection of like-structured records. Imagine a string of information that consists of a student's name, address, telephone number, and social security number. When you stack a number of these records on top of each other, you get a conceptual picture of a database table. Each row contains the data for one student and each column contains a specific type of information about all of the students in the table.

All of the other objects in a database act on the table to define, protect, access, view, manipulate, and traverse the data. SQL Server has two categories of tables. These categories are system tables, in which SQL Server stores all of the information it uses to coordinate and manage database activities, and user tables, which are normally created by a database designer to serve one or more of the applications that use databases. A database commonly has many tables that are related to one another by common columns of information. For example, the social security number column in the student table described previously could be a link to another table that, in addition to the social security number column, contains a course number and a grade. Figure 3-4 shows a little database and the relationship among just three tables linked to each other in this way.

SQL Server gives you a lot of control over how a user can interact with a table, as you'll see in Chapter 8, Database Objects: Tables and Data Integrity. For example, you can insist that a user insert valid data into a column, or they get an error message and the column is not updated. If the data entry clerk in the admissions department at the university enters all of the information in the student database except for the social security number column and, when you created the table, you specified that no nulls are allowed in that column, SQL Server gives the clerk an error message.

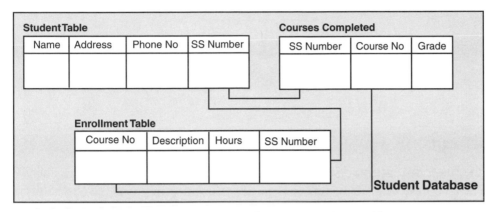

Figure 3-4. *The relationships among three tables*

Datatypes

Datatypes give you a way to tell SQL Server about the characteristics of the data you put in the tables you create. They classify the type of data (character, money, integer, and so forth), the size limits, and how that data is stored in the column with which you associate it. SQL Server provides a set of *system-supplied datatypes*, which include standard ANSI datatypes. In addition, you can make any custom datatype you need by creating a user-defined datatype based on the system-supplied datatypes. The Transact-SQL Quick Reference included at the back of this book lists all system-supplied datatypes.

Rules

Rules specify the domain of legal values for a particular column or datatype. When a user enters data, SQL Server checks whether the table owner has created a rule for columns being updated. If it finds one, SQL Server checks to ensure that the new data does not violate the rule. For example, in the *student* database you might create a rule on the *courseno* column of the *enrollment* table to force the course number to be entered as a specific combination of alpha and numeric digits. Figure 3-5 illustrates a rule on the *courseno* column that requires the first two digits to be uppercase alpha characters between *A* and *Z*, and the last three digits to be integers from *0* through *9*.

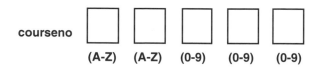

Figure 3-5. *A rule on the* **courseno** *column*

Defaults

Like *rules*, defaults are useful for maintaining data integrity within a database. When you create a table, you can specify to what some or all of the columns default if the user does not enter a value.

Indexes

A database *index* offers the same benefits as a book's index. Rather than searching through all of the pages in a book hoping to find a definition that you know is buried somewhere, you can turn to the index to find a comprehensive summary of the book's contents and corresponding pointers to specific locations. The major deviation from the analogy between a book's index and indexes on tables in SQL Server is that, after the index in SQL Server is created, the user never deliberately accesses the index or directs SQL Server to use it. With rare exceptions, SQL Server makes those decisions itself.

SQL Server uses the index to point directly to the location of a column for which it is looking on disk. Without the index, SQL Server would have to look for the table, then search through the table. Some production environments have thousands of tables, and some of those tables have millions of rows. Consider a database that holds market research on five million American households. The time to identify specific consumer types in this database can be greatly reduced by an index.

In a database, an index is an independent object with a structure similar to that of a data table. Sybase provides clustered indexes and nonclustered indexes. In addition to their usefulness in implementing primary key constraints for data integrity, indexes are generally useful database objects for several reasons. They improve performance by reducing the number of pages to search when looking for data; they help to correlate data across tables; and they order query results.

Stored Procedures and System Procedures

A *stored procedure* is one or more SQL statements and flow-of-control commands that accomplishes a task. The unique thing about a stored procedure is that it is *pre*compiled and stored in a user or system database. Stored procedures reduce network traffic and eliminate the costly overhead of compiling SQL statements each time they are invoked.

System procedures are part of SQL Server's enhanced version of SQL, Transact-SQL. Transact-SQL commands are specialized to give you access to all of the unique features that only Sybase SQL Server offers. Among the numerous advantages they provide over ANSI-standard SQL are that they help you accomplish database administration and performance analysis, and give you access to SQL Server's system tables. You don't have to do anything special to execute system procedures; they execute in sequence with standard SQL commands.

Triggers

A *trigger* is a special, event-driven stored procedure associated with a specific table; it executes whenever a user or application tries to insert, update, or delete information in a table associated with the trigger. In our student database example, illustrated in Figure 3-4, we could have installed a trigger on the social security number column of the *courses completed* table. The trigger would then fire whenever an instructor updates the table for a particular social security number. The procedure associated with the trigger could calculate the student's new GPA and update an honors database if the GPA is above 3.5.

Views

Views give you alternative ways to look at the data in tables. A view can be any combination of rows and columns from a single table or from multiple tables. It is a stored **select** command that behaves like a table, but is actually a virtual table and has no capabilities for storing data.

You can use views to focus, simplify, and customize a user's perception of a database. For example, say that an instructor is looking for information about a student in the *student* database. The instructor's view of the database may be limited to the name and social security number columns in the *student* table combined with the course number column from the *courses completed* table, but not include the student's address or telephone number. The university could have decided that this limited view was necessary to protect the privacy of students.

How SQL Server Manages Storage

Figure 3-6 shows how SQL Server stores data. The *database device* is a specially prepared disk or file device where databases are stored. It is the *physical device*. A *device fragment* is contiguous space allocated on a device for a database. (Chapter 6, Database Devices and Fault Tolerance, discusses these concepts in detail.) Each device fragment for a database is represented by a row in the *master..sysusages* system table. (The preceding construct, *master..sysusages*, indicates the *sysusages* table in the *master* database. The *database..table* construct is commonly used in Sybase documentation.)

The smallest unit of storage in the SQL Server system is a *page*. A page is 2KB, or 2,048 bytes of data (except on Stratus machines, where a page is 4KB). SQL Server has a virtual page (the actual offset on a device for a page within a database) and a logical page (a unique address for pages in the context of each database). SQL Server uses the system tables *sysusages* and *sysdevices* to map virtual to logical pages.

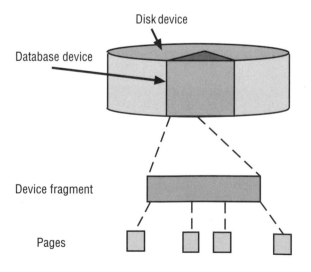

Figure 3-6. *Data storage on SQL Server*

Each page is composed of a body (where the data is stored) a header (which contains information about a page's physical placement relative to other pages), the type of page, status information, and how much space remains. Table 3-2 defines the seven types of pages that SQL Server uses.

Table 3-2. *SQL Server page types*

Page type	What it contains
Data pages	Table data or log data
Index pages	Index data (keys, page pointers, and row identifiers)
Allocation pages	Management information about a group of pages
GAM pages	Management information about allocation pages
OAM pages	Management information about objects
Text/Image pages	Text or image data
Distribution pages	Information about index key values used to optimize queries

SQL Server uses allocation pages, OAM pages, and GAM pages to manage data, indexes, and text.

How a Page Is Allocated

When you do anything that creates, moves, or removes data in a database, such as to create a table or index, add rows to an existing table, or delete rows from an index or a table, SQL Server allocates pages and deallocates pages accordingly in units called *allocation units* and *extents*.

When you use the **disk init** command to prepare physical device space for SQL Server tables, the command creates allocation units containing 256 contiguous logical pages each. SQL Server uses an *allocation page* to manage all of the pages in the allocation unit. Figure 3-7 illustrates two allocation units. The allocation page is the first page of each allocation unit. So in the figure, the allocation pages are page 0 and page 256. The allocation page stores information about all of the extents in the allocation unit.

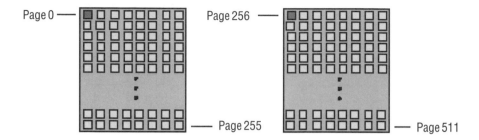

Figure 3-7. *Two allocation units*

Pages are allocated from the unit to a table or index in a blocks of eight pages, called an *extent*. Therefore, each allocation unit contains 32 extents, calculated by dividing the 256 pages in an allocation unit by eight pages per extent.

The Object Allocation Map

The *object allocation map* (OAM) tracks which allocation units contain data for an object. For each unit of allocation, the OAM also tracks the number of pages that are used and unused in the extents allocated to the object. OAM pages facilitate good performance, because they provide a concise map of used and available space so that SQL Server does not have to scan all of the allocation units to find what it needs. OAM pages also help SQL Server allocate new pages in close proximity to those already allocated to the object. This helps improve performance when scanning for an object's pages.

Linking Data Pages

After a page is allocated to a table or an index, it is linked to the other pages associated with the object. Data pages are chained in a double-linked list. The page header fields *nextpg* and *prevpg* indicate next and previous pages. Figure 3-8 shows a new page, Page C, being linked to two existing pages in a chain, Page A and Page B. The lighter, straight arrow shows the original link. Page A's *nextpg* header field points to Page B's address and Page B's *prevpg* header field points to Page A's address. The darker, crooked arrows show two new links from Page A to Page C to Page B. The original link is replaced by the new links.

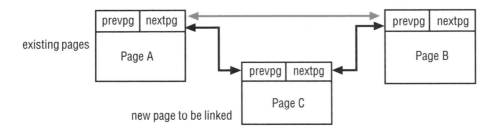

Figure 3-8. *Linking a new page*

In all tables, a field in the *sysindexes* table called *first* points to the first data page of the table. For a table without a clustered index, the *sysindexes* field called *root* points to the last data page. For a table with a clustered index, *sysindexes' root* field points to the root page of the clustered index. Chapter 8, Database Objects: Tables and Data Integrity, more fully discusses these concepts.

How Data Updates Occur

Updates change the data in one or more rows; they don't remove or add rows. SQL Server has two ways to update data. A *direct update*, sometimes called *update in place*, can update data where it is without intermediate steps that require moving the data. In contrast, a *deferred update* method requires deleting the old row and inserting a new one. The direct update method is preferred, because it requires less overhead and is generally faster.

For a direct update, SQL Server uses the table's index to locate the data rows to be updated. Then, because SQL Server uses write-ahead logging (as Chapter 2, System 11 Architecture, explained), it writes the update to the log, then changes the actual data and index pages. There are three types of direct updates, as follows.

- In-place direct updates are updates in which other rows on the page do not move; that is, the row IDs and the pointers do not change.

- Cheap direct updates are the best when SQL Server can't perform an in-place direct update. This type of update rewrites the changed row at the same address, but the surrounding rows move up or down to accommodate any change in length. So row pointers change for the rows that move.

- Expensive direct updates require that the changed row and associated index entries are deleted, then the modified row and index entries are reinserted. SQL Server is forced to use this type of update when the changed data will not fit on the same page as the original data.

SQL Server uses deferred updates when it cannot use direct updates. This situation includes updates that involve joins and updates to columns that are used to protect the data in a table. (This method is discussed with respect to data integrity in Chapter 8.) Deferred updates require more overhead than direct updates, because SQL Server is forced to read from the log to finalize the change to the row and the associated indexes. Update triggers are used on tables that cause deferred updates for trigger processing.

Summary

This chapter gave an overview of how SQL Server's data is organized. It described how the data in SQL Server resides in system databases, if SQL Server uses them to manage the system, or in user databases. User databases can contain a variety of objects, the most important being the table where data is stored. In addition to the table object, you can use other objects to manage and protect user data in a user database. These objects include views, procedures, triggers, indexes, system and user-defined datatypes, defaults, and rules. This chapter also discussed how SQL Server stores and updates data, introducing the concepts of database devices, physical device, and object allocation maps.

Sections II and III of this book discuss these topics in detail, but understanding these ideas now will help you develop a more sophisticated comprehension as the concepts evolve.

4

System 11 Features Provide New Solutions

Sybase SQL Server 11 introduces many features that promote high-performance systems with excellent scalability. This chapter discusses System 11 features and what we mean by scalable. It also provides a different perspective on many of the features that we introduced in Chapter 2, System 11 Architecture, and describes a few features we have not mentioned yet. The difference in this chapter's presentation is that, while Chapter 2 discusses features from an architectural perspective, this chapter considers the features with respect to the types of application solutions they facilitate.

The features this chapter discusses include the following.

- Capabilities to use large I/O sizes that improve performance for I/O-intensive and OLTP applications by allowing more data to be transferred using fewer disk I/O operations

- A user log cache that improves performance for OLTP applications with a fast strategy for transaction logging

- Table partitioning that improves performance for applications with a high number of operations that result in row inserts to tables

- A way to influence the memory manager by creating user-named data caches that improve performance for applications that keep some tables very busy

- A mechanism that allows SQL Server to minimize spinlock contention between processes acquiring locks on data pages or tables

- A network I/O strategy that distributes network I/O tasks to multiple network engines

- An extensive set of configuration parameters that give you the option to influence or control many aspects of SQL Server operation that let you micromanage SQL Server performance if your application calls for it

A Scalable Database System

Scalability in a database system is a way to quantify the ability to maintain performance as the system grows and changes. The growth can be due to an increase in applications or in the number of users, and it usually results in increased use of operating system resources. A scalable system can use new resources, such as CPUs or memory, efficiently to improve performance, or at least to maintain it at a constant level.

Most factors that affect how fast a system responds to queries also affect scalability. For example, more processes involve more competition for shared resources. Without many System 11 features, a query might be slow, because it must await its turn for data or some other shared resource. Many of the features relieve query performance bottlenecks. The multiple network engine feature in particular purely addresses scalability. The following sections explain how System 11 features address query performance and scalability bottlenecks.

Relief for I/O-Intensive Applications with Large I/O

When an application issues a call to read data, SQL Server uses a default I/O size of 2KB. The overhead associated with an I/O operation is constant and consists mostly of queuing, seeking, positioning heads on the disk, and so forth. Large I/O yields better performance, because for the same overhead, SQL Server can read or write more data. Consider an application that uses an I/O size of 2KB to read 160KB of data. The same application configured for a 16KB I/O size takes an eighth of the time to read the same 160KB of data, assuming that there is no seek time latency, because the I/O size has been increased eight fold.

You can also use large I/O for the transaction log. The default I/O size for a database's transaction log is 4KB. If the *syslogs* system table is bound to a data cache that does not support a 4KB log, SQL Server uses only 2KB as the I/O size. OLTP applications spend a relatively large amount of processing time writing data from the transaction log in cache to disk. If SQL Server uses a 2KB cache size, it has to perform more I/O operations than it would if the log is configured to perform 16KB I/O blocks. Again, with the larger I/O size, SQL Server performs fewer I/Os to write the same amount of data.

Fast Transaction Logging with ULCs

In a DBMS, any change to the data should be recoverable. The mechanism SQL Server uses to ensure that data is recoverable is the transaction log (introduced in Chapter 2, System 11 Architecture). In a typical OLTP system, many users insert and modify data at a high rate. To avoid contention for the transaction log, SQL Server keeps the data changes in a user log cache, or ULC. The user log cache is transferred to the on-disk transaction log at a suitable time.

In pre-System 11, the records generated by the data modification commands, **insert**, **update**, and **delete**, are appended directly to the transaction log. When log records from many transactions accumulate, all of them might be written to the transaction log at the same time. If this happens, all of the tasks writing to the transaction log try to acquire a lock on the transaction log at the same time, which results in competition, or contention, on the transaction log. Because only one task can write to the log at one time, the others must wait, which negatively impacts performance.

Consider an example in a sales order entry application. Sixty users are performing data modification: 20 users insert orders, 20 users update orders, and 20 users delete orders. In traditional logging algorithms, the tasks associated with all 60 users could try to write to the transaction log at the same time. Such a situation creates contention for access to the transaction log (which is actually the system table *syslogs*), because only one transaction can write to it at a time. As the number of transactions increases, the time it takes to access the transaction log also increases, resulting in performance degradation.

System 11 eliminates this performance bottleneck by holding the log records for each transaction in a user log cache. (Each user log cache holds information pertaining to one transaction.) So for our example, in which there are 60 users and 60 active transactions, there would be 60 user log caches. As each transaction completes, the data in a user log cache is written to the transaction log. After the user log cache is written, it ceases to exist. SQL Server improves performance for multiple transactions in a given database by maintaining separate caches for each transaction.

Figure 4-1 compares pre-System 10 and System 11 transaction logging. In the top half of the figure, all transactions write to the transaction log. In the lower half of the figure, each transaction has its own user log cache. Database administrators can configure the size of each ULC using the SQL Server configuration parameter *user log cache size*.

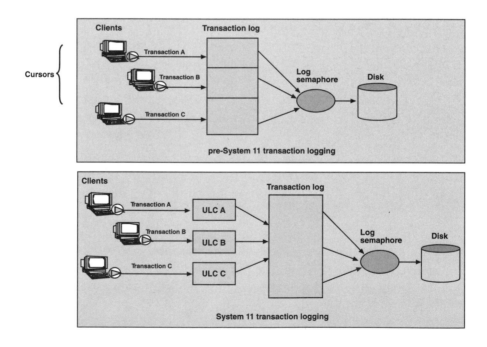

Figure 4-1. *Data logging in pre-System 10 and System 11*

Fast Row Inserts with Table Partitioning

SQL Server 11's *table partitioning* feature overcomes the performance problems that can occur when many users perform operations that result in simultaneous row inserts. To illustrate, consider again the example of the sales order entry application. Say that many sales people place new orders that result in simultaneous requests for row inserts to the *orders* table. The conventional algorithm for inserting a row excludes the possibility of simultaneous inserts. So the more simultaneous insert requests there are, the longer it takes for SQL Server to fulfill the requests, because whenever a row is inserted, SQL Server locks the whole data page that contains the new inserted row. No other process can insert a row into that page until the first process releases the lock. Table partitioning lets you configure heavily used tables to greatly improve performance for simultaneous inserts.

Table partitioning creates many "last" pages and distributes them such that a different task can access each last page. This allows multiple simultaneous inserts. Chapter 17, Performance Tuning at the Database Level, discusses this issue in more detail.

Continuing with our example, if you partition the *orders* table into 10 partitions, even if 200 people enter orders, the contention is at least greatly reduced. Instead of 200 users contending for the single last data page, each of 20 users contends for one of the 10 last data pages. Figure 4-2 illustrates the difference between pre-System 10 and System 11 logging for three transactions writing to a table.

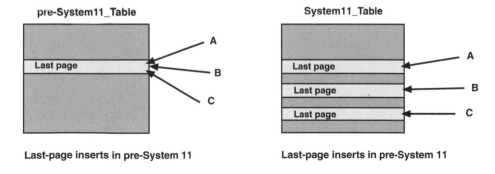

Last-page inserts in pre-System 11   Last-page inserts in pre-System 11

Figure 4-2. *Last page inserts in pre-System 10 and in System 11*

You cannot partition a table that has a clustered index, because the leaf level for a clustered index is the same for both the data and the index pages. You'll learn more about data and index pages in Chapter 11, Installing SQL Server.

Control over Memory Management with Named Data Caches

When a query needs data that isn't already in data cache, SQL Server performs disk I/O to bring the data into cache. For example, suppose that queries that the *sales* application makes frequently result in data access from a *customer* table. To execute these queries, SQL Server performs I/O to read data from the *customer* table on disk into cache. Suppose another query (initiated after the first query is done processing) accesses data from an *orders* table and requires access to different data that is not in cache. As is common, in this example not enough cache is available to accommodate the data needs of both queries. So, SQL Server flushes the *customer* table's data to accommodate the *order* table's data, then processes the second query. If a third query (initiated after SQL Server flushes the *customer* table data) requires the *customer* table data again, SQL Server again must retrieve the *customer* table data. This time-consuming cycle of reading the *customer* table from disk seriously degrades performance.

System 11's named caches give you a way to tell SQL Server what you want it to keep in cache, letting you tune to eliminate time-consuming I/O. You can decide which tables are busy or high priority, and create special named caches for those tables. Then, you *bind* a table to its cache using commands given in Chapter 17. For our sales application example, we would create a cache for the *customer* table called *customer_cache*, then bind the *customer* table to it. When SQL Server starts, it reads the *customer* table into cache. Thereafter, any query requiring data from that table will find it in cache 100 percent of the time, which offers a big performance advantage over traditional caching technology. In SQL Server 11, named caches are controlled by the Logical Memory Manager (LMM). You can also bind an index to a named cache to improve performance by reducing contention for index pages.

Control over Lock Management

Conceptually, *locking* controls access to some set of data in a database. In a typical multiuser environment, locking ensures that simultaneous transactions do not interfere with each other. In this way, locking data ensures its consistency, but locking also reduces the availability of the data to other processes. As you might guess, this results in a performance disadvantage, because when Process A needs data that Process B has locked, Process A must wait for Process B to release the lock. SQL Server gives you control over locking mechanisms, so you can balance the need for data consistency with *concurrency,* or data availability and its effect on performance.

When you execute a query, the SQL Server optimizer determines locking methods. For example, it decides whether to lock a data page that contains a requested row or to lock the entire table. SQL Server always acquires a lock on the data page that contains the row. In pre-System 11, if the number of locked data pages exceeds 200 pages, SQL Server locks the entire table. So if the table on which you issue a query contains more than 200 data pages (which is common with queries that use very large tables), SQL Server locks the entire table, which has a negative impact on performance. In SQL Server 11, this problem is solved by giving database administrators control over how SQL Server performs locking. The database administrators can now determine the page number limit after which SQL Server escalates from page locks to a table lock. In our example, we can configure page lock limits so that SQL Server escalates to a table lock only after acquiring locks on 2,000 data pages.

Parallel Lock Manager

Pre-System 11 SQL Server products used a single spinlock for acquiring and releasing locks. SQL Server 11's parallel lock manager uses multiple spinlocks to reduce contention for shared resources that use locking. The parallel lock manager acquires and releases locks in a parallel mode by utilizing all spinlocks.

Housekeeper

System 11 takes advantage of the times when SQL Server is not doing any useful work by writing any changed information in cache to disk. Writing changed data during idle cycles reduces the need to write it later during the checkpoint operation, when the system might better use the time to perform well. This feature was discussed in Chapter 2.

Dirty Reads

A *dirty read* is a read made to an uncommitted transaction in cache. For example, say that you initiated a transaction that modifies the current balance of a savings bank account number 101 to 20,000, and you have not committed the transaction (that is, the transaction is still active). If another person accesses savings bank account 101, he or she would not see 20,000. Instead, that user would see only the value present before this modification. In other words, the transaction that modified the balance of savings account number 101 to 20,000 is not visible to any other transaction. This is called *read committed*, which means that only after you commit the transaction are the values updated by the committed transaction and visible to other transactions.

Some financial applications require access to the data modified by uncommitted transactions. SQL Server 11 supports this feature. You can access the data modified by an uncommitted transaction by setting the transaction isolation level to 0 before you initiate a transaction. Chapter 10, Transaction Management, explains more about transaction isolation levels.

Scalability

If the load on a system grows, for example because of an increase in the number of users, disk I/Os, or processing capability, and if you add resources such as CPUs, a scalable system can use the added resources to improve performance. Several factors contribute to performance and scalability. In some cases, it is necessary for the architecture to support scalability; in other cases, you can employ methods to improve scalability. This section addresses bottlenecks in pre-System 11 and describes how these bottlenecks have been removed.

If multiple database engines need to perform network I/O and they have to compete for access to a single network I/O manager, the end result is poor scalability. System 11 avoids this type of bottleneck using a multiple network engine strategy. This strategy is one of the features that make System 11 the highly scalable database system that it is. Because all engines handle network I/O (not just a limited number of "special" engines), as you add more CPUs and engines to a system, the ability to handle more users automatically grows. The multiple network engine feature also addresses scalability issues by distributing processing evenly across all available CPUs.

In pre-System 11, the scalability bottleneck was multiple engines requiring concurrent access to common data structures. Let's say that a process that is running in engine 1 has finished executing the I/O and is ready to return results to client applications. This process fills the TDS buffer with data to be transferred back to applications. (For more information about TDS, see the "Transact-SQL and TDS" section in Chapter 2.) Because engine 0 must physically call the network *send* function (engine 0 is the only engine that can do this), engine 1 grabs the *network I/O request* structure and fills information about the network I/O to be performed. The filled data structure is then posted to a list of pending network I/Os. There is only one pending network I/O queue. Again, after the pending network write is issued, the corresponding network I/O request structure is removed from engine 0. A process like this that grabs the network I/O request and removes the network I/O structure doesn't pose a prob lem with a lesser number of processes using a system. But as the number of users increases, more processes need to grab the network I/O request structure and post network I/O requests simultaneously. This is clearly a scalability issue, as other engines must await engine 0.

In SQL Server 11, this bottleneck has been removed by distributing the network I/O load among engines. This feature is described in the new system as Multiple Network Engines and is discussed in Chapter 2. In SQL Server 11, each engine can now physically call the network *send* function, grab *network I/O request,* and save information about the pending network I/O queue. This task is linked to its own list of pending network I/Os. The Multiple Network Engine architecture provides the following benefits.

- As more engines are added, it increases the overall number of simultaneous user connections that a single SQL Server can handle

- This architecture allows all engines to handle the network operations of user connections and distributes CPU utilization evenly across all engines

- This architecture distributes the network I/O load among engines and transparently migrates "network affinity" for each incoming connection to the engine serving the least number of connections

Configuration Parameters for Fine Tuning

In pre-System 11 releases, some configuration parameters are configured using the SQL Server configuration stored procedure **sp_configure**, and some configuration parameters are done using a utility called **buildmaster**. In System 11, all of the SQL Server configurable parameters can be configured using **sp_configure**. Another improvement is that System 11 combines the configurable options of SQL Server into a hierarchy of logically grouped categories. These categories help a database administration to control and assign the configuration to various categories of users. The three groups of categories are basic, intermediate, and comprehensive. You'll learn more about configuration in Chapter 12, Configuring SQL Server.

Another feature of System 11 is that you can even tune simple parameters like query I/O size, a cache strategy that contributes greatly to the performance of a query.

Summary

This chapter gave you a practical introduction to the features that make System 11 one of the most scalable and versatile RDBMSs on the market today. This chapter illustrates how System 11 features solve real-world problems, many of which might be difficult or impossible to solve with another RDBMS. The next chapter concludes the overview section of this book by explaining how you can interact with SQL Server.

5

Interacting with SQL Server

The **isql** utility is one of the most useful client interfaces available for interact ing with SQL Server. Although the **isql** interface is not elegant, it is easy to learn and use, and it allows you to perform all SQL Server operations at any level of sophistication.

Your knowledge of SQL, Transact-SQL, and other Sybase utilities determines your level of control over SQL Server and your understanding of its behavior. The **isql** utility simply provides you with an interface through which you can connect to SQL Server applications, store query output, and fully configure and fine tune SQL Server for high performance. Using SQL Server resources through the **isql** interface, you can also monitor the intricacies of query, database, and system behavior. This chapter discusses how to use the **isql** interface. The rest of the book assumes the use of **isql** for performing almost all SQL Server tasks.

Here are the topics this chapter covers.

- The **isql** utility for UNIX presents **isql** syntax, options, and parameters, and information about using **isql** interactively

- Using scripts with **isql**

- The **wisql** utility—the Microsoft Windows and Windows NT version of **isql**—describes the **wisql** utility interface and how to use it

Third-party alternatives to **isql** and **wisql**, such as RAPIDSQL and DBArtison, give programmers and database administrators an equal amount of control through a graphical user interface.

If you are a Windows or Windows NT user, you can skip to the section of this chapter titled "The *wisql* and *wisql32* Utilities."

The isql *Utility for UNIX*

In a UNIX environment, you connect to SQL Server by entering the command **isql** at the operating system prompt. The command has a long list of parameters that give you many options for connecting to SQL Server and for specifying input and output characteristics and behavior. Although the syntax includes a large number of options, commands typically require some small subset of them. Table 5-1 lists the **isql** syntax and its commonly used parameters.

Table 5-1. *Syntax and options for the* **isql** *command*

isql [-e] [-F] [-p] [-n] [-v] [-X] [-Y]
[-a *display_charset*] [-c *cmdend*] [-E *editor*]
[-h *headers*] [-H *hostname*] [-i *inputfile*]
[-I *interfaces_file*] [-m *errorlevel*]
[-o *outputfile*] [-P *password*]
[-S *server*][-U *username*]
[-w *columnwidth*] [-y *sybase_directory*]
[-A *size*]

-a *display_charset*	Lets you choose a different character set than that used by the machine on which **isql** is running. The **-a** option used with **-J** specifies the character set translation file (*.xlt* file) required for the conversion. Use **-a** alone only if the client character set is the same as the default.
-c *cmdend*	Changes the command terminator.
-E *editor*	Specifies an editor other than the default editor, **vi**.
-h *headers*	Specifies the number of rows to print between column headings. The default prints headings only once for each set of query results.
-H *hostname*	Sets the client *hostname*.

(continued)

Table 5-1. *(continued)*

-i *inputfile*	Specifies the name of an operating system file to use for input to **isql**. Using **-i** is equivalent to using input redirect, < *input-file*.
-I *interfaces_file*	Specifies the name and location of the interfaces file to search when connecting to SQL Server. Without **-I**, **isql** looks for a file named *interfaces* in the directory specified by the SYBASE environment variable. This variable is described in Chapter 11, Installing SQL Server.
-m *errorlevel*	Customizes the error message display.
-o *outputfile*	Specifies the name of an operating system file in which to store **isql** output. Using **-o** is equivalent to use the output redirect, > *outputfile*.
-P *password*	Specifies the current SQL Server password. If you do not specify the **-P** option, **isql** prompts for a password.
-S *server*	Specifies the name of the SQL Server to which to connect.
-U *username*	Specifies a login name. Logins are case sensitive.
-w *columnwidth*	Sets the screen width for output. The default is 80 characters.
-y *sybase_directory*	Specifies a SYBASE directory other than the default *$SYBASE* directory.
-A *size*	Specifies the network packet size to use for this **isql** session.

Point to Note: Several pairs of **isql** options use the same letter (-i and -I, -p and -P, and so forth). Case is important for all **isql** options.

Table 5-2 shows the valid commands you can use within **isql**.

Table 5-2. *ISQL commands*

isql **Command**	**Description**
reset	Resets the buffer, clearing commands so you can start again.
vi or **edit**	Calls the editor with your last set of commands. The **vi** editor is the default, but you can change that using the EDITOR environment variable.
!! *command*	Executes the operating system *command* you specify.
:r *filename*	Reads an operating system file into an interactive **isql** session.
:w *filename*	Writes the buffer to an operating system file called *filename*.
Ctrl-C	Cancels the job and returns to the **isql** prompt.
quit or **exit**	Exits from **isql**.

Setting Up for UNIX *isql*

You might find that all you need to do to invoke **isql** is to type the command as described in the Using *isql* section that follows. However, if typing the command results in an error, the problem may involve the points listed here. Check them if in doubt before you begin to use **isql**.

- Check the login name and password. If you do not have a login account, ask your Sybase database administrator to create one for you.

- Do you need to set the operating system *path*? You might need to set a path so the operating system knows where to find the **isql** program. After a normal SQL Server installation, the **isql** program resides in *$SYBASE/bin*. Chapter 11, Installing SQL Server, describes the installation process and says more about the SYBASE variable. But for now, all you need to know is that SYBASE is the directory path to the SQL Server software. If the operating system indicates that it cannot find **isql**, set the SYBASE environment variable to the SQL Server installation directory in the appropriate configuration file.

- Do you need to connect to a specific SQL Server? **Isql** uses the value of the UNIX environment variable DSQUERY to determine to which SQL Server to connect. If the server on which you have an account is different from the one set in DSQUERY, you can use the -S option to specify the correct server.

Using *isql*

This section describes many of the interactions users commonly have with the **isql** utility. Typically, you begin an **isql** interactive session in the UNIX environment using the following form of the command.

```
unixOS% isql -Uusername
Password: password
1> { ...a SQL command... }
2> go
```

In this simple interaction, you specify your user name with the -U option, after which the **isql** program prompts you for your password. After **isql** connects you to SQL Server, you can issue standard SQL and Transact-SQL commands at the **isql** prompt. By default, the prompt is an integer followed by a "greater-than" symbol: >.

The **isql** utility increments the value of the prompt for each carriage return until you type the *command terminator*, **go**. The command terminator is **isql**'s cue to send the command to SQL Server to execute. The examples in this section illustrate the use of the command terminator and how you can change it from the default value of **go** to some other character or string of characters.

You can also start **isql** using the *-P* option and entering your password on the command line, as the next example illustrates. Your password is echoed to the screen when you invoke **isql** in this way. In this example, the SQL command on line 1 tells SQL Server to use the database called *my_database*.

```
unixOS% isql -Uamanda -PNot2Late!
1> use my_database
2> go
1>
```

The next command connects user *sa* with password *2MyMuM0* to SQL Server and changes the command terminator from **go** to a semicolon using the *-c* option. Note that the backslash that precedes the semicolon overrides the fact that UNIX uses the semicolon as a delimiter. The command on line 1 queries for the current database name using the **db_name()** function, while the output that follows the commands indicates that the user is currently in the *master* database.

```
unixOS% isql -Usa -P2MyMuM0 -c\;
1> select db_name()
2> ;

 - - - - - - - - - - - - - - - - -
 master
 (1 row affected)
```

Point to Note: No matter what you use to represent the command terminator, it must exist on a line by itself. It cannot be on the same line as a Transact-SQL command.

You can also specify to which SQL Server you want **isql** to connect using the *-S* option. When you don't use this option, **isql** looks up the value of the DSQUERY variable, which you set as a preinstallation step (discussed in Chapter 11, Installing SQL Server). This next example makes an **isql** connection with the server called *SWAMI*.

```
unixOS% isql -Uamanda -PNot2Late! -SSWAMI
```

Using an Editor

As Table 5-2 shows, you can invoke an editor from within an **isql** session. The default editor is **vi**, but you can specify a different editor using the EDITOR environment variable. The ability to call an editor from within **isql** is useful in several ways. You can use it to correct a typing error, compose a complicated query, save a query you've just created to an operating system file, or open a file to modify and execute.

Here's an example that uses **vi** to correct an error entered while typing a command. Let's say that you were typing the **create table** SQL command in an **isql** session as follows.

```
1> create table pests
2> (species varchar(40) not null,
3> genus varcar(40) not null,
4> victim varchar (50) null,
5> repellent varchar (40) null)
6> go
Msg 2715, Level 16, State 1:
Server 'snipe', Line 1:
Column or parameter #2: Can't find type 'varcar'.
1> vi
```

After you submit the command with the command terminator **go** on line 6, SQL Server reports an error, and indeed you see that there is a typo on line 3 where it says *varcar* rather than *varchar*. So you type **vi** on the next line and press the Return key. The **vi** editor executes with the current command. Here's what it looks like.

```
create table pests
(species varchar(40) not null,
genus varcar(40) not null,
victim varchar (50) null,
repellent varchar (40) null)
~
~
~
~
"/tmp/Isqla000K3" 5 lines, 132 characters
```

You can edit the file as you would any **vi** file. When you finish, exit using **:wq** as you normally would. The corrected command is then ready to execute from **isql**.

Using the reset Command

The alternative to using an editor to correct an error is to use the **reset** command. This command simply erases all SQL statements from the buffer so that you can start again. For example, if you had used **reset** on the last example instead of **vi**, it would have looked like this.

```
1> create table pests
2> (species varchar(40) not null,
3> genus varcar(40) not null,
4> victim varchar (50) null,
5> repellent varchar (40) null)
6> reset
1>
```

If you wanted to execute this command, you would need to retype it.

Using Scripts with isql and Redirection

You can place any SQL or Transact-SQL command or set of commands in a script for **isql** to use as input. This capability has important implications for defining database objects and creating user accounts, because a well-controlled set of scripts used by all database administrators and programmers goes a long way towards maintaining consistency and accuracy across a database system. A script is an operating system text file that contains a batch job—one or more SQL or Transact-SQL commands, each punctuated with the command terminator **go**. Here's a small script in a file called *pets.sql* that creates a table called *pet_record* and an index on that table called *pet_idx*. (Indexes are discussed in Chapter 8, Database Objects: Tables and Data Integrity.)

```
create table pet_record
(pet_id char(6),
pet_name char(30),
owner_lname char(30),
phone_no int(9)
)
go

create unique clustered index pet_idx on pet_record(pet_id)
go
```

You can submit a script as input to **isql** in two ways in UNIX: use the *-i* option or use redirection. Using the *-i* option, a user called *michelle* with password *enReeKa* could use the following command to run the *pets.sql* script. This command opens an **isql** session with SQL Server and runs the *pets.sql* script creating the table called *pet_record*.

unixOS% isql -Umichelle -PenReeKa -ipets.sql

The other way to submit the preceding file to **isql** is to redirect the file just as you could do with many UNIX commands. So, the other way to run the same script is as follows.

unixOS% isql -Umichelle -PenReeKa < pets.sql

You can also redirect query results to an operating system file using output redirection. For example, say that another file called *pet_list.sql* contains the following script that queries the *pets* table for all *pet_id*s and *pet_name*s.

```
select pet_id, pet_name
 from pets
go
```

The next command shows how user *michelle* can query the *pets* table and store the results in a file called *pet_list*.

unixOS% isql -Umichelle -PenReeKa < pet_list.sql > pet_list

Point to Note: Avoid using passwords in scripts if you are concerned about security.

If you use a SQL command to create an object that already exists in a database, SQL Server issues an error message. This is especially important to remember when you are using scripts to create objects, because the scripts will fail.

Sybase-Supplied Scripts

The Sybase software installation creates a *$SYBASE/scripts* directory and places several ready-to-use scripts in it. $SYBASE is an environment variable for the SQL Server installation directory. The SyBooks CD we've included with this book contains more information about how to use Sybase-supplied scripts.

This example installs the Sybase sample database, *pubs2*. It uses the Sybase-supplied *installpubs* script as input to **isql**.

unixOS% isql -Usa -P -i$SYBASE/scripts/installpubs

Using Stored Procedures

You can use any system-supplied or user-created stored procedure in an interactive **isql** session or script. You should precede the stored procedure with the **execute** command or its abbreviated equivalent, **exec**. The following example illustrates how to execute a system stored procedure. It uses the procedure **sp_help** (described in Chapter 7, Creating and Managing Databases) to get information about the *pet_record* table.

```
1> exec sp_help pet_record
2> go
```

isql Output

Isql output can look cryptic if you are new to the utility. The next example is output from the last command, **exec sp_help** *pet_record*. At the moment, it isn't necessary for you to understand everything about this specific output. The point is to introduce you to **isql** output, which, as you'll notice, can be somewhat difficult to read because it often wraps around. This is a default format that is typical for **isql** output. However you can use the -w option to reformat the column width so the output is more readable.

```
Name      Owner    Type
-----     -----    ----
pet_record         dbo      user table
Data_located_on_segment          When_created
-----------------------          ------------
default Jul 25 1996     7:10PM
Column_name      Type     Length   Prec  Scale   Nulls    Default_name
        Rule_name        Identity
-----------      ----     ------   ------- --    -----    ------------
        ---------        --------
pet_id char      6        NULL     NULL            0       NULL
        NULL             0
pet_name char    30       NULL     NULL            0       NULL
        NULL     0
owner_lname char 30       NULL     NULL            0       NULL
        NULL     0
phone_no int     4        NULL     NULL            0       NULL
        NULL     0
index_name       index_description
        index_keys
        index_max_rows_per_page
-----------      -------------------------------------------------------
        -------------------------------------------------------
        -------------------------------------------------------
```

```
pet_idx          clustered, unique located on default
        pet_id
        0
No defined keys for this object.
Object is not partitioned.
(1 row affected, return status = 0)
```

The wisql *and* wisql32 *Utilities*

The **wisql** utility is the Windows and Windows NT version of **isql**, and the **wisql32** utility is the version available for Win32S. Because they are identical to the user, this section will use **wisql** to describe both interfaces. These Microsoft Windows applications give you all of the same capabilities that **isql** provides (including the capability to run scripts), but they do it through a user-friendly, point-and-click, menu-driven interface.

After installing the SQL software, you can open **wisql** by double-clicking the WISQL icon in the Sybase for Windows program group. The **wisql** GUI comes up as the next section discusses.

Configuring the *sql.ini* File

The SQL Server installation program creates a *sql.ini* file. You'll need to configure this file for **wisql** before you can establish a connection to SQL Server from the client. This file contains information such as IP address and port number. Here is a sample *sql.ini* file.

[APOLLO]
WIN3_QUERY=WNLWNSCK,198.100.100.100,2100
[OPEN_SERVER]
WIN3_QUERY=WNLWNSCK,198.217.68.16,5212

The number 198.100.100.100 is the IP address, 2100 is the port number, and WNLWNSCK is the network loadable Windows socket file.

The *wisql* GUI

Figure 5-1 shows the basic graphical user interface through which you can perform any **isql** operation. The **wisql** window is divided into a workspace area on the top, in which you enter SQL or Transact-SQL commands, and an output area on the bottom, in which **wisql** output is displayed unless you redirect it using a File menu option.

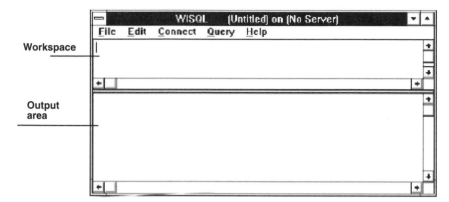

Figure 5-1. *The **wisql** main menu with sample input and output*

The main menu items provide the following functionality.

- The File menu lets you open files, save input and output, specify options, and end the **wisql** session.

- The Edit menu lets you undo, cut, paste, and delete.

- The Connect menu lets you open, close, and switch connections. You use the Connect menu to open a connection to SQL Server. It presents a new dialog box into which you type your user name, password, and a default database. You also can specify the SQL Server.

- The Query menu lets you execute all or part of the text in the workspace area.

Summary

This chapter has given you information about how to connect to and interact with SQL Server using the **isql** and **wisql** utilities. This chapter concludes the overview and context portion of the book. In Section II, SQL Server Fundamentals, which follows next, we give you practical information about creating and managing databases.

SECTION **II**

SQL Server
Fundamentals

This section of the book shows you how to create databases and data tables within them that protect the correctness and completeness of the data they hold. It explains how to create all of the objects associated with tables, which you use to establish data integrity, efficiency, and good performance.

Implementing databases and tables to hold your data doesn't simply start with the **create database** command. Before you can create a database, you need to prepare a physical home for it on a disk or in an operating system file. You also want to ensure that your database environment can protect production data from unexpected, but inevitable resource failures. This section gives the range of information you need to create database devices, backup devices, and mirror devices for fault resilience. It presents the fundamental concepts, theory, and procedures associated with each topic, and reinforces them with simple, but realistic examples. At the end of each chapter, you can test your knowledge by doing the exercises that we have provided, then checking your solutions against ours.

Chapter 6, Database Devices and Fault Tolerance, explains your options for configuring physical devices for SQL Server's use. This chapter provides information about database devices, mirroring, and dump devices for backups. In Chapter 7, Creating and Managing Databases, you learn all about how to create and manage databases on physical devices. This chapter gives tips on data placement and how to plan database requirements in advance. Chapter 7 also describes segments and how to use them to make databases as fast and effective as possible. Chapter 8, Database Objects: Tables and Data Integrity, describes how to create tables that enforce data integrity and perform efficiently for the applications they serve.

Chapter 9, Transact-SQL and Its Extensions, describes Sybase's enhanced version of SQL, Transact-SQL and its extensions—which include local and global variables, cursors, stored procedures, and triggers. These enhancements are the basic constructs you use to develop transaction handling code. Chapter 10, Transaction Management, discusses transaction management, concurrency, and locking in the System 11 environment.

Section II is about how to *implement* a physical database design; it is not about the *theory* of database design. Physical relational database design involves data-oriented activities such as defining a table's column names and establishing relationships between tables. It also involves preplanning for database performance to build in efficiency from the start. Logical database design encompasses understanding and describing transactions, and coding them using data definition language statements in Transact-SQL. For the purpose of learning, you can certainly jump into this section without having designed an entire database. You'll easily be able to understand the text and examples, and can create your own databases and database objects. However, if you are embarking on the creation of a production database system from scratch, you will need to go through a separate physical and logical design process—a subject discussed in publications that specifically address those topics.

6

Database Devices and Fault Tolerance

The *database device* is the physical disk space allocated for the database. This chapter discusses the database device—the home for the database. It covers foundation concepts and practical considerations, such as the following.

- Where to put the database device

- How to create the database device

- How to get information about existing database devices

- How to cope with inevitable hardware failures

After you create a database device using the information in this chapter, you can create one or more databases using the information that Chapter 7 provides.

Foundation Topics

The next sections explain background concepts for the rest of the chapter. They describe the difference between logical and physical devices, and the relationship between a database device and a database.

Because we normally think of a device as a physical object, this term can be misleading. Imagine a database device as a container for a database. It is a logical device that you initialize for use by SQL Server. You can create it either in an operating system file or on a partition on a disk—the physical (hardware) device. Figure 6-1 illustrates the idea.

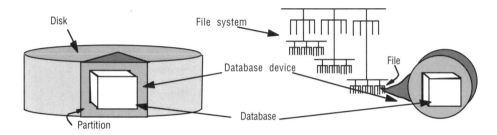

Figure 6-1. *The database device on a disk partition or as a file*

You prepare a database device using the Transact-SQL command **disk init**. This command initializes the physical disk or operating system file and maps it to a name that you specify. It also makes an entry for the new database device in the *sysdevices* table in the *master* database.

Relationships Between Database Devices and Databases

After you initialize a database device, you can allocate it for use by one or more databases. The number of database devices relative to the number of databases distinguishes the physical configuration in an important way. The terms *one-to-one*, *one-to-many*, *many-to-many*, and *many-to-one* describe the relationship of the database device to database.

- In a one-to-one relationship, one database device holds one complete database.

- In a one-to-many relationship, a database device is divided into fragments, each holding a database. A *device fragment* is a portion of a database device allocated to a database.

- In a many-to-many relationship, many databases span many database devices.

- In a many-to-one relationship, a database spans more than one database device. This is a subset of the many-to-many relationship. When a database spans several database devices, you can partition the data across more than one disk to make I/O more efficient.

Figure 6-2 is a conceptual representation of these four types of relationships. Keep in mind that, although this figure shows the physical device as a disk, it could instead be an operating system file. The two graphics in the lower half of the figure represent the "many" database devices positioned next to each other and all on the same physical device; these database devices could just as well be spread over different physical devices. The relationship between a database device and a physical device is usually one to one.

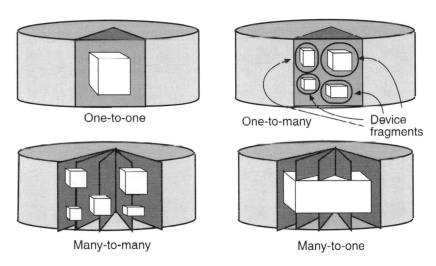

Figure 6-2. *Relationships between database devices and databases*

Example: Allocating Disk Space

Figure 6-3 illustrates three ways to allocate disk space to a database. The database devices named *sy_dev1*, *syb_dev2*, and *syb_dev3* map to a disk partition or to an operating system file as follows.

- A portion of the space on database device *syb_dev1* is allocated to Database A and another portion of *syb_dev1* is allocated to part of Database B; *syb_dev1* maps one to many

- All of the space on database device *syb_dev2* is allocated to part of Database B

- All of the space on database device *syb_dev3* is allocated to the complete Database C; *syb_dev3* maps one-to-one to Database C

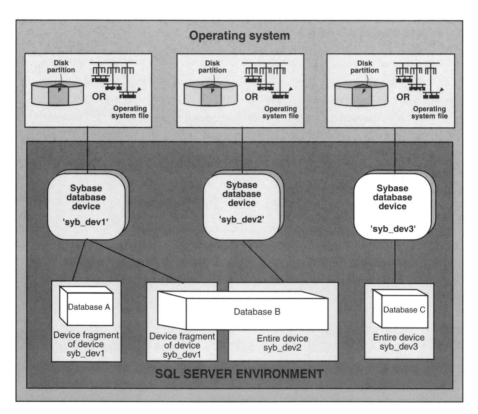

Figure 6-3. *Three ways to allocate disk space*

What Happens in the Server

SQL Server manages database devices using the *sysdevices* table in the *master* database. It stores one row in the *sysdevices* table for each database device or backup device. Each row in the table contains several pieces of information. The following list mentions just a few of these items of information. (See the Sybase documentation on your *SyBooks* CD for complete information about system tables.)

- Name of the logical device

- Name of the physical device

- Name of the primary device (described later in this chapter)

- Device controller type

Deciding Where to Put the Database Device

You can create a database device in an operating system file, or on a *raw (disk) partition*—that is, a devoted chunk of disk with explicitly specified boundaries. The characteristics of the database device you need usually make the choice clear. This section explains what you need to know about operating system files and raw partitions so that you can make that decision.

UNIX Operating System Files

Using UNIX operating system files as a database device is fine if all you consider is its ability to store data; but there is an issue with the way the operating system performs disk I/O. The operating system might temporarily store the data in a buffer cache rather than immediately write it to disk. The operating system has a good reason for doing this: It reduces the number of disk I/Os, which improves performance for many applications. So UNIX operating system files have a performance advantage over raw partitions.

Raw Partitions

As noted, a raw partition is disk space devoted to a database device. After you allocate a partition as a database device, no part of it is available for other use, even when no database device resides on it. Depending how a database uses the partitioned space this can be fine—or, it can be serious waste of disk resources.

Our Recommendation for a Production Database

When you use an operating system file as a database device, data transfer can be unreliable if the system crashes while SQL Server is processing transactions. When SQL Server completes a transaction, it writes to a file and assumes that the transaction is complete; however, if the transaction is still in the buffer cache during a crash, the transaction is lost. What's worse is that SQL Server has no way of knowing it. (This only applies to platforms that do not support asynchronous I/O. We describe asynchronous I/O below in the section titled Mirroring and Asynchronous I/O.)

Therefore, if you are creating a production database on a platform that does not support asynchronous I/O, we recommend that you use a raw partition. When the database device is on a raw partition, SQL Server is in control of disk I/O, so it knows exactly where the data is at all times. This makes transaction recovery possible after a system crash. You also avoid the buffered-data issues associated with using an operating system file as a database device.

Our Recommendation for a Test Database

In most cases, operating system files are a good place to create a database device for test purposes, because they don't monopolize resources in the same way that raw partitions do. However, because SQL Server is not in control of writing data directly to disk, files are not the best place to put the database device if you can't tolerate some loss of test data as a result of a system crash.

Using Both Operating System Files and Raw Partitions

In a UNIX operating system, you can also choose to divide the database device between a raw partition and a file to improve performance for a production database. Temporary databases, such as *tempdb*, are often good candidates to put in a file-based database device even in production environments because recovery is not crucial. However, it is a good idea to store the transaction log on a raw partition.

Our experience at various sites shows that SQL Server performance improves when we place the *tempdb* database in an operating system file. You don't risk anything by doing so because *tempdb* is recreated every time SQL Server restarts.

Creating and Dropping Database Devices

The Transact-SQL commands you use to create and drop a database device are **disk init** and **sp_dropdevice**. To execute them, you must have the *sa* role.

Before creating a database device, you must ensure that permissions are set correctly for writing to the physical device and that the raw partition contains enough physical space for the database device you plan to put there. You must also determine the virtual device number, a parameter that the **disk init** command requires. After that, you can use **disk init** to initialize the disk.

Preparation

1. At the UNIX prompt, use the **ls** command to check the operating system permissions. For example, if the UNIX physical device name is */dev/rsybdev1*, enter the following command.

    ls -l /dev/rsybdev1

    Verify that the owner of the file is *sybase*, as it should be. *Sybase* is the login that SQL Server uses to initialize.

2. Ensure that the size of the database device is the same as the size of the UNIX device if you are creating the database device on a raw partition.

3. Choose a virtual device number that is not in use and that is less than the highest device number. This is a three-step process.

    3a. The first of these steps is to execute the following **select** command to list all the virtual device numbers that SQL Server is using.

    ```
    select name, low/16777216
      from master..sysdevices
      where contrltype = 0
    go
    ```

    The output looks something like this.

    ```
    name
    -------------------          ----------
    syb_dev3             8
    syb_dev5                     6
    master                       0
    sprocdev                     2
    syntaxdev                    5
    syb_dev2                     4
    syb_dev1                     3
      (7 rows affected)
    ```

3b. Execute the system procedure **sp_configure** to obtain the maximum device number that can be used to create a new device, as indicated next.

```
exec sp_configure "device"
go
```

This command generates output like the following.

```
Parameter Name      Default Memory Used Config Value  Run Value
--------------      ------- ----------- ------------  ---------
number of devices   10      #4          10            10
```

3c. Choose a device number that the output from the command in step 3a does not list. The device number must not exceed the maximum number of devices listed in step 3b. In this example, you can choose a device number of 1, 7, or 9. (If all the available device numbers are in use, you can add new devices by reconfiguring SQL Server. Refer to Chapter 13, SQL Server Security Features, to increase the maximum number of devices.)

Creating a Database Device

Next, you use the **disk init** command, which in one step initializes the physical device for SQL Server and creates the database device. Table 6-1 gives the syntax and parameters for this command.

Table 6-1. *Syntax and parameters for the **disk init** command*

disk init name = *'logical name'*,
 physname =*'physical_name'*,
 vdevno = *virtual_device_number*,
 size = *number_of_2k_blocks*,
 vstart = *virtual_address*,
 cntrltype = *controller_number*

logical_name   Logical name for the database device. Use a unique name to identify the database device when it is issued during creation of the database or transaction log.

(continued)

Table 6-1. *(continued)*

physical_name	Name of the UNIX physical device.
virtual_device_number	Virtual device number associated with the device. The virtual device number cannot be greater than the maximum number of devices for which SQL Server is configured.
number_of_2k_blocks	Size of the database device in 2KB blocks. The minimum size of the device is one allocation unit (512KB) if you are creating a log device. Otherwise, the minimum size is the size of *model* database or SQL Server's *minimum database size* configuration parameter.
virtual_address	Starting virtual address or the starting offset in 2KB blocks. The default value is 0.
controller_number	Specifies the controller. The default is 0.

Point to Note: UNIX creates a *sparse* file (a filename that has no space allocated to it) when you create a database device in an operating system file. Because the **create database** or **alter database** command allocates space for the file, it is possible for **disk init** to succeed even if there is insufficient disk space on the file system.

Examples: Creating Database Devices

These examples create database devices in a file and on a partition.

Example 1: The following command creates a database device named *test_dev* in a UNIX operating system file called */usr/syb_dev/test_dev.dat*. It has a virtual device number of 7 and a size of 20MB. Because the command does not specify the controller type, the system takes the default value 0.

```
disk init name='test_dev',
  physname='/usr/syb_dev/test_dev.dat',
  vdevno=7, size=10240
go
```

Example 2: The next command creates a device using a UNIX raw partition as the physical device. It has a size of 1GB and a virtual device number of 8.

```
disk init name = 'test_dev2',
  physname = '/dev/rdsk/c0t0d0s1',
  vdevno = 8, size = 524288
go
```

Example 3: The next command creates a device using an operating system file as a physical device in a Windows NT environment. The size is 5MB.

```
disk init name = "syb_dev1",
  physname = "C:\SYBASE\DATA\sybdev1.dat",
  vdevno = 3, size = 2560
go
```

Point to Note: You cannot reuse a virtual device number without shutting down and restarting (or recycling) SQL Server. So if **disk init** fails for any reason, either recycle or choose a new number that is not in use. You must recycle SQL Server if you drop a database device and want to reuse its virtual device number.

What Happens in the Server

When a **disk init** command is issued, SQL Server adds a new row with the database device name to the system table *sysdevices* in the *master* database. It then divides the database device space into 256 allocation units of pages. Refer to Chapter 3, The SQL Server Engine, for more information about allocation units.

Dropping a Database Device

When you no longer need a database device or a dump device that you were using for backups, you can drop it. Use the system procedure **sp_dropdevice**; verify but before you do, make sure that no other database is using that device. The next command shows how to verify this.

```
select distinct db_name(dbid)
  from sysusages usg, sysdevices dev
  where usg.vstart >= dev.low
  and usg.vstart <= dev.high
  and dev.name ='name_of_device'
go
```

Name_of_device is the name of the database device that you want to drop. The output lists all of the databases that reside on that database device. If the result shows that there are no databases in use, you can drop the database device using the system procedure **sp_dropdevice** with the syntax in Table 6-2.

Table 6-2. *Syntax and parameters for the* **sp_dropdevice** *system procedure*

sp_dropdevice *device_name*	
device_name	The name of the logical device to drop

Example: This command drops a database device named *test_dev* from SQL Server.

```
sp_dropdevice test_dev
go
```

Point to Note: SQL Server issues an error message if you try to drop a database device that is in use. Dropping a file that is being used as a database device makes the file inaccessible to SQL Server but does not remove the file from the file system, so you must remove the file manually to deallocate its space. Consider a database device *testdev* on the file *testdb.dat*. If *testdev* is dropped, you must remove the file *testdb.dat* manually with an operating system command.

What Happens in the Server

When you issue a **sp_dropdevice** command, SQL Server deletes the row from the *sysdevices* table in the *master* database that has the name of the device that was just dropped.

Fault Resilience with Mirroring

Mirroring is a technique that protects data against the perils of hardware failures. With Sybase mirroring, you establish a duplicate of the original database device (or the primary device), and simultaneously perform I/O to both the primary and the duplicate devices. The duplicate is referred to as the *mirror*, or *secondary*, device. If either the primary or the mirror device fails, the other contains an up-to-date copy of the data, providing instant recovery capability.

Some hardware vendors provide mirroring capability at the operating-system level, but Sybase's capability to mirror at the database-device level allows for better database administration and database recovery. The SQL Server **mirror** command does not mirror unallocated space on a primary database device. Unallocated space is space available on the device for a subsequent **create data-**

base or **alter database** command. The **mirror** command mirrors space that becomes allocated after the command is issued.

SQL Server lets you mirror database devices, not the database. However, if the primary device fully contains a database, SQL Server can effectively mirror the database. Here is how mirroring works, depending on the database's distribution over database devices.

- If SQL Server mirrors a primary database device that fully contains a database, it effectively mirrors the database

- If SQL Server mirrors a primary database device that stores multiple databases, it mirrors all of the databases that use that database device

- If SQL Server mirrors a database that is part of a set of database devices, it must mirror all of the database devices to fully mirror the database

---

Tip! Mirror both a database and its transaction log to give SQL Server a higher degree of fault tolerance.

Point to Note: Too much mirroring can result in poor performance, because each write takes place twice. You must balance the performance cost of mirroring with fault tolerance and recovery.

How Disk Writes Work with Mirroring

There are two kinds of data writes: *serial writes* and *nonserial writes*. With serial writes, SQL Server waits for the write to the primary database device to complete before it writes to the secondary database device. With nonserial writes, SQL Server writes to both the primary and secondary devices in parallel. Figure 6-4 illustrates this concept.

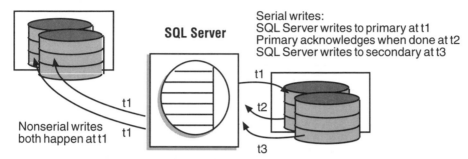

Figure 6-4. *Two ways to write to mirrored disks*

Tip! We use serial writes in a production environment because they are more reliable than nonserial writes. Serial writes ensure that data on at least one of the disks is safe even if the other device is damaged.

Mirroring might not achieve its objective if the primary and secondary database devices are on the same physical device. Normally, primary and secondary devices reside on different disks. You might also associate them with different disk controllers. We recommend that you mirror at least the *master* device and the transaction log device of critical databases for continuous recovery capability. However, if there is sufficient disk space, it's a good idea to mirror the data area of critical user databases too.

Mirroring and Asynchronous I/O

Asynchronous I/O is interrupt driven rather than scheduled at regular intervals as synchronous I/O is. An operating system that performs asynchronous I/O does not poll for data or send data on a regular, scheduled basis. Instead, data transmission occurs on a variable basis as needed. SQL Server uses asynchronous I/O to maximize performance.

To retain the use of asynchronous I/O, always mirror devices that are capable of asynchronous I/O to other devices capable of asynchronous I/O. In most cases, this means mirroring raw devices to raw devices and operating system files to operating system files. If the operating system cannot perform asynchronous I/O on files, mirroring a raw device to an operating system file produces an error message. Mirroring an operating system file to a raw device works, but you lose asynchronous I/O capability.

Point to Note: If there is a media failure on a transaction log device, you can recover the database only up to the last transaction. (Chapter 7, Creating and Managing Databases, describes the transaction log and the transaction log device.)

Implementing a Mirror Device

You can issue any mirroring command while SQL Server is running without interfering with ongoing activities. A user with system administrator permission can issue the mirror commands **disk mirror**, **disk remirror**, and **disk unmirror**. Table 6-3 gives the syntax and parameters for the **disk mirror** command.

Table 6-3. *Syntax and parameters for the* **disk mirror** *command*

---

disk mirror name = *'db_device_name'*,
  mirror = *'physical_device'*
  [,writes = {serial | noserial}]

db_device_name	Database device to mirror
physical_device	Physical mirror file or device name
serial, nonserial	Optional choice of whether to enforce serial writes

---

Point to Note: SQL Server mirroring requires that primary and secondary devices are of equal size.

Examples: Creating Mirror Devices

The following examples illustrate the use of the **disk mirror** command to mirror a database device to a file, to a raw partition, and in an NT environment.

Example 1: The following command mirrors the database device named *test_dev* to a UNIX operating system file */usr/sybase_dev/test_mir_dev.dat*. It uses the serial writes option.

```
disk mirror name='test_dev',
  mirror ='/usr/sybase_dev/test_mir_dev.dat',
  writes = serial
go
```

Example 2: The next command creates a mirror for a database device named *test_dev2* on the raw partition disk */dev/rdsk/c0t1d0s4*.

```
disk mirror name='test_dev2',
  mirror='/dev/rdsk/c0t1d0s4'
go
```

Example 3: This example shows how to mirror a *master* device in a Windows NT environment. In this command, the write option is set to *serial* by default.

```
disk mirror name=master,
  mirror ='C:\SYBASE\DATA\mst_mir.dat'
go
```

What Happens in the Server

SQL Server maintains a row in the system table *sysdevices* for each database device. When the **disk mirror** command is issued, SQL Server updates the row in *sysdevices* that corresponds to the database device being mirrored. It also sets a code in the *sysdevices* status column. Table 6-4 lists the status code values that you see when you query the *sysdevices* table.

Table 6-4. *Status control bits in the **sysdevices** table*

Decimal	Status
1	default disk
2	physical disk
4	logical disk (not used)
8	skip header
16	dump device
32	serial writes
64	device mirrored
128	reads mirrored
256	secondary mirror side only
512	mirror enabled

Tips for Successful Mirroring

- It's a good idea to mirror the *master* device to protect data in the event of a SQL Server crash. SQL Server uses the *master* device during initialization, so if it is lost or damaged, SQL Server might not be able to restart.

- Mirroring the production database transaction log gives SQL Server a higher degree of recoverability.

- Always backup the *master* database after issuing mirror commands.

How to Stop and Restart Mirroring

The **disk unmirror** command temporarily stops mirroring or deactivates mirroring for hardware maintenance when a hardware device needs to be replaced. (Disk mirroring is deactivated automatically when one of the mirror devices fails.) The syntax for **disk unmirror** follows in Table 6-5.

Table 6-5. Syntax and parameters for the **disk unmirror** command

disk unmirror name = '*database_device*' [, side = {primary | secondary}] [, mode = {retain | remove}]	
database_device	Name of the logical database device
secondary, primary	Specifies whether to disable the primary device or the secondary device; secondary is default
retain, remove	Determines whether the unmirroring is temporary (retain) or permanent (remove); default value is retain

Examples: Unmirroring Devices

The following three examples illustrate the use of the **disk unmirror** command to temporarily suspend and permanently deactivate mirroring.

Example 1: The following command temporarily suspends mirroring of the device named *test_dev* and retains the device. By default, the mode is *retain* and side is *secondary*. The mirroring can be activated by executing the command **disk remirror**.

```
disk unmirror name ='test_dev'
go
```

Example 2: The next command permanently deactivates mirroring of the device named *test_dev*. By default, the mirror is deactivated on the secondary device.

```
disk unmirror name='test dev', mode=remove
go
```

Example 3: This command temporarily suspends mirroring of the device named *test_dev* and retains the device. This command is commonly used when a hardware error or the primary device needs maintenance. You can reactivate mirroring using the **disk remirror** command.

```
disk unmirror name ='test_dev',
  side = primary,
  mode=retain
go
```

What Happens in the Server

When the **disk unmirror** command is used, SQL Server updates the column status of the row containing the device name and sets the appropriate bits, which it retrieves from the *sysdevices* table in the *master* database. Table 6-4 above shows the details of the status control bits that result

Tip for Recovery with Mirroring

Sometimes, only a portion of a disk containing multiple database devices becomes damaged, so some of the database devices on the disk are still functional and can continue processing transactions. Figure 6-5 illustrates a scenario in which three database devices on a production disk hold the production database. The database device named *DBDA* is damaged, so the disk must be replaced.

One way to replace the disk is to backup *DBDB* and *DBDC*, then halt production to make the replacement. Another way is to mirror the two good database devices, *DBDB* and *DBDC*, to another disk. Then, you can deactivate the primary database device using the command that follows. After the command executes, any I/O to the *DBDB* device is stored on the mirror device, *DBDB*. After mirroring the two devices, the damaged disk can be removed for maintenance.

```
disk unmirror name='DBDB',
 side=primary,
 mode=remove
go
```

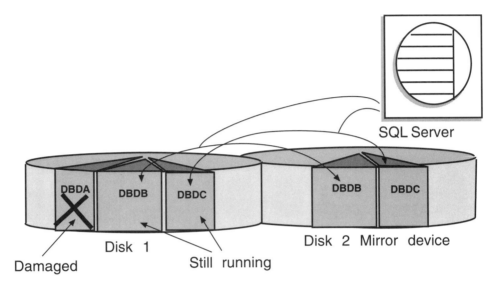

Figure 6-5. One of three database devices is damaged

Restarting Suspended Mirroring

Use the **disk remirror** command to restart suspended mirroring. Table 6-6 shows the syntax.

*Table 6-6. Syntax and parameters for the **sp_dropdevice** system procedure*

disk remirror name =*'device_name'*	
device_name	The name of the database device to resume mirroring

Point to Note: If you permanently deactivate mirroring, the **disk remirror** command won't work, but you can restart mirroring using the **disk mirror** command.

Example: The following command restarts the mirroring of device *test_dev* that was suspended earlier with the **disk unmirror** command with the mode *retain*.

```
disk remirror name ='test_dev'
go
```

Dump Devices for Backups

SQL Server writes backups to the *dump device*. When backing up data on a local SQL Server, you have two choices. You can specify the physical file (for example, an operating system file or device file), or you can specify a logical dump device name.

Tip! If you use a logical dump device name rather than a physical filename, you do not need to backup scripts when new UNIX dump devices are added to the local server.

For backups on a local server, you must specify a logical dump device name. The system procedure **sp_addumpdevice** assigns a UNIX physical dump device to a database device. For backups to a remote server, you must specify the operating system physical dump device name rather than the Sybase logical device name.

You create a logical dump device using the system procedure **sp_addumpdevice**. Table 6-7 lists the syntax and parameters for this command.

Table 6-7. *Syntax and parameters for the* **sp_addumpdevice** *system procedure*

sp_addumpdevice {"tape"|"disk"},
   logical_name,
   physical_name,
   [tapesize]	

tape	For tape devices
disk	For disk devices
logical_name	Name of the logical dump device
physical_name	Name of the physical device
tapesize	The capacity of the tape dump device in megabytes

Examples: Adding a Dump Device

The next two commands show how to add tape and disk dump devices.

Example 1: The following command adds a tape dump device named *dumptape1*. The physical device is *dev/nrmt0*.

```
sp_addumpdevice "tape",
  dumptape1,"/dev/nrmt0"
go
```

Example 2: The next command adds a disk dump device file named *usr/diskdump.dat*.

```
sp_addumpdevice "disk",
  dumpdisk1,"/usr/diskdump.dat"
go
```

What Happens in the Server

The **sp_addumpdevice** system procedure inserts a row into the *sysdevices* table. If the dump device is a tape device, it is assigned the value of 3 in the *cntrltype* column; disk devices are assigned the value of 2.

A Pool of Default Database Devices

When a user creates or alters a database without specifying the device name, SQL Server allocates space from the default database device to the new database. The system procedure **sp_diskdefault** marks a database device as a default device and creates a pool of default database devices available to all users.

*Table 6-8. Syntax and parameters for the **sp_diskdefault** system procedure*

sp_diskdefault *database_device*, {defaulton | defaultoff}	
database_device	Name of the logical database device
defaulton	Designates the database device as a default database device
defaultoff	Designates that the specified database device is not a default database device

Examples: Adding Default Disks

The following examples illustrate how to mark a database device as a default database device or a nondefault database device.

Example 1: The following command marks the device *syb_dev1* as a default database device.

```
sp_diskdefault syb_dev1, defaulton
go
```

Example 2: The next command marks the *master* database device as a non-default device.

```
sp_diskdefault master, defaultoff
go
```

Example 3: The next two commands illustrate the use of the *defaulton* and *defaultoff* parameters.

```
sp_diskdefault syb_dcv1, defaulton
go
sp_diskdefault master, defaultoff
go
```

The last example illustrates two points. First, assigning *defaulton* to database device *syb_dev1* does not mean that subsequent **create database on default** commands will allocate space from this device. When a pool of default devices are available, SQL Server uses space from the default pool of devices in the alphabetical order of the device names. So, although *syb_dev1* is marked *default-on*, SQL Server uses the *master* device (if space is available) because *master* alphabetically precedes *syb_dev1*. For that reason, the above example assigns *defaultoff* to the *master* device immediately after marking the other device. The second point this example illustrates is that, by default, SQL Server assigns the *master* device as the default device after a SQL Server installation.

Tip! Assign the *master* device *defaultoff* immediately after SQL Server installation.

Getting Information About Devices

You use the **sp_helpdevice** system procedure to list one or more database devices, dump devices, and mirror devices available in SQL Server. When you use the system procedure **sp_helpdevice** without a device name, it lists all the devices. Here's an example with output.

```
sp_helpdevice
go
```

```
device_name                              physical_name
            description
            status    cntrltype   device_number    low      high
----------  ------    ---------   -------------    ----     ----
master                                   /dev/rmaster
            special, MIRROR ENABLED, mirror = '/dev/rmaster_mir',
serial writes, reads mirrored, physical disk, 52.00 MB
                738   0           0  0             0        26623
tapedump1                                /dev/rmt1.1
            tape,     2200 MB,    dump device
            16        3           0                0        70400
tapedump2                                /dev/rst0
            disk, dump device
            16        2           0                0        20000
test_dev                                 /dev/rtest_dev
            special, physical disk, 200.00 MB
            2         0           4         67108864        67211263
            (4 rows affected, return status = 0)
```

Listing a Particular Device

For information about a specific device, use the system procedure **sp_helpdevice** with the name of the device in which you are interested as a parameter. Here's an example with output.

sp_helpdevice test_dev
go

```
device_name                              physical_name
            description
            status    cntrltype   device_number    low          high
----------  -------   ---------   -------------    -----        -----------
test_dev                                 /dev/rtest_dev
            special, physical disk, 200.00 MB
            2         0           4     67108864    67211263
(1 row affected, return status = 0)
```

Listing Mirrored Devices

You can use the system procedure **sp_helpdevice** to list mirror devices, or you can use the following Transact-SQL **select** command. Its output follows.

select name,
  physname from master..sysdevices
  where status &64 = 64
go

```
name        physname      mirrorname
------      -----------   ----------------
master      /dev/rmaster  /dev/rmaster_mir
(1 row affected)
```

Listing Dump Devices

The following command lists all of the dump devices. Its output follows.

select name, physname from master..sysdevices
  where cntrltype != 0
go

```
name         physname
---------    -------------
tapedump1    /dev/rmt1.1
tapedump2    /dev/rst0
(2 rows affected)
```

Exercises

6-1.   Which of the following devices would you use to create a production database if the platform does not support asynchronous I/O: a raw partition disk, or a UNIX operating system file?

6-2.   Which device is preferred for the *tempdb* database?

6-3.   Which Transact-SQL command would you use to create a new database device?

6-4.   Which devices would you mirror, in order of importance?

6-5.   A database device is on a disk */dev/rdsk/c0t0d0s3* of size 200MB. There is free disk space available on disk */dev/rdsk/c0t0d0s5* (same controller and same disk, different area). Is it advisable to mirror the logical device on the same disk?

6-6.   The database *testdb* is on the device *tstdb_dev1* and *tstdb_dev2* with a *tstdb_log* of size 200MB each. What commands would you issue to mirror the entire database on devices */dev/rdev1*, */dev/rdev2*, and */dev/ rlog* of size 200MB each?

6-7.   What is the SQL Server command to temporarily stop mirroring database device *syb_dev5*?

6-8.   What command would you use to permanently stop mirroring a device named *tstdb_dev1*?

6-9.   What is the Transact-SQL command that lists all of the virtual device numbers of the devices in use by SQL Server?

6-10.   What is the Transact-SQL command that lists all of the devices that are mirrored?

6-11.   What is the Transact-SQL command that lists all of the dump devices in use by SQL Server?

6-12.   Which command lists all of the devices that are in use by SQL Server?

Answers to the Exercises

6-1.   Raw partition disk

6-2.   UNIX operating system file

6-3.   **disk init**
        go

6-4.   1. *Master* device
        2. Transaction log device of critical databases with transaction orientation
        3. Data device of user databases

6-5.   No

6-6.   **disk mirror name = 'tstdb_dev1', mirror = '/dev/rdev1' writes = serial**
        go
        disk mirror name = 'tstdb_dev2', mirror = '/dev/rdev2' writes = serial
        go
        disk mirror name = 'tstdb_log', mirror = '/dev/rlog' writes = serial
        go

6-7.   **disk unmirror name = 'syb_dev5'**
        go

6-8.   **disk unmirror name = 'tstdb_dev1', mode = remove**
        go

6-9.   **select name, low/16777216**
        ** from master..sysdevices**
        go

6-10.   **select name, physname
    from master..sysdevices
    where status &64 = 64
go**

6-11.   **select name, physname
    from master..sysdevices
    where cntrltype != 0
go**

6-12.   **sp_helpdevice
go**

7

Creating and Managing Databases

The SQL Server database is home to a variety of objects, which are organized into three distinct areas. These areas are the *system data*, the *user data*, and the *transaction log*, as Figure 7-1 illustrates. The transaction log is where SQL Server records all changes within a database.

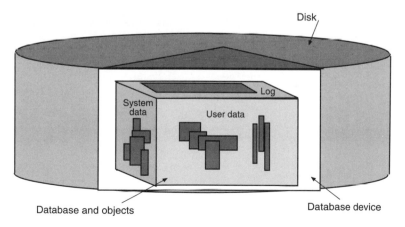

Figure 7-1. *The database and its objects*

Segments are logical names that allow you to assign objects to different database devices. You make the association using the **create table** and **create index** commands. Segments are just names; they do not occupy space. When you use the **create database** command, SQL Server creates a database for you and organizes it into at least the three segments that follow. Figure 7-2 is a conceptual representation of how SQL Server allocates segments by default.

- The *system* segment stores the database's system tables, such as *sysusers* and *sysobjects*.

- The *logsegment* stores the database's transaction log. If one transaction log spans many database devices, SQL Server creates a *logsegment* for each database device. So a transaction log that spans four database devices has four *logsegments*, all with the same name.

- The *default* segment stores all other database objects (unless there is one or more user-defined segments on which you explicitly place objects).

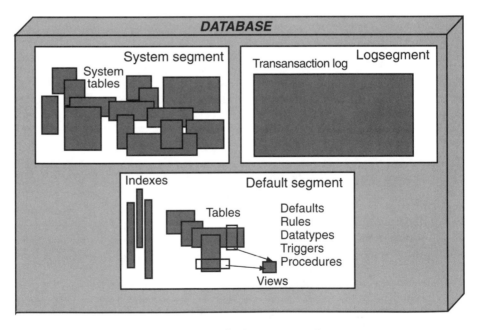

Figure 7-2. *SQL Server's default segment allocation strategy*

Deciding Where to Place Data and logsegments

When you create a database without specifying data or transaction log options, by default SQL Server places the data and log together on the same database device. For production databases, we recommend that you place the data and transaction log on different database devices for many reasons.

- It limits the log size so the log can't compete with other objects for disk space.

- It improves performance.

- It ensures full recovery if the disk with the data crashes.

- It allows the use of the threshold manager to prevent the transaction log from filling. (See Chapter 10, Transaction Management, for more information about the threshold manager.)

You use the **dump tran** command to back up incremental changes to the transaction log, which helps to ensure recoverability.

Tip! We recommend that you place the transaction log and the data on different database devices in production environments. This is because SQL Server cannot use the threshold manager on the *logsegment* if the log is stored on the same device as the data.

How System Tables Manage Disk Storage

SQL Server directs the placement of database objects within user databases using the system tables *sysdevices*, *sysusages*, and *sysdatabases* in the *master* database, and the system tables *syssegments* and *sysindexes* in all databases. Table 7-1 lists what each table manages, and Figure 7-3 illustrates the relationship between these system tables.

Table 7-1. *System tables that manage database objects*

System table	SQL Server adds	What it manages
sysdevices	• One row to *sysdevices* every time **disk init** creates a database device. • One row every time **sp_addumpdevice** adds a dump device.	• Database devices and dump devices. • Maintains the mapping between the physical device and the database so that device reflects N-N mapping.
sysusages	• One row to *sysusages* for every database allocation. Every row in *sysdatabases* can have one or more rows in *sysusages*.	• Space allocated to every database. • Maps a device fragment to its possible segment assignments in a user database. • Maps *syssegments* table in the user database.
sysdatabases	• One row for every database.	• Databases.
syssegments	• One row to *syssegments* every time **sp_addsegment** adds a new segment.	• Tracks segments as they are created and removed.
sysindexes	• One row for each table, index, or table with text.	• Tracks where each clustered index, nonclustered index, and chain of text or image pages is stored.

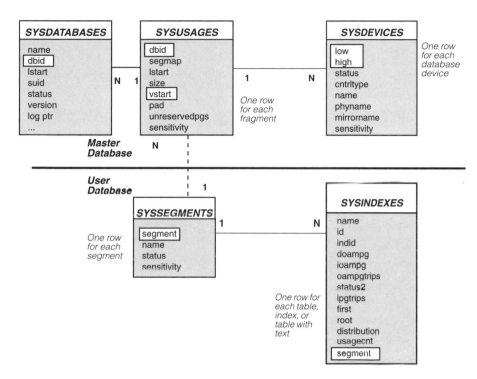

Figure 7-3. *Relationship between system tables used for disk management*

Estimating Database Size

You need to know the approximate size of a database before you create it. Normally, you have a documented database design plan that includes all tables, indexes, integrity constraints, and relationships between tables. This plan should also include scripts to create all of the database tables and indexes.

You can use the database design to create a prototype database and run the system procedure **sp_estspace** to calculate the size of each table and its index. The section "Using the System Procedure *sp_estspace*" later in this chapter explains how to use this system procedure.

Procedure for Estimating Database Size

Use a worksheet like the example in Figure 7-4 to estimate database size using the following procedure.

1. Create a test database with minimum size on any test or development database device. (See "Creating a Database" later in this chapter for database creation syntax.)

2. Create a text file that creates the tables and indexes, and run this file.

3. Decide the *fillfactor* level. *Fillfactor* specifies the percentage of data with which each page is filled. For a read-only database running data warehouse or DSS applications, a *fillfactor* of 100 percent is recommended.

4. Execute the **sp_estspace** system procedure on each of the tables with an approximate number of rows.

5. Add all of the results from running **sp_estspace** on each table.

6. Estimate approximate disk space to store other database objects such as triggers, stored procedures, views, defaults, rules, and datatypes. Add this estimate to your result from step 5.

7. Estimate space for system tables that will grow, especially tables like *sysusers*, where the user names are stored, and the table *sysprotects*, where SQL Server stores permissions on each database object. Add this estimate to your result from step 6.

8. Estimate the space that will be needed for the transaction log and add this estimate to the result from step 7. Figure 7-4 gives you more details for calculating transaction log space.

9. Estimate a percentage of the result in step 9 as a growth factor. Add this estimate to your result in step 8.

Point to Note: It is important to review the database size of each table and index at least every six months to make sure that the database can accommodate growth.

	Table Name	Row total (sp_estspace)	Data (A)	Index (B)	Total (C)
1.					
2.					
3.					
			Total (C)		
	Database objects such as procedures, triggers, etc.		Total (D)		
	Transaction log space		Total (E)		
	Buffer for growth — a percentage of (C+D+E)		Total (F)		
	Total Database Size = C + D + E + F		**TOTAL**		

Figure 7-4. *Template of worksheet for calculating database size*

Using the System Procedure *sp_estspace*

Run the system procedure **sp_estspace** on the test database before creating the production database to estimate how much space a table and its indexes require. The **sp_estspace** procedure also tells you the time needed to create the index. Table 7-2 gives the syntax.

Table 7-2. *Syntax and parameters for the **sp_estspace** system procedure*

sp_estspace *table_name,*
   est_num_of_rows
   [*fill_factor*
   [, *cols_to_max*
   [, *textbin_lin*
   [, *iosec*]]]]

table_name	Name of the table for which you are estimating space.
est_num_of_rows	Estimated number of rows that the table will contain.
fill_factor	Index *fillfactor*. If not specified, SQL Server uses its default *fillfactor*. *Fillfactor* specifies the percentage of data with which each page is filled for creating an index. For a clustered index, this is the percentage filled for data pages. For a nonclustered index, this is the percentage to be filled for index pages.

(continued)

Table 7-2. *(continued)*

cols_to_max	A comma-separated list of the variable-length columns for which to use the maximum rather than the average length. The default value is the average declared length of the variable-length columns.
textbin_len	Length per row of all text and image columns. The default value is 0. There is no need to specify this value unless the table stores text or image data. In the actual table, each row stores a pointer to this data. The data is stored in a separate set of data pages from the rest of the table's data. The **sp_estspace** procedure prints a separate line of information about the size of the text or image pages for a row.
iosec	The number of disk I/Os per second on this machine. This is used to calculate the amount of time required to create the indexes.

Examples: Estimating Database Size

The examples in this section show commands and a script for creating tables, and illustrate the use of the **sp_estspace** procedure.

Example 1: The following command creates a table.

```
create table
  vendor (vend_id char(10),
  vend_name char(50))
go
```

Execute the following command to estimate the space needed for the table in this example that will have about 100,000 rows.

```
sp_estspace vendor, 100000
go
```

This example uses the default *fillfactor* value. This is a sample of its output.

```
name    type   idx_level  Pages  Kbytes
------  -----  ---------  -----  ------
vendor  data       0      3176   6351

Total_Mbytes
------------
      6.20
(return status = 0)
```

Example 2: The following script creates a table called *prod_mast*.

```
create table prod_mast
 (prod_id char(10),
 prod_name char(50),
 vend_id char(10),
 prod_cat int)
go
create clustered index idx0
 on prod_mast(prod_id)
go
create nonclustered index idx1
 on prod_mast(vend_id)
create nonclustered index idx2
 on prod_mast(prod_cat)
sp_estspace prod_mast, 100000
go
```

This creates a table named *prod_mast*, then creates a clustered index and two nonclustered indexes on the table. After creating the table, the script estimates the size of the table for 100,000 rows. This results in the following output.

```
name            type            idx_level   Pages    Kbytes
-----  ------    -----------     ---------   -----    ------
prod_mast       data               0        7740
idx0            clustered          0         30        60
idx0            clustered          1         1          2
idx1            nonclustered       0        863       1726
idx1            nonclustered       1         10        20
idx1            nonclustered       2         1          2
idx2            nonclustered       0        553       1106
idx2            nonclustered       1         5         10
idx2            nonclustered       2         1          2
Total_Mbytes
------- ------------
           10.42
```

Example 3: This example calculates the size of a table with 50,000 rows and a *fillfactor* of 75 percent. The second command uses the **average** function with the *datalength* parameter to calculate the length of an image data column to pass this value to execute the **sp_estspace** procedure.

```
declare @txt_len int
 select @txt_len = avg (datalength(pic))
 from au_pix
go
exec sp_estspace au_pix, 50000, 75, null, @txt_len
go
```

Here's the output from the **sp_estspace** system procedure.

```
name            type            idx_level   Pages     Kbytes
-----------     ---------------  ----------- --------  ------
au_pix          data            0           2018      4036
au_pix          text/image      0           150000    300000

Total_Mbytes
------------------
        296.91

(return status = 0)
```

Estimating Transaction Log Space

SQL Server logs all data modification operations (insert, update, and delete) in transaction logs, except for operations that result from the use of the *fast bcp* utility, which generates transaction log entries only for allocation and deallocation.

It is important to calculate transaction log size to ensure that you allocate enough space. If a database's transaction log becomes full, all operations that modify data will be suspended for that database until the transaction log is allocated more space.

SQL Server does not offer a method or procedure for calculating the optimal size of the transaction log as it does for tables and indexes, but your estimation will be more accurate if you consider the factors listed in Table 7-3.

Table 7-3. *Factors to consider for estimating log size*

Factor	Description
Dump frequency	If the transaction log will be dumped frequently to save completed transactions, a database can tolerate a smaller log size.
Database option	How the database option *truncate log on checkpoint* is set.
	If this database option is set to true, you can't dump the log and the log will be cleared when a checkpoint is executed on that database. You will not be able to recover a database using the transaction log (not good for production databases). You can manage a database with less space for the transaction log, because it is cleared at checkpoints.

(continued)

Table 7-3. *(continued)*

Factor	Description
Modification frequency	If there is a high frequency of insert, update, and delete transactions, the transaction log will fill faster and will require more space. Modification frequency is application dependent.
Transaction duration	If transactions are kept open longer, they tend to fill the log faster.
Bulk copy method	If you use **bcp** to transfer data from a UNIX file to a database table with indexes or triggers, SQL Server uses *slow bcp*, which produces many transaction log pages. The database must have more space for a log if the application uses slow bcp.
Data replication	If the database is the primary source of data for replication, the Replication Server replicates the data modifications. LTM (Log Transfer Manager) of Replication Server maintains the secondary log truncation point, and this point is moved forward in the log as transactions are replicated. If the LTM fails for any reason, the transaction log cannot be truncated until the LTM is up and running. So you need more transaction log space to hold transactions in the event of LTM failure.
Transactions affecting all tables	If there are transactions that affect entire tables, the transaction log fills quickly and requires space dependent on the size of the tables.

Example: The transaction in this example affects the entire *Price-master* table. This updates statement logs before and after images of every row.

```
update Price-master
 set cost_price = cost_price * 1.2
go
```

The size of the transaction log depends on the application and the nature of the transactions. However, if the application does not use transaction logging, the size of the transaction log can be very small. For example, data warehouse and DSS applications require no transaction logging. The operations are read only, so the transaction log space can be minimal.

Creating, Altering, and Dropping Databases

You create user databases with the **create database** command. **Create database** allocates disk space on database devices to a database. It clears every page of the database device that it will use before it creates the database, so the time it takes is proportional to the size of the database. It's not unusual for the operation to take several minutes.

Preparation

Here are a few things to check before you execute the **create database** command.

- Do you have permissions that allow you to create a database? If you don't, ask the database administrator to grant **create database** permission to your login.

- Are you a user in the *master* database? You must be a user in the *master* database to create a database. To check, execute the system procedure **sp_helpuser** from the *master* database using your login name as the parameter, as the following example illustrates.

```
use master
go
sp_helpuser <login>
go
```

- Is there enough space on the database device to create the database?

```
select b.name,
  disk_space = (high - low - (sum(size))) / 512
from sysusages a, sysdevices b
where a.vstart between b.low and b.high
and b.name = <enter database device name>
group by b.name
go
```

Creating a Database

After you estimate the size of the database that you want to create, use the **create database** command. Table 7-4 gives the syntax for this command.

Table 7-4. *Syntax and parameters for the* **create database** *command*

---

create database *database_name*
  [on {default | *database_device*} [= *size*]
  [, *database_device* [= *size*]] ...]
  [log on *database_device* [= *size*]
  [, *database_device* [= *size*]] ...]
  [with {override, dbmaxhold[=] "label1" }]

database_name	The name of the database.
default	Instructs SQL Server to create the database on the default database device. You can list default database devices using the command: **select** *name* **from master..sysdevices** where (status & 1) = 1.
database_device	Name of the logical database device on which the database will be created. A database can span multiple database devices.
size	The amount of disk space, in megabytes, that is to be allocated to the database on the specified database device. By default, the size of the database is the size specified by the default database size configuration parameter or the size of the model database, whichever is larger.
log on	Indicates that the transaction log is to be stored separately on the specified logical database devices. This is an optional keyword.
with override	Mandatory when the same device is specified in the *on* and *log on* clauses of the create database command.
for load	This option expedites the **create database** operation by avoiding the page initialization at create database time.

Tip! Because the **create database** command modifies system tables in the *master* database, back up the *master* database every time you create a new database.

Examples: Creating Databases

These examples illustrate the versatility of the **create database** command. They show how to create databases on default and specified database devices, how to specify the database size, and how to allocate transaction log space for the database.

Example 1: The following command creates a database on the default device. The size of the database is determined by the default database size configuration parameter or the size of the *model* database, whichever is larger.

```
create database test_db
go
```

Example 2: The next command creates a database called *test_db* and allocates 20MB for both the data and transaction log on the default device.

```
create database test_db
 on default = 20
go
```

Example 3: The following command creates a database named *test_db* on logical device *data_dev*. The size of the database is determined by the size of the *model* database or the SQL Server configuration parameter default database size, whichever is larger.

```
create database test_db
 on data_dev
go
```

Example 4: This example creates a database named *test_db* with 40MB of space on device *data_dev1* and 40MB on device *data_dev2* for data, and 20MB on device *log_dev* for the transaction log. The data size is 80MB and the total database size is 100MB.

```
create database test_db
 on data_dev1 = 40, data_dev2 = 40,
 log on log_dev = 20
go
```

Example 5: The next command creates a database named *test_db* with 40MB of space reserved for data and 20MB for transaction log. Both data and transaction log reside on device *data_dev1*. Because the data and the transaction log reside on same device and the size of transaction log is specified, it is necessary to specify the option *with override*.

```
create database test_db
 on data_dev1 = 40,
 log on data_dev1 = 20 with override
go
```

Example 6: This last example creates a database named *test_db* with 40MB of space reserved for data and 20MB for transaction log. The *for load* option determines that the user must load the database from backup media.

```
create database test_db
 on data_dev1 = 40,
 log on log_dev = 20 for load
go
```

Point to Note: To assign ownership of a database to a user, the system administrator should create the database and change the ownership to the user with the system procedure **sp_changedbowner**.

What Happens in the Server

SQL Server performs the following actions when it executes the **create database** command.

1. Verifies that the database name specified in the command is unique.

2. Ensures that the database device names specified in the command are available.

3. Obtains an unused identification number for the new database from *master.dbo.sysdatabases*.

4. Assigns space to the database on the specified devices and updates the *sysusages* table in the *master* database to reflect these assignments.

5. Inserts a row into the *sysdatabases* table.

6. Copies the *model* database to a new database, thereby creating all of the database objects in the *model* database in the new database.

7. Initializes the remaining database pages. When the option *for load* is used, the process of initializing data pages does not take place except for the allocation pages.

8. Creates the *sysegments* table with three default entries, one for each segment: *system*, *default*, and *logsegment*.

Changing Database Size

You allocate additional space using the **alter database** command when a database object or transaction log outgrows its available space; however, you can not decrease database space. The **alter database** command is also useful to prepare to load a database from backup media. Table 7-5 gives the syntax for this command.

Table 7-5. *Syntax and parameters for the **alter database** command*

---

alter database *database_name*
  [on {*default*|*database_device*}[= *size*]
  [, *database_device* [= *size*]] ...]
  [log on {*default* | *database_device*} [= *size*]
  [, *database_device* [= *size*]] ...]
  [*with override*][*for load*]

database_name	Name of the database.
on	Indicates that you want to specify a size or location for the database extension. If log and data are on separate devices, use this clause for the data device and *log on* for the log device.
default	Instructs SQL Server to alter the database on the *default* database device. You can list default database devices using the command: **select** *name* from **master..sysdevices**.
database_device	Name of the logical database device on which the database will be created.
size	The amount of disk space, in megabytes, to be allocated to the database on the specified database device. The default value is the same as the minimum size, 1MB.
log on	Indicates the transaction log is to be stored separately on the specified database devices. The *log on* clause uses the same defaults as the *on* clause.
with override	Must be included when the same device is specified in the *on* and *log on* clauses.
for load	Mandatory when the user wants to load the database from backup immediately after altering the database.

Points to Note: Successful Database Management

- The *master* database can be extended only on the *master* device.

- You cannot drop a corrupted database using **drop database**. Instead, use **dbcc dbrepair** (*dbname*, **dropdb**) as described in Chapter 15, Database Administration Tools.

(continued)

- To recreate a database, issue **create database** and **alter database** commands in the same order that you previously used to extend the database. If you don't use the same order, you will not be able to load the database from back-up media.

Examples: Altering the Database

The following examples show how to use the **alter database** command to add space to a database, to specify its use, and to increase the transaction log space. They also illustrate how to use some of the **alter database** options.

Example 1: The following command adds 1MB of space to the database *testdb* on the default disk. If the database and the log are on separate devices, the new space (1MB) is added to the data area. Otherwise, it is available to both the data-base and the log.

```
alter database testdb
go
```

Example 2: The next command adds 10MB of space to the database *testdb* on the database device *syb_dev1*. If the database and the log are on separate devices, the new space (1MB) is added to the data area. Otherwise, it is available to both the database and the log.

```
alter database testdb
 on syb_dev1=10
go
```

Example 3: This next command increases the transaction log size by 10MB. It increases only the transaction log space, not the database space.

```
alter database testdb log
 on log_dev1=10
go
```

Example 4: This example extends the database *testdb* by 40MB, 30MB for data and 10MB for transaction log.

```
alter database testdb
 on syb_dev2 =20, syb_dev3 = 10,
 log on log_dev1=10
go
```

Example 5: This example extends the database *testdb* by 20MB, 10MB for data and 10MB for transaction log. The option *with override* must be specified because the data and log reside on the same device.

```
alter database testdb
 on syb_dev2 =10 log
 on syb_dev2=10
 with override
go
```

Example 6: This example extends the database *testdb* by 30MB, 20MB for data and 10MB for transaction log. The option *for load* is specified because the database will be loaded using backup media.

```
alter database testdb
 on syb_dev2 = 20 log
 on syb_dev2=10
 for load
go
```

The *for load* option in the **alter database** command is used in conjunction with a **create database** command that uses the *for load* option. The *dbo* or *sa* could have created the database with the *for load* option and subsequently decide that the database should be extended or modified. The *dbo* or *sa* can use the **alter database** command with the *for load* option to avoid zeroing out the pages, which saves time.

Tip! Always save the scripts you use to create and alter a database. To recreate a damaged database, you must create and alter the database in the same order it was originally created and extended, which could be difficult to do without the scripts. Additionally, you can use the **bcp** utility to save a copy of the *sysusages*, *sysdevices*, and *sysdatabases* system tables, so that if necessary the *sa* or *dbo* will have a reference from which to recreate the database.

What Happens in the Server

When SQL Server executes **alter database**, it performs the following the activities.

1. Verifies that the database name is available in the *sysdatabases* table.

2. Ensures that the specified database devices are available and that there is enough space in them.

3. Assigns space to the database on the specified device and updates the *sysusages* table in the *master* database to reflect these assignments.

4. Initializes the newly extended database pages, except when the *for load* option is specified. In the latter case, the process of initializing the data pages does not occur. Only allocation pages are initialized.

Dropping a Database

When a database is not in use, you can use the following command to remove it and free the space allocated to it. The *dbname* parameter is the name of the database you are dropping.

*Table 7-6. Syntax and parameter for the **drop database** command*

drop database *dbname*	
dbname	The name of the database to drop.

Example: The following example illustrates the **drop database** command by dropping a database named *testdb*.

```
drop database testdb
```

What Happens in the Server

When SQL Server executes the **drop database** command, it removes the row containing the database name and the space allocated to the database by deleting the rows containing the database ID from the *sysdatabases* table.

Tip! Back up a database before you drop it and back up the *master* database after executing the **drop database** command, because **drop database** completely removes the database.

Database Options

Database options control characteristics of a database, such as transaction handling, defaults and identity for table column usage, access restrictions, transaction log behavior, bulk copy operations, and recovery. You can set the following options using **sp_dboption** as described later in this chapter in the section called "Setting Up Database Options."

- The *abort tran on log full* option tells SQL Server what to do for in-progress transactions when the last-chance threshold is crossed. If this option is set to true, all of the user operations that need to write to the transaction log are aborted until space in the transaction log has been freed or extended.

- The *allow nulls by default* option, when set to true, tells SQL Server to change the default type of a column definition from not null to null for any tables created. By default, the columns in a table do not allow null values unless you specifically request that they are allowed when you create the table.

- The *auto identity* option, when set to true, tells SQL Server to add a 10-digit identity column to each new table that is created without a specification for a primary key, a unique constraint, or an identity column.

- The *dbo use only* option, when set to true, allows only the database owner to use the database.

- The *ddl in tran* option, when set to true, tells SQL Server to allow the commands listed in Table 7-7 to be used inside a user-defined transaction.

- The *identity in nonunique index*, when set to true, tells SQL Sever that there will be at least one identity column already defined in your table schema. If you set this option and create a nonunique index, it will automatically add the existing identity column to the index and make it unique internally.

- The *nochkpt on recovery* option, when set to false (the default condition), tells SQL Server to add a *checkpoint* record to the database if it is recovered during a SQL Server restart. This checkpoint changes a sequence number in the database, which ensures that recovery is not unnecessarily rerun.

- The *no free space acctg* option, when set to true, tells SQL Server to suppress free space accounting and execution of threshold actions for the nonlog segments. It also disables updating of the rows-per-page value stored for each table. The system procedures that estimate space usage (**sp_spaceused** and **sp_helpdb**) may report inaccurate values when this value is set to true.

- The *read only* option, when set to true, lets users retrieve data from a database, but it does not let them modify that data.

- The *select into/bulkcopy* option, when set to true, tells SQL Server to perform minimal logging when the following operations take place: **write-text** utility, *select into* a permanent table, and **bulk copy** to a table that has no indexes or triggers.

  - Using this process, SQL Server records only page allocations and reallocations in the transaction log, but not the actual changes that are made on the data pages. Because a transaction log dump cannot recover these unlogged operations, dumping a transaction to a dump device is prohibited. However, you can still issue **dump tran** with *no log* and **dump tran** with *truncate_only*

  - It is important that, after making minimally logged changes, you perform a **dump database** command, because the changes are not recoverable from transaction logs. It is not necessary to set *select into/bulkcopy* to true when selecting rows into a temporary table, when using the **bulk copy** utility to copy to a table that has indexes or triggers, or when using **bulk copy** to copy data from a table.

- The *single user* option, when set to true, dictates that only one user at a time can access the database.

- The *trunc log on chkpt* option, when set to true, tells SQL Server to truncate all committed transactions from the transaction log whenever the checkpoint process occurs. The **checkpoint** command can also be manually issued by the database owner or system administrator. You cannot dump the transaction log, because it is truncated every time the **checkpoint** command is executed; so it is not possible to recover the transaction log. This option is recommended only for development databases; it should not be set for production databases. The *tempdb* database always has the *trunclog on chkpt* option set to true.

Table 7-7. *DDL commands allowed in transactions*

Alter commands	Create commands	Drop commands	Privilege commands
alter table (columns other than partition and unpartition are allowed)	create default create index create procedure create rule create schema create table create trigger create view	drop default drop index drop procedure drop rule drop table drop trigger drop view	grant revoke

Point to Note: It is not necessary to set the *select into/bulkcopy* option to true when selecting rows into a temporary table, when bulk copying to a table that has indexes or triggers, or when using **bulk copy** to copy data from a table to a file.

Setting Up Database Options

The **sp_dboption** system procedure sets the database options to true or false. By default, all options are set to false. When **sp_dboption** executes, SQL Server updates the row containing the database name with internal values for each database option. The syntax for this system procedure is given in Table 7-8.

Table 7-8. *Syntax and parameters for the **sp_dboption** system procedure*

sp_dboption [*dbname, optname,* {true | false}]	
dbname	Name of the database for which to set the option.
optname	Name of the option to set or unset. Use quotation marks around the option name if it is a keyword, or if includes includes embedded blanks or punctuation. Options are listed in the "Database Options" section earlier in this chapter.
true, false	True sets the option and false unsets it.

Tip! After executing the system procedure **sp_dboption** on a database, issue a **checkpoint** command from within the database so that the settings take effect.

Examples: Setting Database Options

These examples show how to list all available options and how to set the *select into/bulkcopy* and *trunc log on chkpt* options.

Example 1: The following command lists all of the options that you can set.

```
sp_dboption
go
```

Example 2: The following series of commands set the *select into/bulkcopy* option on. The option *select into* uniquely identifies the *select into/bulkcopy* option among all available database options.

```
sp_dboption testdb,
 "select into", true
go
use testdb
go
checkpoint
go
```

Example 3: This example unsets the database option *trunc log on chkpt*.

```
sp_dboption testdb,
 "trunc log on chkpt", false
go
use testdb
go
checkpoint
go
```

Getting Information About Database Options

To view information about database options, execute the system procedure **sp_helpdb**. This sample output from **sp_helpdb** indicates that *trunc log on chkpt* is set to true.

```
name      db_size     owner   dbid    created       status
------    --------    ------  ------- -----------   --------------------
testdb    100.0 MB    sa      11      Dec 27, 1995  select into/bulkcopy,
    trunc log on chkpt

device_fragments      size        usage           free kbytes
----------------      --------    ---------------  ---------------
syb_dev4              100.0 MB    data and log     33720
device                            segment
----------------------------      -------------------------------
```

```
syb_dev4                          default
syb_dev4                          logsegment
syb_dev4                          system
 (return status = 0)
```

Working with Segments

Segments associate database objects with database devices. The "Segments" section earlier in this chapter gives the conceptual background for the current discussion.

Each database can have a maximum of 32 segments, including the system segments. You can store a database's data and transaction logs on separate devices, or they can share the same device. (They share the same device when you create the database on a single database device.)

Point to Note: If you store data and the transaction log on the same device, you jeopardize reliability. The section called "Deciding where to Place Data and Logsegments" at the beginning of this chapter discusses this point.

You can create user-defined segments to store database objects that SQL Server would otherwise store on the default segment. Use the system procedure **sp_addsegment** to create a segment. Then, place a table or an index on a specific user-defined segment with the **create table...on** and **create index...on** commands. For example, the following script places data on one device and text on another device. The script creates a table with data and text columns on *data_seg1*, and places the text column on a separate device, *data_seg2*.

```
create table
   vendor (vendor_id char(8), vend_text text)
   on data_seg1
go
sp_placeobject data_seg2,
   "vendor.tvendor"
go
```

You may place multiple segments on a database device, but we recommend only one segment per database device for easier database administration.

Why Use User-Defined Segments?

If you add a new database device to a database using **alter database**, it increases the space available to the database, but it does not determine which objects occupy the new space. If a table or index could grow to fill all of the device space, other critical tables that share that space will not have room to grow. One solution is to place a potentially large table or index on a separate physical device. However, segments are the best solution for this problem. You can put the object on a segment that is associated with many database devices so it can use any of the devices in that segment, but it will not be allowed to grow into any segments that contain other objects. Figure 7-5 shows an example of how to assign objects to different segments.

In Figure 7-5, the database spans four database devices. Each device is one segment, with the database objects distributed as follows.

- Segment 1 is a *user-defined* segment, which holds a table and an index that are expected to grow very large

- Segment 2 is the *logsegment,* which holds only the transaction log

- Segment 3 is the *default* segment, which holds other user data

- Segment 4 is the *system* segment, which holds all of the system tables and indexes

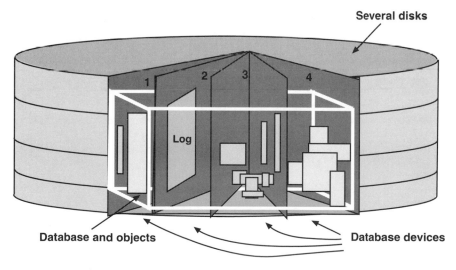

Figure 7-5. *A database spans four database devices*

Tip! If you know that a table or index could grow to fill a large portion of a shared segment, place it on a segment of its own.

Adding a Segment

The **sp_addsegment** system procedure adds a segment to a database. The maximum size of the data within a segment is the size of the database device with which it is associated. The data within the segment can also grow to just a fraction of the available space. (Recall that the segment itself does not take up space. It is the object with which it is associated that does.)

Use the system procedure **sp_helpsegment** to list the objects and potential space available on a segment. Because segments can share a common database device, the total available space is equal to the space available on the database device. Table 7-9 shows the syntax for **sp_helpsegment**.

Table 7-9. Syntax and parameters for the **sp_addsegment** system procedure

sp_addsegment *segname, dbname, devname*	
segname	Name of the segment. It is used in **create table** and **create index** statements.
dbname	Name of the database in which the segment is to be added.
devname	Name of the database device on which the segment is to be labeled.

We recommend that you back up both *master* and *user* databases before using the **sp_addsegment** system procedure because it updates the *master* database.

Tip! Creating one user segment per database device makes database administration simpler and more effective.

Example: Adding Segments

The following is partial output from **sp_helpdb** when it is run before adding a segment.

```
device                   segment
--------------------     ----------------
syb_dev1                 default
syb_dev1                 system
```

```
syb_dev2              default
syb_dev2              idx_seg2
```

The next command creates segment *data_seg1* on the *syb_dev1* database device.

sp_addsegment data_seg1, testdb, syb_dev1
go

Here is partial output from **sp_helpdb** when it is run after adding the segment.

```
device                segment
-------------------   -------------
syb_dev1              data_seg1
syb_dev1              default
syb_dev1              system
syb_dev2              default
syb_dev2              idx_seg2
```

What Happens in the Server

When a new segment is added to a database, SQL Server performs the following activities.

1. Verifies the name of the device and database.

2. Verifies that the segment name is unique.

3. Adds a row with the segment name to the table *syssegments*.

4. Updates the bitmap column *segmap* of the system table *sysusages* with the value of the segment ID of the segment in the *syssegments* table.

Extending a Segment

The growth of a table or index on a segment is limited by the maximum space specified for the segment. When a segment is full, the table or index that is stored in that segment cannot grow and SQL Server reports an error if an application tries to insert a row into the table.

The system procedure **sp_extendsegment** increases the size of a segment by adding additional database devices to the segment. Before extending a segment, check to ensure that there is sufficient space available on the database device. Table 7-10 gives the syntax for this system procedure.

Table 7-10. *Syntax and parameters for the* **sp_extendsegment** *system procedure*

sp_extendsegment *segname, dbname, devname*	
segname	The name of the segment. It is used in **create table** and **create index** commands. This segment must already be present in the *syssegment* table.
dbname	The name of the database in which the segment is to be added.
devname	The name of the database device on which the segment is to be labeled.

Examples: Extending Segments

These examples show how to use the **sp_extendsegment** system procedure to extend user and default segments.

Example 1: This example extends the segment *data_seg1* on database *syb_dev2*.

```
sp_extendsegment data_seg1, testdb, syb_dev2
go
```

Example 2: This example extends the segment *default* in another device, *syb_dev1*. *Default* is a reserved word, so it must be specified within quotes.

```
sp_extendsegment "default", testdb, syb_dev1
go
```

What Happens in the Server

When the system procedure **sp_extendsegment** executes, the column *segmap* in the *sysusages* table is updated with the segment ID stored in the *syssegment* table.

Placing an Object in a Segment

The system procedure **sp_placeobject** causes all future disk allocation for an object to occur on a new segment. Note that the procedure does not remove existing objects from the original segment or move them to the new segment. Only future allocations are placed on the new segment. You can also use **sp_placeobject** to place text or image columns on a separate chain of text pages. Table 7-11 gives the syntax for the **sp_placeobject** system procedure.

Table 7-11. *Syntax and parameters for the **sp_placeobject** system procedure*

sp_placeobject *segname, objname*	
segname	The name of the segment on which to locate the table or index.
objname	The name of the table or index for which the future allocations are to be placed on the specified segment.

Examples: Placing an Object on a Segment

These examples illustrate how to allocate a table's data to a specific segment and how to use scripts to specify data and text placement.

Example 1: The following command allocates all future data of a table named *vendor* to the segment *data_seg2*.

```
sp_placeobject data_seg2,
vendor
go
```

Example 2: This command places all subsequent space allocation for the index *supp_id* of the table named *vendor* on the segment *data_seg3*.

```
sp_placeobject data_seg3,
"vendor.supp_id"
go
```

Example 3: This script places data on one database device and text on another database device. The script creates a table with data and text columns on *data_seg2*, then it places the text column on a separate device, *data_seg3*. Notice that the text column name is not specified in the system procedure **sp_placeobject**, so the procedure places all of the text columns of the table named *vendor* on device *data_seg3*. Had we not used **sp_placeobject**, the data and text pages would have been stored on the same device by default.

```
create table
 vendor (vendor_id char(8), vend_text text)
 on data_seg2
go
sp_placeobject data_seg3, "vendor.tvendor"
go
```

Dropping a Segment

You use the system procedure **sp_dropsegment** to drop a segment from a database. However, before you drop a segment, make sure that there are no objects assigned to it. Otherwise, you receive an error message and the segment will not be dropped. You need to move the objects to another segment before you drop it. Table 7-12 gives the syntax for the **sp_dropsegment** system procedure.

Table 7-12. *Syntax and parameters for the* ***sp_dropsegment*** *system procedure*

sp_dropsegment *segname*, *dbname*, device	
segname	The name of the segment to be dropped.
dbname	The database name.
device	The name of the database device associated with the segment to be dropped.

Examples: Dropping Segments

The following examples drop segments from a database and from the *default* segment.

Example 1: This example drops the segment *data_seg2* from the database *testdb*.

```
sp_dropsegment data_seg2, testdb
go
```

Example 2: This example drops only the *default* segment of *syb_dev1* device. The *default* segment may be present in other devices.

```
sp_dropsegment "default", testdb, syb_dev1
go
```

What Happens in the Server

When SQL Server executes the **sp_dropsegment** system procedure, it checks whether any other device uses the named segment. SQL Server deletes the row containing the segment name from the system table *syssegments* of the user database only if the segment is not in use by any other device.

Getting Information About Segments

You can use the system procedures **sp_helpsegment**, **sp_helpdb**, **sp_help**, and **sp_helpindex** to get information about segments and their associated objects. Table 7-13 describes the information each of these system procedures delivers.

Table 7-13. *System procedures that give information about segments*

Procedure name	Information that it gives you
sp_helpsegment	Lists the names of all segments, and the tables or indexes associated with a particular segment name. This procedure is useful in controlling the objects in a segment.
sp_helpdb	Lists all database devices and the segments in each database device.
sp_help	With a table name as the parameter, displays information about the table and its index.
sp_helpindex	With a table name as the parameter, lists information about the indexes and location of the index (segment name).

Examples: Getting Information About Segments

These examples illustrate how to get information about all segments in a database or table, segments with database and database device information, and segments and indexes.

Example 1: The following command lists all of the segments that are available in the database from which you execute it. Notice that the output that follows the command shows the *system* segment, the *default* segment, the *logsegment*, and user-defined data segments.

```
sp_helpsegment
go
```

```
segment          name          status
------------     -----------   --------
     0           system           0
     1           default          1
     2           logsegment       0
     3           data_seg1        0
     4           idx_seg1         0
     5           data_seg2        0
     6           idx_seg2         0
     7           data_seg3        0
     8           idx_seg3         0
(return status = 0)
```

Example 2: The output that follows this command lists the objects that are stored in the *default* segment. When you specify the *default* and *system* segments, you must place them within quotes.

```
sp_helpsegment "default"
go
table_name                  index_name            indid
-----------------------      -------------------   ---------
vendor                       vend_idx               1
test1_tab                    test1_tab              0
syscomments                  syscomments            1
sysusermessages              csysusermessages       1
sysusermessages              ncsysusermessages      2
(return status = 0)
```

Example 3: This example lists three pieces of information provided by the **sp_helpdb** command. The first of these elements displays information about the *testdb* database. The second item lists information on each device that is allocated to the database. The third portion of the output displays the segments that are logically labeled to each database device.

```
sp_helpdb testdb
go
name    db_size     owner   dbid    created
------  -------      ------  ----    -------
   status
------------
testdb  100.0 MB sa  11  Dec 27, 1995 select into/bulkcopy,
   trunc log on chkpt
device_fragments    size      usage          free kbytes
----------------    --------  ------------   ---------------
syb_dev4            100.0 MB  data and log   33720
  device         segment
  ----------     ----------
syb_dev4         default
syb_dev4         logsegment
syb_dev4         system
(return status = 0)
```

Example 4: The **sp_helpindex** command used in this example lists general information about indexes. The *index_description* column lists information about segment details.

```
sp_helpindex vendor
go
```

```
index_name    index_description              index_keys
----------    ----------------------------   ----------
vend_idx      clustered, unique located on data_seg2   vend_id
(1 row affected, return status = 0)
```

Example 5: This example lists information about a table and its segments through use of the **sp_help** command.

```
sp_help vendor
go
```

```
Name       Owner     Type
------     --------  ----------
vendor     dbo       user table
 Data_located_on_segment     When_created
 -----------------------     ------------
 data_seg1                   Jan  7 1996    9:01AM
Column_name    Type    Length  Prec  Scale  Nulls  Default_name
       Rule_name    Identity
-----------    -----   -------  -----  ------  ------  -------------

       ----------   --------
vend_id        char    4       NULL  NULL   1      NULL
       NULL         0
vend_desc      char    20      NULL  NULL   1      NULL
       NULL         0
index_name     index_description                  index_keys
----------     -----------------                  ----------
vend_idx       clustered, unique located on data_seg2   vend_id
(1 row affected, return status = 0)
(return status = 0)
```

Exercises

7-1.   Name the system tables that manage database storage and objects.

7-2.   Name the system procedure that is used to estimate the size of a table.

7-3.   Name the segments that are created by SQL Server through a **create database** command.

7-4.   What is the size of a database when the size is not specified in the **create database** command?

7-5. Which options will you use if you need to create a database with data and log on the same device?

7-6. The default pool of devices includes *master* and *syb_dev2*. Suppose you create a database allocating disk space from default devices. On which device will SQL Server allocate space for the database?

7-7. What is the advantage of storing the data and transaction log on separate devices?

7-8. Under what circumstance should the *for load* option of **create database** command be used?

7-9. If a database is created with data and transaction log on the same device, what is the maximum size to which the transaction log can grow?

7-10. Give the command to extend the *master* database by 4MB.

7-11. What database option should be set when *fast bcp* is to be used?

7-12. If a segment is full and there is space available on other devices of this database, which stored procedure would you execute?

7-13. Name the command to remove a database.

7-14. How do you increase the space of a segment?

7-15. The database *testdb* has two data devices, *syb_dev1* and *syb_dev2*, on separate disks. Where would you place a table that has one clustered index and five nonclustered indexes?

7-16. Table *test_table* has 10,000 rows. List all of the steps to split the table into two separate segments, *data_seg1* and *data_seg2*.

7-17. Name the system procedure to list all of the databases that are managed by SQL Server.

Answers to Exercises

7-1. The system tables are *sysusages*, *sysdevices*, and *sysdatabases* in the *master* database, and *syssegments* and *sysindexes* in the user database.

7-2. **sp_estspace**

7-3. The segments are *default*, *system*, and *logsegment*.

7-4. The size of the *model* database or value of the configuration parameter *default database size*, whichever is larger.

7-5. The option *with override*.

7-6. The *master* device.

7-7. Transaction recoverability.

7-8. When you want to load the data after creating the database.

7-9. The size of the database device.

7-10. **alter database master on master = 4.**

7-11. Use the option *select into/bulk copy*.

7-12. Either **sp_extendsegment** or **sp_placeobject.**

7-13. **drop database**

7-14. By executing the system procedure **sp_extendsegment.**

7-15. The table will be placed on one device (for example, *syb_dev1*) and the nonclustered indexes on the other device (such as *syb_dev2*).

7-16. The four required steps are as follows.
   1. Create the table on *data_seg1*
   2. Load the first 5000 rows to the table using the **bcp** command
   3. Execute **sp_placeobject data_seg2, test_table**
   4. Load the last 5000 rows using the **bcp** command

7-17. **sp_helpdb**

8

Database Objects: Tables and Data Integrity

Chapter 3, The SQL Server Engine, introduced database objects, which include tables, indexes, datatypes, rules, defaults, triggers, views, and stored procedures. This chapter builds upon that foundation by focusing on how you use **create table** and other commands with database objects to create and maintain tables that protect the integrity of the data they hold. Stored procedures, which have a range of uses, are covered in Chapter 9, Transact-SQL and Its Extensions.

Foundation Topics

Database applications that involve data access by several to thousands of users require some way to ensure that users and other applications don't interfere with the integrity of the data stored in the database. *Data integrity* refers to the correctness and completeness of data within a database.

One way to enforce data integrity is to include input checking of data and constraints in every application that accesses the data. The other way is to use SQL Server's centralized capabilities to consistently enforce integrity for every application, user, or tool that can affect the data. Using a centralized approach to enforce data integrity is the more efficient method and ensures consistency that would otherwise be difficult to realize.

A well designed database can reliably manage data accessed by any number of applications and users. Using SQL Server database objects, you can establish tables with built-in integrity enforcement to constrain or restrict the data values that users insert, delete, or update in the database. Figure 8-1 shows how database objects interact as integrity enforcement mechanisms. You can refer back to this figure as you read about each object's role.

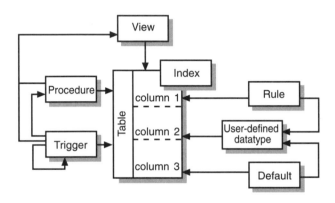

Figure 8-1. *Objects in their roles as integrity enforcers*

Table 8-1 is an overview of the constraints you can implement to maintain data integrity in a SQL Server environment. The methods to enforce the first three types of data integrity are discussed in the rest of this chapter.

Table 8-1. *Types of data integrity*

Integrity type	How it constrains data	Methods for enforcement
Validity or check integrity	Limits or restricts the data values that may be inserted in a table.	The **create table** command. (See the "Tables" section in this chapter.)
		Datatypes bound to rules and defaults. (See the "Datatypes" section.)
		Rules and defaults. (See the "Rules and Defaults" section.)

(continued)

Table 8-1. (continued)

Integrity type	How it constrains data	Methods for enforcement
Uniqueness and primary key integrity	Requires that no two table rows have the same nonnull values for one or more table columns.	The **create table** command. (See the "Tables" section.) Indexes and primary key. (See the "Indexes" section.)
Referential integrity	Requires that data inserted into a table column already have matching data in another table column or another column in the same table.	The **create table** command. (See the "Tables" section.) Use triggers with primary and foreign keys. (See the "Triggers" section.)
Consistency integrity	Requires that a set of one or more SQL commands are treated as a single unit, and that users never see or operate on data associated with the unit if the work of the whole unit is not complete.	The **create table** command. (Transactions, which are described in detail in Chapter 10, Transaction Management.)

Validity Check Constraints

Validity check constraints are enforced for every SQL update or insert into a row. These constraints restrict the values that can be inserted into a table by following rules that the table designer associates with columns in the table. Examples of this type of constraint include a list or set of values, a range of values, and a *like* clause in a SQL command.

Using a check constraint, you might mandate that a column can only accept the values 100, 200, and 300. Or, you might make a rule that a column can only accept values that have four digits starting with the number 55. You implement the last example with the command below. Each *[0–9]* indicates that the digit is valid if it is an integer between 0 and 9. So, the value 5537 would be a valid entry for this column.

column_name like "55[0-9][0-9]"

Point to Note: You can define multiple check constraints on a column.

Unique and Primary Key Constraints

The *primary key constraint* ensures that no two rows in the primary key column are the same. A table's primary key must have a unique value for each row. For example, say that newborns in a hospital are identified by their baby IDs, and *baby_id* is the primary key column in a database table that associates *baby_id* with the *parent_name* column. It would be unacceptable to have two or more of the same *baby_id* values, because parents might go home with someone else's child.

In addition to the requirement that no two rows have the same value within the primary key column, no row in the primary key can have a null value. If you were able to insert a null into the primary key column, SQL Server would not be able to figure out whether this primary key duplicates one that is already in the table.

Similarly, you can impose a *uniqueness constraint* on any column other than the primary key. Unique constraints ensure that no two rows in a table have the same values in specified columns. They permit one (and only one) null value in the column. In that way, unique constraints are less restrictive than primary key constraints.

Each of these constraints creates an index by default. A unique constraint creates a unique nonclustered index, while a primary key constraint creates a unique clustered index on the primary key column. This subject is discussed in more detail in the "Indexes" section later in this chapter. We use unique constraints all the time in our daily lives to select one item out of millions. Here are some examples.

- Driver's license number—uniquely identifies a single driver

- Bank account number—uniquely identifies a single account

- Bar code—uniquely identifies a supermarket item

- Employee number—uniquely identifies an employee in a company

We can define a unique constraint on a column named *emp_no* in an employee table as long as the column is not the primary key. This automatically creates a nonclustered index on *emp_no* and does not allow duplicate values for *emp_no* to be entered in the table. There can be only one row in the table with a null value for column *emp_no*.

Consider a table called *sales* that has three columns: *stor_id*, *ord_num*, and *date*. We can define a primary key constraint on *stor_id* and on *ord_num*. This constraint enforces nonnull values in the columns and ensures that they are unique by creating a unique clustered index on the columns. In this example, the constraints are defined at the table level.

Referential Integrity Constraints

Referential integrity ensures that vital data in your database remains accurate. It refers to the rules governing data consistency across tables. You can declare referential integrity constraints to require that data inserted into a *referencing* table that defines the constraint must have matching values in a *referenced* table. A referential integrity constraint is satisfied if any column in the referencing table included with the constraint contains a null value, or if columns in the referencing table included with the constraint match the corresponding columns in the referenced table.

The following example gives you a preview of the SQL **create table** command (described in more detail in the Tables section below) and of the use of datatypes (described in the "Datatypes" section later in this chapter). The referential integrity constraint in the following example is indicated in italic type. Figure 8-2 conceptually shows what the tables generated by the following command might look like.

```
create table publishers
      (pub_id    char (4),
      pub_name varchar (40)
      references my_titles (pub_id))
```

This SQL command creates a table called *publishers* with two columns. *Pub_id* is a four-character entity, while *pub_name* is a variable character string that can contain up to 40 characters.

The *pub_id* column plays a different role in each of the tables that we created with the above command. It is the primary key for the *publishers* table, so every row in the *pub_id* column must be unique in the *publishers* table. In the *my_titles* table, *pub_id* is a foreign key. By the referential integrity constraint, this means that *pub_id* in *my_titles* must match a *pub_id* value in publishers.

My_titles is referencing publishers, so it is the referencing table, which makes publishers the referenced table. The referenced table cannot be dropped without first dropping the referencing table. Also, the rows in the referenced table cannot be deleted if one or more rows are matching in the referencing tables.

my_titles table		publishers table	
title_id	pub_id	pub_id	pub_name
BU1032	1389	0736	New Age Books ...
BU111	1389	0877	Binnet & Harley
BU2075	0736	1389	Algodata Infosystems
BU7832	1389		
MC2222	0877		
MC3021	0877		

Foreign key values   **Primary key values**

Figure 8-2. Two SQL Server tables that illustrate referential integrity

Points to Note: Referential Integrity Constraints

Keep the following points in mind when working with referential integrity constraints.

- SQL Server does not enforce referential integrity constraints on temporary tables that include any tables in the *tempdb* database.

- Objects in *tempdb* are only temporary and are deleted whenever SQL Server is shut down.

- The datatypes of the referencing table columns must be exactly identical to those of the columns in the referenced table.

- A table can include a referential integrity constraint on itself.

- If referential integrity is enforced using both referential integrity constraints and triggers, SQL Server first checks for referential integrity constraints before the triggers are fired.

- Error messages cannot be created and bound to constraints.

Implementing Data Integrity Constraints

As you might have noticed, Sybase Transact-SQL provides several mechanisms for enforcing integrity. You can categorize these methods into two groups, those that define rules, defaults, indexes, and triggers; and those that define **create table** integrity constraints. Choosing one of these methods rather than the other depends on your requirements. The **create table** method for implementing integrity constraints during table creation is the simpler alternative. However, **create table** integrity constraints are more limited in scope and less comprehensive than defaults, rules, indexes, and triggers. Triggers provide more rigorous handling of referential integrity than the **create table** command. Also, the integrity constraints defined by **create table** are specific for that table—unlike rules or defaults, which can be bound to several tables. You can only drop or change **create table** constraints using the **alter table** command. Constraints cannot contain subqueries or aggregate functions, even on the same table.

The two methods for implementing constraints are not mutually exclusive. You can use integrity constraints along with defaults, rules, indexes, and triggers. This gives you the flexibility to choose the method that works best for your application. The next sections describe how to use **create table** integrity constraints, defaults, rules, indexes, and triggers.

Datatypes

Datatypes give you a way to tell SQL Server about the characteristics of the data you put in your tables. Datatypes also help to enforce validity checking. When a table is created, each column in the table is assigned a datatype, and SQL Server ensures that only data that adheres to the properties of that type is inserted into the column. For example, if a *patient_no* column is defined as an integer using the datatype *int*, SQL Server produces an error if a SQL **insert** or **update** command tries to store a character string or a decimal number in that column.

There are two categories of datatypes. *System-supplied datatypes* come with SQL Server, while *user-defined datatypes* don't exist until you create them. The system table *systypes* contains one row for each system-defined datatype and one row for each user-defined datatype. So every time you create a user-defined datatype, SQL Server adds a row to *systypes*. Each system-supplied datatype name is associated with a fixed property for the number of storage bytes it uses, which also determines the range of values it can take.

System-Supplied and User-Defined Datatypes

SQL Server provides the system-supplied datatypes—a group of predefined datatypes that characterize many types of data typically used in databases. The categories of system-supplied datatypes include numbers, date and time, characters, money, binary values, and images and text. A complete list of system-supplied datatypes is found in Appendix C.

User-defined datatypes are custom datatypes that you create using system-supplied datatypes as building blocks. You can bind your own mix of rules and defaults to a user-defined datatype, then associate the datatype with columns. In this way, datatypes help enforce consistency among the columns of different tables by allowing different database designers to work with the same set of custom datatypes. A user-defined datatype is available for tables in all databases if you create the datatype in the *model* database.

Creating User-Defined Datatypes

You create a new user-defined datatype in one step with the **sp_addtype** system procedure. The format for **sp_addtype** is followed by a description of its parameters in Table 8-2.

*Table 8-2. Parameters used by the **sp_addtype** system procedure*

sp_addtype typename,
   phystype [(length) | (precision [, scale]) |
   [, "identity" | nulltype]

typename	Name of the new datatype.
phystype	Existing system-supplied datatype on which to base the new datatype.
length	The number of bytes the new char-based datatype requires.
precision, scale	For numeric and decimal datatypes, specifies the degree of accuracy required.
identity	Establishes identity for the datatype. Should have an underlying type of numeric and a scale of 0.
nulltype	Establishes whether the datatype is nullable; legal values are null and not null (default).

Examples: Creating User-Defined Datatypes

These examples illustrate how to create user-defined datatypes that can and cannot take null values.

Example 1: This example creates a character datatype called *tid* that can be six bytes long and is not nullable. After the *tid* datatype exists, anyone can use it to define a column when he or she creates a table in the database in which *tid* was defined.

```
sp_addtype tid, "char(6)", "not null"
go
```

Example 2: This example creates an integer datatype called *ud1* that can take null values.

```
sp_addtype ud1, int, "null"
go
```

Example 3: This example creates a datetime-based datatype called *ud2*.

```
sp addtype ud2, datetime
go
```

Example 4: This example creates a datatype called *ud3* based on the numeric system-supplied datatype.

```
sp_addtype ud3, "numeric(10,0)", "identity"
go
```

Points to Note: User-Defined Datatypes

Keep the following points in mind when working with user-defined datatypes.

- Sybase provides two ready-made user-defined datatypes: *timestamp* and *sysname*. (Note: You cannot create another user-defined datatype based on the timestamp datatype.)

- A user-defined datatype is only available in the database in which it was created.

- You cannot create a datatype based on another user-defined datatype.

- You cannot drop a user-defined datatype that is in use.

Getting Information About Datatypes

The **sp_help** system procedure displays information about the properties of both system and user-defined datatypes. For example, **sp_help** *employee* lists all of the columns and datatypes for a table called *employee*. The **sp_help** report indicates the column types, whether the datatype allows nulls, the names of any rules and defaults bound to the datatype, and whether it has the identity property described later in this chapter. The following illustrates an **sp_help** report for a table called *titles*.

```
1> sp_help titles
2> go

Name          Owner           Type
-------       ---------------  --------------------
titles        dbo             user table

Data_located_on_segment       When_created
-------------------------      --------------------------
default                        Apr 10 1996   6:04PM
```

Column_name	Type	Length	Prec	Scale	Nulls	Default_name	Rule_name	Identity
title_id	tid	6	NULL	NULL	0	NULL	title_idrule	0
title	varchar	80	NULL	NULL	0	NULL	NULL	0
type	char	12	NULL	NULL	0	typedflt	NULL	0
pub_id	char	4	NULL	NULL	1	NULL	NULL	0
price	money	8	NULL	NULL	1	NULL	NULL	0
advance	money	8	NULL	NULL	1	NULL	NULL	0
total_sales	int	4	NULL	NULL	1	NULL	NULL	0
notes	varchar	200	NULL	NULL	1	NULL	NULL	0
pubdate	datetime	8	NULL	NULL	0	datedflt	NULL	0
contract	bit	1	NULL	NULL	0	NULL	NULL	0

index_name	index_description	index_keys	index_max_rows_per_page
titleidind	clustered, unique located on default	title_id	0
titleind	nonclustered located on default	title	0

```
(2 rows affected)
```

keytype	object	related_object	object_keys	related_keys
foreign	roysched	titles	title_id, *, *, *, *, *, *, *	title_id, *,
*, *, *, *, *, *				
foreign	salesdetail	titles	title_id, *, *, *, *, *, *, *	title_id, *,
*, *, *, *, *, *				
foreign	titleauthor	titles	title_id, *, *, *, *, *, *, *	title_id, *,
*, *, *, *, *, *				
foreign	titles	publishers	pub_id, *, *, *, *, *, *, *	pub_id, *, *,

```
*, *, *, *, *
 primary  titles        — none —title_id, *, *, *, *, *, *, *    *, *, *, *, *, *, *, *
Object is not partitioned.
```

Tables

This section gives background, functions, and examples for creating, altering, and dropping tables, and for enforcing integrity constraints using the **create table** command. You obtain information about a table using the system procedure **sp_help** with the table name as a parameter. For example, the **sp_help** *employee* lists information about a table called *employee*.

Creating Tables

When you create a table, you specify a name for each column and the column's datatype. You also can use parameters to establish the **create table** integrity constraints described in the "Foundation Topics" section early in this chapter. For every new table, SQL Server adds a new row to *sysobjects* and inserts a value of *U* into *sysobjects' type* column, indicating that the new table is user created. The simplest form of using the **create table** is as follows.

create table *table_name*
  (column_name datatype)

To create a table called *drivers* with one column called *driver_id* in which IDs can be up to 20 characters long and another column called *driver_name*, the contents of which can be a string up to 40 characters long, you enter the following command.

```
create table drivers
  (driver_id varchar(20),
   driver_name varchar(40))
go
```

Below is an abbreviated syntax for the **create table** command, followed by a description of its parameters in Table 8-3. (See Appendix C for the complete syntax.) Many of the options of this command are for enforcing integrity. You'll understand them better as you read this chapter.

Table 8-3. *Parameters used by the create table command*

```
create table [table_name
  (column_name datatype
  [default] {[{identity | null | not null}]
  | [[constraint constraint_name]
  {{unique | primary key}
  clustered | nonclustered]
  with {fillfactor | max_rows_per_page} = x]
  | references ref_table
  | check (search_condition)]} ...
  | [constraint constraint_name]
  {{unique | primary key}
  [clustered | nonclustered]
  (column_name [{, column_name} ...])
  [with {fillfactor | max_rows_per_page}=x]
  [on segment_name]
  | foreign key (column_name)
  references ref_table
  [(ref_column [{, ref_column}...])]...}
```

table_name	Name of the table you are creating. Must be unique within a database and to the owner. Temporary tables can be created either with a pound symbol (#) or as *tempdb*.
column_name	Name of the column in the table.
datatype	Datatype of the column. Can be either a system-defined or a user-defined datatype.
default	The default value for a column. SQL Server inserts this value if the user does not provide one.
constant_expression	Constant expression used as a default value for the column.
user	null	Inserts the user name, or null if not specified.
identity	Use to indicate that the column has the *identity* property. Identity columns store sequential numbers, such as employee numbers in a payroll application.
null	not null	User must enter a value if not *null* is specified. If *null* is specified, SQL Server assigns a null value if a user does not provide a value during insertion; no default exists for the column.
constraint	Name of an integrity constraint.
constraint_name	Name of the unique constraint or primary key constraint. *Unique* is used to constrain the values of the indicated columns to disallow two rows from containing the same value.

(continued)

Table 8-3. *(continued)*

clustered | nonclustered	Specifies that the unique or primary key constraint is a clustered or nonclustered index.
fillfactor	Specifies how full SQL Server will make each page when creating a new index on data that already is present. *Fillfactor* is a percentage be-tween 1 and 100. The default value for fillfactor is 0.
max_rows_per_page	Limits the number of rows on data pages and the leaf pages of indexes. Valid values for *max_rows_per_page* are between 0 and 256. The default is 0.
on segment_name	Creates the index on the named segment. (See Chapter 7 for more information on segments.)
references	Creates a referential integrity constraint on the specified list of columns.
foreign_key	Specifies that the columns are foreign keys in the table whose target keys are listed in the *references* clause.
ref_table	Name of the table that has the referenced columns.
ref_column	Name of the columns in the referenced table check used to create check constraints on columns and specifies a *search_condition*.
search_condition	Check constraint on the values of the columns. These constraints can include *in*, *like*, and *between* clauses.
next_column | *next_constraint*	Include additional column definitions or table constraints.
on segment_name	Places the table on the specified segment.

Examples: Creating Tables

The following examples illustrate how to create a variety of integrity constraints.

Example 1: This command creates a table called *compute* with three columns, *max*, *min*, and *sum*, that accept only integer values. Because *compute*, *max*, *min*, and *sum* are reserved words in SQL Server, you must enclose them in quotation marks.

```
create table "compute"
  ("max"    int,
   "min"    int,
   "sum"    int)
go
```

Example 2: This command creates a table with two columns in the *sampdb* database. The first column accepts integers, while the second column accepts strings of 20 characters. The name of the user creating the table is *user1*. The command must be executed from the *master* database. Neither column allows null values.

```
create table sampdb.user1.test_table
  (int1        int,
   char1       char(20))
go
```

Example 3: This is a generalized version of the preceding command that you can use to create the table in a different database. Only *ownername.tablename* must be unique. In other words, two different users, *joe* and *fred,* can create a table with the same name, because they have different owner names.

```
create table database.owner.table_name
go
```

Example 4: This command creates a table with a float column and a character column that can accept a string with a maximum length of 20. We use *varchar (20)* for the character column, because the data can be of varying length.

```
create table math_table
  (float1       float,
   vchar1       varchar(20))
go
```

Example 5: This command creates a table that declares a default value of 100 for a column. The table includes a character column that can store values of 80 characters. In this example, the column *int2* is given a value of 100 unless the user explicitly defines some other value.

```
create table int_char
  (int2        smallint default 100 null,
   char2       char(20))
go
```

Example 6: This command creates a table for an application that stores a company's stock prices along with the date.

```
create table money_table
  (date1       datetime default not null,
   money1      money)
go
```

Example 7: This example shows how to implement a column-level constraint that restricts column input to the values 100, 200, or 300.

```
create table small_money
  (value_id  int not null
  constraint value_constraint
  check (value_id in (100, 200, 300)),
  amount1    smallmoney)
go
```

Example 8: This command illustrates how to implement a table-level check constraint. The table-level check constraint *high_low_check* checks whether the value of one column is less than or equal to the value of another column.

```
create table art_table
  (art_id        char(4) not null,
  lowqty         smallint null,
  highqty        smallint null,
  constraint high_low_check
  check (lowqty <= highqty))
go
```

Example 9: This command defines a unique constraint on column *comp_id*. It creates a nonclustered index on this column, because the default index for a unique constraint is nonclustered index. This is a column-level unique constraint.

```
create table comp_table
  (comp_id        char(4) null unique,
  comp_name      char(30))
go
```

Example 10: This example creates a table-level unique constraint on two columns, *comp_id* and *comp_num*.

```
create table comp2_table
  (comp_id char(4) not null,
  comp_num int,
  comp_name char(30),
  unique clustered (comp_id, comp_num))
go
```

Example 11: This command implements column-level referential integrity for two tables, *comp3_table* and *comp4_table*. *Comp3_table* is the referencing table, because its *comp_id* column refers to the *comp_id* column in *comp4_table*. Because column *comp_id* of *comp4_table* is being referenced, *comp4_table* is the referenced table.

```
create table comp3_table
  (comp_id char(4) not null,
  comp_num int,
  comp_name char(30)
  constraint comp_id_const
  references comp4_table (comp_id))
  create table comp4_table
  (comp_id char(4) not null,
  state char(30))
go
```

Example 12: The next command creates a temporary table in SQL Server's temporary system database, *tempdb*. The pound symbol that is used as the first letter of a table name indicates to SQL Server that the table is temporary. SQL Server therefore automatically creates the table in the *tempdb* database.

```
create table #temp_table
  (comp_id char(4) not null,
  state char(30))
go
```

Example 13: This example creates a table on segment *seg1*.

```
create table seg1_table
  (emp_id char(4) not null,
  city char(30)) on seg1
go
```

Example 14: This command creates a table with a fillfactor of 10 and a *max_rows_per_page* value of 10.

```
create table comp5_table
  (comp_id char(4) not null,
  state char(30))
  with fillfactor = 10,
  max_rows_per_page = 10
go
```

Points to Note: Creating Tables

Keep the following points in mind when working with user-defined datatypes.

- A table can have a maximum of 250 user-defined columns. A database can have up to two billion tables.

- Column names must be unique within a given table, but you can use the same column name in different tables in the same database.

- The maximum row length in a table cannot exceed 1962 bytes.

(continued)

- Only columns with variable-length datatypes can have null values.

- By default, columns do not allow nulls.

- You can rename tables or columns using system procedure **sp_rename**.

Tip! Be sure to put parentheses around the list of column names, and commas after each except the last column definition.

Tables with Identity Columns

Identity columns store sequential numbers, such as employee numbers, in an employee database. SQL Server generates the numbers automatically starting from the default, which is one. However, you can change this value using the option *set identity_insert on* to insert any value into the *identity* column. SQL Server then increments starting from the value you insert.

Sometimes identity values can have gaps due to server failures or shutdowns. The gaps in identity values can be controlled by using the following command.

sp_configure "identity burning set factor", value

In the above command, the *value* parameter is expressed as a percentage; it specifies the percentage of entities in a column that you want to make available at one time multiplied by 10^7. For example, to release five percent of the potential column values at the same time, value is 500,000 (0.05 times 10^7).

The default datatype of identity columns is numeric with a scale of 0. For example, a three-digit identity column can have values ranging from 1 to 999. Say that SQL Server makes values 1 through 500 available for the first set of insertions. The second set of insertions can then have values from 501 through 999. The first time you insert a row, SQL Server assigns the identity column a value of 1; the second insert results in a value of 2. If SQL Server fails at this point, it discards the remaining numbers in the block (3 through 500). When you restart SQL Server, it makes a new block of numbers available, 501 through 999.

Example: The payroll processing group of a company wants to design a table with three columns: *emp_no*, *emp_name*, and *gross_pay*. The *emp_no* column should have sequential values starting from 1. The company uses the following command to do so. Because *emp_no* is sequential, the company can use the identity column. In this example, *emp_no* is an identity column of type numeric (2,0). This means that the values of *emp_no* can be from 1 to 99 because the 2 represents a two-digit range and the 0 means zero decimal places.

```
create table employee_table
  (emp_no       numeric(2, 0) identity,
   emp_name     varchar(20),
   gross_pay    money)
go
```

Creating Tables Using select into

Another way to create tables is to use the Transact-SQL command **select into**. Using this method, you create a table by selecting its values from an existing table or a combination of existing tables. The new table inherits the integrity constraints of the original table or tables. You can also use this option to select into a nontemporary table if the *select into/bulkcopy database* option is turned on. The following example illustrates these ideas.

Example 1: This example creates a new table, *cases*, that has exactly the same table definition as *case_history*. Its data is composed of two columns, *case_no* and *litigator*, which are copied from the *case_history* table. First, you execute the system procedure **sp_dboption** from within the *master* database. **Sp_dboption** allows you to select into a permanent table in the *lawsuits* database.

```
use master
go
sp_dboption "lawsuits",
  "select into/bulkcopy",
  "true"
go
```

Next, change databases from *master* to *lawsuits* and execute a **checkpoint** command so changes requested with the **sp_dboption** system procedure take effect.

```
use lawsuits
go
checkpoint
go
```

Finally, create the *cases* table.

```
select case_no, litigator
  into cases
  from case_history
go
```

Example 2: The following command copies the structure of a table called *abc*. This creates a table with the same integrity constraints, but one that has no rows.

```
select * into abc_dup
  from abc
  where 1=2
go
```

Altering Tables

The **alter table** command is useful when you change your mind about an established table's structure and decide to restructure it. You can use **alter table** to do the following.

- Add new columns with variable lengths that allow null values

- Add, drop, or modify constraints

- Partition or unpartition an existing table that has no clustered index

The **alter table** command cannot be used to do any of the following.

- Add a column that is of *not null* type

- Drop columns

- Modify a datatype

- Modify a column property

The abbreviated syntax for the **alter table** command that we present here is followed by a description of its parameters in Table 8-4. Appendix C lists the complete syntax for the **alter table** command.

Table 8-4. *Parameters used by the* **alter table** *command*

---

alter table *table_name*
  {add *column_name datatype*
  [[constraint *constraint_name*]
  references [[*database.*]*owner.*] *ref_table*
  [(*ref_column* [{, *ref_column*}...])] |
  check (*search_condition*)} |
  drop constraint *constraint_name* | *replace column_name*
  partition number_of_partitions | unpartition}

(continued)

Table 8-4. *(continued)*

table_name	Name of the table that you want to change.
add	Indicates the name of the column or constraint you want to add to the table.
column_name	Name of the column in the table.
datatype	Refers to the datatype of the column.
constraint	Specifies the name of the integrity constraint.
constraint_name	Name of the constraint that is being added to the table.
clustered | nonclustered	Specifies that the unique or primary key constraint is a clustered or nonclustered index.
ref_table	Name of the table that has the referenced columns.
ref_column	Name of the columns in the referenced table check used to create check constraints on columns and specifies a *search_condition.*
search_condition	Check constraint on the values of the columns. These constraints can include *in, like,* and *between* clauses.
next_column | next_constraint	Used to include additional column definitions or table constraints.
drop	Specifies the name of the constraint to drop from the table. *Replace* indicates the name of the column whose default value to modify.
partition	Creates multiple page chains for the table. (For more details on partitioning, see Chapter 17.)
number_of_partitions	Must be a positive integer greater than or equal to two. *Unpartition* creates a single page chain for the table by coalescing all of the multiple page chains.

Examples: Using the alter table *Command*

These examples illustrate some of the kinds of changes you can make to existing tables, including adding columns, modifying default values, and adding and dropping constraints.

Example 1: This command adds a character column to a table that can store a character string with a length up to 100. The datatype of the column is *varchar* to accommodate the varying length of the column. The *null* parameter is specified so that it is not mandatory for users to enter values. If the parameter had been specified as *not null* when the *dept_name* column was created, you would not be allowed to execute an **alter table** command on the *dept_table*.

```
alter table dept_table
add dept_name varchar(100) null
go
```

Example 2: This command modifies the default value of the *state* column. If new rows are added for which the *state* value is undefined, they default to *CA*. Existing rows that have values other than *CA* are not affected.

```
alter table address_table
replace state default "CA"
go
```

Example 3: This command shows how to add a column-level check constraint so that the value of the first column must be less than or equal to the second column.

```
alter table temp1_table
  add constraint table_const
  check (lorange <= hirange)
go
```

Example 4: This command drops the constraint created in the preceding example.

```
alter table temp1_table
drop constraint table_const
go
```

Example 5: Here's how to add a unique constraint on two columns, *stor_id* and *ord_num*.

```
alter table temp2_table
  add constraint stor_ord_constr
  unique (stor_id, ord_num)
go
```

Example 6: This command adds a primary key constraint for the table given in the preceding example.

```
alter table temp2_table
  add constraint stor_p_constr
  primary key (stor_id, ord_num)
go
```

Example 7: This example adds an identity column that can accept values between 1 and 99,999.

```
alter table temp3_table
  add comp_num numeric (5, 0) identity
go
```

Example 8: The next command creates a partitioned table with five partitions.

```
alter table temp4_table
  partition 5
go
```

Example 9: This command modifies the number of partitions for the table in the preceding example. To do this, the table must first be unpartitioned. Chapter 17, Performance Tuning at the Database Level, discusses the details about how to unpartition a table.

```
alter table temp4_table unpartition
alter table temp4_table partition 4
go
```

Dropping Tables

The **drop table** command removes a table and all of the data, triggers, and permissions associated with it from a database. Internally, the command removes all of the rows from system tables associated with the table being dropped. The system tables affected are *sysobjects*, *sysindexes*, *sysprotects*, *syscolumns*, *sysreferences*, *sysconstraints*, *syskeys*, and *syscomments*. The parameter *table_name* is the name of the table to drop.

drop table *table_name*
  [, *table_name*] ...

Examples: Dropping Tables

These examples illustrate how to drop an unpartitioned table and a partitioned table.

Example 1: Here's how to drop a table owned by a user called *user1* that was created in the *sampdb* database. The table is dropped from the *master* database.

```
drop table sample_db.user1.test_table1
go
```

Example 2: To drop a partitioned table, you must first unpartition it. This example shows how to drop a partitioned table.

```
alter table test_table2 unpartition
drop table test_table2
go
```

Points to Note: Dropping Tables

- System tables cannot be dropped.

- A partitioned table must be unpartitioned before you can drop it.

- Referencing tables can be dropped, while referenced tables can be dropped only if they do not reference anything.

Rules

You can use rules and defaults to limit or restrict the data values that may be inserted in a table. Rules let you define what is legal for update and insert operations. You can define rules on a specific column or on any column with a given, user-defined datatype.

For example, you can define a rule that says a column named *state* can have the value of *CA* or *WA*, but it can not accept any other value. You can then associate (or *bind*) the rule to the state column using the system procedure **sp_bindrule**. After that, any time a user enters new data to the state column or updates it, SQL Server checks the data to make sure it follows the rule. If the user enters *CA* or *WA*, the entry is accepted. If the user enters anything else, SQL Server will not insert the value and will generate an error message.

SQL Server does not check to ensure that a rule you create and bind makes sense. For instance, SQL Server would not generate an error if you create an integer rule and bind it to a character datatype. However, any insert or update operation will fail and SQL Server will issue an error message.

SQL Server adds a row to the *sysobjects* table in the *master* database that has the name of a new rule. The operation defined by the rule is saved in the *sysprocedures* table. SQL Server also adds a row to the *syscolumns* table to indicate that a specific column has a row bound to it. Before SQL Server performs an insert or update operation on a column, it checks the *syscolumns* table to see if rules are bound to the column. If so, the rules become part of the insert or update operation.

Point to Note: You can view a rule's definition using the system procedure **sp_help** *rule_name*.

Creating, Renaming, and Dropping Rules

You create, rename, and drop rules with the commands listed in this section. A description of their parameters is provided in Table 8-5. After creating a rule, it's a good idea to verify that it works the way you expect by inserting or updating values in the relevant column. Testing like this prevents errors due to incorrect rules.

Use the following command to create a rule.

create rule *rule_name* as *condition_expression*

Use this command to rename a rule.

sp_rename *rule_name*, *new_name*

Here is the command to drop a rule.

drop rule [*owner.rule_name*] [, [*owner.*]*rule_name*] …

Table 8-5. *Parameters used by the* **create rule***,* **rename rule***, and* **drop rule** *commands*

rule_name	Name of the rule that you are defining
new_name	New rule name to which you are renaming an existing rule
condition_expression	Definition of the rule

Examples: Rules

These examples illustrate how to establish rules for columns or datatypes, how to modify rules, and how to remove them. You must bind a rule for it to take effect. We describe binding later in this chapter in the section "Binding and Unbinding Rules and Defaults."

Example 1: If you bind the following rule to a column or a user-defined datatype, that column or user-defined datatype accepts only one value, *CA*. If you try to insert any value other than *CA* for *state*, it is rejected and the SQL command fails.

```
create rule state_rule
  as @state = "CA"
go
```

Example 2: The following rule rejects values of *qty* that are less than 1 or greater than 100.

```
create rule qty_rule
  as @qty between 1 and 100
go
```

Example 3: This rule accepts only phone numbers that are exactly 10 characters in length and that start with *510*.

```
create rule phone_rule
  as @phone like '510-------'
go
```

Example 4: In this case, only names with uppercase characters that are six characters in length and those that are lesser than or equal to ZZZZZZ are accepted. Typical valid values include *AAAAAA*, *MMMMMM*, and *ZZZZZZ*.

```
create rule char_rule
  as @name <= "ZZZZZZ"
go
```

Example 5: Here, the rule checks if the values of *discount* are between 1 and 20, but not equal to 10. Typical valid values include *1*, *5*, and *19*.

```
create rule discount_rule
  as @discount between 1 and 20 and @discount !=10
go
```

Example 6: The following command drops the rule named *phone_rule*.

```
drop rule phone_rule
go
```

Example 7: The next command renames rule *discount_rule* to *sales_rule*.

```
sp_rename discount_rule, sales_rule
go
```

Point to Note: You cannot create a rule in any database other than the current database.

Defaults

Like rules, defaults are useful for maintaining data integrity within a database. When you create a table, you can specify the defaults for some or all of the columns. SQL Server will use the defaults if the user does not enter values. For example, the cells of a column with a default of 100 will contain the value 100 whenever the user does not specify a value.

SQL Server adds the name of each new default within a new row in the *sysobjects* system table. The actual definition of the default is saved as a row in the *syscomments* system table. The operation defined by the default is saved in the *sysprocedures* table.

Point to Note: You can obtain default definitions using the system procedure **sp_help** *default_name*.

Creating, Renaming, and Dropping Defaults

You can create, rename, or drop a default using the commands listed next. The parameters used by these commands is provided in Table 8-6. It's worthwhile to check your defaults after you create them to ensure that they work properly and to prevent errors due to incorrect defaults.

Use the following command to create defaults.

create default [*owner.*]*default_name*
  as *condition_expression*

Use this command to rename defaults.

sp_rename *default_name*, *new_name*

Here is the command to drop defaults. Before dropping a default, you must unbind it from all columns and user datatypes. If you don't first unbind it, you receive an error message and the command fails.

*Table 8-6. Parameters used by the **create default**, **sp_rename**, and **drop default** commands*

drop default [*owner.default_name*] [, [*owner.*]*default_name*] …	
default_name	Name of the default that you are defining
new_name	New default name to which you are renaming an existing default
constant_expression	Definition of the default

Examples: Defaults

These examples illustrate how to create string and numeric defaults. You still need to bind the default before it takes effect. We describe binding in the next section.

Example 1: This command creates a default called *name_dft* that has the value of *JOHNNY*.

```
create default
  name_dft as "JOHNNY"
go
```

Example 2: This example creates a default in which, after the default is bound to the column, the value of *100* will be inserted as the default.

```
create default
  lorange_dft as "100"
go
```

Example 3: This command drops the default called *name_dft*.

```
drop default name_dft
go
```

Point to Note: You can only create a default in the current database.

Point to Note: A default name must be unique for each user within a database.

Binding and Unbinding Rules and Defaults

You must bind new rules and defaults to make them active on the columns and user-defined datatypes that you want them to affect. The **sp_bindrule** and **sp_bindefault** commands make these associations.

If you no longer want a rule bound to a column or user-defined datatype, you unbind it using **sp_unbindrule**. If you bind a new rule to a column or datatype that already has a rule associated with it, the old rule is automatically unbound. Similarly, you can unbind a default either with **sp_unbindefault** or by binding a new default to that column or datatype.

When a default or a rule is bound to a column, the object ID of the default or rule is stored in the *syscolumns* table. If a default or a rule is bound to a user-defined datatype, the object ID of the default or rule is stored in the *systypes* table.

SQL Server issues an error message if you try to bind using a rule or default name that does not exist. Likewise, you experience an error message if you try to unbind a rule or default that does not exist. When a rule is bound to a user-defined datatype, every time that datatype is associated with a column, the rule is also bound to that column.

Here are the commands to bind and unbind rules and defaults, followed by descriptions of their parameters in Table 8-7.

Use this command to bind rules.

sp_bindrule *rulename, objectname* [, futureonly]

This command unbinds rules.

sp_unbindrule *objectname* [, futureonly]

Use this command to bind defaults.

sp_bindefault *defaultname, objectname* [, futureonly]

This command unbinds defaults.

sp_unbindefault *objectname* [, futureonly]

Table 8-7. Parameters used by **sp_bindrule, sp_unbindrule, sp_bindefault,** and **sp_unbindefault** commands

rulename	Name of the rule to bind.
objectname	Name of the object to which to bind (such as column).
defaultname	Name of the default to bind.
futureonly	Existing columns with a user-defined datatype will not inherit the rule or default. The rule or default applies only when created after binding or unbinding.

Examples: Binding and Unbinding Rules and Defaults

These examples illustrate how to use the bind and unbind commands to attach rules and defaults to columns and other objects.

Example 1: In this command, *authors.state* is the *objectname*, which is of the form *table_name.column_name*.

```
sp_bindrule state_rule,"authors.state"
go
```

Example 2: This command binds a rule to the user-defined datatype *tid*.

```
sp_bindrule char_rule,"tid"
go
```

Example 3: Before dropping a rule, it must be unbound from the column. This example illustrates these commands.

```
sp_unbindrule "authors.state"
drop rule state_rule
go
```

Example 4: This command creates a rule and binds it to a column. Because rules bound to columns take precedence over rules bound to datatypes, in this example rule *ge_rule* is activated during insert and update operations.

```
create rule ge_rule
 as @name > "ZZZZZ"
go
 sp_bindrule ge_rule, "stores.city"
go
```

Example 5: These commands bind the *name_dft* default to the *au_fname* column in table *authors*.

```
Create default name_dft
 as "JOHNNY"
go
 sp_bindefault name_dft,
  "authors.au_fname"
go
```

Points to Note: Binding and Unbinding
Rules and Defaults

Keep the following points in mind when binding and unbinding rules and defaults.

- A default can be defined and bound to one or more columns.

- You can bind the same default to both columns and user-defined datatypes.

- You can bind a default to a column or datatype without unbinding an existing default.

- You can't bind a rule to a text, image, or timestamp datatype column.

- Defaults bound to identity columns are ignored.

- A default remains in a database until it is dropped, even if it is not bound to a column or user-defined datatype.

- A column that you are binding should be made large enough to hold default values. For example, a char(10) column cannot hold a default value that is 20 bytes long.

Relationships Between Rules, Datatypes, Defaults, and Nulls

Rules bound to columns take precedence over rules bound to user datatypes. If a column has both a default and a rule associated with it, the default value must not violate the rule. If a default contradicts the rule, SQL Server generates an error message whenever a default is inserted. Any data existing in the table before binding a default or rule is not affected after the binding, but future operations on that column are affected by the rule.

Table 8-8 summarizes the outcome when rules and user-defined datatypes are bound, and a user then attempts to rebind new rules and user-defined datatypes. Table 8-9 summarizes the relationship between nulls and column defaults.

Table 8-8. *Rule-binding outcomes*

If you bind a rule to a:	...and a rule already was bound to the column, the affect on the column is:	...and a rule already was bound to a user-defined datatype, the affect on the datatype is:
Column	The new rule replaces the old rule	The new rule replaces the old rule
User-defined datatype	No change	The new rule replaces the old rule

Table 8-9. *Relationships between defaults and column nulls*

If a column was created with:	If there is no default and the user does not enter a value:	If there is a default and user does not enter a value:	If there is no default and user enters a NULL:	If there is a default and user enters a NULL:
NOT NULL	SQL Server issues an error	The column value is set to the default	SQL Server issues an error	SQL Server issues an error
NULL	The column value is set to NULL	The column value is set to the default	The column value is set to NULL	The column value is set to NULL

If you bind a default to a user-defined datatype, then bind another default to a column of the same user-defined datatype, the column default replaces the user-defined datatype default.

Indexes

A database index offers the same benefits as a book's index. Rather than searching through a 350-page book hoping to find what you want, you turn to the index to find a comprehensive summary of the contents and a corresponding pointer to the location of the material that you seek. In a database, an index is an independent object with a structure similar to that of a data table. Sybase supports clustered indexes and nonclustered indexes. In addition to their usefulness in implementing primary key constraints for data integrity, indexes are generally useful database objects because they improve performance by reducing the number of pages to search when looking for data, and they help to correlate data across tables.

SQL Server uses an index to point directly to the location of a column it is seeking on disk. Without an index, SQL Server would have to find the table, then search its entire contents. Some production environments have thousands of tables, and some of those tables have millions of rows. Those environments get enormous performance benefits from indexes. Other than the performance gains, the index on a table does not affect the user's perception of that table.

By default, when tables are created SQL Server creates a row in *sysindexes* with a value for the index id of *indid* = *0*. For a new, clustered index, the *sysindexes* row for this value is replaced with a new *sysindexes* row containing *indid* = *1*. For a new, nonclustered index, the *sysindexes* row is replaced with a new *sysindexes* row containing *indid* = *2*.

So, if two nonclustered indexes, *ind_i1* and *ind_i2*, are created in a table, the row corresponding to *ind_i1* has a *sysindexes.inid* value of 2. For the index *ind_i2*, another row is added with a value of *sysindexes.indid* set to 3. The *sysindexes* catalog also keeps information on the root node of the b-trees of clustered and nonclustered indexes. B-trees are discussed below.

Composite Indexes

If an index is created with more than one column in a table, it is called a *composite index*. Composite indexes are helpful when two or more columns are best searched as a unit. Up to 16 columns can be combined in a single composite index, and those columns can be in any order.

Unique Indexes

A unique index ensures that each row contains unique data for the columns on which the index is defined. SQL Server checks for duplicate data values whenever an index is created and whenever data is added. If you attempt to create a unique index on a table that has duplicates, SQL Server displays an error message with the first duplicate. Here's an example.

```
create table test_table (i int, c char(10))
  insert test_table values (1, "TEST1")
  insert test_table values (2, "TEST2")
  insert test_table values (2, "TEST3")
create test_table index test_ind on test_table(i)
go
```

After the last command, SQL Server issues the following error message.

```
Create unique index aborted on duplicate key. Primary key is '2'.
```

Clustered and Nonclustered Indexes

Both clustered and nonclustered indexes are based on a binary tree, or *b-tree*, structure. A b-tree offers direct access to sets of rows, eliminating the need for SQL Server to read each page of data for the table until it finds the row it needs. A simple b-tree structure is shown in Figure 8-3. This example has two intermediate levels. A basic b-tree structure has the following characteristics.

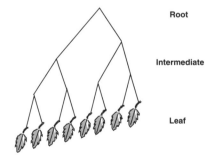

Figure 8-3. *Basic b-tree structure*

- Pages contain ordered pointers to pages the next level down

- The lowest level is the *leaf level*

- The highest level is called the root level

- Everything between the leaf and root levels is called intermediate levels

In a clustered index, the leaf level holds the data pages. In a nonclustered index, the leaf level holds the index pages that point to the data pages. You count levels as you go up from the leaves to the root. (Think of it as an upside down tree.) This convention for counting levels is illustrated in Figure 8-4.

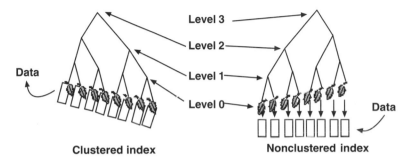

Figure 8-4. *Level conventions for clustered and nonclustered indexes*

A table can have only one clustered index, but up to 249 nonclustered indexes. Clustered indexes should be created before any nonclustered indexes, because nonclustered indexes are automatically rebuilt when a clustered index is created. When a table and its clustered index are created on two different segments, the table migrates to the segment on which the clustered index is created. This is not the case with nonclustered indexes.

Clustered Indexes

SQL Server sorts rows so that the data's physical order is the same as its logical, or indexed, order, which means that SQL Server continuously sorts and re-sorts the rows of a table. When you create a clustered index on a table, about 120 percent of the table size is required for initial sorting. Figure 8-5 illustrates a clustered index.

Because the leaf level of a clustered index has the actual data pages of a table, the table can only have one clustered index. Clustered indexes speed up the most important queries that would benefit from ordered data, because the data rows are physically ordered by the index key. Clustered indexes are a good choice when queries use range searches or sequential searches, or when data has a high percentage of duplicates. You should define a clustered index on the most common *join* column or on the *primary key* columns. Clustered indexes should also be defined on columns that queries use for range searches or sequential searches.

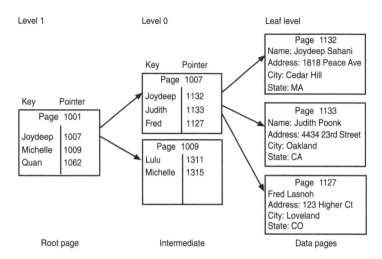

Figure 8-5. *A clustered index*

Point to Note: Tables with clustered indexes cannot be partitioned, because the physical order of rows on a database device is the same as the indexed order of the rows in clustered indexes.

Nonclustered Indexes

Nonclustered indexes have an extra index page level beyond clustered indexes, so they are larger than clustered indexes. Nonclustered indexes are a good choice when columns are involved in joins or queries, and a clustered index is not available. Nonclustered indexes also are good for queries that return single row matches. Figure 8-6 illustrates a nonclustered index.

Creating a nonclustered index does not reorder the data or affect data pages; the index just gives pointers to rows in the table and makes the pointers appear ordered. As noted earlier, a table can have up to 249 nonclustered indexes.

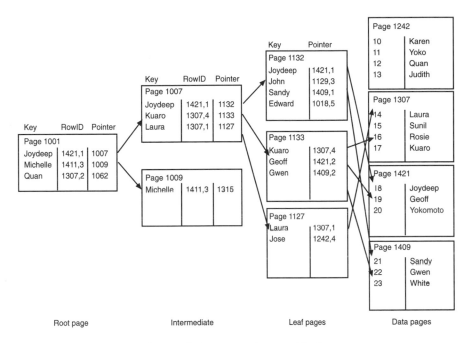

Figure 8-6. *A nonclustered index*

Creating Indexes

Indexes are created on the columns of a table. Here's the command that creates indexes, followed by a description of some of its parameters in Table 8-10.

Table 8-10. *Some of the parameters used by the* **create** *command*

create [unique] [clustered | nonclustered]
  index *index_name*
  on table_name (*column_name*
  [, column_name]...)
  [with {{fillfactor | max_rows_per_page} = x,
  ignore_dup_key, sorted_data,
  [ignore_dup_row | allow_dup_row]}]
  [on segment_name]

unique	Prevents duplicate key values in a table during the creation of index and during an update or insert
clustered	Physical order of rows is the same as the indexed order of rows

(continued)

Table 8-10. (continued)

nonclustered	Adds an additional level of indirection between index structure and the data itself, which helps performance in some cases
index_name	Name of the index being created; must be unique within a table, but need not be unique in a database
table_name	Name of the table that has the indexed columns

Options

The **create index** command has many powerful options. Let's consider the most important of them individually.

fillfactor

The *fillfactor* option specifies how full each page can be when creating an index on existing data. It is expressed as a percentage and is relevant only at the time the index is created. The default *fillfactor* value is zero. The extreme cases are as follows.

- A *fillfactor* value of zero creates clustered indexes and nonclustered indexes with completely full pages on every level.

- A *fillfactor* value of 100 creates clustered and nonclustered indexes with each page 100 percent full. A *fillfactor* of 100 is suitable only for read-only tables. A *fillfactor* of 10 might be a reasonable choice for creating indexes on a table that will ultimately hold a great amount of data.

max_rows_per_page

The *max_rows_per_page* option limits the number of rows on the data pages and the leaf pages of indexes. It is expressed as an integer between 0 and 256. The default value is 0, which creates clustered indexes with full data pages and non-clustered indexes with full leaf pages. Setting *max_rows_per_page* creates both clustered and nonclustered indexes one row per page at the leaf level. Low values for *max_rows_per_page* create new indexes with pages that are not full and require more storage space.

ignore_dup_key

The *ignore_dup_key* option gives control on batch inserts that might have duplicate key values in them. If this option is set, the duplicate key rows are ignored and only rows that have unique values of key column are inserted.

sorted_data

The *sorted_data* option is used to accelerate the creation of an index when the data already is sorted. Tables containing large amounts of data (approximately 1GB or more) see notable performance gains using this option. If you specify this option and the data is not sorted, SQL Server displays an error message and aborts the command. The *sorted_data* option is useful only when creating clustered and unique, nonclustered indexes. If you use the option for a nonunique, nonclustered index on a table that has duplicate keys, you receive an error and the command is aborted.

ignore_dup_row *and* allow_dup_row

The *ignore_dup_row* and *allow_dup_row* options are used while creating nonunique clustered indexes. Setting the *ignore_dup_row* option eliminates rows with duplicate values from a batch of data. Setting the *allow_dup_row* option allows creation of a nonunique clustered index on a table that has duplicate rows. The allow *dup_row* and *ignore_dup_row* options are mutually exclusive. Table 8-11 describes the effects of using the options that handle duplicate rows in various circumstances.

Table 8-11. *Options for handling duplicate rows*

Option set	Insertion of duplicate rows in a table with index	Creating index on a table with duplicate rows
allow_dup_row	Insertion completes	Create index completes
ignore_dup_row	All rows except duplicates are inserted	Create index completes, but duplicate rows are eliminated
Neither option	Insertion fails	Create index fails

on segment_name

The on *segment_name* option specifies the name of the segment on which the index is to be created.

Examples: Creating Indexes

The examples in this section illustrate commands that create unique, clustered indexes and nonclustered indexes.

Example 1: In this example, a nonclustered, nonunique index, *name_ind,* on table *name_list* is created on column *soc_number*. If no options are specified in a **create index** command, a nonclustered, nonunique index is created.

```
create index name_ind_1
  on name_list (soc_number)
go
```

Example 2: The following command creates a unique, nonclustered index, *emp_ind* on table *employees*.

```
create unique emp_ind
  on employees (emp_no)
go
```

Example 3: The following command shows how to create a clustered, composite index on two columns, *ord_id* and *ord_num,* of table *orders*. Because the default for a clustered index is nonunique, a nonunique clustered index is created.

```
create clustered index ord_ind
  on orders (ord_id, ord_num)
go
```

Example 4: You can create a unique index on a table into which a batch of **insert** commands having duplicate keys is inserted using the following command. After the index is created on the table, only the rows with unique keys can be inserted. Attempts to insert rows with duplicate values result in error messages and corresponding **insert** commands are aborted.

```
create unique index dupkey_ind
  on dupkey_tab (soc_no) with ignore_dup_key
go
```

Example 5: The next command creates a clustered index, *emp_ind*, on the *employee* table that does not allow inserts of duplicate values for the *emp_no* column. Unique values of *emp_no* may be inserted into table *employee*.

```
create clustered index no_dup_ind
  on employee (emp_no) with ignore_dup_row
go
```

Example 6: The following command shows how to create a clustered index on a table for which duplicate values are acceptable.

```
create clustered index dup_ok_ind
  on employee (emp_no) with allow_dup_row
go
```

Example 7: This last example creates a nonclustered index on the table *sales* with a *fillfactor* of 25. This means that only 25 percent of the index pages will be filled with index data.

```
create nonclustered index sales_ind
  on sales (sales_no) with fillfactor = 25
go
```

Points to Note: Using Indexes

Keep the following factors in mind when using indexes.

- Building indexes takes time and storage space
- A composite index can have up to 16 columns
- Indexes can be created on temporary tables

Tip! While creating an index on a table, it can be useful to find out if the table has duplicate keys. The following command lists duplicate keys in a table.

```
select emp_no, count(*)
  from tab1
  group by emp_no having count(*) > 1
go
```

This table would have been created using the following command.

```
create table tab1 (emp_no int, emp_name char(30))
go
```

Dropping Indexes

You drop indexes using the **drop index** command, which has the following syntax. The *table_name* parameter is the name of the table that has the index, and the *index_name* parameter is the name of the index that is about to be dropped.

```
drop index table_name.index_name
  [, table_name.index_name]...
```

When you drop an index, you regain all of the space that was occupied by the index, and SQL Server also drops the row corresponding to the index in system table *sysindexes*. You cannot drop an index on a system table in the *master* database or in user databases. Similarly, you cannot drop indexes that support unique indexes or indexes that are currently used by any open cursor. (Chapter 11, Installing SQL Server, provides more information about cursors.)

Point to Note: Indexes that support unique constraints cannot be dropped using the **drop index** command, but you can drop them using the **alter table** command.

Example: Dropping Indexes

Example: The command in this example drops the index *emp_ind*, which was created on table *employee*.

```
drop index employee.emp_ind
go
```

Getting Information About Indexes

Using the **sp_helpindex** system procedure with a table name as a parameter lists all of the indexes that are available on the named table. Used with the name of a table or a view as a parameter, this command gives information about the indexes associated with that table or view. The following example illustrates use of **sp_helpindex**.

```
1> sp_helpindex titles
2> go
```

index_name	index_description	index_keys	index_max_rows_per_page
titleidind	clustered	unique located on default titleid	0
titleind	nonclustered	located on default title	0

Triggers

Triggers are a more rigorous way to handle referential integrity than the native **create table** options. The integrity constraints defined by **create table** are specific to the table you create using those constraints. Triggers, on the other hand, can facilitate database-wide referential integrity. Because Sybase created triggers, they are Transact-SQL extensions and are not ANSI compatible.

What Are Triggers?

Triggers are a special type of stored procedures. But unlike stored procedures, triggers cannot be directly executed. A trigger is an event-driven procedure that is executed whenever a table or column is modified with an **insert**, **update**, or **delete** command.

Triggers have a number of interesting and useful applications. Consider an application that alerts a stock broker if the value of a particular stock rises or falls 15 percent from a given value. You can implement such a notification application using a trigger.

Triggers and Referential Integrity

Triggers enforce the referential integrity of data across a database. Referential integrity can also be coordinated through the use of primary and foreign keys. Triggers help to keep the values of foreign keys in line with the values of primary keys. When a data modification command affects the primary key column, triggers compare the new value with the related key columns. This is done by creating temporary tables, which we refer to as *trigger test tables*.

While writing triggers, the data stored in these trigger test tables can be used for comparison. Two special trigger tables are called the *inserted table* and the *deleted table*. These tables are temporary. The data in these tables cannot be altered, but it can be used to determine the effects of a data modification command such as **insert**, **update**, or **delete**.

Triggers can cascade changes through related tables in a database. For example, a delete trigger on the *title_id* column of a *titles* table could cause a corresponding deletion of matching rows in other tables, such as *titleauthor*, *sales*, and *roysched*, using *title_id* column as a unique key.

Triggers can enforce complex restrictions by referencing other database objects. Triggers can also roll back or continue a transaction depending on referential integrity requirements. Chapter 10, Transaction Management, more fully describes triggers.

Views

A view is a stored **select** command that behaves like a normal table but is actually a virtual table. Because it is virtual, it cannot store data. You create views by using the **select** command so the view can be any combination of rows from a single table or from multiple tables. The tables from which you create the view are called *base tables*, which can be updated through views if you only attempt to update a single table at a time.

A user with **create view** permission or with *dba* or *sa* role can create views that customize the user's perception of the database. Say that a table contains all employee information including monthly salaries. You might want users to access employee names, numbers, and job descriptions, but not salary information. You can create a view on employee tables that includes a subset of the columns. This provides security by hiding certain confidential information about the employees. Views simplify data manipulation and provide for logical data independence.

Figure 8-7 depicts *view v1* that is created from two tables, *table1* and *table2*. *Table1* has two columns, *emp_no* (the primary key) and *emp_name*. *Table2* has three columns, *emp_no* (a foreign key), *dep_name*, and *gross_pay*. We can create a view of a particular department with *emp_no* and *emp_name* of *table1,* and *dept_name* of table2. The view hides the information about *gross_pay*. The user of the view need not have permissions on *table1* and *table2*.

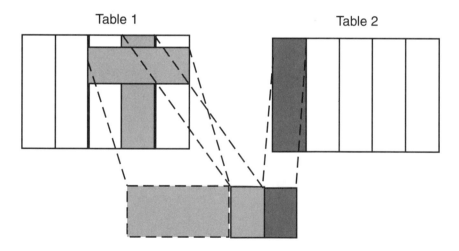

Figure 8-7. *A two-table view that hides selected data*

Creating Views

View definitions can include aggregate functions, joins, and up to 16 levels of views. The number of columns referenced by a view cannot exceed 250. Views cannot include the *order by* clause, the *compute* clause, or the *select into* clause. They can be created only in the current database, and you can't create them on temporary tables. Triggers cannot be defined on a view.

To retrieve the text of a view definition, use the **sp_helptext** system procedure with the name of the view as a parameter. You can get other information about a view using the **sp_help** system procedure with the name of the view as a parameter.

SQL Server does not check for permissions on objects such as tables and views that are referenced by the view while creating a view. Permissions are checked only when a user invokes the view.

When a view is created, a new row is added to system table *sysobjects*. The *type* column will have a value of V, indicating that it is a view. The view's query tree (or execution plan) is stored in *sysprocedures,* and the view text is stored in *syscomments*.

Here is the command to create a view, followed by a description of its parameters in Table 8-12.

Table 8-12. *Parameters used by the* **create view** *command*

create view [owner.]*view_name*
    [(*column_name* [, *column_name*]...)]
    as select [distinct] *select_statement*
    [with check option]

view_name	Name of the view being created
column_name	Name of the columns in the view
as select	Begins the select that defines the view
distinct	Refers to a view that does not contain duplicate rows
select_statement	Completes the select command that defines the view
with check option	All data modification commands will be validated against the new view

Examples: Creating Views

The following examples illustrate how to create views on tables using various options and parameters.

Example 1: This example creates a view on an *authors* table that has only two columns, *au_lname* and *au_fname*.

```
create view author_view
  as select au_lname, au_fname from authors
go
```

Example 2: This example creates a view on an *authors* table that has information about authors living in the state of CA.

```
create view aut_state_view
  as select au_lname, au_fname, phone
  from authors
  where state = "CA"
go
```

Example 3: In this example, columns are renamed to *last_name*, *first_name,* and *phone_number* in a view. (If the column names are omitted, the columns in the view inherit the headings of the columns in the **select** command.)

```
create phone_view
  (last_name, first_name, phone_number) as
  select au_lname, au_fname, phone
  from authors
  where state = "CA"
go
```

Example 4: In this example, *with check option* restricts the rows that can be updated or inserted based on the *where* clause. If a user or application attempts to update or insert a value for *state* other than *CA* in the view *author_details*, the insert or update fails.

```
create view author_details
  (last_name, first_name, phone_number) as
  select au_lname, au_fname, phone
  from authors
  where state = "CA"
  with check option
go
```

Inserting, Updating, and Deleting Through Views

You can insert into or update the tables from which the view is created through the view as long as the affected columns belong to the same base table. You cannot insert rows into views created with the *distinct* or the *check* option.

You cannot insert a row through a view that includes a computed clause. You also cannot insert or update into a view defined with the distinct clause.

If a view is created on a table that has nonnull columns, values of all nonnull columns must be provided during the insert operation.

Delete commands are not allowed on views created on more than one base table.

Exercises

8-1. Create a user-defined datatype, *ud4*, that can take variable strings with a length not exceeding 200 characters. Values for this column are not mandatory.

8-2. Create a user-defined datatype, *ud5*, that has a *timestamp* datatype.

8-3. Create a rule named *hitrange_rule* that accepts integers that are equal to or greater than 10, but less than 100.

8-4. A certain integer column can take only three values, -1, 0, and 1. Create a rule for this and name it *int_rule*.

8-5. Create a rule called *be_rule* that accepts characters that are less than *aaaaa* but greater than *FFFFF*, and that are five characters in length.

8-6. Create a default named *royalty_deft* that has a value of 20.

8-7. The default in exercise 8-6 is bound to a column. If you update the column with a value of 30, what value will that column contain?

8-8. Based upon the following commands, can you insert a value of 70 in column *qty*?

```
create rule qty1_rule
  as @qty < 100
sp_bindrule qty_rule,
  "salesdetail.qty"
create rule qty1_rule
  as @qty < 50
```

8-9.   Based upon the following commands, what will happen if no data is specified on an insert for the column *authors.state*?

```
create default state1_dft as "NY"
sp_bindefault state_default,
  "authors.state"
create rule state_rule
  as @state_rule of ("CA", "WA", "MI")
sp_bindrule state_rule,
  "authors.state"
```

Consider the following commands for your answers to questions 8-10 through 8-14.

```
create table ex_table
  (i int not null, b int default 10 null)
go
create rule ex_rule
  as @val between 0 and 100
go
sp_bindrule ex_rule, "ex_table.b"
go
create view ex_view
   as select * from ex_table
go
alter table ex_table
add c varchar(20)null
go
alter table ex_table
add constraint ex_check
check (b between -10 and 10)
go
```

8-10. What value will be inserted into the table for the following **insert** command?

```
insert ex_table values (1, null)
```

8-11. If the table already had 100 rows when the default was bound and 50 of those rows had no value for column **b**, what value will those rows have for column **b** after the default is bound?

8-12. What columns will a user see if the following command is run?

```
select * from ex_view
```

8-13. What values are allowed in column **b** during insert or update?

8-14. What is the command to change the default in column **b** to 50?

8-15. What is the major difference between a clustered index and a nonclustered index?

8-16. How many columns with *identity* property can be created in a table?

8-17. What system datatype can be used for *identity* columns?

8-18. What is the difference between *char* and *varchar* datatypes?

8-19. What does *null* means within the context of a SQL Server environment?

8-20. If a table is created with a unique constraint on a column, will that column allow null values?

8-21. If a view is created on a table called *tab1* and that table is renamed to *tab2*, will the view work?

8-22. If you add a column to a table after a view is created on that table, will the view work?

8-23. What system tables contain information on system and user-defined datatypes?

8-24. How many triggers may a table have?

Answers to Exercises

8-1. **sp_addtype ud4, "varchar(200)", "null"**

8-2. User-defined datatypes based on *timestamp* cannot be created, because SQL Server generates *timestamp* values.

8-3. **create rule hitrange_rule**
      as @i between 10 and 100

8-4. **create rule int_rule**
      as @i in ("-1", "0", "1")

8-5. **create rule be_rule**
      as @c between "aaaaa" and "FFFFF"

8-6. **create default royalt_deft as "20"**

8-7. The column will have a value of 30, because defaults are not affected during updates.

8-8. Yes, because the second rule is not yet bound to the column.

8-9. The insert will fail, because the default value conflicts with the value defined by the rule.

8-10. The insert will fail, because the number of values supplied does not match the table definition. The table has three columns.

8-11. Because the rule affects only the new rows that are inserted, the existing null values of column *b* will still be *null*.

8-12. The view will have only two columns.

8-13. Column b can take values only from 0 to 10.

8-14. **alter table ex_table**
      replace b default 50

8-15. The leaf level of a clustered index contains the data pages, while the leaf level of a nonclustered index contains pointers to the data pages.

8-16. A table can contain only one identity column.

8-17. Identity columns can contain only numeric datatypes. However, user-defined datatypes that contain underlying *numeric* datatype can also be used to create identity columns.

8-18. Datatype *char* can be used to store fixed length strings, while datatype *varchar* is used for storing variable length strings.

8-19. *Null* does not have any explicitly assigned value, including blanks and zeros.

8-20. Yes, because unique constraints create unique nonclustered indexes by default; they allow *null* values.

8-21. The view will work until SQL Server recompiles the view.

8-22. If the view is defined with a **select** * command, the new columns will not appear. To see the new columns, you must drop and recreate the view.

8-23. System table *systypes*.

8-24. A maximum of three triggers can be defined on a table.

9

Transact-SQL and Its Extensions

Sybase offers an enhanced version of SQL called Transact-SQL (T-SQL) that provides a more powerful and versatile language set than other versions of SQL. The T-SQL implementation aims to minimize or eliminate the need to use any other programming language within the Sybase environment. Sybase refers to its enhancements to SQL as Transact-SQL extensions. This chapter discusses the following ANSI SQL and Transact-SQL extensions.

- *Local and global variables* Entities that store values

- *SQL batches* One or more T-SQL commands that SQL Server processes as a group

- *Control-of-flow commands* Keywords that control the flow of execution

- *Cursors* Symbolic names you can associate with a **select** command to manipulate results row by row

- *Stored procedures* A precompiled collection of SQL commands stored in a SQL Server database

- *Triggers* A special stored procedure used to maintain referential integrity in a database

We have already discussed the following SQL and Transact-SQL topics in Chapter 8, Database Objects: Tables and Data Integrity.

- Create table integrity features

- User-defined and system datatypes

- Defaults and rules

In the following sections, we turn to a discussion of the additional extensions that we have listed here.

Local and Global Variables

While a batch program or stored procedure runs, it needs a mechanism for holding the data values it processes—variables are that mechanism. T-SQL has two types of variables, local and global, which we discuss in the next two sections.

Local Variables

Local variables serve as temporary containers (commonly used for counters) that hold data while it is being processed. For example, if you want to manipulate table values, you can declare a local variable, assign it the result of the column query, perform processing on the variable, and return the processed variable value to the table using an **update** command. These variables are called *local*, because they are only valid locally—within the batch or procedure in which they are created, and only for the time during which the batch or procedure is active.

Using Local Variables

After you declare a local variable, you identify it in a program by preceding its name with the @ sign, like this: *@variable_name*. Declare a local variable right in the batch or stored procedure that needs to use it with a **declare** keyword. The declaration associates the local variable with a user-defined datatype or system datatype, and often with an initial value. If you don't assign an initial value, the local variable takes on a value of NULL. You can use local variables in expressions, and a procedure or batch can perform conditional branching based on its value.

Table 9-1 gives a simplified syntax for declaring local variables. See the Quick Reference at the back of this book for the complete syntax.

Table 9-1. *Syntax and parameters for the* **declare** *command*

declare *@variable_name datatype*	
@variable_name	The name of the variable that is being declared
datatype	The datatype (either system defined or user defined) of the local variable being declared

Getting Information About the Contents of Local Variables

To obtain the current value of a local variable, use the following command, where *variable_name* is the name of the local variable for which you want to see a value.

select @variable_name

Examples: Using Local Variables

These examples illustrate local variable declaration, using a local variable to store a returned value and basing decisions on that value. They also show what happens if you do not assign an initial value to a local variable.

Example 1: This example declares a local variable called *vchar1*, which is a *varchar* datatype. It is assigned an initial value of *Sybase 11.0 SQL Server.*

```
declare @vchar1 varchar(30)
select @vchar1 = "Sybase 11.0 SQL Server"
go
```

Example 2: This example declares three local variables: *product, value1,* and *value2,* all of type *float. Value1* and *value2* are assigned 9.2 and 10.5, respectively. The *product* variable is assigned a value equal to the product of *value1* and *value2.* The last **select** command displays the value of *product.*

```
declare @product float
declare @value1 float
declare @value2 float
select @value1 = 9.2
select @value2 = 10.5
select @product = @value1 * @value2
/* Display the value of variable product */
select @product
go
```

Example 3: This example shows how to use variables to store values returned from table queries. The example declares a variable *total_income* and assigns the product of values in the columns *price* and *total_sales* for a particular *title_id*.

```
declare @total_income money
select @total_income = price * total_sales
  from titles
  where title_id = "BU2075"
/* Display the value of variable total_income */
select @total_income
go
```

Example 4: This example shows how action can result based on a variable's value. In this example, the value of variable *max_advance* is set to the maximum value of column *advance* in a *titles* table. The **print** command displays a message that depends on whether the value of *max_advance* is greater than 10,000.

```
declare @max_advance money
select @max_advance = max (advance)
from titles
/* Now do some processing */
if @max_advance > $10000
  print "Advance is too high!"
else
  print "Advance is reasonable!"
go
```

Example 5: This example illustrates what happens when you do not assign an initial value to a local variable. The variable defaults to NULL, because it is not assigned a value. The query will not return any rows if no rows have a NULL value in the *state* column.

```
declare @s char(2)
select au_id, city
  from authors
where state = @s
go
```

Example 6: In this example, variable *char_value* is assigned several initial values. It will only store the last assigned value. In this case, *char_value* contains the value *SECOND*.

```
declare @char_value char(20)
select @char_value = "FIRST"
select @char_value = "SECOND"
/* Display the value of the variable */
print @char_value
go
```

Points to Note: Local Variables

Observe the following points when working with local variables.

- A local variable must be declared in the batch, stored procedure, or trigger that will use it. It is only available within the batch, stored procedure, or trigger in which it was declared

- A local variable takes the last value assigned to it

- Local variables cannot be associated with *text*, *image*, or *sysname* datatypes

- You cannot substitute names of tables, columns, other database objects, or keywords for a local variable

---

Global Variables

Like local variables, global variables are useful for decision-based processing. Global variables are used in batches, stored procedures, triggers, and cursors.

The difference between local and global variables is that global variables are supplied by SQL Server and have a predefined value—they are not user defined. In addition, although they are called global *variable*, they are read-only—that is, you cannot directly update them. Use the @@ sign to identify a global variable. Table 9-2 shows some of the most commonly used global variables. For a complete list of global variables, see the Quick Reference appendix.

Table 9-2. *Commonly used global variables*

Global Variable	Description
@@error	Error number returned by the last command
@@rowcount	Number of rows affected by the last command
@@version	SQL Server version number
@@trancount	Nesting level of transactions
@@transtate	Current level of transaction after execution of a command

What Happens in the Server

The stored procedure **sp_monitor** displays the current values of some of the global variables.

Examples: Using Global Variables

These examples show how to obtain and use information that global variables store.

Example 1: This command displays the SQL Server version number.

```
select @@version
go
```

Example 2: This example uses the global variable *rowcount* to determine the number of rows in the *authors* table whose value for *state* is *CA*.

```
select au_lname, au_fname, address
  from authors
  where state = "CA"
if @@rowcount = 0
  print "No authors living in California!"
else
  print "There are authors living in California."
go
```

Example 3: This example shows how to determine the number of authors living in the state of *CA* by saving the value of global variable *rowcount* to a local variable.

```
declare @count int
select au_lname, au_fname, address
  from authors
  where state = "CA"
select @count = @@rowcount
if @count = 0
  print "No authors living in California!"
else
  print "The number of authors living in CA is:"
    select @count
go
```

Example 4: This example gives you a preview of transaction processing, which Chapter 10, Transaction Management, discusses in detail. The global variable *trancount* displays the transaction nesting level. The first *trancount* is set to zero, because it is not in a transaction. The second *trancount* contains the value *1*, because the **select** command is within a transaction. The beginning of a transaction is marked by a *begin tran* and a *commit* marks the end of a transaction. The third *trancount* contains a zero value, because it is outside the transaction.

```
select @@trancount      /* 1st trancount   */
begin tran
  select @@trancount    /* 2nd trancount */
commit
select @@trancount      /* 3rd trancount   */
go
```

Points to Note: Global Variables

Note the following points about global variables.

- You *cannot* create global variables or assign values to them

- You *can* save the values of global variables to local variables

- You *cannot* update global variables directly using the **select** command

Transact-SQL Batches

One of the most basic T-SQL extensions to SQL is the ability to create programs by batching T-SQL commands, executing one or more commands as a group either interactively or from an operating system file. You must identify the boundaries of every batch using an end-of-batch command so that SQL Server knows which commands you want to process as a group. T-SQL uses **go** as the end-of-batch command. SQL Server processes the following group of commands as a batch.

```
declare @txt_len int
select @txt_len = avg (datalength (pic))
  from au_pix
go
```

In the preceding example, SQL Server executes the local variable declaration as a batch with the **select** command so that the local variable *txt_len* is in effect when the **select** command is processed. See Chapter 5, Interacting with SQL Server, for a discussion of how to use the **go** terminator with **isql**.

Submitting Batches

Batches can be submitted to SQL Server either interactively, for example using **isql**, or from an operating system file.

You can group the commands **create database**, **create table**, and **create index** together in a batch. However, you cannot drop an object and recreate or reference the same object in the same batch.

SQL Server parses all commands in the batch before it processes them, so if there is an error in the batch, SQL Server does not process any portion of the batch. SQL Server checks for object permissions only during the execution phase, not during the compilation phase. Therefore, you should verify object permissions before executing a batch.

Point to Note: You cannot use a rule or default in the same batch in which you bind it.

Examples: Submitting Batches

The examples in this section are simple illustrations of batches.

Example 1: This example selects from two tables and returns the number of rows in tables *sales* and *authors*.

```
select count(*) from sales
select count(*) from authors
go
```

Example 2: This example shows how you can create a table and reference it in the same batch.

```
create table emp
  (emp_no int, emp_name varchar(50))
insert emp values (100, "ADAMS")
go
```

Example 3: If there is a syntax error in any of the commands in a batch, none of the commands in the batch is executed. The third **insert** command has a typo (*isert* rather than *insert*), so the batch is aborted.

```
insert emp values (101, "ROBERT")
insert emp values (102, "MARK")
isert emp values (103, "DAVE")
go
```

Control-of-Flow Keywords

The Transact-SQL control-of-flow language gives you control over the order in which Transact-SQL commands execute in the same way that other programming languages do. Transact-SQL provides **begin...end**, **if...else**, and **while** constructs so you can define the comparisons and rules that your program uses to perform operations.

Table 9-3 summarizes Transact-SQL control-of-flow keywords and their descriptions.

Table 9-3. *Transact-SQL control-of-flow keywords*

Keyword	Description
begin	Begins a command block.
end	Ends a command block.
begin command block **end**	The **begin...end** construct is normally used in combination with **while** or **if...else** constructs. It enables execution of two or more commands (the command block) following the **if** or **else** command.
if	Defines conditional execution.
else	Defines alternate execution when the **if** condition is false.

if *logical_expression*
    commands
[**else**
    [**if** *logical_expression*]
    command]
	Imposes conditions on the execution of a SQL command. If the condition of the **if** keyword is true, the command immediately following that **if** keyword is executed. If the condition is false, the control of flow skips to the command following the **else** keyword.

while *logical_expression* command	Sets a condition for the repeated execution of a command or a command block. The commands are executed repeatedly as long as the condition specified in the **while** clause is true. *Logical_expression* is any expression that returns TRUE, FALSE, or NULL.
break	Exits from a **while** loop, but not the batch. If the loops are nested, it exits one level of nesting. Any commands after the **end** keyword that marks the end of the loop are subsequently executed.
continue	Restarts a **while** loop.

while *logical_expression*
    command
  break
    command
  continue
	Logical_expression is any expression that returns TRUE, FALSE, or NULL.

(continued)

Table 9-3. *(continued)*

Keyword	Description
declare	Declares local variables.
label: **goto label**	**Goto label** jumps to a position specified by label in a command block.
print	Prints a user-defined message on the console.
{*format_string* | *@local_variable*	*Format_string* can be either a variable or a string up to 255 bytes.
| *@@global_variable*} [, *arg_list*]	*Local_variable* is a local variable with any of the character system datatypes.
	Global_variable is a global variable with any of the character system datatypes.
	Arg_list is a series of variables or constants separated by commas.
return	Unconditionally exits from a batch or stored procedure. Any commands following **return** are not executed.
return [*integer_expression*]	Unconditionally exits from a batch or stored procedure. Any commands following **return** are not executed. Returns the integer value *integer_expression* to the calling entity.
waitfor {*delay time*	Sets delay for command execution.
| **time** *time* | **errorexit** | **processexit**	The **delay** option tells SQL Server to wait until the specified amount of time has passed. The maximum permitted delay is 24 hours.
| **mirrorexit**}	The **time** option instructs SQL Server to wait until the specified time.
	The **errorexit** option instructs SQL server to wait until a kernel or user process terminates abnormally.
	The **processexit** option instructs SQL Server to wait until a kernel or user process terminates for any reason.
	The **mirrorexit** option instructs SQL Server to wait for a mirror failure.

(continued)

Table 9-3. *(continued)*

Keyword	Description
/* Comment */ or --- Comment	Inserts a comment anywhere in a SQL command. Comment is a series of words or symbols.

Points to Note: Control-of-Flow Keywords

Here are some points to note for creating batches using the control-of-flow keywords.

- **Begin...end** blocks can be nested within other **begin...end** blocks.

- **If...else** blocks can be nested within other **if...else** blocks or following an **else** block.

- When you include a **create table** or **create view** command within an **if...else** block, SQL Server creates the schema for the table or view before determining whether the condition is true. (A *schema* is a collection of objects associated with a name.)

- You can use the **break** and **continue** keywords to control the flow of execution within a **while** loop.

- If two or more **while** loops are nested, the inner **break** exits to the next outer-most loop, so the break in loop 2 in Figure 9-1, transfers execution to loop 1.

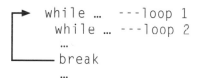

```
      ┌──► while …   ---loop 1
      │      while … ---loop 2
      │      …
      └───── break
             …
```

Figure 9-1. *Nesting loops*

- The **return** keyword can be used to exit from anywhere within a batch or stored procedure.

- A **waitfor** keyword suspends the availability of the associated SQL Server connection until the **waitfor** time elapses.

- The output string length used in a **print** keyword cannot exceed 512 bytes.

Error Messages

You can use the **raiserror** keyword to identify errors. Error numbers are separated into three levels: 1-17000 are for SQL Server error messages, 17001-20000 are used by SQL Server in system procedures, and error numbers starting at 20001 are for user-defined procedures or queries. (You can use the system procedure **sp_addmessage** to calculate the message number. See documentation on your *SyBooks* CD.) The syntax and parameters for the **raiserror** keyword are listed in Table 9-4.

Table 9-4. *Syntax and parameters for the **raiserror** keyword*

raiserror *error_number*
  {format_string
  | @local_variable}]
  [, arg_list]

error_number	An integer value greater than 17000
format_string	A character string up to 255 bytes

Point to Note: If you want a client to capture a message, use a **print** or **raiserror** keyword.

What Happens in the Server

All system error messages are stored in the *sysmessages* table in the master database. All user-defined error messages are stored in the *sysusermessages* table in the database from which the query or stored procedure originates.

Comments in Transact-SQL

You can specify comments in Transact-SQL using an opening slash and asterisk combination or a double hyphen. If you use a slash and asterisk pair to open a comment, you must close the comment with an asterisk and a slash. If a comment spans a line, you must use the slash and star style; otherwise, the style is a matter of choice.

Example 1: This example uses the slash and asterisk style for a brief comment on a single line and for a comment that span lines.

```
/* This is a comment */ /* ...and so
is this */
```

Example 2: This example uses the double-hyphen style for a comment that does not span lines.

```
-- This is also a comment
```

Examples: Using Transact-SQL Control-of-Flow Keywords

This section illustrates how to use the control-of-flow keywords listed in Table 9-3. The examples that follow show how to query system and user tables, and base decisions on the query results. They illustrate how to perform data processing using loops, **if** commands, and labels.

Example 1: This **if** keyword will always print a message, because the condition is always true.

```
if 100 >10
  print "100 is greater than 10!"
go
```

Example 2: This example determines whether the current database contains any user-created objects. It queries the *sysobjects* table and prints a message if any objects have an ID greater than 100, because user-created objects have *sysobjects* IDs greater than 100.

```
If (select max (id) /* Search for user-created objects */
  from sysobjects) < 100
  print "No user created objects in this database"
else
begin
  print "There are user objects created in the database"
  select name, type
    from sysobjects
    where id > 100
end
go
```

Example 3: This example increments the *discount* column of the *salesdetail* table by two for any row in *salesdetail* that has an average discount of less than 55. The **while** loop checks for the rows satisfying the condition, and the **begin... end** block updates the column *discount*.

```
while (select avg (discount) — Search for average discounts less than 55
from salesdetail) < 55
begin -- Increase discount by two if it meets search criteria
```

```
    select title_id, discount
    from salesdetail
    update salesdetail
    set discount = discount + 2.0
end
go
```

Example 4: This example illustrates what happens when a **break** keyword is encountered during processing within a **while** loop. When the value of local variable *count* reaches 5, the flow of execution transfers to outside the **while** loop, as demonstrated by the fact that the **select @count** command, which is outside the **while** loop, executes.

```
declare @count int
select @count = 1
while (@count > 0)
begin
  print "looping!"
  if @count = 5
    break
  select @count = @count + 1
end
select @count
go
```

Example 5: This example uses the **if** keyword to query the *authors* table and print a list of authors who live in California.

```
if exists (select state
  from authors
  where state = "CA")
print "There are authors living in California!"
go
```

Example 6: This example illustrates the use of the **label** keyword to branch when the value of *count* is less than 100.

```
declare @count int
select @count = 95
label:
  select @count = @count +1
  print "The count is less than 100!"
while @count < 100
  goto label
go
```

The query output is as follows.

```
The count is less than 100!
The count is less than 100!
```

```
The count is less than 100!
The count is less than 100!
The count is less than 100!
```

Example 7: This example shows how to add a user-defined error message using the system procedure **sp_addmessage**. The following example inserts a message with number 30000 to display an error message if an invalid user tries to log in to SQL Server. *%1!* is a placeholder for the first argument, which is the name of the user. *%2!* is a placeholder for the second argument, which is the name of the server.

```
sp_addmessage 30000,
  "User '%1!' cannot log in to server '%2!'."
go
```

The output of this example is as follows.

```
User '<arg1>' cannot log in to server '<arg2>'.
The message has been inserted.
(return status = 0)
```

To activate the error condition, you can use **raiserror**, as given below.

```
raiserror 30000, george, myserver
go
```

The output of the above command follows.

```
Msg 30000, Level 16, State 1:
Line 1:
User 'george' cannot log in to server 'myserver'
```

Example 8: This example illustrates use of the **waitfor** keyword. This series of commands instructs SQL Server to wait until midnight, then update *clk_table*.

```
begin
   waitfor time "00:00:00"
   update clk_table
   set clk_time = "It's midnight!"
end
go
```

Example 9: This example uses a **while** loop to insert 100 rows into the *temp* table.

```
declare @count int
select @count = 1
while (@count < 101)
begin
   insert into temp values (@count, "TEST")
```

```
    select @count = @count + 1
end
go
```

Cursors

A *cursor* is similar to a UNIX file handle that you can use in C programming. When a C program opens a file and works with its content, the file handle keeps track of the program's location within the file. Similarly, a cursor points to a row in a table to track the process in a query. You associate a cursor with a particular query by defining the cursor for a **select** command. When you execute a **select** command that doesn't have a cursor, SQL Server processes the results for every row selected and returns the result as a unit. The *cursor result set* is a set of rows chosen by a **select** command with an associated cursor. The *cursor position* indicates the row in the cursor result set to which the cursor points.

A select operation with cursors offers two advantages over a select operation without cursors. A program can take action row by row rather than on the entire set of selected rows. Cursors bridge the gap between the set-oriented approach to RDBMS and row-oriented programming. Using cursors involves declaring the cursor, opening it, and fetching the row to which it points. We explain the process in more detail in the "Using Cursors" section later in this chapter.

How Cursors Work

Figure 9-2 illustrates how a cursor steps through a result set consisting of three rows. Initially, the cursor points to the row that has an *emp_no* value of 1000. The cursor moves to the next row after every **fetch** command. This process continues until all of the rows of the cursor result set are returned.

Cursor position	emp_no	emp_name	dept_name
→	1000	Andy	Server
	1001	Cindy	Engg
	1002	David	Admin

Figure 9-2. How cursors work

Cursor Scope

A cursor is only known within specific boundaries that define its *scope*. Table 9-5 describes the three valid scope regions for a cursor. Cursors are local to the region in which they are declared, so a cursor declared in a stored procedure cannot be accessed from a batch.

Table 9-5. *Cursor scope and boundaries*

Scope Region	Region Boundaries
Session	Starts when a client logs into SQL Server and ends when the client logs out
Stored procedures	Starts when a stored procedure begins execution and ends when it completes execution
Trigger	Starts when a trigger begins execution and ends when it completes execution

Using Cursors

Using cursors involves the following process.

1. Use the **declare** command to declare the cursor for the select operation. This checks the syntax of the SQL command.

2. Use the **open** command to open the cursor. This executes the query plan and creates the cursor result set by scanning the underlying base tables. It also positions the cursor before the first row of the cursor result set.

3. Use the **fetch** command to fetch the row to which the cursor points. This fetches one row of the result set. The cursor result set is generated as a cursor's fetch operations return rows.

4. Perform Step 3 repeatedly until all the rows in the cursor result set are fetched, or an error occurs and the operation aborts. When the cursor is no longer needed, its resources should be deallocated by performing Steps 5 and 6.

5. Use the **close** command to close the cursor. This closes the result set, but the compiled query plan still resides in memory so that you can use it again.

6. Use the **deallocate** command to deallocate the cursor. This drops the query plan from memory so that it is no longer available.

The next sections give the commands for carrying out each part of this process.

Declaring a Cursor

There are four types of cursors: *server cursors*, *language cursors*, *client cursors*, and *execute cursors*. You declare one of these types depending where you need to use the cursor. The parameters and local variables referenced in the **declare cursor** command do not have to contain valid values until the cursor is opened. Here is where you declare each of the four types of cursors.

- Language cursors are declared within batches

- Server cursors are declared within stored procedures

- Client cursors and execute cursors are declared through Open Client calls

This section discusses how to declare language cursors, and the next section explains server cursors. Client and execute cursors are associated with Client-Library, which we do not go into here. See your Open Client Client-Library documentation if you need information on client and execute cursors. Table 9-6 lists the syntax for declaring language cursors.

Table 9-6. *Syntax and parameters for the **declare cursor** command*

declare *cursor_name* **cursor**
  for *select_command*
  [for {read only | update [of *column_name_list*]}]	

cursor_name	The name of the cursor you are creating
select_command	The query that defines the cursor result set
read only	Specifies that the cursor result set is for select only and cannot be updated or deleted
for update	Specifies that the cursor result set can be updated or deleted
of *column_name_list*	Specifies the names of columns from the **select** command that can be updated

---

Points to Note: Cursor Usage

Bear the following in mind when working with any cursor

*   A cursor name must be unique within its scope

*   You must deallocate a cursor before you can declare another cursor with the same name

---

Example 1: This example declares a read-only cursor, which only can perform **select** operations.

```
declare emp_cursor cursor
   for select emp_no, emp_name
   from emp
   where dept = "Engg"
go
```

Example 2: This example shows a cursor used to update a table. The cursor is used to update the value of the *advance* column for rows that satisfy the **select** criteria.

```
declare titles_cursor cursor
   for select title, total_sales
   where total_sales > 4000
   from titles for update of advance
 go
```

Opening a Cursor

Table 9-7 gives the syntax for opening a cursor. When the cursor is first opened, it is positioned before the first row of the cursor result set.

Table 9-7. *Syntax for opening a cursor*

open *cursor_name*	
cursor_name	The name of the cursor you want to open

Example: The following command opens the cursor *titles_cursor* declared in the preceding example.

```
open titles_cursor
go
```

Fetching Rows

By default, the **fetch** command returns only one row at a time. However, you can specify the number of rows for each fetch to return using the **set** command. A cursor moves forward (never backward) through the result set after each fetch. The datatypes and the order of the variables must match that of the column values for fetched columns. Table 9-8 shows the syntax for using a cursor to fetch a row.

Table 9-8. *Syntax and parameters for the **fetch** command*

fetch *cursor_name* [into *fetch_list*]	
cursor_name	Name of the cursor
into *fetch_list*	Specifies that the column data returned by the cursor should be placed into the variables identified by the *fetch_list*

Figure 9-3 illustrates how a cursor is positioned before and after a series of fetches. F0 is the position of the cursor after it is opened. F1 is the cursor position after the first fetch, which returns the first row. F2 is the cursor position after the second fetch, which returns the second row. F3 is the position of the cursor after the third fetch, which returns the last row of the cursor result set.

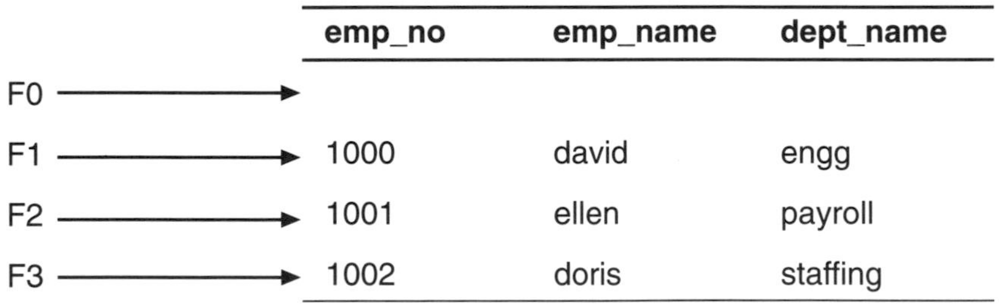

	emp_no	emp_name	dept_name
F0 ───────────→			
F1 ───────────→	1000	david	engg
F2 ───────────→	1001	ellen	payroll
F3 ───────────→	1002	doris	staffing

Figure 9-3. *Cursor positioning before and after a series of fetches*

Example 1: This example illustrates how to fetch three rows at a time from a table. The **set cursor** command specifies the number of rows to fetch.

```
set cursor rows 3
   for titles_cursor
fetch titles_cursor
go
```

Example 2: This example illustrates how to fetch column values into variables. After the fetch, *@emp_no* contains the value of the column *emp_no,* and *@emp_name* contains the value of column *emp_name.*

```
declare @emp_no varchar(10)
declare @emp_name varchar(30)
declare emp_cursor cursor
   for select emp_no, emp_name
   from emp
   where dept = "Engg"
open emp_cursor
fetch emp_cursor into @emp_no, @emp_name
go
```

Global Variables Affected by Fetch

Every fetch operation affects the *sqlstatus* and *rowcount* global variables as described by Tables 9-9 and 9-10.

*Table 9-9. Values held by the **@@sqlstatus** global variable*

Global Variable	Description
@@sqlstatus	Holds status that indicates whether the fetch was successful. The status values are: 0: Successful fetch 1: An error resulted from an attempt to fetch 2: There is no more data to fetch

*Table 9-10. Values held by the **@@rowcount** global variable*

Global Variable	Description
@@rowcount	Holds the cumulative number of rows fetched by a particular cursor.

Example: This command shows a SQL status value for a successful fetch and is followed by a display of its output.

```
select @@sqlstatus
go
 -------------
0
(1 row affected)
```

Closing and Deallocating a Cursor

You should close a cursor set using the syntax specified in Table 9-11 after fetching all results. Similarly, after you close a cursor, you should deallocate its used resources as specified in Table 9-12 so that the resources can be reused.

Table 9-11. *Syntax and parameter for the **close cursor** command*

close *cursor_name*	
cursor_name	The name of the cursor to close

Table 9-12. *Syntax and parameter for deallocating cursor resources*

deallocate cursor *cursor_name*	
cursor_name	Name of the cursor holding resources to deallocate

Example: This command closes cursor *titles_cursor* and deallocates the resources held by the cursor.

```
close cursor titles_cursor
deallocate cursor titles_cursor
go
```

Using Cursors to Update Tables

By default, you cannot update and delete a table's rows using cursors, but you can create *updatable cursors* using the *for update* option in the **declare cursor** command. Refer to the "Declaring a Cursor" section earlier in this chapter. The following example illustrates how to create an updatable cursor.

Example: The cursor in this example updates column *royaltyper* in table *titleauthor*. The *royal_cursor* increments the value of *royaltyper* by 100 every time it fetches a row.

```
declare royal_cursor cursor
   for select au_id, title_id, royaltyper
    from titleauthor
   for update of royaltyper
go
fetch royal_cursor
update titleauthor
set royaltyper = royaltyper + 100
   where current of royal_cursor
go
```

If you do not explicitly specify *for read only* or *for update*, SQL Server checks to see whether the cursor is updatable. If you omit the *for read only* option, the cursor is implicitly *read only* if the **select** command contains any of the following clauses (otherwise, it is implicitly updatable).

- The *distinct* option

- A subquery

- Aggregate functions, such as *sum*, *avg*, and *max*

- The *union* operator

- A *group by* clause

- An *at isolation read uncommitted* clause

- An *order by* clause

Updatable Columns

If you do not specify a *column_name_list* with the *for update* option when you use cursors to update a table, all of the columns specified in *select_command* are updatable. However, if you specify a list of columns in the *column_name_list*, only the columns in the list can be updated.

SQL Server tries to use *unique* indexes for updatable cursors when scanning the *base tables* (the tables that the cursors are updating). A table must have a *unique* index if you want to modify its data based on cursor position.

Table 9-13 summarizes the rules for using cursors to scan base tables. For example, the first line in the table says that if you specified the *for update* option and there is a *unique* index on the table, the update will succeed. The second line indicates that if you specified the *for update* option but the table has no *unique* index, the update will not succeed.

Table 9-13. *Cursor rules for scanning base tables*

Did you specify the *for update* option?	Is there a *unique* index on the table?	Result
Yes	Yes	Update succeeds
Yes	No	SQL Server issues error
No	Yes	Update succeeds
No	No	Update succeeds

Point to Note: If you specify the *read only* option with a **delete** or **update** command, the cursor result set cannot be updated.

Deleting Rows with Cursors

You can use cursors to delete rows from tables by specifying the *for update* option in cursor declarations. The following example declares a cursor that deletes all rows in the *emp* table for which the *dept* column has a value of *misc*.

```
declare royal_cursor cursor
   for select emp_id, emp_name
   from emp
   where dept = "misc"
   for update
go
fetch royal_cursor
delete from emp
   where current of royal_cursor
close royal_cursor
go
```

Example: Using Transact-SQL and Its Extensions

This section presents an example that uses all of the T-SQL extensions that you've learned up to now. It is a batch that involves local and global variables in flow-of-control constructs with cursors. The example updates the salary of all employees based on their present salary. If the salary is more than $100,000, the employee gets a 10 percent raise; all others get a raise of 20 percent.

Cursors facilitate the row-by-row operations appropriate for this type of processing. Using SQL commands would require selecting an entire set of rows, which would not have been as efficient.

```
/* Declare a cursor for update */
declare sal_update cursor
   for select emp_name, salary
   from emp
   for update
go
/* Declare variables for holding the column values */
declare @emp_name varchar(30)
declare @salary money
/* Open the cursor */
open sal_update
begin tran
fetch sal_update into @emp_name, @salary
```

```
    while @@sqlstatus != 2  /* Loop through until all rows are fetched */
begin
      if (@@sqlstatus = 1)   /* Raise error if the fetch is not successful */
        begin
          raiserror 30001 "Fetch failed in cursor"
          close sal_update
          deallocate cursor sal_update
          return
        end
      if @salary < 100000 /* If salary is less than 100,000 update emp  */
        set salary = salary * 1.20
        where current of sal_update
      else
        update emp
        set salary = salary * 1.10
          where current of sal_update
        if @@transtate = 2    /* If the previous  fetch was aborted, rollback
                                          transaction */
        begin
           rollback tran
           close sal_update
           deallocate cursor sal_update
           return
        end
        fetch sal_update into @emp_name, @salary
      end
  commit tran
go
```

Getting Information About Cursors

The system procedure **sp_cursorinfo** displays information about a cursor. Table
9-14 provides the syntax and parameters for this procedure.

*Table 9-14. Syntax and parameters for the **sp_cursorinfo** procedure*

sp_cursorinfo *nesting_level, cursor_name*

cursor_name	The name of the cursor for which you want information
nesting_level	The nesting level can be one of the following:
	N is any cursor declared inside a stored procedure at a specific procedure nesting level
	O (zero) is any cursor declared outside stored procedures
	-1 is any cursor declared either inside or outside the stored procedure from either N or O

Example: This example uses **sp_cursorinfo** to get information about cursor *sal_update*. The command is followed by a partial output of what it generates.

```
sp_cursorinfo 0, sal_update
go
Cursor name 'sal_update' is declared at nesting level '0'.
The cursor id is 65539.
The cursor has been successfully opened 0 times.
The cursor was compiled at isolation level 1.
The cursor is not open.
The cursor will remain open when a transaction is
  committed or rolled back.
The number of rows returned for each FETCH is 1.
The cursor is updatable.
This cursor is using 4188 bytes of memory.
There are 4 columns returned by this cursor.
The result columns are:
Name = 'emp_no', Table = 'emp', Type = VARCHAR,
  Length = 30 (updatable)
Name = 'emp_name', Table = 'emp', Type = VARCHAR,
  Length = 30 (updatable)
Name = 'dept', Table = 'emp', Type = VARCHAR,
  Length = 10 (updatable)
Name = 'salary', Table = 'emp', Type = MONEY, Length = 8 (updatable)
```

Stored Procedures

There is nothing unusual about the "procedure" part of a stored procedure; it has all of the characteristics of a normal SQL Server batch program. It is that the procedure can be "stored" that makes it so useful. When you create a stored procedure, SQL Server does the following.

- Associates the procedure with the name that you supply when you create it

- Compiles the procedure by processing the query. From that, SQL Server prepares a query plan, which it uses to run the procedure each time it is called

- Stores the normalized query tree in the *sysprocedures* table in the *master* database

Figure 9-4 shows a client invoking a stored procedure. SQL Server processes the request, executes the stored procedure, and returns the results to the client.

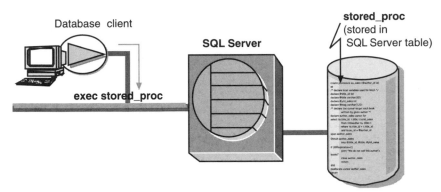

Figure 9-4. *Processing a request for a stored procedure*

Benefits of Stored Procedures

Stored procedures offer the following advantages over batches.

- Stored procedures run much faster than a normal batch, because SQL Server uses precompiled versions of the stored procedures. A batch needs to be parsed and normalized; a procedure does not.

- Stored procedures improve performance when you use them to implement frequently run queries, because they are precompiled and cached.

- Stored procedures reduce network traffic, because the client can issue a single command (**exec procedure_name**) that sends the batch as a single I/O request rather than sending each command in the batch as a separate I/O request. However, SQL Server should be configured with an optimal value of default network packet size. (The actual value depends on your network.)

- Stored procedures aid in consistent, modular application development.

- Stored procedures eliminate redundancy, because they can be reused.

- Stored procedures provide security, because users don't access the table directly—they receive a processed result. Users can execute a stored procedure even if they do not have permissions to modify tables that the procedure affects.

- Stored procedures can be executed remotely if the local server and the remote server are set up for remote operations.

Creating and Dropping Stored Procedures

A stored procedure is stored in the database in which it is created and may reference objects in other databases. Table 9-15 gives the syntax for creating a stored procedure.

Table 9-15. *Syntax and parameters for* **create procedure**

create procedure [*owner.*] *procedure_name* [*;number*]
  [[(]@*parameter_name*
  datatype [(*length*) | (*precision* [, *scale*])]
  [= *default*] [output]
  [, @*parameter_name*
  datatype [(*length*) | (*precision* [, *scale*])]
  [= *default*] [output]]...[)]]
  [with recompile] as *SQL_commands*

procedure_name	Name of the stored procedure.
number	An optional integer used to group different procedures that will share the same name.
parameter_name	The stored procedure parameter name. This parameter must always be preceded by an @ sign. A stored procedure can have up to 255 parameters, and parameter names can be up to 30 characters in length (including the @ sign).
datatype [(*length*) | (*precision* [, *scale*])]	Datatype of the parameter. The *length* parameter is used for character datatypes such as *char, nchar, nvarchar,* and *varbinary.* Datatypes of parameters can be either user defined or system datatypes. A database object name cannot be passed as a parameter. The *precision* and *scale* parameters are used by *numeric* and *decimal* datatypes.
output	Indicates that the parameter is a return parameter, whose value can be returned to the client.
with recompile	Tells SQL Server not to save a plan for this procedure. (The stored procedure generates a new plan every time it is called.)
SQL_commands	The set of SQL commands that dictate the stored procedure's actions.

Points to Note: Creating Stored Procedures

Consider these points when creating stored procedures.

- Stored procedures cannot include **create default**, **create rule**, **create trigger**, **create procedure**, or **create view** commands

- Sixteen megabytes is the maximum amount of text that you can use to create a stored procedure

- You cannot create tables and access them in the same stored procedure

- You must drop a stored procedure before you can create a new one with the same name

Example: This example creates the stored procedure *proc_state*, which returns information about authors who live in *MI*.

```
create proc proc_state
as
   select au_id, au_lname
   from authors
   where state = "MI"
return
go
```

Table 9-16 shows the syntax for dropping stored procedures.

Table 9-16. *Syntax and parameters for the **drop procedure** command*

drop procedure [*owner.*]*procedure_name* [, [*owner.*]*procedure_name*]...	
procedure_name	The name of the stored procedure to drop
owner	The name of the user who owns the stored procedure

Example: This command drops the *emp_proc* stored procedure.

```
drop proc emp_proc
go
```

However, you cannot drop a particular procedure from a group. For example, the following command is not allowed.

```
drop proc emp_proc;1     /* Not Allowed */
go
```

Tip! While creating procedures, set up defaults for all parameters so that you can catch errors due to invalid combinations.

Invoking Stored Procedures

Table 9-17 gives a simplified syntax for invoking a stored procedure from within a batch. You can use one of two forms for this command, either **execute** or **exec**. (Appendix C gives the complete syntax.)

Table 9-17. Syntax and parameters for executing a procedure

execute [*server_name*].[*database_name*].[*owner*].*procedure_name*	
exec *server_name*.[*database_name*].[*owner*].*procedure_name*	
server_name	Name of the SQL Server that has the stored procedure
database_name	Name of the database in which the procedure is stored
owner	Name of the user who owns the stored procedure

You don't always need to use the **execute** or **exec** command to invoke a stored procedure, although you always can if you prefer. Here are the rules about how you can execute a stored procedure simply by using its name. You can do so when you invoke it within an **isql** session or as the first command in a batch. In contrast, you must use an **exec** or **execute** command when you invoke it from a batch and it is not the first command.

Tip! Passing parameters by name is more self-documenting and flexible than passing parameters by position.

Example 1: You can execute the stored procedure *proc_state* using the following methods.

```
proc_state   /* From an isql session or as the first command in batch */
go
execute proc_state  /* From within a batch */
go
exec proc_state  /* From within a batch */
go
```

Example 2: If a stored procedure is stored in database *pubs2* on a server called *loc*, it can be executed from a remote server using the following command.

```
execute loc.pubs2.dbo.proc_state
go
```

Stored procedures can also be executed using variable names, as the following commands illustrate.

```
declare @sp char(20)
select @sp = "loc.pub2.dbo.proc_state"
exec @sp
go
```

Point to Note: Stored procedures can be called from a batch, another stored procedure, a trigger, an Open Client program, or a third-party client program.

Stored Procedures and Passed Parameters

A stored procedure behaves much like any software procedure and has the ability to take parameters. You can optionally declare one or more parameters for a stored procedure. Parameter names must be preceded by an @ symbol, because they are local variables—they are only meaningful within the procedure that declares them. The parameter name must have a system or user-defined datatype and cannot exceed 30 characters. If you don't initialize a stored procedure parameter, its initial value defaults to NULL.

Example 1: The following stored procedure obtains the list of employees working in a particular department. The **create proc** command declares the parameter *deptname* with no initial value.

```
create proc dept_info @deptname varchar(20)
as
   select emp_name, dept
   from emp
   where dept = @deptname
return
go
```

Example 2: The following command executes a stored procedure and displays a list of all employees working in *engg*.

```
exec proc_dept "engg"
go
```

Stored Procedures and Default Parameters

You can assign a default value for a parameter in the **create proc** command. If the user does not supply any value for this parameter, it takes the default value.

Example: This example shows a new version of an earlier example that has a default value for *deptname*. If the user does not specify a value for *deptname*, the procedure uses the default value **engg**.

```
create proc dept_info
@deptname varchar(20) =  "engg"
as
  select emp_name, dept
  from emp
  where dept = @deptname
return
go
```

Default parameters can have NULL values. In this case, SQL server executes the procedure without giving errors if the user does not supply a parameter. When multiple parameters are used in stored procedures, you can call values in parameters by position or by name.

Example: This examples shows a declaration for three parameters in a new stored procedure called **param_proc**.

```
create proc param_proc (@i int, @j int = 10, @k
  varchar(30))
  as
  {commands that define the procedure ...}
go
```

The following illustrates the execution of the procedure using position.

```
exec param_proc 2, null, 10
go
```

This command shows execution of the procedure using names.

```
exec param_proc @i = 2, @j = null, @k =10
go
```

Because these execution commands specify a null value for *j*, its value will be *10*—it defaults to its assigned initial value.

Using the *with recompile* Option

SQL Server usually stores the query plan in a stored procedure when it first compiles the procedure. However, a change in the data or parameter values can result in the need for SQL Server to come up with a new query plan. Using the **create procedure** command with the *with recompile* option forces SQL Server to recompile the procedure each time it executes. This is sometimes necessary, such as when data is frequently inserted, updated, or deleted. The general format for using the *with compile* option looks like the following.

```
create proc author_proc
...
with recompile
```

When procedures are created using the *with recompile* option, SQL Server does not save a plan for the procedure. Use this option only when you need a new plan; that is, when you expect the execution of the procedure will not be normal. When this option is used, please keep the following two points in mind. First, the advantage of executing a procedure from the procedure cache is lost, because the procedure is not cached. Second, compilation is an expensive CPU operation.

Recompilation occurs automatically for several reasons. For example, if a change occurs in the data or in the parameter values supplied for subsequent executions, SQL Server could recompile the stored procedure and come up with a new query plan. Procedures created without the *with recompile* option can also be recompiled at the execution phase of the procedure using the following command.

```
exec ..... with recompile
```

Example: Here's an example that uses the *with recompile* option on the command line.

```
exec dept_info with recompile
go
```

Return Status

Stored procedures automatically return status. A stored procedure returns a zero value when it completes successfully. If the stored procedure detects an error, it returns a number between -1 and -99, which depends on the nature of the error. When several errors occur during execution, a stored procedure returns a status equal to the highest absolute value of all errors.

You can use return status values to determine appropriate actions to take. You can define your own return status in stored procedures by adding a parameter to the **return** command. This parameter may be any positive integer.

Tip! End each procedure with a **return** command. This helps accelerate the debugging of stored procedures.

Example 1: This example creates a stored procedure that checks if a specific employee name is valid. If the employee name matches a record in the *emp* table, the stored procedure returns a value of *1*. When the employee name is not found, the stored procedure returns a value of *100*.

```
create proc empvalid @empname varchar(30)
as
   if (select count(*) from emp
     where emp_name = @empname) = 1
   return 1
else
   return 100
go
```

To execute this stored procedure, use the following command.

```
exec empvalid "ADAM"
go
```

Example 2: The following stored procedure uses conditional clauses to check return status.

```
create proc checkemp @empname varchar(30)
   as
      declare @retvalue=checkemp @empname
if (@retvalue=1)
  Print "The employee record was found!"
else
  Print "The employee record was not found."
go
```

Return Values

Stored procedures can return the results of calculations, queries, or other processing to the caller for use in subsequent processing. You enable a stored procedure's return capability by specifying the *output* option when creating or calling the stored procedure. (The caller can be a SQL batch or another stored procedure.)

Example: In this example, parameters *stock_price* and *num_shares* are input parameters, and *result* is an output parameter. The procedure returns the product of *stock_price* and *num_shares* in the output parameter *result*. The variable *result* contains the output.

```
create proc stock_proc @stock_price float, @num_shares float, @result float
  output
   as
```

```
        select @result = @stock_price * @num_shares
return
go
```

These commands execute this stored procedure and retrieve the value in *result*. The result is *2012.5*.

```
declare @result float
exec stock_proc 20.125, 100, @result output
go
```

Nested Stored Procedures

When one stored procedure calls another, the process is called nesting. There can be up to 16 levels of nesting, and you get the current nesting level by querying the *@@nestlevel* global variable. The nesting level is incremented when the called procedure begins execution and decremented when the called procedure finishes executing.

Figure 9-5 shows *proc1* calling the nested stored procedure *proc2*. The value of *nestlevel* is initially *0*. The nesting level before executing *proc2* is set to *1*, because the execution of the first stored procedure has commenced. The value of *nestlevel* inside *proc2* is *2*.

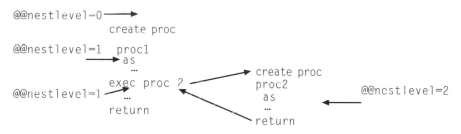

Figure 9-5. An example of nested stored procedures

Server Cursors: Cursors in Stored Procedures

Server cursors are cursors used in stored procedures. A cursor is local to the stored procedure that declares it, so it follows that you cannot open, fetch, or close a cursor in a stored procedure unless you declare the cursor in that stored procedure.

Example: This example illustrates how you can use a cursor in a stored procedure. This procedure returns information about all employees who work in the *dept* with a value of *engg*.

```
create proc emp_proc
as
   declare @emp_no varchar(30), @emp_name varchar(30)
   declare emp_cursor cursor
   for select emp_no, emp_name
     from emp
     where dept = "engg"
open emp_cursor
while @@sqlstatus !=2    /* Loop through until all
   the rows are processed */
   begin
     fetch emp_cursor into @emp_no, @emp_name
     select @emp_no, @emp_name
   end
close emp_cursor
deallocate cursor emp_cursor
return
go
```

Renaming Stored Procedures

You can rename a stored procedures using the system procedure **sp_rename**. The **sp_rename** procedure is a useful general system procedure, because it renames any object specified as *objname* (such as table or column). The syntax for **sp_rename** is as follows.

```
sp_rename objname, newname
```

Example: Here's a command that renames stored procedure *emp_proc* to *emp_detproc*.

```
sp_rename emp_proc, emp_detproc
go
```

Procedure Groups

You can group a series of stored procedures by giving them the same name and differentiating them by their number in the series. An example of a group of procedures is *deptname;1*, *deptname;2*, and *deptname;3*. When you group procedures like this, you can drop the whole group using its common name in a **drop proc** command. If you want to drop the group of procedures called *deptname*, you issue the following command.

```
drop proc deptname
go
```

System Procedures

System procedures are stored procedures that Sybase supplies to simplify SQL Server administration tasks. You can use system procedures to retrieve information from system tables in any database. All system procedures begin with *sp_* and are stored in the *sybsystemprocs* database.

Point to Note: System procedures can be run from any database.

What Happens in the Server

When a stored procedure is created, SQL Server parses and compiles all of the database objects. It performs the following steps in doing so.

- It adds a row with the procedure name to the *sysobjects* system table and sets the value of the *type* column to *P*.

- It stores the actual procedure in the *syscomments* system table.

- It stores the compiled version of the procedure in the database in which the procedure is defined.

Point to Note: The *sybsystemprocs* database has useful system procedures that access system tables. Refer to Chapter 3, The SQL Server Engine, for more information about the *sybsytemprocs* database.

Getting Information About Stored Procedures

Sybase provides three system procedures that you can use to get information about stored procedures.

- **sp_help** *proc_name* Displays information about a stored procedure.

- **sp_helptext** *proc_name* Displays the entire text of a stored procedure.

- **sp_depends** *object_name Object_name* is the name of a stored procedure or a table. This system procedure lists all the objects that *object_name* references.

Example: In this example, if either *state_name* or *city_name* is not specified by the user, the procedure returns an appropriate message and exits. The procedure then displays a list of all authors who live in the given state and city.

```
create proc state_proc @state_name char(2) = null,
  @city_name varchara(30)=null
as
  if @state_name is null
    print "Please specify the state!"
  if @city_name is null
    print "Please specify the city!"
  return
select au_id, au_lname
  from authors
  where state = @state_name and city = @city_name
return
go
```

Triggers

A trigger is an event-driven stored procedure associated with a specific table. It executes when a data modification command such as **insert**, **update**, or **delete** attempts to affect that table; that is, the trigger "fires" even if no rows are affected. Depending which data modification command drives the trigger, it is referred to as an *update trigger*, *insert trigger*, or *delete trigger*.

Figure 9-6 shows a delete trigger called *del_emp* created on an *emp* table. The trigger fires whenever anything attempts to delete a row in the *emp* table.

The trigger aspect together with the batch aspect of a trigger make triggers very useful. Here are the most common way in which triggers are used.

- To enforce referential integrity

- To enforce complex restrictions

- To notify

- To automate a process based on an insert, update, or delete operation

Enforcing Referential Integrity and Complex Restrictions

Triggers enforce referential integrity by keeping the values in a foreign key consistent with those in the primary key they reference. The trigger compares the new column values with the key column values and takes appropriate action based on the trigger procedure defined during trigger creation. For example, if the *title_id* column is a unique key, an update trigger on the *title_id* column of a *titles* table can cause an update of the corresponding row in any table that reference *titles*, such as *titleauthor*, *sales*, and *roysched*.

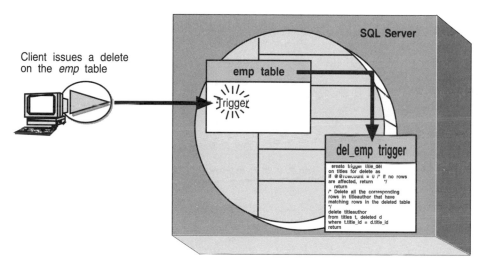

Figure 9-6. *A trigger driven by a **delete** command*

Triggers cascade changes through related tables in a database. For example, an update trigger defined on the *titles* table that affects the unique key *title_id* could cascade changes through the corresponding rows in other tables, such as *titleauthor*, *sales*, and *roysched*. Referential integrity constraints created using the **create table** command do not cascade updates and deletes, so you can more rigorously enforce referential integrity using triggers.

Triggers can also enforce complex restrictions by referencing other database objects. An example of a complex restriction is that employees should not get a raise of more than 10 percent in one update. For example, a trigger can roll back (undo) updates that attempt to increase the employee salary by more than 10 percent if the employee works for the sales department.

Notification

Another application for triggers is notification. Say that an update trigger on a column holds up-to-the minute stock prices. The trigger fires, executing its procedure every time the column is updated. The trigger procedure can check the column value and send e-mail to notify any interested stock broker when the price falls below a certain value.

Creating Triggers

Table 9-18 gives the syntax for creating triggers.

*Table 9-18. Syntax and parameters for the **create trigger** command*

```
create trigger [owner.] trigger_name
  on [owner.] table_name
  for {insert, update, delete}
        as SQL_commands
  [if update (column_name)
  [{and | or} update (column_name)]...]
    SQL_commands
    [if update (column_name)
    [{and | or} update (column_name)]...
      SQL_commands]...
```

trigger_name	Name of the trigger that is being created. Insert, update, and delete refer to the types of triggers based on their effects.
SQL_commands	Specify the trigger actions and conditions. They determine if the attempted actions cause the trigger to fire. Trigger actions take effect when a data modification command such as delete, insert, or update is attempted.
if update	This clause is used to test whether the specified column is included in the set list of an **update** command.

Example: This example creates a trigger for notification. It creates a delete trigger on *emp* table that issues a warning message whenever a row is deleted from *emp*.

```
create trigger emp_del on emp
  for delete
as
  print "You have just deleted a row from emp!"
return
go
```

How Triggers Work

Whenever a data modification affects a key column, SQL Server creates two temporary work tables called *trigger test tables*: a deleted table, which holds any rows that were deleted to a table due to a delete or update operation; and an inserted table, which holds any rows that were added to a table as a result of an **insert** or **update** command.

There is no need for a separate updated table, because an update is a delete followed by an insert when there are triggers defined on the table.

When a trigger fires, the following process takes place.

- SQL Server creates the trigger test tables

- During delete or update operations, SQL Server deletes rows from the trigger table (the table on which the trigger is defined) and places the rows in the deleted table

- During insert or update operations, SQL Server simultaneously adds rows to the trigger table and to the inserted table

The Delete Trigger

You can create a delete trigger to enforce referential integrity as follows. If a user or application attempts to delete a primary key row referenced by foreign key rows, the delete is either disallowed or the corresponding foreign key rows in referencing tables should also be deleted to preserve referential integrity.

Example 1: In this example, a trigger on the table *titles* has a primary key called *title_id*, as shown in Figure 9-7. The foreign key column *title_id* of the *titleauthor* table references the primary key *title_id*. If any rows in the *titleauthor* table have a match in *title_id*, the primary key cannot be deleted without first deleting all the matching rows in the *titleauthor* table to maintain referential integrity.

Example 2: Refer again to Figure 9-7. Say a user attempts to delete the row with *title*_id of *BU1032* in the *titles* table. Two rows in the *titleauthor* table have the same value for *BU1032*. The following actions occur as a result of the create trigger operation defined below: The deleted rows are placed in the deleted table and all the corresponding rows in *titleauthor* are deleted using a join operation on *title_id*.

```
create trigger title_del
  on titles for delete as
if @@rowcount = 0  /* If no rows are affected, return    */
  return
/* Delete all the corresponding rows in
  titleauthor that have matching rows in the
  deleted table */
delete titleauthor
  from titles t, deleted d
  where t.title_id = d.title_id
return
go
```

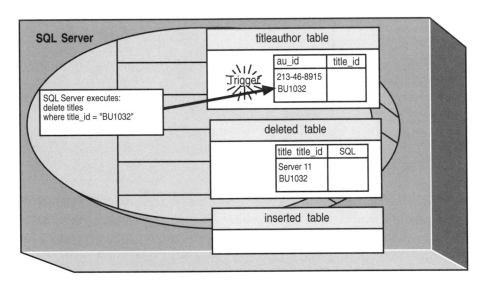

Figure 9-7. *Using a delete trigger*

The Insert Trigger

To preserve referential integrity when a foreign key is inserted, the trigger procedure can ensure that a matching row exists in the primary key table, depending whether the user wants to accept the transaction.

Example: The trigger shown in Figure 9-8 uses an inserted table to compare against the key values in the primary key table.

Example: In Figure 9-8, a user attempts to insert a row in the *titleauthor* table. The inserted row should have a matching key column *title*_id in the *titles* table.

When the trigger fires, the row to insert is placed in the inserted table. The trigger then compares the rows with a matching row in the *titles* table. If there is a matching row, the insert succeeds. If there is no match, an error is raised and the insert transaction is rolled back to its original value.

```
create trigger titleauthor_ins
  on titleauthor for insert as
/* Find out how many rows were modified */
declare @num_rows int
select @num_rows = @@rowcount
/* Ensure that all title_ids match with those in
   titles table */
if (select count(*) from titles t, inserted i
  where t.title_id = i.title_id) != @num_rows
begin
  raiserror 30002 "Attempt to insert invalid
  title_id into titleauthor"
  rollback transaction
  return
end
return
go
```

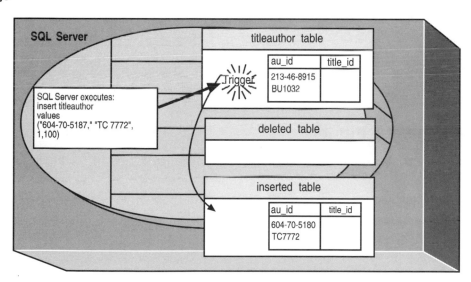

Figure 9-8. *Using an insert trigger*

The Update Trigger

The update trigger is very useful for initiating a series of actions based on a column update. For example, you could use a trigger on an inventory column for items in stock. Whenever the column is updated for an item that has been removed from stock, the trigger fires and initiates a procedure to compare the current inventory amount with the reorder amount. When the inventory amount of the item falls below its reorder value, the trigger initiates actions that prepare and print a purchase order to reorder the item.

Example: The following example uses the *if update* clause to determine if a particular column was updated on weekends. The function **datename** (**dw, getdate()**) displays the day of the week.

```
create trigger emp_trig
on emp
for update
as
   if update(emp_salery)
   and datename(dw, getdate())
   in ("saturday", "sunday")
begin
   print "Employee salary adjustments not allowed
     on weekends!"
   rollback transaction
end
go
```

Point to Note: You can update triggers on a primary key column, but we don't recommend it because such updates can cause far-reaching referential integrity violations. If for some reason you must update a primary key value, do it very carefully.

Rolling Back Triggers

Triggers can be rolled back using either the **rollback trigger** or **rollback transaction** command. The roll back operation undoes whatever was done so that the affected objects return to their preoperation state. The **rollback triggers** operation rolls back only the effect of the trigger, not of the entire transaction. **Rollback transaction** rolls back the entire transaction. The syntax of **rollback trigger** is presented in Table 9-19.

Table 9-19. Syntax and parameters for the **rollback trigger** command

rollback trigger [with *raiserror_keyword*]	
raiserror_keyword	Specifies a **raiserror** keyword (discussed earlier in this chapter)

Point to Note: A **rollback trigger** command executed outside a trigger, but inside a transaction, generates an error and causes SQL Server to roll back the transaction and abort the current batch. For more information about how transactions work, see Chapter 10, Transaction Management.

Example: This example rolls back the effect of a trigger after an attempt to insert a row into the *titleauthor* table.

```
create trigger titleauthor_ins
  on titleauthor
  for insert
  as
  if (select count(*) from titles, inserted
    where titles.title_id = inserted.title_id) !=
         @@rowcount
    rollback trigger with raiserror 30004
         "Row was not added to titleauthor because
         there was no matching row
         in titles table: Rolling back the trigger ..."
return
go
```

Nesting Triggers

A trigger is nested if it calls another trigger. Triggers can nest to a depth of up to 16 levels. Nesting attempts beyond 16 levels result in aborted transactions. Figure 9-9 illustrates the nesting concept. The insert trigger in table A fires if a row is inserted in table A. If the trigger procedure in trigger A inserts a row in table B (which has another insert trigger defined on it), trigger B fires. Trigger B results in a row insert into table C.

You can enable or disable nesting using the **sp_configure** system procedure as follows.

sp_configure "allow nested triggers", 1

Use the following command to disable nesting.

sp_configure "allow nested triggers", 0

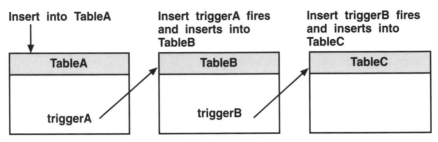

Figure 9-9. *The effects of nested triggers*

Self-Recursive Triggers

An update trigger can call itself in response to a second update to the same table within the trigger. This is called *self-recursion*. By default, a trigger cannot call itself recursively, but you can enable self-recursion using the following command.

set self_recursion on | off

Example: This example illustrates the concept of self-recursion. Consider table *t1* with two columns, *c1* of datatype char and *c2* of datatype int.

```
create trigger t1_ins on t1
for insert as
begin
  set self_recursion on
  if @@nestlevel > 4
    set self_recursion off
      insert into t1 values ("From t1, Nest Level:", @@nestlevel)
end
go
```

When a row is inserted into table *t1*, the insert trigger fires and inserts another row into *t1*. This triggers another insert, which inserts another row into *t1*. This continues until there are five more rows, after which the self-recursion halts.

insert t1 values ("Self Recursion", 100)

The table *t1* has five rows, as shown here.

```
c1                                  c2
--------------------------------    -------
Self Recursion                      100
From t1, Nest Level:                  1
From t1, Nest Level:                  2
From t1, Nest Level:                  3
From t1, Nest Level:                  4
From t1, Nest Level:                  5
```

What Happens in the Server

When a procedure or trigger is created, SQL Server adds a new row to the system table *sysobjects*. The text of the procedure or trigger is stored in the *syscomments* system table and its normalized tree is stored in the *sysprocedures* table.

Getting Information About Triggers

You can obtain a listing of all the database objects that a trigger references using system procedure **sp_depends** *trigger_name*. Use **sp_help** to get information about the trigger and **sp_helptext** to list the text of the trigger.

Example: The following example defines three triggers on a table—one each for inserts, updates, and deletes. If an attempt is made to update the primary key column, the update trigger fires and disallows the update. During the insertion or deletion of rows in the table, an appropriate message is dispatched.

```
create trigger emp_trigger on emp
  for  insert, update, delete
  as
    declare @rows_del int, @rows_ins int
    select @rows_ins = count(*) from inserted
    select @rows_del = count(*) from deleted
  if @rows_del = @rows_ins   /* trigger was fired by update  */
  begin
    if update (emp_no)
    begin
      print "Update of primary key not allowed! Rolling
              back .."
      rollback tran
    return
    end
  end
if @rows_del < @rows_ins /* trigger was fired by insert  */
begin
  print "New employees are being added!"
  return
end
if @rows_del > @rows_ins /* trigger was fired by delete */
begin
  print "Employees are being deleted!"
  return
end
go
```

Points to Note: Triggers

Note the following important information about triggers.

- A trigger fires only once for a single SQL data modification command regardless of the number of rows affected.

- The temporary trigger tables *inserted* and *deleted* are available only to triggers.

- Triggers do not take parameters and cannot be executed directly.

- Overhead for triggers is normally very low, as the database objects referenced by the trigger are either in memory or on the database device.

- A table can have a maximum of three triggers: *delete, update,* and *insert.*

- Triggers cannot be created on temporary tables and system tables.

- You cannot use SQL commands such as **create**, **drop**, **alter table**, or **alter database** in trigger procedures.

- Triggers must be dropped and recreated if any database object that is referenced by the trigger is renamed. However, if a user creates another object with the same name in a different schema, the server will raise errors.

- When you drop a table, all triggers associated with that table are also dropped.

- Trigger can be renamed using system procedure **sp_rename** *trigger_name, new_trigger_name*.

Dropping Triggers

Use the syntax described in Table 9-20 to drop a trigger. When a table is dropped, all triggers associated with the table are automatically dropped.

*Table 9-20. Syntax and parameters for the **drop trigger** command*

drop trigger [*owner.*] *trigger_name* [, [*owner.*] *trigger_name*]...	
trigger_name	Name of the trigger to drop

Exercises

9-1. Which global variable gives the number of rows affected by a previous command?

9-2. How do you assign values to global variables?

9-3. How are local variables defined in SQL? What is the duration of local variables?

9-4. If a local variable is defined, what is its initial value?

9-5. What is the output of the following commands?

```
declare @i int, @j int
select @i = 100, @j = @i/2
select @i, @j
```

9-6. What variable do you use for checking error status?

9-7. What is the value of *k* in the following batch?

```
declare @k float
select @k = 10.0
select @k = 20.0
```

9-8. What is the maximum number of local variables and global variables for a stored procedure?

9-9. The table *samp* has the following schema.

```
i int
c1 char(255)
```

Write a SQL Script that does the following.
*   Declares two variables, @*i* and @*c1*
*   Assigns values 10 and "HELLO" to @*i* and @*c1*, respectively
*   Inserts a row int table *samp* using these variables

9-10. Table *samp_tbl* has 100 rows in database *samp_db*. What will be the output of the following query?

```
use samp_db
select count(*) from samp_tbl
```

9-11. What is the difference between **break** and **return** commands?

9-12. What is the output of the following batch?

```
select count(*) from titleauthors
select count(*) from titles
slect count(*) from salesdetail
```

9-13. What is the main difference between language cursors and server cursors?

9-14. A cursor is declared and opened as given in the following batch. Will this work?

```
declare samp_cursor cursor
    for select * from tab_name
        open samp_cursor
```

9-15. Can a cursor be moved backward?

9-16. Which of the following is or are untrue. Using cursors, we can:
   a. delete rows
   b. insert rows
   c. update rows
   d. create indexes

9-17. What global variable can be used to display the number of rows fetched by a cursor?

9-18. Why should cursors be deallocated?

9-19. Where are system stored procedures located?

9-20. How do you rename a stored procedure?

9-21. The table names that a stored procedure references have been renamed. Will the stored procedure work? What happens if the stored procedure is automatically recompiled?

9-22. Can a stored procedure create another stored procedure within itself?

9-23. In the following procedure, if you add columns to the table *ex_tab1*, can the stored procedure be executed?

```
create proc ex_proc1
as
    select * from ex_tab1
return
```

9-24. How do you execute remote stored procedure *ex_rproc* that is created on server *ex_svr*, in database *ex_db*. Assume that the procedure is created by *ex_user1*.

9-25. In stored procedures, what values for *return* are reserved for use by SQL Server?

9-26. What is the maximum number of nesting levels permitted in a stored procedure?

9-27. What is the maximum number of triggers that can be defined on a table?

9-28. An insert on table A fires a trigger that inserts a row into table B, and table B has an insert trigger created on it. Will the trigger on table B be executed?

9-29. If an insert of a row in table A fires a trigger that inserts another row in table A, will the trigger on table A be executed again?

9-30. When a trigger is created:
   a. What are the two temporary tables that are created?
   b. What is the structure of these tables?
   c. Where are these tables located?

9-31. An insert trigger is created on a table. If 1,000 rows are inserted into a table, how many times does the insert trigger fire?

9-32. A table that has a delete trigger created on it contains 100 rows. How many times does the delete trigger fire when the following command is executed? (Hint: The command **truncate** deletes all of the rows from a table.)

   truncate ex_tbl2

9-33. A table that has an insert trigger defined on it is dropped and recreated. Which of the following is true?
   a. The trigger is automatically recreated.
   b. The trigger is recreated when the table is recreated.
   c. The trigger is not automatically recreated.

Answers to Exercises

9-1. *@@rowcount*

9-2. Global variables cannot be assigned values directly by the user.

9-3. Local variables are defined using the following syntax: **declare @var_name datatype**. (Local variables are visible only in a batch or stored procedure, or in a trigger in which they are declared.)

9-4. Local variables initially have a value of NULL.

9-5. The output is: 100 NULL

9-6. *@@error*

9-7. Variable *@k* will contain the value 20.0.

9-8. There is no maximum limit for the number of local or global variables that a stored procedure can have. This number is limited only by the available memory.

9.9. /* Declare the local variables */
declare *@i* int, *@c1* char(255)
/* Assign values to the local variables */
select *@i* = 10
select *@c1* = "HELLO"
/* Insert the row into the table */
insert samp values (*@i, @c1*)

9-10. None, because **use sampdb** cannot be executed in a batch.

9-11. A **return** command exits a batch unconditionally, while **break** causes an exit from the outermost **while** loop.

9-12. The batch will abort, because the last query has a typo (**slect** instead of **select**).

9-13. Language cursors are declared in a batch, and server cursors are declared in stored procedures.

9-14. No, because the **declare** statement must be the only statement in a batch.

9-15. No

9-16. *b* and *d*

9-17. *@@rowcount*

9-18. Deallocating a cursor releases all the resources associated with the cursor. Also, a cursor with the same name cannot be declared unless it is deallocated.

9-19. All the system stored procedures are located in *sybsystemprocs* system database.

9-20. Using **sp_rename**

9-21. No. The stored procedure will seem to be working until it is recompiled. If the stored procedure is automatically recompiled, it will fail because the objects to which it refers do not exist.

9-22. No

9-23. The stored procedure will not pick up the new columns. Drop and recreate the stored procedure.

9-24. **exec ex_svr.ex_db.ex_user1.ex_rproc**

9-25. Numbers 0 to -99 are reserved for use by SQL Server.

9-26. A maximum of 16 levels

9-27. A table can have a maximum of three triggers.

9-28. Yes

9-29. By default, a trigger does not call itself when there is a second data modification statement within the same trigger. However, setting the following option will cause the trigger to fire again: **set self_recursion on.**

9-30. Inserted and deleted. These tables have similar schema to the table on which the trigger is defined. The inserted and deleted tables are created in the *tempdb* database.

9-31. Only once

9-32. The **truncate** command does not cause the trigger to fire, because truncate operation is not logged.

9-33. *c*

10

Transaction Management

Many business rules are defined by a group of SQL statements and require that each statement in the group executes successfully; otherwise, none of the statements affects the database. In addition, if some of the statements execute, there must be a way to undo their effect if other statements subsequently fail.

Transaction is the construct that ensures that these requirements are met. *Transaction management* is a method for coordinating transactions. The basic concepts associated with transactions are transaction processing, beginning and committing transactions, recovery from failure during transactions, and rolling back transactions. This chapter describes transaction concepts and the transaction management tools that Sybase provides. The topics that we discuss in this chapter are as follows.

- Transaction fundamentals, including more information on the transaction log, which was introduced in Chapter 2, System 11 Architecture

- How to begin, roll back, and save transactions

- How transaction nesting works

- Ways to obtain information about transactions

- Concurrency and locking, including isolation levels

- Using transactions in stored procedures, cursors, and triggers

- Executing DDL commands in transactions

Transaction Fundamentals

A transaction is a *logical unit of work* that contains at least one data modification command, such as **insert**, **update**, or **delete**. Either all of the commands inside the transaction execute successfully or none of them does. (An exception is an insert or update that causes a duplicate key condition.) Here are the basic components of a transaction.

```
begin transaction
  {set of transaction commands}
end transaction
```

The **begin transaction** and **end transaction** commands define the logical unit of work made up by the set of transaction commands between them.

Transaction Processing

Transaction processing is a method for coordinating transactions that modify databases. An important aspect of transaction processing is that it keeps a running log of all of the modifications made to a database during a period of time. Every database has a transaction log that records all the transactions occurring in that database.

Transactions are governed by the ACID properties (atomicity, consistency, isolation, and durability). The ACID properties are as follows.

- *Atomicity* All portions of a transaction either succeed and are saved (*committed*), or they are rolled back and have no effect.

- *Consistency* If a transaction is rolled back, all resources that the transaction affected return to their state before the transaction took place. (This includes integrity constraints.)

- *Isolation* Although transactions may run concurrently, each transaction's dependencies will be before, after, or independent of another transaction's dependencies.

- *Durability* After a transaction commits, all of the affected resources are permanent and cannot be altered by subsequent system failures.

Transaction Boundaries

SQL Server uses the **begin transaction** and **commit transaction** commands to determine the boundaries of the set of commands to process as a single unit. The **begin transaction** command indicates the start of a transaction, and the **commit transaction**, **commit work**, or **rollback work** command indicates the end of a transaction. Table 10-1 shows the syntax for the **begin transaction**, **commit transaction**, and **commit work** commands.

Table 10-1. *Syntax and parameters for the **begin** and **commit** commands*

begin {**transaction** | **tran**} [*transaction_name*] **commit** {**transaction** | **tran** | **work**} [*transaction_name*]	
transaction_name	Name of the transaction
transaction, tran, work	Syntax allows you to use either the full or abbreviated word

Example: Here's a simple example of a transaction. Both **update** commands are processed as a single unit. That is, both of them execute or neither one does. If either update fails, neither is committed and the table reverts to its pretransaction state.

```
begin transaction
update savings
   set amount = amount - $400.00
   where acct_no = 1939-4434
update checking
   set amount = amount + $400.00
   where acct_no = 5820-1960
commit transaction
go
```

The Two-Phase Commit Protocol

When an application program issues a **commit tran** command for a distributed transaction (one that affects databases in more than one location), a transaction manager uses a *two-phase commit protocol* to guarantee transaction atomicity. A transaction manager is a software product available through a third party, such as BEA's TUXEDO.

Transaction completion using the two-phase commit protocol ensures atomicity, integrity, and consistency for all databases affected by a distributed transaction. Transaction completion takes place in two phases, the *prepare phase* and the *commit phase*.

- In the prepare phase, the transaction manager requests that SQL Server prepare to commit its distributed portions of the transaction.

- In the commit phase, the transaction manager instructs SQL Server to commit or abort its branches of the transaction. If all transaction branches are prepared, the transaction manager commits the entire transaction. If SQL Server reports that any branch of the transaction failed or did not respond, the transaction manager rolls back the entire transaction.

Saving Transactions and Roll Back

As mentioned earlier, if a transaction does not succeed in its entirety, it must be undone. The capability to undo a transaction is called *roll back*.

We can deliberately cancel a transaction before it is committed using the **rollback transaction** or **rollback work** command. This undoes every part of the transaction that was executed. Table 10-2 gives the syntax for the **rollback transaction** command.

Table 10-2. *Syntax and parameters for the **rollback** command*

rollback {transaction | tran | work}
  [*transaction_name | savepoint_name*]

transaction_name	Name of the transaction
transaction | tran	You may use either the full or abbreviated word
savepoint_name	A marker you can use within a transaction to indicate the point to which a transaction may be rolled back

The *savepoint* mechanism used as a parameter as described in Table 10-2 is useful in complex transactions that involve many commands. The application can save its status as the transaction progresses. If problems develop later during the transaction, the application does not have to abort the entire transaction. It can roll back to any of its savepoints and proceed from there. Insert savepoints using the **save transaction** command within the transaction. If *savepoint_name* is omitted, the transaction is rolled back to the first **begin transaction** command in a batch. Table 10-3 gives the syntax and parameters for the **save transaction** command.

Table 10-3. *Syntax and parameters for the* **save transaction** *command*

save {**transaction** | **tran**} [*savepoint_name*]	
savepoint_name	A marker you can use within a transaction to indicate the point to which a transaction may be rolled back

The **rollback tran** and **save tran** commands give you control over what is and is not committed or rolled back.

Example: This example illustrates the use of the **save tran** command. The **insert** command inserts a row in the *emp* table. The savepoint is marked as *save1*. The **update** command raises the salary of all employees by 10 percent. If the total salary of all employees exceeds $1,000,000, the transaction rolls back to *save1*. This rolls back the update operation. The insert operation is not rolled back. If the total salary of all employees does not exceed $1,000,000, the update succeeds and the entire transaction (marked by **begin tran**) is committed.

```
begin tran
   insert emp values ("1004", "Meryl", "engg", 60000)
save tran save1
   update emp set salary = salary * 0.10
if (select sum(salary) from emp) > 1000000
   rollback tran save1
else
commit tran
go
```

Points to Note: Successful Use of the Rollback Command

Here are several points you should bear in mind about the **rollback** command.

- The **rollback tran** command does not produce any error messages. Use **print** and **raiserror** commands if you need to roll back error messages.

- The **commit tran** and **rollback tran** commands do not affect SQL Server in a transaction that is not currently active.

- The **rollback tran** command without a *savepoint* name rolls back the entire transaction.

- A transaction cannot be rolled back after it is committed.

Recovery

Recovery addresses the need to recreate and finish a transaction that was in progress when a system failure occurred, such as a hard disk crash or a power outage. SQL Server records transaction changes in the transaction log to enable recovery when necessary.

Every database has a transaction log that is implemented as the system table *syslogs*. SQL Server records the transaction's ID and its specific characteristics for transactions involving update, delete, or insert as soon as it detects a **begin transaction** command. SQL Server will not write the log records until an update or insert takes place for transactions that begin with a read-only query. The transaction takes the following series of actions.

- Takes locks for isolation (discussed in the "Types of Locks" section later in this chapter)

- Writes to the log for consistency and durability

- Updates data pages for consistency

- Associates data pages to either the ULC discussed in Chapter 2, System 11 Architecture, or the log for durability

As the transaction progresses, SQL Server updates the *syslogs* table for every insert, update, and delete. Changed data pages are finally written to disk when a checkpoint occurs or when cache space is needed for other operations. (See Chapter 2, for more information about caches and checkpoints.) A checkpoint process takes place on a configurable periodic basis to write all modified pages in memory to disk.

The transaction manager can either roll forward or roll back the transaction. If there is enough information in the transaction log to complete the transaction, it is rolled forward and the transaction is committed. Otherwise, the information about the changes the transaction made before it was interrupted are read from the transaction log, the changes are reversed, and the database is restored to its prefailure state.

A Write-Ahead Transaction Log

The transaction manager uses a *write-ahead log protocol* to write to the log before making any change to a table. This ensures that you can always either complete the transaction or roll it back, depending on the circumstances at the time of the failure. For example, suppose you are transferring money from your savings account to your checking account. If an earthquake temporarily interrupts processing after the money is removed from your savings account and before it is added to your checking account, the transaction is rolled back. Any modifications done to the savings and checking accounts are undone.

Point to Note: Keep in mind that *syslogs* (the transaction log) is updated even before the change is applied to the table itself. This impacts how your code handles errors and transaction failures.

Example: The single transaction in this example is composed of the Transact SQL commands **insert** and **update**.

```
begin tran
insert into emp
   values (100, "JOHN", "staffing", 30000)
update emp
   set salary = salary + .10*salary
commit tran
go
```

Transaction Nesting

Transactions can be nested within each other. In nested transactions, the outermost pair begin and commit the transaction. Nested groups of commands are not committed until the final **commit tran** command. SQL Server uses the inner pairs of **begin tran** and **commit tran** commands to track which level it is currently processing.

SQL Server tracks the nesting level using the global variable @@*trancount*. The first transaction sets @@*trancount* to 1. Each subsequent **begin tran** command increments @@*trancount* by 1, and each **commit tran** or **rollback tran** command decrements @@*trancount* by 1.

Example: Figure 10-1 shows an example of nested transactions and illustrates how the value of @@*trancount* varies.

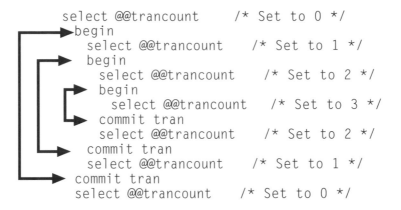

```
select @@trancount     /* Set to 0 */
begin
  select @@trancount     /* Set to 1 */
  begin
    select @@trancount     /* Set to 2 */
    begin
      select @@trancount     /* Set to 3 */
    commit tran
    select @@trancount     /* Set to 2 */
  commit tran
  select @@trancount     /* Set to 1 */
commit tran
select @@trancount     /* Set to 0 */
```

Figure 10-1. *Nested transactions*

Point to Note: You cannot use transaction names in nested transactions.

Getting Information About the Transaction State

SQL Server tracks the current state of transactions in the global variable *@@transtate*. You can use *@@transtate* for status checking and to base decisions. The legal values and their meanings for *@@transtate* are shown in Table 10-4.

Table 10-4. *Status values for the **@@transtate** global variable*

@@*transtate* Value	Meaning
0	Transaction is in progress
1	Transaction succeeded and committed
2	Previous command aborted and transaction still in progress
3	Transaction is aborted and rolled back

Examples: Getting Information About Transaction State

These examples illustrate how to use the *@@transtate* global variable to determine decision outcome.

Example 1: In this example, a transaction is in progress, so the first @@*transtate* is set to zero. After the transaction completes successfully, the value of the second @@*transtate* is set to one.

```
begin tran trnstate_01
   insert into emp values ("1006", "Lisa", "Doc", 4000)
   select @@transtate     /* This should be 0 */
commit tran trnstate_01
go
select @@transtate        /* This should be 1 */
go
```

Example 2: In this example, a transaction is aborted, because the primary key is a duplicate. So @@*transtate* has a value of 2. When the transaction rolls back, @@*transtate* has a value of 3.

```
begin tran trnstate_23
   insert into emp values ("1006","Lisa", "Doc", 4000)
   select @@transtate     /* This should be 2 */
commit tran trnstate_23
go
select @@transtate        /* This should be 3 */
go
```

Example 3: This example demonstrates how you can base decisions on the value of @@*transtate*. If the update command in this example is aborted and the transaction is still in progress, the transaction is rolled back (@@*transtate* = 2). If the transaction is aborted and rolled back (@@*transtate* = 3), the batch simply returns. If the transaction succeeds, the transaction is committed.

```
begin tran
   update emp set salary = salary * 0.20
   if @@transtate = 2
     begin
        rollback tran
        return
     end
   if @@transtate = 3
     return
commit tran
go
```

Point to Note: The global variable @@*transtate* is updated only after an insert, update, or delete. It retains its previous value until another data modification occurs.

Transaction Modes

SQL Server provides two transaction modes, or environments, in which transactions can be defined. These transaction modes are *chained* and *unchained*. We discuss each of these modes separately in the next two sections.

Unchained Mode

Unchained mode is SQL Server's default mode. This mode requires an explicit **begin tran** to begin a transaction. The **begin tran** command should be paired with a corresponding **rollback tran** or **commit tran** command.

Example: This example sets the environment to the unchained transaction mode and executes a transaction. The **begin tran** command begins the transaction. The **commit tran** commits the transaction.

```
set chained off   /* "off" is the default mode */
go
begin tran
   insert emp
   values ("1005", "vinay", "sales", 70000)
commit tran
go
```

Point to Note: Because the default mode is unchained, you need not execute the command **set chained off** unless you previously set chained transaction mode.

Point to Note: In unchained transactions, the number of **begin tran** commands must match the number of **commit tran** and **rollback tran** commands.

Chained Mode

In chained mode, any data retrieval or data modification mode implicitly begins a transaction. The commands that implicitly begin a transaction are **select**, **insert**, **update**, **delete**, **open**, and **fetch**. However, you should explicitly specify a **commit tran** or **rollback tran** command for ending a transaction. The command to enable chained transaction mode is as follows.

```
set chained on
```

Example: The preceding example executed in *unchained* mode looks like this in *chained* mode. In this example, the **insert** command implicitly begins the transaction. The **commit tran** command commits the **insert** command and ends the transaction.

```
set chained on
go
insert emp
  values ("1005", "Vinay", "sales", 70000)
commit tran
go
```

Point to Note: You can nest transactions only when you explicitly use a **begin tran** command.

Getting Information About Modes

The global variable *@@tranchained* contains a code for the transaction mode. *@@tranchained* has a value of *1* for chained transactions and a value of *0* for unchained transactions. Use the **select** command to see the mode, as shown here.

```
select @@tranchained
go
```

Concurrency and Locking

Concurrency issues arise when more than one user simultaneously access a database. SQL Server prevents simultaneous queries and data modification requests from interfering with one another using a *locking* strategy. Locking restricts access to data or modification of a set of data in the database. Locking is primarily used for the following.

- *Maintaining data security* You can use locks to restrict access to confidential data

- *Handling concurrent access* In a multiuser environment, locks prevent simultaneous modification and access to data by more than one user

Without locking in a multiuser environment, data inconsistency and incomplete data changes are common. For example, in a theater ticket reservation system, if more than one person accesses and books a particular seat in the concert hall, multiple patrons could be assigned the same seat.

The Impact of Locking on Performance

Locking impacts SQL Server system performance in two significant ways, reduced data availability and reduced performance.

While data restriction is obviously necessary for consistency, it can also reduce data availability. The granularity of locks specifies how much data is locked at one time. Granularity refers to the number of rows or pages each lock locks (see Figure 10-2).

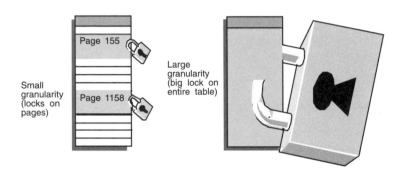

Figure 10-2. Large and small lock granularity

SQL Server needs to work to process each lock. The larger the lock granularity, the less work SQL Server has to do. But large granularity restricts more records during the locked time period. Users must wait for the lock to be released before they can access the data, which degrades performance. On the other hand, decreasing lock granularity results in a larger number of locks and more overhead for SQL Server. A good locking mechanism balances the needs of concurrency and performance.

Types of Locks

SQL Server uses *page locks* and *table locks*. A page lock locks all the rows on a page, while a table lock locks an entire table. SQL Server determines which lock type to use depending how the query will execute. SQL Server uses a table lock if several page locks are to be acquired on a table. Consider the following query.

```
update emp
set dept = "engg"
   where emp_no = "1010"
go
```

If the table has no index, the query executes using a *table scan* to scan the entire table. SQL Server tends to use a table lock for this type of query execution. If the table has a defined index, the execution query uses an *index scan*. In this case, SQL Server acquires a page lock.

SQL Server uses the page-locking strategy, then switches to a table lock after a certain number of pages are locked. See Chapter 18, SQL System-Level Performance and Tuning, for more information about this subject.

Page Locks

The page lock category includes *shared page locks*, *exclusive page locks*, and *update locks*. We look at each separately in this section.

Shared page locks are applied only for read operations. When a page has a shared lock, any other transactions can also acquire a shared lock on that page even before the first transaction completes. However, no other transactions can acquire an exclusive lock on the page until the first shared lock is released. Shared page locks are normally released after the page is scanned, rather than when the transaction completes.

Example: The following query uses a shared page lock. Assume that the table has an index defined on the *dept* column.

```
select * from emp
  where dept = "sales"
go
```

Exclusive page locks are applied for data modification operations. When a page has an exclusive lock, no other transaction can acquire any type of lock on that page. Until the exclusive lock is released, other transactions must wait.

Update locks are applied during the initial phase of an update, delete, or fetch cursor (when the fetch cursor is used with the *for update* clause). An update lock is an internal lock that allows shared locks on a page, but does not allow other update locks or exclusive locks. The update lock is promoted to an exclusive page lock when the actual data modification takes place.

Example: The following command uses an update lock, which is promoted to an exclusive page lock. Assume that an index is defined on *emp* for column *emp_no*.

```
delete emp
  where emp_no = "1010"
go
```

Table Locks

There are also three types of table locks: *shared table locks*, *intent locks*, and *exclusive table locks*. Shared table locks behave similarly to shared page locks, except that a shared table lock applies to the entire table.

An intent lock indicates the intention to acquire a shared or exclusive lock on a data page. A shared lock can also be acquired on a data page that has an intent lock. The intent lock is promoted to an exclusive lock when data modification actually occurs. Intent table locks are applied with each shared or exclusive page lock. Therefore, an intent lock can be either an intent exclusive lock or an intent shared lock. Other transactions cannot acquire a shared lock or an exclusive lock on a table that has an intent table lock.

Exclusive table locks behave similarly to exclusive page locks. However, the exclusive table lock affects an entire table.

Demand Lock

If several overlapping shared locks are held on a table, a write transaction waits indefinitely to obtain its exclusive lock. To prevent such situations, SQL Server uses a *demand lock* technique to indicate that a given transaction is next in the queue to lock a table or a page. As soon as the existing read transactions complete, the write transaction is allowed to proceed. Any new read transaction must wait until the write transaction completes.

Using the *holdlock* Keyword with *select*

You can use the *holdlock* keyword in the **select** command to make a shared page or shared table lock more restrictive. With *holdlock*, the shared lock is held until the transaction completes. The *holdlock* option is useful for applications that require that no change be made until a row is updated or the transaction is canceled.

Example: This query uses the *holdlock* keyword. No other transaction can update the specified row until the current transaction releases the lock. If the query uses an index, SQL Server applies a shared page lock. If there is no index, it applies a table lock.

```
select salary
  from emp holdlock
  where emp_no = "1010"
go
```

Summary of Different Lock Types

Tables 10-5, 10-6, and 10-7 summarize lock behavior as a result of various SQL commands. The meaning of these behavior types is described in the subsconent section.

Table 10-5. *Effect of SQL statements on locks (with index on table)*

SQL Statement	Table Lock	Page Lock
select	Intent Shared	Shared
select with holdlock	Intent Shared	Shared
update	Intent Exclusive	Update, Exclusive
delete	Intent Exclusive	Update, Exclusive

Table 10-6. *Effect of SQL statements on locks (without index on table)*

SQL Statement	Table Lock	Page Lock
select	Shared	No Lock
select with holdlock	Shared	No Lock
update	Exclusive	No lock
delete	Exclusive	No lock

Table 10-7. *Effect of **insert** an **create index** statements on locks*

SQL Statement	Table Lock	Page Lock
insert	Intent Exclusive	Exclusive
create clustered index	Exclusive	No Lock
create non clustered index	Shared	No Lock

Lock Promotion Thresholds

A *lock promotion threshold* sets the number of page locks allowed by a command before the lock is promoted to a table lock. SQL Server defines the three lock promotion thresholds as shown in Table 10-8. Use the system procedure **sp_setpglockpromote** to set lock promotion thresholds. You can set thresholds server-wide, database-wide, or only for a particular table using the system procedures given in this table.

Table 10-8. *Setting lock promotion thresholds*

sp_setpglockpromote **"server"**, null, *LWM, HWM, PCT*
sp_setpglockpromote **"database"**, *database_name, LWM, HWM, PCT*
sp_setpglockpromote **"table"**, *table_name, LWM, HWM, PCT*

Lock promotion HWM (high water mark)	When the number of page locks exceed this number, the lock is promoted to a table lock
Lock promotion LWM (low water mark)	Sets the minimum number of page locks allowed on a table before a table lock can be acquired
Lock promotion PCT (percent)	Sets the percentage of page locks above which SQL Server tries to acquire a table lock

The following examples illustrate lock promotion thresholds with server-wide, database-wide and table-only effects.

Example 1: This example sets a server-wide lock promotion threshold.

```
sp_setpglockpromote "server", null, 200, 2000, 50
go
```

Example 2: This example sets a lock promotion threshold for the *master* database.

```
sp_setpglockpromote "database", master, 1100, 1100, 50
go
```

Example 3: This example sets lock promotion thresholds for the database *cars*.

```
sp_setpglockpromote "database", cars, 200, 2000, 50
go
```

Example 4: This example sets the lock promotion threshold for table *emp*.

```
sp_setpglockpromote "table", emp, 100, 1000, 50
go
```

Deadlock

When each of two processes holds a lock on a page that the other process needs, each waits for the other process to release the lock so it can continue processing. Figure 10-3 illustrates what happens in a deadlock.

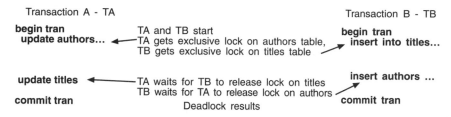

Figure 10-3. *A deadlock scenario*

In this example, transaction TA updates the *authors* table by acquiring an exclusive lock on the *titles* table. Simultaneously, transaction TB inserts a row into the *titles* table and acquires an exclusive lock on the *authors* table. When transaction TA tries to update the *titles* table, it must wait for transaction TB to release its exclusive lock on the *titles* table. When transaction TB tries to insert a row into the *authors* table, it must wait for transaction TA to release its exclusive lock on the *authors* table. This results in a deadlock.

SQL Server checks for deadlocks. When it finds one, it identifies the transaction that has accumulated the least amount of CPU time as its victim. SQL Server then rolls back the victim transaction and raises error 1205. Therefore, in a multiuser environment, each user's thread application should check for message 1205 during transactions that modify data. The victim must restart the transaction.

Long-running transactions are more susceptible to deadlocks, because locks in them can be held for longer periods of time, increasing the possibility that another transaction needs to use the data. Deadlock becomes more common as the lock contention increases between such transactions. Observe the following guidelines to minimize deadlocks.

- Order your table references so that the locks are also ordered

- Commit transactions as often as possible

- Use holdlock as little as possible

- Avoid human interaction within transactions or while a table has a holdlock

Isolation Levels

A transaction's *isolation level* indicates the read and write operations that are not allowed during transaction processing. The ANSI 89 SQL standard defines four isolation levels: level 0, level 1, level 2, and level 3. SQL Server supports all levels except level 2. SQL Server's default transaction isolation level is 1. The following sections give an overview of the three isolation levels that SQL Server supports.

Level 0

When a transaction is in progress, level 0 prevents other transactions from overwriting the data that the first transaction is using; however, other transactions are allowed to read the data before the transaction is committed. Reading uncommitted data is referred to as a *dirty read*. Dirty reads are described later in a section of this chapter, "Allowing Dirty Reads."

Examine transactions A and B in Figure 10-4, which illustrates a dirty read scenario. Transaction A updates a column of a table. The **select** and **insert** commands in transaction B occur before the update commits in transaction A. In this transaction, the select succeeds, but the insert is blocked until transaction A commits. Other transactions can read transaction A's uncommitted data.

Transaction A	Transaction B
| ```
begin tran
  update table_name ......


commit tran
``` | ```
begin tran
  select * from table_name
  insert into table_name ....

commit tran
``` |

Figure 10-4. A dirty read scenario

Setting Isolation Level 0

To set the transaction isolation level to 0, use the following command.

set transaction isolation level 0

You can use the isolation option *read uncommitted* to change the isolation level at the query level.

Example: The following query behaves as though the transaction isolation level were set to 0.

```
select * from emp
  at isolation read uncommitted
go
```

Level 1

Isolation level 1 prevents both writing and reading of uncommitted data. If isolation level 1 were set in the example shown in Figure 10-4, the **select** command in transaction B would be forced to wait until transaction A commits, because isolation level 1 does not allow dirty reads.

Setting Isolation Level 1

Isolation level 1 is SQL Server's default. But if the isolation level has been set to something else and you want to reset it to level 1, use this command.

```
set transaction isolation level 1
```

To set isolation level 1 at the query level, use the option *read committed*.

Example: This example sets isolation level 1 at the query level.

```
select * from authors
  at isolation level read committed
go
```

Level 3

Isolation level 3 prevents a transaction from performing a read that uses the same set of search conditions used in a previous read performed by the same transaction. That is, isolation level 3 prevents repeated reads, because they can result in *phantoms*. Phantoms occur when one transaction performs a read, a second transaction modifies the same data that was read, then the first transaction repeats the read. The result of the second read is different from that of the first. The transactions in Figure 10-5 illustrate this point.

```
Transaction A                        Transaction B
begin tran                           begin tran
  select * from emp
     where emp_no = "1002"

                                        update emp set salary =
                                          salary * 1.10
                                        where emp_no = "1002"
                                     commit tran

  select * from emp
    where emp_no = "1002"
commit tran
```

Figure 10-5. *A phantom scenario*

In the example illustrated in Figure 10-5, transaction A reads information about an employee whose *emp_no* is 1002. Suppose transaction B updates the same row at the same time that transaction A is reading it. If transaction A tries to read that same row again, the result would be different. This is another example of phantom reads. However, isolation level 3 prevents phantom reads. Isolation level 3 instructs SQL Server to apply a *holdlock* automatically to all **select** operations.

Setting Isolation Level 3

Use the following command to set the isolation level to 3.

set transaction isolation level 3

To set isolation level 3 at the query level, use the option *serializable*.

Example: This example sets isolation level 3 at the query level with the *serializable* option.

```
select * from titles
   at isolation serializable
go
```

Getting Information About Isolation Levels

The global variable *@@isolation* contains the isolation level of a transaction. You can use the **select** command shown here to see isolation levels.

```
select @@isolation
go
```

Points to Note: Using Isolation Levels

Here is advice about when to use each isolation level.

- Isolation level 0 requires the least stringent type of lock, so its use results in better performance than any other type of lock. Use isolation level 0 for applications that can tolerate, or require, dirty reads (as some financial applications do), which only isolation level 0 allows. For such applications, set the transaction to isolation level 0 before issuing the query.

- Isolation level 1 prevents dirty reads, so you use it for applications that cannot tolerate dirty reads. For example, an application that updates a stock inventory level based on a quantity measured accurately at the time it is checked cannot tolerate dirty reads.

- Isolation level 3 is used when you need to guarantee consistent, repeatable reads. For example, an application that generates invoice numbers based on incrementing a previous invoice number requires isolation level 3 to prevent another process from modifying the data before it generates the new number.

Allowing Dirty Reads

As mentioned earlier, setting isolation level 0 enables dirty reads. Multiple applications that use dirty reads experience better concurrency and a reduced incidence of deadlocks when they access the same data. For example, an airline reservation system may want to use the data for reservation availability for a particular flight and time concurrently, even though another transaction in progress might not have committed. Setting isolation level 0 would make this application possible.

You can enable dirty reads either at the session level or at the query level. At the session level, use the following command.

```
set transaction isolation level 0
```

At the query level, you set isolation level 0 using the *read uncommitted* option, as shown next.

```
select * from emp
  at isolation read uncommitted
go
```

Using Cursors in Transactions

By default, a cursor remains open after a **rollback tran** or **commit tran**. However, SQL Server provides the *set close on endtran* option to modify this behavior. If *set close on endtran* is on, the cursor is closed after a **rollback tran** or **commit tran**. If *set close on endtran* is off, the cursor remains open after a **rollback tran** or **commit tran**. The syntax of *set close on endtran* is as follows.

set close on endtran {on | off}

For chained transactions, SQL Server implicitly begins a transaction before fetching and opening a cursor.

Example: In this example, a cursor is declared in chained transaction mode with *set close on endtran* set to on.

```
set close on endtran on
go
declare emp_curs cursor for
select * from emp
go
open emp_curs
fetch emp_curs
commit tran    /* Cursor emp_curs is closed */
go
```
Any exclusive locks acquired by a cursor in a transaction are held until the end of that transaction.

Cursors and Isolation Level

A cursor declared with *read uncommitted* (isolation level 0) will be a read-only cursor. You cannot specify the **update** command with the *read uncommitted* option.

The cursor's isolation level is determined when it is opened, not when it is declared. After the cursor is opened, the SQL server determines the isolation level based on the following.

- The cursor declared with the *at isolation* option overrides the isolation level in which it is opened. For example, if a cursor is declared with isolation level 1 and opened in a transaction with isolation level 0, the cursor's isolation level is 1.

- The cursor uses the isolation level with which it was opened if the cursor was not declared with the *at isolation* option. For example, if a cursor is not declared with *at isolation* and opened in a transaction with isolation level 0, the cursor's isolation level is 0.

- Cursors declared with an isolation level of 1 or 3 cannot be opened in a transaction with isolation level 0.

All Sybase system procedures operate at isolation level 1 regardless of the transaction or isolation level of the session. User-stored procedures execute with the isolation level of the transaction that executes it. If a stored procedure changes the isolation level, the new isolation level remains in effect only during the execution of the stored procedure.

Using Stored Procedures in Transactions

When a stored procedure that rolls back a transaction is called from within a batch, all of the commands in the batch prior to the execution of the stored procedure are rolled back. However, all of the commands in the batch are executed after the stored procedure executes. Figure 10-6 illustrates a transaction using a stored procedure.

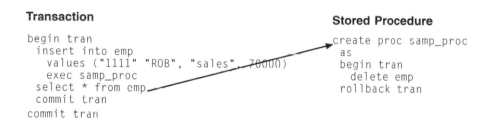

Transaction
```
begin tran
  insert into emp
    values ("1111" "ROB", "sales", 70000)
    exec samp_proc
  select * from emp
  commit tran
commit tran
```

Stored Procedure
```
create proc samp_proc
as
  begin tran
    delete emp
  rollback tran
```

Figure 10-6. *A transaction uses a stored procedure*

The batch represented in Figure 10-6 inserts a row in the *emp* table, then executes the stored procedure **samp_proc**. If there were a **rollback transaction** command in the stored procedure, both the procedure and the **insert** command before the procedure call would be rolled back. However, the **select** command that comes after **exec samp_proc** command in the batch would be executed. If there were a **commit tran** command in the stored procedure, all of the commands prior to calling the stored procedure and the command in the stored procedure would be committed.

Point to Note: You cannot execute system stored procedures that alter the *master* database or create temporary tables in user-defined transactions.

Stored Procedures and Transaction Modes

Stored procedures written using chained transaction mode might not be compatible with other transactions that use unchained mode. In chained transaction mode, SQL Server implicitly executes a **begin tran** command before executing any data retrieval or modification commands, such as **delete**, **insert**, **update**, **fetch**, **select**, and **open**. For example, the following group of commands produce different results depending on the transaction mode in which they are executed.

```
update emp set dept = "engg"
  where emp_no = "1000"
begin tran
  delete from emp where emp_no = "1000"
rollback tran
go
```

In unchained mode, the rollback affects only the **delete** command, so the update succeeds. In chained mode, the **insert** command implicitly begins a transaction, and the **rollback tran** command rolls back all of the commands including the **update** command.

The stored procedure **sp_procxmode** determines if a procedure can run in chained transaction mode, unchained transaction mode, or both. The syntax for the **sp_procxmode** appears in Table 10-9.

Table 10-9. Syntax and parameters for the **sp_procxmode** procedure

sp_procxmode *procedure_name, mode*

procedure_name	Name of the stored procedure for which you are checking possible modes
mode	Transaction mode is *chained* for chained transaction mode, *unchained* for unchained transaction mode, or *anymode* for both chained and unchained transaction modes

Executing **sp_procxmode** without any parameters returns the list of stored procedures in the current database and their transaction modes.

Using Triggers in Transactions

Triggers execute at isolation level 0 or isolation level 1, whichever is higher than the level of the command that causes it to fire. Recall that only data modification commands fire triggers. If a trigger fires as a result of a level 0 command, the isolation level of the trigger is set to 1 before executing its first command.

If a transaction in a batch fires a trigger and the trigger has a **rollback tran** command, the entire batch is aborted. Consider the following example.

```
begin tran
    insert emp .....
    update emp ...
    delete emp ....
commit tran
```

If a **delete trigger** command is defined on table *emp* in this example and contains a **rollback tran** command, the batch is aborted. That is, the **insert** and **update** commands are also rolled back.

DDL Commands in Transactions

By default, SQL Server does not allow data definition language (DDL) commands within transactions. DDL commands are **create table**, **create rule**, **create procedure**, and so on. However, you can use some DDL commands after setting **sp_dboption**'s *ddl in tran* option to true. Use the following command to set *ddl in tran* to true. The *database_name* parameter identifies the database in which the transaction is defined.

sp_dboption *database_name*, **"ddl in tran", true**

When the *ddl in tran* option is set to true, the DDL commands shown in Table 10-10 are allowed in transactions. Table 10-11 shows the DDL commands not allowed within transactions.

Table 10-10. *DDL commands allowed in transactions when* **sp_dboption**'s ***ddl in tran option*** *is set to true*

alter table (except partition and unpartition clauses)			
	create default	**drop default**	**grant**
	create index	**drop index**	**revoke**
	create proc	**drop proc**	
	create rule	**drop rule**	

(continued)

Table 10-10. *(continued)*

create table	drop table
create trigger	drop trigger
create view	drop view
create schema	

Table 10-11. *DDL commands not allowed in transactions*

alter database	disk init	load transaction	select into
alter table ..partition	dump database	load database	update statistics
alter table ..unpartition	dump tran	reconfigure	truncate table
create database	drop database		

Point to Note: Avoid setting the *ddl in tran* option in any database, because DDL commands result in system table contention.

If you need to issue DDL statements in transactions in databases, enable the *ddl in tran* option in the *model* database.

Exercises

10-1.   What global variable checks the current status of a transaction?

10-2.   Why is transaction log known as a write-ahead log?

10-3.   Which of the following is true?
a. Table *syslogs* exists only in the *master* database.
b. Each user database has a *syslogs* table.
c. Every database has a *syslogs* table.
d. All databases except *master* database have a *syslogs* table.

10-4.   Define a transaction.

10-5.   How do you determine if a transaction is chained or unchained?

10-6.   Which mode is the default transaction mode—chained or unchained?

10-7.   If a user executes the following set of commands, what rows will be displayed if **select * from tab1** is executed?

```
create table tab1 (i int)
begin tran
   insert tab1 values (10)
   save tran savept
   insert tab1 values (20)
   rollback tran savept
   insert tab1 values (30)
commit tran
```

10-8.   Based on the following batch of SQL commands, answer the questions that follow.

```
begin tran user_tran
print "updating emp .."
update emp set salary = salary * 1.10
if (select avg(salary) from emp) > 100000
   print "Average salary exceeds 100,000. Raise not allowed!"
   rollback tran user_tran
   return
commit tran
print "All employees have got a raise of 10%!"
```

a. What will be displayed if the average salary after the update is greater than 100,000?

b. What will be displayed if the average salary after the update is less than 100,000?

10-9.   What will be the value of *@@trancount* in the following batch?

```
begin tran
select @@trancount
   begin tran
      select @@trancount
   rollback
select @@trancount
commit tran
```

10-10. When does a transaction begin and end in chained transaction mode?

10-11. After how many page locks does a table lock get set? Assume that the lock promotion thresholds are set to their default values.

10-12. What is a deadlock?

10-13. Which SQL statement is a major cause of deadlocks?

10-14. How can you overcome deadlocks?

10-15. How can you check the isolation level in a transaction?

10-16.   Which isolation level prevents dirty reads?

10-17.   How can you determine in which transaction mode a stored procedure can be executed?

10-18.   Assume that the server uses the default *dboption* option. Will the following batch succeed?

```
begin tran
   create default samp_dft as 100
commit tran
```

Answers to Exercises

10-1.   *@@transtate*

10-2.   Because changes are made to the *syslogs* table before the actual data modifications occur.

10-3.   c

10-4.   A transaction is a SQL operation that has at least one data modification statement.

10-5.   Use the global variable *@@tranchained*. A value of *0* indicates the transaction is unchained and a value of *1* means that the transaction is chained.

10-6.   Unchained

10-7.   The output will have two rows, *10* and *30*.

10-8.   The batch prints the message:

```
Average salary exceeds 100,000. Raise not allowed!
```

The transaction is then rolled back. The transaction is committed and the batch prints the message:

```
All employees have got a raise of 10%!
```

10-9.   The first *@@trancount* will display *1*, the second will display *2*, and the third will display *0*.

10-10.   In a chained transaction, any data modification or data retrieval statement begins a transaction. Only the **rollback** statement ends a chained transaction.

10-11. 200

10-12. Deadlock is a situation in which two concurrent users attempt to acquire conflicting locks on the same page.

10-13. **select with holdlock**

10-14. Deadlocks can be minimized by avoiding the *holdlock* option, by not leaving transactions in an uncommitted state for a long duration, and by using procedures for transactions.

10-15. Use the global variable *@@isolation*.

10-16. Isolation level 1

10-17. Use the stored procedure **sp_procxmode**.

10-18. No, because *ddl in tran* is not enabled in the default mode.

SECTION **III**

Language, Management, and Control

After you've established a database and its tables, then filled those tables with data, you can put the system to work. You can use Transact-SQL to develop transaction processing code, manage transactions, establish and maintain security in the SQL Server system, and perform backup and recovery. The chapters in this section describe the tools and procedures you will use to install and configure SQL Server, and put the system to work.

Chapter 11, Installing SQL Server, guides you through the preinstallation and post-installation steps necessary to establish a SQL Server for the first time, while Chapter 12, Configuring SQL Server, describes various configuration parameters and how to use them. Chapter 12 also discusses some of the more commonly used configuration parameters.

Chapter 13, SQL Server Security Features, explains how to set up a secure system and auditing procedures. Chapter 14, Backup and Recovery, gives information to help you backup system and user databases, and about how to perform recovery. Finally, Chapter 15, Database Administration Tools, describes some of the more useful tools and utilities System 11 offers to help you with configuring and tuning your system.

11

Installing
SQL Server

This chapter will help you to achieve a smooth SQL Server installation. It discusses what we think are the essential activities that you need to perform before, during, and after SQL Server installation. In addition, we offer some advice garnered from our years of experience with Sybase in the field.

Refer to the Sybase SQL Server Installation Guide on the CD-ROM for your platform for installation procedure details. Then, supplement that knowledge with this chapter, which includes the following information.

- Background information on reading and using the *interfaces* file

- How clients connect to SQL Server

- Preinstallation tasks, which include planning, adding login accounts, checking operating system patches, configuring shared memory, configuring for asynchronous I/O, and verifying the network

- Installing SQL Server software

- Post-installation activities, which involve changing the *sa* password, increasing the size of the *master* and *tempdb* databases, mirroring the master database device and removing it from the pool of devices, modifying configuration parameters to fine-tune your system, adding logins, and starting the executable

Foundation: The Client/Server Interface

SQL Server communicates with other SQL Servers, Open Server applications (such as Replication Server and Omni SQL Gateway), and client software using a file called *interfaces*. The installation program *sybinit* creates entries in the *interfaces* file for the new SQL Servers and Backup Servers. *The interfaces* file is an ASCII file that serves as an address book with the names of Sybase servers and their network addresses.

Format of an *interfaces* File Entry for UNIX

The *interfaces* file for UNIX is composed of two entries, which describe a server entity. The first line is the server entry, which contains server information. The second line is the query master entry, which contains network information. (There can be more than one of these lines.) A UNIX interfaces file entry has the following general format.

```
server_name   retry   delay
type_of_service  protocol network  machine  port
```

Table 11-1 summarizes the fields in *interfaces* file entries for UNIX.

Table 11-1. Interfaces *file entries for UNIX*

Field	Description
server_name	Client applications identify Sybase servers by this name. You must choose a unique name. The name can be up to 11 characters in length, and should not be a Sybase reserved name.
retry	The number of times a client can attempt to connect to the server before giving up.
delay	The length of time between each attempt to connect to a server.

(continued)

Table 11-1. *(continued)*

Field	Description
type_of_service	The type of service can be either *query* or *master*. Query entry is used by the client program to log into SQL Server. Master entry is used by the SQL Server program to listen to login requests from clients.
protocol	Specifies the network protocol. Usually TCP/IP for UNIX.
network	Specifies the network; for example, Ethernet.
machine	The network name of the machine on which the server will run.
port	The port number of the machine that was assigned to this server during installation. Port numbers are between 5000 and 65535. The port number must be unique across servers on the same machine. (Ports on a Solaris machine are hex numbers.)

Example: Figure 11-1 shows a sample *interfaces* file for an RS/6000 UNIX machine. It has entries for a SQL Server, called APOLLO, and its backup, APOLLO_BS.

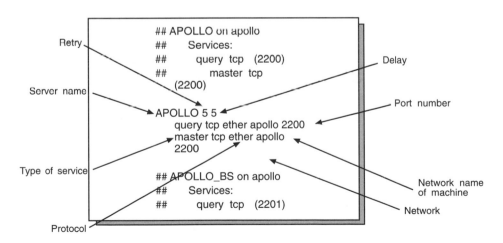

Figure 11-1. *Sample* interfaces *file for an RS/6000 UNIX machine*

Format of an *interfaces* File Entry for Windows NT

The *interfaces* file for Windows NT is composed of two entries that describe a server entity. The first line is the server entry, which contains the name of the SQL Server. The second line is the query master entry, which contains network information. (There can be more than one of these lines.) A Windows NT *interfaces* file entry has the following general format.

```
[database_server_name]
 <link_type> = <network_driver>, <connection_info>
```

Table 11-2 summarizes the fields in *interfaces* file entries for Windows NT.

Table 11-2. Interfaces *file entries for Windows NT*

Field	Description
database_server_name	Client applications identify SQL Servers by this name. You must choose a unique name. The name can be up to 11 characters in length and should not be a Sybase reserved name.
link_type	One of either *master* or *query*.
network_driver	NLMSNMP specifies the name of the network library driver to use for the connection. The driver name must correspond to the a valid entry in the Windows NT LIBTCL.CFG file.
connection_info	Named pipe is the protocol that specifies the connection information. The named pipe protocol consists of the unique pipe name for the server. Valid pipe names begin with */pipe* and follow the same naming restriction as MS-DOS file names. The default pipe name for SQL Server is */pipe/sybase/query*. Examples of nonunique pipe names are */pipe/sqql* and */pipe/sql/query*.

Example: This is an example of an *interfaces* file for NT. It establishes the GURU SQL Server, the GURU_BS backup SQL Server, and the GURU_MS Monitor Server.

```
;;Sybase Interfaces file
;;
;;[<database_server_name>]
;;<link_type>=<network_driver>, <connection_info>
```

```
;;
;;
;;Examples:
;;[JUPITER]
;;QUERY=NLMSNMP,\\JUPITER\pipe\sybase\query
;;WIN3_QUERY=WNLNMP,\\JUPITER\pipe\sybase\query
;;
[GURU]
$BASE$00=NLMSNMP,\pipe\sybase\query
$BASE$01=NLWNSK,guru,5000
MASTER=$BASE$00;$BASE$01;
$BASE$02=NLMSNMP,\pipe\sybase\query
$BASE$03=NLWNSK,guru,5000
QUERY=$BASE$02;$BASE$03;
[GURU_BS]
$BASE$00=NLMSNMP,\pipe\sybase\backup
$BASE$01=NLWNSK,guru,5001
MASTER=$BASE$00;$BASE$01;
$BASE$02=NLMSNMP,\pipe\sybase\backup
$BASE$03=NLWNSK,guru,5001
QUERY=$BASE$02;$BASE$03;
[GURU_MS]
$BASE$00=NLMSNMP,\pipe\sybase\monitor
$BASE$01=NLWNSK,guru,5001
MASTER=$BASE$00;$BASE$01;
$BASE$02=NLMSNMP,\pipe\sybase\monitor
$BASE$03=NLWNSK,guru,5001
QUERY=$BASE$02;$BASE$03;
```

How Client Applications Connect to SQL Server

Client applications use two environment variables, DSQUERY and SYBASE, to connect to SQL Server. DSQUERY is the name of the SQL Server to which the clients connect, and SYBASE is the directory location that contains SQL Server software. When a client application, or a server acting as a client, needs to connect to SQL Server, the client performs the following three steps.

1. It finds the server name in DSQUERY, the command line, or SYBASE

2. It uses that name to find the SQL Server network address in the *interfaces* file

3. It then connects to SQL Server, as illustrated in Figure 11-2

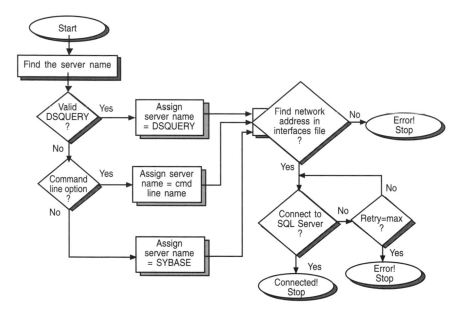

Figure 11-2. *The process for clients, or servers acting as clients, to connect to SQL Server*

Query Entries for Standbys

The *interfaces* file contains one master entry and at least one query entry for each SQL Server. You can also add a query entry for a standby SQL Server to ensure that, if a SQL Server fails or is unavailable, the client automatically and invisibly connects to the standby SQL Server.

For example, here is an entry with two query lines in an environment in which APOLLO_WARM is the warm standby SQL Server for the APOLLO SQL Server. APOLLO_WARM is on a machine called *apollo_warm_host* and APOLLO is on a machine called *apollo_host,* as shown in Figure 11-3.

```
APOLLO 5 5
query tcp ether apollo_host 2200
query tcp ether apollo_warm_host 2200
master tcp ether apollo_host 2200
```

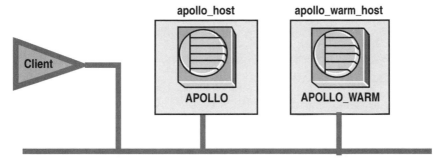

Figure 11-3. *A SQL Server and its standby*

When a client application needs to connect to the APOLLO SQL Server, it attempts first to connect to APOLLO on *apollo_host*. If APOLLO is unavailable, the connection is redirected to APOLLO_WARM on *apollo_warm_host*. In either case, it appears to the client that it is connected to APOLLO.

Preinstallation Tasks

A number of tasks must be performed before you can install SQL Server. The nature of these tasks varies according to the operating environment in which you are installing. This section outlines the preinstallation process for a UNIX environment, the general steps for UNIX are as follows. If you are an NT user, skip to the section called "Installing SQL Server."

1. Plan

2. Set environment variables

3. Create a Sybase login account

4. Install any necessary operating system patches

5. Configure shared memory values

6. Configure asynchronous I/O

7. Verify the network

You must have *root* permissions on the UNIX system to perform these tasks. We now consider each of these issues in more detail in the sections that follow.

Planning and Environment Considerations

Before you can do anything else, you must perform the following steps.

- Choose a name for the SQL Server (unless you are installing software to upgrade an existing SQL Server)

- Choose where to put the SQL Server software (whether or not the SQL Server is new)

Planning Ahead

Our experience installing SQL Server has taught us that taking the time up front to plan pays off in time saved later. Planning includes advance consideration of issues such as location, size, and defaults for the database devices, databases, and objects within the database. Planning also involves gathering the detailed information that you need to provide during the installation, such as names, identifiers, and network port locations. Here is a list of some of the information you should gather before you start the actual installation.

- SQL Server name

- Port number

- Size and location of the *master* device

- Size and location of the *sysprocdev* database device

- Name and location of the error log file

- Default language, character set, and sort order. Size and location of the *sybsecurity* device, if you need to install auditing. If you will use this feature, you can find more information in Chapter 13, SQL Server Security Features.

You also need to install Backup Server, a product included with the SQL Server software, which helps you manage regular backups. For that, you need the following additional information.

- Backup Server name

- Backup Server alias name

- Port number for Backup Server

- Name and location of the Backup Server error log

Environment Variables

You need to set the environment variables that SQL Server uses. These environment variables are as follows.

- **$SYBASE** The full path to the installation directory. Many sites choose a default location of */usr/sybase*.

- **$DSQUERY** The name that a client (such as **isql**) uses to identify SQL Server.

- **$DSLISTEN** The name that SQL Server uses to detect clients during start-up.

How you set these environment variables depends upon whether you use the Bourne shell or C-shell. If you use the C-shell, set the environment variables in the *.cshrc* file using the *setenv* parameter. If you use the Bourne shell, add the following lines (filling in the necessary information, shown in italics) to the *.profile* file.

export SYBASE = *<directory containing the installation files>*
export DSQUERY = *<name of the server to which clients connect>*
export DSLISTEN = *<name the server uses to listen for input from clients>*

Add the Sybase Login Account

When SQL Server starts, it opens files for writing. If the files are owned by various logins, SQL Server may be unable to start. So Sybase recommends that all SQL Server installation activities be performed through a single login account to ensures that all of the files created during installation have consistent ownership and access permissions. For a standard UNIX installation, the UNIX system administrator creates an account with the login name of *sybase*, which is used for all SQL Server tasks.

Check Operating System Patches

Make sure that any operating system kernel patches required for SQL Server 11 are installed. Contact Sybase technical support for the exact patch numbers for your operating system.

Configure Shared Memory

If you have an SMP environment running multiple SQL Server engines, the engines communicate using shared memory. You must configure the UNIX kernel shared memory parameters for SQL Server and Backup Server to function properly.

When SQL Server starts, it reads the operating system parameters' shared memory value from the kernel. If the operating system does not have enough shared memory, SQL Server might not start. (Please refer to your operating system manuals for information on assigning shared memory values.)

For example, on Sun Solaris you can configure the shared memory parameter by adding the following line to the UNIX file */etc/system*.

set shmsys:shminfo_shmmax = <shminfo_shmmax>

The *shminfo_shmmax* field is the maximum allowed shared memory segment size. The *shminfo_shmmax* parameter is the maximum allowed shared memory, not the current amount of shared memory. *Shminfo_shmmax* must be higher than the *total memory* configuration parameter; otherwise, SQL Server will not start. You can set *shminfo_shmmax* higher if needed.

Configure for Asynchronous I/O

Asynchronous I/O is interrupt driven rather than scheduled at regular intervals like synchronous I/O. An operating system that performs asynchronous I/O does not poll for data or send data on a scheduled basis. Instead, data transmission occurs as needed.

SQL Server uses asynchronous I/O to maximize performance. If the system is not configured for asynchronous I/O, a user with *root* permissions, such as the UNIX system administrator, must reconfigure to enable asynchronous I/O.

Verify the Network

SQL Server is built around networking, so even when you install it on a standalone system (one not connected to a network), you need to verify that network software is properly configured. To do this, enter the UNIX command telnet *<host_name>*. If the system is properly configured for network interaction, the telnet command asks you for a login name. If it is not correctly configured, you get an error message.

Installing SQL Server

With System 11.0.1 and forward, Sybase ships a utility that replaces **sybload** and **sybinit**, the load and setup utilities. The replacement utility is called **sybsetup**, which makes the installation processes much faster and simpler. The major tasks in this section involve **sybsetup**, or **sybload** and **sybinit** (which you can still use if you prefer).

Load the Software

Before installing SQL Server, you need to load the software from the media onto your system. To load the software, log into the machine using the *sybase* login for the user account you set up in a prior step.

This is a good time to check that the SYBASE environment variable is set properly. From the UNIX operating system prompt, type **cd $SYBASE**. If this results in moving you to the installation directory, $SYBASE is properly set. Otherwise, please refer to the previous "Environment Variables" section in this chapter.

Follow directions for using the Sybase utility **sybload** to load the software and create the Sybase directory structure.

Sybase Directory Structure

The **sybload** or **sybsetup** utility creates the Sybase SQL Server directory in the location defined by the SYBASE environment variable. It then loads the SQL Server software in that directory, which is commonly referred to as the installation directory. The installation directory contains executable files and utilities.

Figure 11-4 illustrates the SQL Server 11 installation directory structure for a Solaris platform.

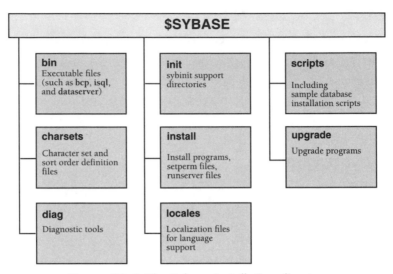

Figure 11-4. *The Sybase installation directory*

Upgrades

If you are upgrading an existing SQL Server, you'll have two installation directories, one for the existing SQL Server installation directory and one that the installation program creates for the new installation.

Tip! It's always good to make a backup before upgrading.

Installation Using *sybinit*

The Sybase **sybinit** utility installs SQL Server (and all other Sybase products). **Sybinit** helps automate SQL Server configuration by guiding you through the configuration process and letting you know if you make invalid menu selections. **Sybinit** prompts you for all of the information given in the list in the prior "Planning Ahead" section of this chapter.

If you encounter errors during installation, **sybinit** writes them to an error log file in the *$SYBASE/init/logs* directory. Check the file for errors and take any necessary action.

After successful installation of SQL Server, use **sybinit** to install Backup Server.

Point to Note: Execute **sybinit** once for each SQL Server you are installing. For example, you must execute **sybinit** twice if you are installing a production server and a test server.

What sybinit Does

The **sybinit** program performs the following actions.

- It creates entries in the *interfaces* file for the new SQL Server and Backup Server

- It creates the *master* and *sybprocdev* devices

- It creates *master*, *model*, *sybsystemprocs*, and *tempdb* databases

- It creates RUNSERVER files described later in this chapter in the section called "The RUNSERVER File"

- Finally, it starts SQL Server itself

Installing SQL Server on the Windows NT Platform

Installing SQL Server on a Windows NT platform is easy. You simply specify the installation directory, and the installation program does the rest.

Post-Installation Activities

The post-installation activities that this section discusses apply to both UNIX and NT environments. A newly installed SQL Server has a default configuration that is fine for bringing the system up, but you usually need to customize SQL Server to optimize it for your environment. The user called *sa* has permissions to configure changes. By default, no password is set for the *sa* account when SQL Server is newly installed. In a UNIX system, you log in using the following command.

```
isql -Usa -P
go
```

After you enter this command, the **isql** prompt appears. You can perform all administration, configuration, and tuning activities from within the **isql** program. See Chapter 5, Interacting with SQL Server, for more information about using **isql**.

Post-installation tasks vary from one environment to the next, but you should perform certain tasks after typical installations. Later sections in this chapter describe how to do the following tasks using the **isql** interface.

- Change the *sa* password
- Alter the size of the *master* database
- Increase the size of the *tempdb* database
- Mirror the *master* database
- Remove the *master* device from the pool of devices
- Modify SQL Server configuration parameters
- Name the local SQL Server and define the remote servers
- Add SQL Server logins
- Install the *sybsyntax* database
- Install the *pubs2* database
- Back up the *master* database
- Create database devices

Point to Note: It is good practice to back up the *master* database immediately after installation and after post-installation activities.

Change the *sa* Password

When you log into SQL Server as *sa*, you have special privileges that allow you to execute any SQL Server command. As mentioned, the *sa* login account has no password when SQL Server is installed, which means anyone can log in as *sa*. There are many reasons to disallow this, so create a password for the *sa* login to maintain a measure of security and accountability as illustrated in the following example.

Example: To change the existing *sa* password to *one0one*, issue the first command below from the UNIX prompt, and the second one from the **isql** prompt.

```
unixOS% isql -Usa -P
1> sp_passwd null, one0one
2> go
```

Increase the Size of the *master* Database

As you create database devices, objects, and logins, the system tables in the *master* database grow. The *master* database's initial size is only 3MB, which in our experience, is never large enough. SQL Server will not perform modifications or additions to objects in the *master* database if you don't provide sufficient space, so we recommend that you increase the size of the *master* database.

Example: This example adds 11MB to the *master* database.

```
1> alter database master on master=11
2> go
```

Increase the Size of the *tempdb* Database

If the *tempdb* database is not big enough to store temporary results, SQL Server processes that use *tempdb* will abort. *Tempdb* is created on the *master* database device with an initial size of 2MB, which is insufficient to hold most temporary results.

We recommend that you increase *tempdb* space by an appropriate amount for your particular SQL Server environment. The more active SQL Servers that use *tempdb*, the more space they need. Determining the exact size is a matter of estimation. Some people begin by increasing *tempdb* to 200MB. If SQL Server processes are frequently aborted for lack of *tempdb* space, allocate more space. Chapter 6, Database Devices and Fault Tolerance, discusses how to create *tempdb* space.

Example: This example creates a 200MB database device on a UNIX operating system file with path */usr/sybase/data/tempdb.dat*. Then, it allocates disk space to the *tempdb* database.

```
1> disk init name="tempdb_dev1",
2> physname ="/usr/sybase/data/tempdb.dat",
3> vdevno=2, size = 102400
4> go
1> alter database tempdb on tempdb_dev1=200
2> go
```

Mirror the Master Database Device

As Chapter 6, Database Devices and Fault Tolerance, describes, it is important to mirror the *master* database device because it stores the *master*, *model*, and *tempdb* databases. SQL Server reads control information from the *master* database during start-up. If the *master* database device is damaged, SQL Server might be unable to start. If you mirror the *master* device, SQL Server will start even if the original device is damaged.

Remove the *master* Database Device from the Pool

After installation, the *master* database device is marked as a default location for new databases unless the new database is specifically stored on another database device. The problem with letting user databases reside on the *master* database device is that when the user databases grow, they do so at the expense of the *master* database; and if the *master* database does not have enough space, SQL Server can't run properly. You should remove the *master* database device from the pool of default database devices to ensure that user databases cannot reside there. Chapter 6, Database Devices and Fault Tolerance, describes how to do so.

Example: The command in this example removes the *master* database device from the pool of default devices.

```
1> sp_diskdefault master, defaultoff
2> go
```

Modify SQL Server Configuration Parameters

The configuration program configures SQL Server to its default values. This configuration is not necessarily the configuration that your installation requires. You can customize many configuration parameters using the **sp_configure** system procedure. Configuration parameters allow you to control many aspects of SQL Server behavior so that the server performs optimally for your system's environment.

Chapter 12, Configuring SQL Server, discusses configuration issues, but here's a preview of some of the configurable settings that we have typically needed to customize.

- Amount of memory available to SQL Server
- Maximum number of on-line engines (applicable only to SMP systems)
- Total number of user connections
- Support for remote access

Example: This command configures 60MB of memory for SQL Server. After configuring the memory parameter, you have to recycle SQL Server for the new memory allocation to take effect.

```
1> sp_configure "total memory", 30720
2> go
```

Add Local and Remote Servers

To execute a remote procedure call on a remote server, the remote server name must exist in the *sysservers* table. You also need to identify the local server name so that SQL Server can use that name when it prints messages. You can use the system procedure *sp_addserver* to name the local SQL Server and to add remote servers to *sysservers*.

Example: If your local server's name is GURU and the remote server's name is APOLLO, the following set of commands add the local and remote server names to *sysservers*.

```
sp_addserver GURU, local
go
sp_addserver APOLLO
go
```

Chapter 13, SQL Server Security Features, provides more information about remote servers.

Add SQL Server Logins

All SQL Server users must have login accounts. There are three different types of login roles, each with its own set of permissions. They are the SA role (system administrator), the SSO role (system security officer), and the OPER role (operator). Chapter 13, discusses these roles in detail.

Use the system procedure **sp_addlogin** from within the *master* database to add new login accounts. We recommend that you use individual logins whenever possible for accountability purposes. We also recommend that you establish one or two special login accounts with *sa_role*, *sso_role*, and *oper_role* to perform system administration tasks.

Example: The following command creates a SQL Server login account with login *shell*, password *MooMu*, default database of *pubs2*, default language of US

English, and a full name of Michelle Anseno. The second command grants permissions to the *shell* login for every role.

```
use master
go
sp_addlogin shell, MooMu, pubs2, us_english, "Michelle Anseno"
go
sp_role "grant", sa_role, shell
go
```

Install the *pubs2* Database

It is unnecessary to install the *pubs2* database, but it is useful for learning and experimentation. Many of the examples listed in SQL Server documentation use *pubs2*.

To install *pubs2*, execute the script *installpubs2* using **isql**. By default, *pubs2* is installed on the default database device. If you want it to reside on any other database device, modify the script in *SYBASE/scripts/installpubs2*. The following command installs *pubs2*.

```
isql -Usa -SGURU -i$SYBASE/scripts/installpubs2
    -PGURU_PSWD
go
```

The RUNSERVER File

The installation program creates a *RUNSERVER* file to boot servers for customized upgrades. It contains only one command line, which invokes the executable *dataserver* (for UNIX) or *sqlsrvr.exe* (for Windows NT). The command parameters include the locations of the *master* database device, the error file, and the shared-memory files directory.

You use the RUNSERVER file to start SQL Server. The following illustrates the contents of a RUNSERVER file in a Windows NT environment. For the UNIX environment, you use *dataserver* instead of *sqlsrvr.exe*.

```
C:\SYBASE\bin\sqlsrvr.exe  -dC:\SYBASE\DATA\MASTER.DAT
  -sGURU -eC:\SYBASE\install\errorlog -iC:\SYBASE\ini
  -MC:\SYBASE
```

Table 11-3 shows the parameters found within a RUNSERVER file.

Table 11-3. RUNSERVER file syntax

Parameter	Description
-d	Location of the *master* device
-s	Name of the SQL Server
-e	Location of the error file
-i	Location of the *interfaces* file
-M	Location of the shared-memory file

The RUNSERVER file naming convention is RUN_<*server name*>. For example, if the SQL Server name is GURU, the RUNSERVER filename will be RUN_GURU. The following is an example of a RUNSERVER file on the AIX operating system.

```
#!/bin/sh
# SQL Server Information:
# name:                    APOLLO
# master device:                          /dev/rmaster
# master device size:                     30720
# errorlog: /opt/sybase/install/errorlog_APOLLO
# interfaces:              /opt/sybase
#
/opt/sybase/bin/dataserver -d/dev/rmaster -sAPOLLO \
  -e/opt/sybase/install/errorlog_APOLLO -i/opt/sybase
```

Point to Note: A RUNSERVER file is created for every SQL Server and Backup Server.

Starting SQL Server

Use the **startserver** utility to start SQL Servers using a RUNSERVER file. Here is an example.

```
startserver -f RUN_GURU
```

If you want to start more than one server at the same time, you can specify multiple server names. In the following example, one command line starts a SQL Server and a backup server. The -*f* option is used to specify a RUNSERVER filename.

```
startserver -f RUN_GURU -f RUN_GURU_BS
```

Starting SQL Server in Single-User Mode

At times, it is necessary to run SQL Server without interference from other users. For example, this single-user mode is necessary to recover a damaged *master* database. Use the *-m* option with **startserver** to start SQL Server in single-user mode. Only one System Administrator will be allowed to log in.

Example: This command starts the GURU SQL Server in single-user mode.

startserver -f RUN_GURU -m

SQL Server Automatic Start-Up

In a production environment, you can modify the operating system. For example, on AIX systems, you can modify the files */etc/inittab* and */etc/rc.nfs* so that SQL Server restarts automatically whenever the operating system restarts.

Automatic start-up varies from platform to platform. In general, network resources must be available before starting SQL Server. Therefore, make sure that the necessary network commands precede any SQL Server start-up commands. For example, here's an excerpt of an *rc.nfs* file for an AIX system that has been modified so that SQL Server starts automatically.

```
#!/bin/bsh
# ------------------------------------------------------------------
# the following lines start SQL Server when UNIX restarts
# ------------------------------------------------------------------
su - sybase "-c /opt/sybase/install/startserver
        -f /opt/sybase/install/RUN_APOLLO"
# ------------------------------------------------------------------
# the following line starts Sybase Backup Server
# ------------------------------------------------------------------
su - sybase "-c /opt/sybase/install/startserver
  -f /opt/sybase/install/RUN_APOLLO_BS"
```

Automatic Recovery During SQL Server Start-Up

When SQL Server starts, it initiates a process called automatic recovery, during which each database is compared to its transaction log. If the transaction log holds more recent information than the corresponding data pages in a database, the changes are applied to the database. For more details on transaction recovery, refer to Chapter 13, SQL Server Security Features.

After recovery completes, a *checkpoint log record* (a record that indicates that a boot-time recovery was done) is added to the database so that the recovery process is not unnecessarily rerun.

SQL Server databases are recovered in the following order.

1. *master*

2. *sybsecurity* (if present)

3. *model*

4. *tempdb*

5. *sybsystemprocs*

6. user databases in ascending order of their database IDs as they exist in the *sysdatabases* table

SQL Server Error Logs

SQL Server reports errors, fatal error messages, kernel error messages, and internal error messages to a log file. It identifies the log file by the filename that you specify after the *-e* parameter in the RUNSERVER file. Each message is identified by a message number. An error message also has a severity number and text that describes the error in words. Table 11-4 provides a summary of SQL Server errors, while Figure 11-5 shows where the error messages appear.

Table 11-4. *SQL Server error messages*

Severity	Description
1 through 9	User errors resulting from a syntax, permission, or other problem
10	These actually aren't errors, they provide additional information to the user
11	Specified data object not found
12	Wrong datatype
13	User transaction syntax error
14	Insufficient permissions to execute command
15	Syntax error in SQL statement
16	Miscellaneous user error

(continued)

Table 11-4. (continued)

Severity	Description
17	Insufficient resources
18	Nonfatal internal error
19	SQL Server fatal error in resource
20	SQL Server fatal error in current process
21	SQL Server fatal error in database process
22	SQL Server fatal error: table integrity is suspect
23	Fatal error: database integrity is suspect
24	Hardware error or system table corruption
25, 26	Miscellaneous internal errors

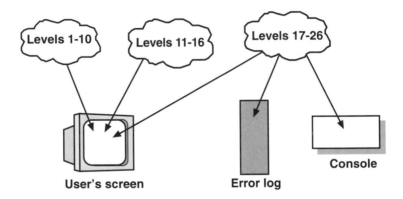

Figure 11-5. *Where error messages appear*

Monitor the Error Log

Many things can cause SQL Server errors. For example, SQL Server writes an error message to the error log if the disk space on the log database device falls below the threshold warning level.

Obviously, it is best to anticipate problems and account for them before they happen, but that isn't always possible. You can still avoid disasters, though, if you monitor SQL Server's error log so that you can take action immediately if an error occurs. The sidebar titled "Automatically Monitoring the Error Log" suggests some ways to help you monitor SQL Server errors.

Automatically Monitoring the Error Log

You can write a shell script to automatically monitor the error log on a periodic basis. The script can issue appropriate warnings and alarms if it finds specific error numbers. Here are some ideas with which you could develop a script that checks the error log every 15 minutes.

- A *cron job* (an event you can schedule in a UNIX environment) that checks the error log every 15 minutes

- Write any error messages that occurred in the last 15 minutes to a script

- Filter error messages that you don't want to monitor

- E-mail the filtered error log to Sybase database administrators

- Search for critical errors

- Page Sybase database administrators if critical errors are found

- Track the last error-log line number that was scanned to use for the next scan

Stopping SQL Server

Use the **shutdown** command, as shown here, to stop SQL Server when there are no processes running.

```
1> shutdown
2> go
```

If processes are running, the above command will not work. You need to terminate the processes before issuing the **shutdown** command. However, if you must shut down SQL Server without terminating processes, you can use the *nowait* parameter with **shutdown** as follows.

```
1> shutdown with nowait
2> go
```

When you execute a **shutdown** command with no parameters, SQL Server performs the following actions.

1. Disables server logins from all users except system administrators

2. Executes a checkpoint, which flushes all dirty buffers to disk for every database

3. Waits for active processes to complete

4. Shuts down SQL Server

When you execute **shutdown with nowait**, SQL Server only performs actions 1 and 4, so **shutdown with nowait** is not the preferred shutdown method. If you must use it, issue the **checkpoint** command manually in all active databases before shutting down, or you will lose data.

Terminating a Process

You might have to terminate a process for various reasons. You can do so using the **kill** command. For example, the following command terminates the SQL Server process *id2*. But, before you terminate a process, you should list the process using the system procedure **sp_who** to make sure it is the one you want to terminate.

```
1> kill 2
2> go
```

Terminating SQL Server Using UNIX Commands

If you can't log into SQL Server and you need to shut it down, you have no option but to terminate the SQL Server process using the UNIX **kill** command.

Point to Note: Terminating SQL Server using the UNIX **kill** command is strictly a last resort, because it will most likely cause a loss of data.

Stopping Backup Server

The **shutdown** command used to shut down SQL Server can also be used to shut down Backup Server. The following command shuts down Backup Server.

```
1> shutdown SYB_BACKUP
2> go
```

Checking Whether SQL Server Is Running

To check whether SQL Server is running, you can execute the **showserver** script, a shell script included with SQL Server software in the *$SYBASE/install* directory. The **showserver** script checks whether both SQL Server and Backup

Server are running. You can modify the script to display information about other Sybase products. Here is sample output from an execution of **showserver** on an AIX platform.

```
USER        PID %CPU %MEM   SZ  RSS    TTY STAT    STIME  TIME
                           COMMAND
sybase    12726  0.0  4.0  464 5864      0 A    13:46:00  1:09
                           /opt/sybase11/bin/dataserver
                            -d/dev/rmaster -sAPOLLO
                            -e/opt/sybase11/install/APOLLO.err
                            -i/opt/sybase11
sybase    14014  0.0  4.0 3564 5252      0 A    13:48:27  0:00
                           /opt/sybase11/bin/backupserver
                            -SAPOLLO_BS
                            -/opt/sybase11/install/APOLLO_BS.err
                            -I/opt/sybase11/interfaces
                            -M/opt/sybase11/bin/sybmultbuf
                            -Lus_english -Jiso_1
                            -c/opt/sybase11/backup_tape.cfg
```

Exercises

11-1. What is the maximum length of a server name?

11-2. Given a chance to select between an operating system file and UNIX raw partition, which one is recommended for the *master* device?

11-3. Which product should you install first, SQL Server or Backup Server?

11-4. How do you prioritize the following activities after you install SQL Server?

    a. Creating user databases

    b. Creating user accounts

    c. Mirroring the *master* database

    d. Installing the *sybsyntax* database

    e. Configuring SQL Server for more memory

    f. Installing Backup Server

    g. Dumping the *master* database

    h. Creating database devices for user databases

11-5. In a UNIX environment, the home directory for Sybase products is */usr/sybase* and Sybase software is installed in */opt/sybase*. (The $SYBASE environment variable is */opt/sybase*.) Where is the *interfaces* file stored?

11-6. Sybase software is installed in *c:\sybase* in a Windows NT environment. Where is the *interfaces* file stored?

11-7. SQL Server S1 is running on UNIX machine A and you just now installed SQL Server S2 on UNIX machine B. What will you do if you want to access SQL Server S1 from machine B using **isql**?

11-8. You have installed one development SQL Server, one production SQL Server (with four engines) and one Backup Server. How many RUN-SERVER files are present?

Answers to Exercises

11-1. The maximum number of characters in a server name is 11.

11-2. UNIX raw partition

11-3. SQL Server

11-4. The prioritization is indicated in the following table

Activity	Priority
a. Creating user databases	5
b. Creating user accounts	6
c. Mirroring the *master* database	2
d. Installing the *sybsyntax* database	3
e. Configuring SQL Server for more memory	7
f. Installing Backup Server	1
g. Dumping the *master* database	8
h. Creating database devices for user databases	4

11-5. In */opt/sybase*

11-6. In *c:\sybase\ini*

11-7. Copy the network address from the *interfaces* file of Server S1 on machine A to the *interfaces* file on machine B, and execute **isql** with the name of Server S1 on the command line.

11-8. 3

12

Configuring SQL Server

Every distributed client/server database system is different. Each system has its own mix of applications, user loads, performance requirements, and associated hardware. Configuring an RDBMS for operability and performance is an important part of establishing a well-functioning environment. Configuration is also an essential maintenance task to keep the system running at specifications as it grows and as the mix of applications change. A good RDBMS must be highly configurable.

SQL Server has an extensive set of configuration options that offer great flexibility for meeting the needs of an enormous variety of system requirements. In this chapter, we discuss some of SQL Server's most frequently used configuration options and summarize their configuration parameters. Refer to the *SQL Server Administration Guide* and the *Performance and Tuning Guide* on your SyBooks CD for in-depth coverage of all SQL Server configuration topics.

This chapter covers the following subjects.

- Configuration fundamentals
- Displaying levels of information about a configuration

- Using the configuration system procedure **sp_configure**
- Common configuration parameters

Configuration Fundamentals

SQL Server gives you control over its behavior through its *configuration para-meters*, which you can set using the system procedure called **sp_configure**. You can set the parameter *total memory*, for example, to designate the amount of memory SQL Server may consume during execution.

The Default Configuration and Changing It

When you first install SQL Server, all of its configuration parameters are set to default values. This configuration is sufficient to make the new installation operable in a configuration environment with the minimum resources to run SQL Server, but you'll want to configure the system for the specific resources and requirements of the system in which it runs. For example, the default SQL Server memory allocation is 15MB, which is the smallest amount of memory you can use to run SQL Server. But if SQL Server is to reside on a machine with 512MB of memory, a memory allocation of 15MB is an unnecessary limitation. The system in this environment gains a relatively large performance benefit if it takes advantage of the rest of the memory resource.

Configuration Categories

Sybase groups configuration parameters by the behavior they affect. This aids in identifying which parameter to adjust to affect a particular area of SQL Server performance. The categories are as follows.

- Backup and recovery
- Cache management
- Disk I/O
- General information
- Languages
- Lock management

- Memory use

- Network communications

- Operating system resources

- Physical memory

- Processors

- SQL Server administration

- User environment

Some parameters may appear in more than one group. For example, the parameter *number of remote connections* belongs primarily in the network communications group, but it also belongs to the SQL Server administration group and the memory use group. This type of organization makes it easier to find the parameter you need.

Dynamic and Static Parameters

Configuration parameters can be either *dynamic* or *static*. When you modify a dynamic parameter, the change takes effect immediately. Static parameters require SQL Server to reallocate memory, which it can only do when you restart SQL Server.

Configuration Parameters

Table 12-1 lists all SQL Server configuration parameters and their properties. The display levels listed in the fourth column of the table are explained in following sections.

Table 12-1. *SQL Server 11 configuration parameters*

Group	Parameter Name	Dynamic or Static	Display Level	Default Value
Backup and recovery	*print recovery information*	static	intermediate	0
	recovery interval in minutes	dynamic	basic	5
	tape retention in days	static	intermediate	0

(continued)

Table 12-1. *(continued)*

Group	Parameter Name	Dynamic or Static	Display Level	Default Value
Cache manager	memory alignment boundary	static	comprehensive	2048
	number of index trips	dynamic	comprehensive	0
	number of oam trips	dynamic	comprehensive	0
	procedure cache cache percent	static	comprehensive	20
Disk I/O	allow sql server async i/o	static	comprehensive	1 (on)
	disk i/o structures	static	comprehensive	256
	number of devices	static	basic	10
	page utilization percent	dynamic	comprehensive	95
General information	configuration file	dynamic	comprehensive	0
Languages	default character set id	static	intermediate	1
	default language id	dynamic	intermediate	0
	default sortorder id	static	comprehensive	50
	number of languages in cache	static	intermediate	3
Lock manager	address lock spinlock ratio	static	comprehensive	100
	deadlock checking period	dynamic	comprehensive	500
	deadlock retries	dynamic	intermediate	5
	freelock transfer block size	dynamic	comprehensive	30
	max engine freelocks	dynamic	comprehensive	10
	number of locks	static	basic	5000

(continued)

Table 12-1. *(continued)*

Group	Parameter Name	Dynamic or Static	Display Level	Default Value
	page lock spinlock ratio	static	comprehensive	100
	table lock spinlock ratio	static	comprehensive	20
Network communication	allow remote access	dynamic	intermediate	1
	default network packet size	static	intermediate	512
	max network packet size	static	intermediate	512
	max number network listeners	static	comprehensive	15
	number of remote connections	static	intermediate	20
	number of remote logins	static	intermediate	20
	number of remote sites	static	intermediate	10
	remote server pre-read packets	static	intermediate	3
	tcp no delay	static	comprehensive	0 (off)
Operating system resources	max async i/os per engine	static	comprehensive	2147483647
	max async i/os per server	static	comprehensive	2147483647
	o/s async i/o enabled	read only	comprehensive	0
	o/s file descriptors	read only	comprehensive	0
	shared memory starting address	static	comprehensive	0
Physical memory	additional network memory	static	intermediate	0
	lock shared memory	static	comprehensive	0 (off)

(continued)

Table 12-1. *(continued)*

Group	Parameter Name	Dynamic or Static	Display Level	Default Value
	total memory	static	intermediate	platform specific
Processors	max online engines	static	intermediate	1
	min online engines	static	intermediate	1
SQL Server administration	allow nested triggers	static	intermediate	1
	allow updates to system tables	dynamic	comprehensive	0 (off)
	audit queue size	static	intermediate	100
	cpu accounting flush interval	dynamic	comprehensive	200
	cpu grace time	static	comprehensive	500
	default database size	static	intermediate	2
	default fill factor percent	static	intermediate	0
	event buffers per engine	static	comprehensive	100
	housekeeper free write percent	dynamic	intermediate	1
	identity burning factor	static	intermediate	5000
	identity grab size	dynamic	intermediate	1
	i/o accounting flush interval	dynamic	comprehensive	1000
	i/o polling process count	dynamic	comprehensive	10
	lock promotion HWM	dynamic	intermediate	200
	lock promotion LWM	dynamic	intermediate	200
	lock promotion PCT	dynamic	intermediate	100
	number of alarms	static	comprehensive	40

(continued)

Table 12-1. *(continued)*

Group	Parameter Name	Dynamic or Static	Display Level	Default Value
	number of extent i/o buffers	static	comprehensive	0
	number of mailboxes	static	comprehensive	30
	number of messages	static	comprehensive	64
	number of open databases	static	basic	12
	number of open objects	static	basic	500
	number of pre-allocated extents	static	comprehensive	2
	number of sort buffers	dynamic	comprehensive	0
	print deadlock information	dynamic	intermediate	0
	runnable process search count	dynamic	comprehensive	200
	partition groups	static	comprehensive	1024
	partition spinlock ratio	static	comprehensive	10
	size of auto identity column	dynamic	intermediate	10
	sort page count	dynamic	comprehensive	0
	sql server clock tick length	static	comprehensive	platform specific
	time slice	static	comprehensive	100
User Environment	*number of user connections*	static	basic	25
	permission cache entries	static	comprehensive	15
	stack guard size	static	comprehensive	4096
	stack size	static	basic	platform specific

(continued)

Table 12-1. *(continued)*

Group	Parameter Name	Dynamic or Static	Display Level	Default Value
	systemwide password expiration	dynamic	intermediate	0
	user log cache size	static	intermediate	2048
	user log cache spinlock ratio	static	intermediate	20

Display Levels

In earlier versions of SQL Server, any user could view the value of any configuration parameter. In some environments, such freedom is a security issue. System 11 lets you associate a display level to a parameter to limit users' views of parameter values and their ability to modify those values. The three levels of display are basic, intermediate, and comprehensive. By default, SQL Server sets a user's display level to comprehensive.

A user with a *basic display level* can modify only a very small set of parameters. This level is suitable for users who intend to adjust the following SQL Server parameters: *recovery interval*, *number of devices*, *number of locks*, *number of open databases*, *number of open database objects*, *number of user connections*, and *stack size*.

A user with an *intermediate display level* has the same capabilities as the user with a basic display level, but can modify an additional 40 percent of the configuration parameters, as identified in Table 12-1.

A user with a *comprehensive display level* can modify all of the configuration parameters. This level is recommended only for users with system administration authority.

You might need to adjust some parameters more often than others. If those parameters happen to be available in the basic or intermediate display level, you can set that display level and automatically limit access. For example, if you are optimizing the number of open objects, setting the display level to basic produces **sp_configure** output that includes only the number of open databases open objects. The examples in the sections below illustrate the effects of using display levels.

Using Display Levels to View Parameter Groups

You can display all of the configuration parameters in a group by using the **sp_configure** command as indicated in Table 12-2.

Table 12-2. *Command for viewing parameter groups*

sp_configure *"group_name"*
group_name   One of the groups listed in the section earlier in this chapter called "Configuration Categories"

If you execute the command **sp_configure** with a comprehensive display level, you see output similar to the following.

```
Group: SQL Server Administration
Parameter Name                   Default   Memory Used   Config Value   Run Value
---------------                  --------  ------------  -------------  ---------
 allow nested triggers              1           0             1             1
 allow updates to system tables     0           0             1             1
 audit queue size                 100          42           100           100
 cpu accounting flush interval    200           0           200           200
 cpu grace time                   500           0           200           200
 deadlock retries                   5           0             5             5
 default database size              2           0             2             2
 default fill factor percent        0           0             0             0
 event buffers per engine         100         #30           100           100
 housekeeper free write percent     1           0             1             1
 i/o accounting flush interval   1000           0          1000          1000
 i/o polling process count         10           0            10            10
 identity burning set factor     5000           0          5000          5000
 identity grab size                 1           0             1             1
 lock promotion HWM               200           0           200           200
 lock promotion LWM               200           0           200           200
 lock promotion PCT               100           0           100           100
 number of alarms                  40           1            40            40
 number of extent i/o buffers       0           0             0             0
 number of mailboxes               30           1            30            30
 number of messages                64           1            64            64
 number of open databases          12         395            12            12
 number of open objects           500         494           500           500
 number of pre-allocated extent     2           0             2             2
 number of sort buffers             0           0             0             0
 partition groups                1024          21          1024          1024
 partition spinlock ratio          10           0            10            10
 print deadlock information         0           0             0             0
 runnable process search count      3           0             3             3
 size of auto identity column      10           0            10            10
 sort page count                    0           0             0             0
 sql server clock tick length  100000           0        100000        100000
```

```
time slice                       100          0       100          100
upgrade version                  100          0      1101         1101
(return status = 0)

The display level for login 'srik' has been changed to 'intermediate'.
(return status = 0)
```

If you execute the command **sp_configure** with an intermediate display
level, you see output similar to the following.

```
Group: SQL Server Administration
Parameter Name           Default  Memory Used  Config Value  Run Value
--------------           -------  -----------  ------------  ---------
allow nested triggers         1          0          1          1
audit queue size            100         42        100        100
deadlock retries              5          0          5          5
default database size         2          0          2          2
default fill factor percent   0          0          0          0
housekeeper free write percent 1         0          1          1
identity burning set factor 5000         0       5000       5000
identity grab size            1          0          1          1
lock promotion HWM          200          0        200        200
lock promotion LWM          200          0        200        200
lock promotion PCT          100          0        100        100
number of open databases     12        395         12         12
number of open objects      500        494        500        500
print deadlock information    0          0          0          0
size of auto identity column 10          0         10         10
(return status = 0)
The display level for login 'srik' has been changed to 'basic'.
(return status = 0)
```

If you execute the command **sp_configure** with a basic display level, you
see output similar to the following.

```
Group: SQL Server Administration
Parameter Name           Default  Memory Used  Config Value  Run Value
--------------           -------  -----------  ------------  ---------
number of open databases     12        395         12         12
number of open objects      500        494        500        500
(return status = 0)
```

Setting the Display Level

Use the system procedure **sp_displaylevel** to set or modify the display level, as
illustrated by the following example.

Example: The following command sets the display level to basic for a user with a login name of *thomas*.

```
sp_displaylevel "thomas", basic
go
```

This command produces the following output.

```
The display level for login 'thomas' has been changed to 'basic'.
(return status = 0)
```

Using sp_configure

You can configure SQL Server using any one of the following three methods. Table 12-3 shows syntax for **sp_configure**.

* By executing the system procedure **sp_configure** with the required values in on-line mode

* By editing the configuration file, then executing system procedure **sp_configure** with the *config file* option

* By providing the name of a configuration file while starting SQL Server

Table 12-3. Syntax for the **sp_configure** system procedure

Syntax	Description
sp_configure	Displays all configuration parameters by group. Gives current values, default value, value before the current value, and amount of memory that the setting uses.
sp_configure *"parameter"*	For all parameters matching the named parameter, displays current value, default value, value before the current value, and amount of memory that the setting uses.
sp_configure *"parameter", value*	Sets the named parameter to the specified value.
sp_configure *"parameter", 0, "default"*	Sets the named parameter to its default value.
sp_configure *"group_name"*	Displays all configuration parameters in the named group. Gives current values, default value, value before the current value, and amount of memory that the setting uses.
sp_configure *"configuration file", 0, "sub_command", "file_name"*	Lets you use **sp_configure** noninteractively. You can invoke it through a configuration file.

Example: To view the current SQL Server configuration, simply execute
sp_configure with no parameters. Here is sample output.

```
Group: Configuration Options
Group: Backup/Recovery
Parameter Name            Default  Memory Used  Config Value   Run Value
--------------            -------  -----------  ------------   ---------
allow remote access          1          0            1             1
 print recovery information   0          0            0             0
 recovery interval in minutes 5          0            2             2
 tape retention in days       0          0            0             0

Group: Cache Manager
Parameter Name            Default  Memory Used  Config Value   Run Value
--------------            -------  -----------  ------------   ---------
memory alignment boundary  2048         0          2048          2048
number of index trips         0         0             0             0
number of oam trips           0         0             0             0
procedure cache percent      20     52818            20            20
total data cache size         0    203648             0        203648
total memory               7500    409600        204800        204800

Group: Disk I/O
Parameter Name            Default  Memory Used  Config Value   Run Value
--------------            -------  -----------  ------------   ---------
allow sql server async i/o    1         0             1             1
disk i/o structures         256        18           256           256
number of devices            10       #38            85            85
page utilization percent     95         0            95            95

Group: General Information
Parameter Name            Default  Memory Used  Config Value   Run Value
--------------            -------  -----------  ------------   ---------
configuration file            0         0             0  /cis1/sybas

Group: Languages
Parameter Name            Default  Memory Used  Config Value   Run Value
--------------            -------  -----------  ------------   ---------
default character set id      1         0             1             1
default language id           0         0             0             0
default sortorder id         50         0            50            50
disable character set conversi 0        0             0             0
number of languages in cache   3        4             3             3

Group: Lock Manager
Parameter Name            Default  Memory Used  Config Value   Run Value
--------------            -------  -----------  ------------   ---------
address lock spinlock ratio  100        0           100           100
deadlock checking period     500        0           500           500
freelock transfer block size  30        0            30            30
max engine freelocks          10        0            10            10
```

```
number of locks                5000      2344          25000          25000
page lock spinlock ratio        100         0            100            100
table lock spinlock ratio        20         0             20             20
```

```
Group: Memory Use
Parameter Name               Default Memory Used   Config Value    Run Value
--------------               ------- -----------   ------------    ---------
additional network memory         0       300          307200         307200
audit queue size                100        42             100            100
default network packet size     512     #3017             512            512
disk i/o structures             256        18             256            256
event buffers per engine        100       #69             100            100
executable code size              0      4812         3252200           4812
max number network listeners     15      1361              15             15
max online engines                1      1267               7              7
number of alarms                 40         2              80             80
number of devices                10       #38              85             85
number of extent i/o buffers      0       803              50             50
number of languages in cache      3         4               3              3
number of locks                5000      2344           25000          25000
number of mailboxes              30         1              30             30
number of messages               64         1              64             64
number of open databases         12       990              30             30
number of open objects          500      2841            3000           3000
number of remote connections     20       618             384            384
number of remote logins          20       137             128            128
number of remote sites           10      1813              20             20
number of user connections       25    135717            1500           1500
partition groups               1024        21            1024           1024
permission cache entries         15      #724              15             15
procedure cache percent          20     52818              20             20
remote server pre-read packets    3      #603               3              3
stack guard size               4096     #6232            4096           4096
stack size                    34816    #62320           40960          40960
total data cache size             0    203648               0         203648
total memory                   7500    409600          204800         204800
```

```
Group: Network Communication
Parameter Name               Default Memory Used   Config Value    Run Value
--------------               ------- -----------   ------------    ---------
additional network memory         0       300          307200         307200
allow remote access               1         0               1              1
allow sendmsg                     0         0               0              0
default network packet size     512     #3017             512            512
max network packet size         512         0             512            512
max number network listeners     15      1361              15             15
number of remote connections     20       618             384            384
number of remote logins          20       137             128            128
number of remote sites           10      1813              20             20
remote server pre-read packets    3      #603               3              3
syb_sendmsg port number           0         0               0              0
tcp no delay                      0         0               0              0
```

```
Group: O/S Resources
Parameter Name             Default Memory Used  Config Value   Run Value
--------------             ------- -----------  ------------   ---------
max async i/os per engine   5000             0           500         500
max async i/os per server   2147483647       0    2147483647  2147483647
o/s asynch i/o enabled         0             0             0           0
o/s file descriptors           0             0          2048        2048
tcp no delay                   0             0             0           0

Group: Physical Resources

Group: Physical Memory
Parameter Name             Default Memory Used  Config Value   Run Value
--------------             ------- -----------  ------------   ---------
additional network memory      0           300        307200      307200
lock shared memory             0             0             0           0
shared memory starting address 0             0             0           0
total memory                7500        409600         04800      204800

Group: Processors
Parameter Name             Default Memory Used  Config Value   Run Value
--------------             ------- -----------  ------------   ---------
max online engines             1          1267             7           7
min online engines             1             0             1           1

Group: SQL Server Administration
Parameter Name             Default Memory Used  Config Value   Run Value
--------------             ------- -----------  ------------   ---------
allow nested triggers          1             0             1           1
allow updates to system tables 0             0             0           0
audit queue size             100            42           100         100
cpu accounting flush interval 200            0           200         200
cpu grace time               500             0          1500        1500
deadlock retries               5             0             5           5
default database size          2             0             2           2
default fill factor percent    0             0             0           0
event buffers per engine     100            69           100         100
housekeeper free write percent 1             0             1           1
i/o accounting flush interval 1000           0          1000        1000
i/o polling process count     10             0            10          10
identity burning set factor 5000             0          5000        5000
identity grab size             1             0             1           1
lock promotion HWM           200             0           200         200
lock promotion LWM           200             0           200         200
lock promotion PCT           100             0           100         100
number of alarms              40             2            80          80
number of extent i/o buffers   0           803            50          50
number of mailboxes           30             1            30          30
number of messages            64             1            64          64
number of open databases      12           990            30          30
number of open objects       500          2841          3000        3000
```

```
number of pre-allocated extent  2                0              2              2
number of sort buffers          0                0              0              0
partition groups             1024               21           1024           1024
partition spinlock ratio       10                0             10             10
print deadlock information      0                0              0              0
runnable process search count 2000               0           2000           2000
size of auto identity column   10                0             10             10
sort page count                 0                0              0              0
sql server clock tick length 100000              0         100000         100000
time slice                    100                0            200            200
upgrade version              1100                0           1101           1101

Group: User Environment
Parameter Name           Default  Memory Used  Config Value   Run Value
--------------           -------  -----------  ------------   ---------
default network packet size  512     3017           512            512
number of pre-allocated extent 2        0             2              2
number of user connections    25   135717          1500           1500
permission cache entries      15      724            15             15
stack guard size            4096     6232          4096           4096
stack size                 34816    62320         40960          40960
systemwide password expiration 0        0             0              0
user log cache size         2048        0          2048           2048
user log cache spinlock ratio 20        0            20             20
(return status = 0)
```

There are two ways to use **sp_configure**. You can execute **sp_configure** commands from the SQL interface prompt or you can create a configuration file, as the next two sections explain.

Configuring from the Command Prompt Using *sp_configure*

You can use **sp_configure** from the command prompt to change parameters on the fly, such as when you are experimenting. Dynamic parameters take effect immediately. Static parameters are changed, but don't take effect until the next time you start SQL Server. Here are examples of setting dynamic and static parameters on the fly.

Example: This command makes it possible for a user to update system tables.

```
sp_configure "allow updates to system tables",1
go
```

Because *allow updates* is a dynamic parameter, the change takes effect immediately. SQL Server displays the following output.

Parameter Name	Default	Memory Used	Config Value	Run Value
allow updates to system tables	0	0	1	1

Example: This command allocates 200MB of memory to SQL Server.

```
sp_configure "total memory", 102400
go
```

Because *total memory* is a static parameter, the new value takes effect only after SQL Server restarts. SQL Server displays the following output after you execute the command and before restart.

Parameter Name	Default	Memory Used	Config Value	Run Value
total memory	7500	15000	102400	7500

Using Configuration Files

The method described in the preceding section only lets you modify one parameter at a time. Configuration files are a more convenient way to set multiple parameters. The **sp_configure** command can read a list of parameters from a file you create. The file contains a list of parameters and their new values.

Configuration File Naming Convention

SQL Server generates configuration files using the following naming convention, for which *<server name>* is the name of the SQL Server and *xxx* is the serial number of the configuration file.

<server name>.xxx

For example, if the SQL Server name is GURU, SQL Server generates a configuration file called *GURU.001*. If a configuration file called *GURU.001* already exists, the serial number for the new file is 002 and the filename is *GURU.002*.

Example: This example, configures SQL Server using a configuration file called *GURU.010*.

```
sp_configure "configuration file", 0, "read", "GURU.010"
go
```

SQL Server performs checking on the values of each parameter in *GURU.010* and configures only the parameters that pass the checks. The other parameters are not modified; the current run values are substituted for them.

Example: Here's a command that copies all of the current configuration values to a file called *curconfig.cfg*.

```
sp_configure "configuration file", 0,
  "write","curconfig.cfg"
go
```

Starting SQL Server Using a Configuration File

Rather than using **sp_configure** to submit the configuration file, you can submit the file during SQL Server start-up. All of the parameters specified in the file take effect as soon as SQL Server is up and running.

Example: This example starts SQL Server from a UNIX prompt with configuration file *GURU.cfg*.

$SYBASE/bin/dataserver -C GURU.cfg

Another way to start up with configuration file *GURU.cfg* is to add *-c GURU.cfg* to the dataserver command in the *RUNSERVER* file.

What Happens in the Server

When you execute the **sp_configure** command to modify a parameter, SQL Server performs the following actions.

1. It copies all SQL Server configuration parameter values to an operating system file called *$SYBASE/<server name>.xxx* before changing the configuration.

2. It updates the configuration parameter with the new value in the system table *master..syscurconfig*.

3. It modifies the run value of the parameter, if it is a dynamic parameter.

What to Do if SQL Server Does Not Start

Sometimes, SQL Server might not start after you modify parameters. This problem most commonly occurs when you change a memory parameter value. It's possible that the resources for the new configuration are not available, or there might be an operating system limitation. In any case, you can revert to the previous configuration file using the *-c* option in the *RUNSERVER* file. For example, suppose you modified the *total memory* parameter and now SQL Server won't start. Here are two actions you can take.

- You can check the error log file to see which parameter caused SQL Server not to start, then investigate and act based on what you discover.

- You can start SQL Server with the previous configuration file using *$SYBASE/bin/dataserver -c <previous_config_file>*. (*Previous_config_file* is the configuration file that SQL Server was using before you made the modification.)

Commonly Configured Parameters

In the following sections, we discuss the most commonly used configuration parameters.

Configuring Total Memory

The *total memory* parameter defines the maximum amount of operating system memory that the SQL Server process can use. *Total memory* is expressed in 2KB units. The default value for this parameter varies from platform to platform. Make sure that the new value to which you want to set *total memory* does not exceed the amount of physical memory available.

Example: This example allocates 200MB of memory to SQL Server.

```
sp_configure "total memory", 102400
go
```

Setting the Maximum Number of Engines

The *max number of engines* parameter specifies the number of SQL Server engines that can run simultaneously in a multiple CPU environment (an SMP environment). The *max number of engines* parameter has a default value of one, so you need to reconfigure it for an SMP system.

Sybase recommends that there should never be more engines than processors. We suggest that you configure this parameter to one less than number of processors, which we believe fully utilizes the SMP processing power and leaves enough additional power for operating system tasks.

As you configure more engines, the amount of overhead for each engine also increases.

Example: This example configures SQL Server for three SQL Server engines.

```
sp_configure "max number of engines", 3
go
```

Setting the Procedure Cache Percentage

The *procedure cache* parameter sets the percentage of memory to allocate for compiling and storing stored procedures. The start-up messages in the SQL Server *errorlog* file (in *$SYBASE/install*) list the amount of procedure cache that SQL Server uses.

If your application uses a large number of stored procedures, you should increase this parameter. You can calculate the amount of *procedure cache* you need using the following equation.

```
procedure cache = procedure percent * (total memory - executable size -
user connection memory)
```

Example: This command sets the *procedure cache* to 10 percent.

```
sp_configure "procedure cache", 10
go
```

Setting the Stack Size

Queries with long *where* clauses, select lists, and deeply-nested stored procedures might cause a SQL Server stack overflow error and roll back the transaction. To avoid this problem, you can either break the large query into smaller ones or you can increase the *stack size* parameter.

Stack size defines the size of the execution stacks used by each SQL Server engine. An execution stack is an area in SQL Server memory that stores information about process context and local data for user processes. When you increase the stack size, you increase it across every user in SQL Server, not just for the query that needs a larger stack size. Each stack size of each SQL Server engine will be equal to the size you set for the *stack size* parameter.

Example: This example configures the *stack size* to 30KB.

```
sp_configure, "stack size", 30720
go
```

Setting the Number of User Connections

As a SQL Server system grows, you'll add user logins for new user connections. However, there is a limit to the number of user connections that SQL Server will accept. This limit is determined by the parameter *number of user connections*. If you meet the limit for the number of user connections and you need to add more logins, you must increase the value of this parameter.

The maximum value for this parameter is based on the operating system parameter file descriptors, which you can view using the SQL command **select @@max_connections**. Each user connection occupies an amount of memory equal to approximately 52KB. So before you increase the number of user connections, you should check to make sure you have enough memory to handle the new users.

Example: This example configures the number of user connections to 50.

```
sp_configure "number of user connections", 50
go
```

Allowing Remote Access

The *allow remote access* parameter is a toggle that opens or closes communication between SQL Servers and other servers, such as Backup Server. By default, this parameter is set for open communication—a setting of *1*. Because SQL Server communicates with Backup Server using remote procedure calls, it's important to keep this parameter set to *1*.

Example: This command opens SQL Server communication to other servers.

```
sp_configure "allow remote access", 1
go
```

Setting Maximum Network Packet Size

The default network packet size is 512KB. Using much larger packet sizes, such as 4096KB, greatly improves performance by reducing the overhead associated with loading and unloading packets. Client applications that want a larger packet size can use the parameter *max network pkt size* at the time they establish their connection with SQL Server. For example, **isql -Usa -A4196**, makes that **isql** client's network packet size 4196KB. If there is not enough data to fill the larger packet size, SQL Server sends a smaller one. But when more data is transmitted, the larger packet size boosts performance.

If you do increase this parameter, you'll need to configure additional network memory using the *additional netmem* parameter. Otherwise, SQL Server uses a network packet size of only 512KB. See the next section for more information about the *additional netmem* parameter.

Example: The following example tells client applications to use 4096KB as the network packet size for communication with SQL Server.

```
sp_configure "max network pkt size", 4096
go
```

Client applications that use a larger packet size must specify the packet size while establishing their connections to SQL Server. For example, an **isql** client requiring a packet size of 4096KB could use the command **isql -Usa -A4096**.

Adding Network Memory

You must modify the *additional netmem* parameter when you change the *max network pkt size* parameter discussed in the preceding section. The *SQL Server System Administration Guide* on your SyBooks CD gives detailed information about how to calculate the amount of additional network memory you need.

Example: This command increases network memory by 30KB—that is, by 30,720 bytes.

```
sp_configure "additional netmem", 30720
go
```

Number of Devices

When you have used the maximum number of database devices and you want to add a new device, you must increase the SQL Server parameter *number of devices*.

Example: This example allows a maximum of 15 database devices.

```
sp_configure "number of devices", 15
go
```

Summary

This chapter gave you an overview of how you can use SQL Server's rich set of configuration parameters to customize SQL Server to run optimally in your particular computing environment. It discussed some of SQL Server's most frequently used capabilities of the **sp_configure** command, including display levels and commonly configured parameters. You'll perform these types of configuration techniques at every phase of the system's life—from configuring for smooth operation after installation to maintaining good performance as the system grows and changes.

Exercises

12-1. What command do you use to find SQL Server's current configuration?

12-2. What command do you use to copy the current SQL Server configuration to an ASCII file?

12-3. What display level do you use if you will only be working with the parameter *number of locks*?

12-4. If SQL Server will not start after you set one or more configuration parameters, how do you start it using a previous configuration?

12-5. Is the configuration parameter *total memory* a static or a dynamic parameter?

12-6. Explain how SQL Server names configuration files.

12-7. What command do you use if you want to view parameters related to the *lock manager* group?

12-8. What configuration parameters do you modify if the client application needs a packet size of 8,192 bytes?

12-9. What configuration parameter do you modify if some long queries report a stack error and do not execute?

12-10. In an SMP environment, which parameter do you configure so that SQL Server utilizes all CPU resources?

Answers to Exercises

12-1.   **sp_configure**
        go

12-2.   **sp_configure "configuration file",0,"write","<name of file>"**
        go

12-3.   Basic level

12-4.   **$SYBASE/bin/dataserver -C <config file name>**

12-5.   Static

12-6.   The naming convention for a configuration file is *<SQL Server Name>.*
        <serial number>

12-7.   **sp_configure "Lock Manager"**
        go

12-8.   *max network packet size* and *additional network memory*

12-9.   *stack size*

12-10. *max online engines*

13

SQL Server
Security Features

SQL Server security features protect sensitive data from unauthorized access. For many people, the idea of securing data from unauthorized access conjures up thoughts of government projects and top secret applications. Actually, there are reasons to secure data in many common database applications, especially in a multiuser environment in which many users might have access to tables that contain sensitive data. An employee database might contain personal and confidential information such as salary, legal history, and health information. Most employees would not feel comfortable if they thought that any interested person could look at this type of private information.

Enterprises are demanding higher security standards as we head into the era of the Internet and other channels for increased access to information, which can leave information systems more vulnerable to unauthorized users. More companies require the stringent standards used by the U.S. Department of Defense (DOD), which has pioneered security computing. The DOD established levels of security from class A2 (the most stringent) to class D (the least stringent). The DOD defines the requirements for all security levels in their book titled *Department of Defense Trusted Computer System Evaluation Criteria*, otherwise known as the Orange Book.

This chapter covers the following SQL Server security topics.

- Roles and role management, SQL Server's basic strategy for assigning privileges based on user status

- User management

- Managing permissions

- Auditing

Basic Security: Roles and Ownership

Requiring authorization to perform SQL Server tasks, and ownership of databases and database objects, are simple ways to define roles and responsibilities within the SQL Server environment. We briefly explore these issues in the following sections.

User Roles for Tasks

The most fundamental level of security in SQL Server is enforced by Sybase user roles. Roles are special privileges granted for individual accountability to users performing tasks within SQL Server. Roles let you to categorize users by the types of tasks they are allowed to perform. Roles provide accountability for users performing administrative tasks. These tasks can be audited and attributed to them.

Three different role categories can be assigned to individual SQL Server login accounts. Users with the system administration role (SA) have permissions to perform administration tasks. Users with the role of system security officer (SSO) can perform security-related tasks, and users with operator role (OPER) have permissions to perform backup and restore procedures. Table 13-1 summarizes the roles and the tasks associated with them.

Table 13-1. *User roles and their permissions*

Role	Description
System Administration (SA)	A user with SA role can perform all administrative tasks commonly required for day-to-day activities. The SA role can be granted to either one user or a group of users. If the SA role is granted to a user group, it is important to coordinate SA functions well. Because SQL Server does not check for permissions when an SA accesses objects, it is important to make sure that only appropriate users are granted SA role. Some of the activities that an SA can perform include the following. • Installing SQL Server • Granting and revoking permissions to SQL Server users • Diagnosing system problems • Managing disk storage • Monitoring SQL Server's recovery activities • Transferring bulk data between SQL Server and other software • Fine-tuning SQL Server performance • Setting up groups • Creating user databases and granting ownership to them • Granting and revoking the SA role to other users
System Security Officer (SSO)	The SSO is responsible for all security related tasks in SQL Server. These tasks include the following. • Creating login accounts • Granting and revoking SSO and OPER roles • Changing passwords of any SQL Server user account • Managing all auditing activities

(continued)

Table 13-1. *(continued)*

Role	Description
	• Setting the configuration option *systemwide* password expiration
	• Only the SSO can access, update, or drop the *sybsecurity* system database. Also, only the SSO can execute certain system stored procedures, such as **sp_modifylogin**, which changes a user's login name.
Operator (OPER)	An operator can perform all backup tasks, such as those listed here.
	• Backups using **dump database** and **dump tran** commands (Chapter 14, Backup and Recovery, details these commands)
	• Restore databases and transaction logs from dumps using **load database** and **load tran** commands

Data Ownership

In addition to the SA, SSO, and OPER roles, which apply to tasks that users perform, SQL Server recognizes database owners (DBO) and database object owners (DBOO). The database owner is a user who creates a database or someone to whom database ownership role has been granted. A database owner can freely access all database objects inside the database he or she owns. The database owner can grant other users permission to create database objects (such as tables, stored procedures, triggers, and so on) within a database. The owner can also grant other users access to a database using the system procedure **sp_adduser** (described later in this chapter in the "Managing User Access" section).

A user who creates a database object owns the object and is referred to as a DBOO. DBOOs can grant or revoke permissions on their database objects to other users.

Granting and Revoking Roles

In general, the SSO can grant SSO and OPER roles to other users. An SA can grant the SA role to other users.

When SQL Server is installed for the first time, it includes an account called *sa*, which is granted complete access to the entire system and can perform any administrative function. The *sa* account has the privileges of the SA, SSO, and OPER roles. As a security precaution, the SSO, who can change SA, SSO, and OPER roles for other logins, should decentralize *sa*'s tasks by granting its roles to three separate logins. Roles can be granted and revoked using the system procedure **sp_role**, the syntax for which is provided in Table 13-2.

Table 13-2. *Syntax and parameters for* **sp_role**

sp_role {"grant" | "revoke"}, {*sa_role* | *sso_role* | *oper_role*}, *login_name*	
login_name *sa_role,* *sso_role,* or *oper_role*	Login name of the user to whom the role is being granted or revoked. When using this command, choose one of *sa_role, sso_role,* or *oper_role* to apply to the user. The newly granted role takes effect the next time the user logs into SQL Server. You cannot revoke a role from a user who is currently logged in.

Example 1: This command grants SA role to user *robin*. The SA role takes effect the next time *robin* logs into SQL Server. However, *robin* can immediately enable the SA role by using the **set role** command, which is discussed after these examples.

```
sp_role "grant", sa_role, robin
go
```

Example 2: This command revokes OPER role from the user with login *gita*.

```
sp_role "revoke", oper_role, gita
go
```

Turning Roles On and Off

When you log in, all roles assigned to you are automatically enabled. To enable or disable roles for the current session, use the command **set role**, the syntax for which is provided in Table 13-3.

Table 13-3. Syntax and parameters for *set_role*.

set role "{sa_role | sso_role | oper_role}" {on | off}	
sa_role, sso_role, oper_role	The role you want to enable or disable
on | off	Use *on* or *off* to enable or disable a role

Example: The following command disables the SA role assigned to user *ruby*. User *ruby* executes this command.

```
set role "sa_role" off
go
```

Getting Information About Roles

The system procedure **sp_displaylogin** and the functions **show_role** and **proc_role** allow you to check roles granted to you or others. The **sp_display-login** procedure displays all of the information about a particular *login_name*. The syntax is as follows.

sp_displaylogin *login_name*

Example: Here's an example for a user with the SA role, followed by its resulting output.

```
sp_displaylogin sa
go
Suid: 1
Loginame: sa
Fullname:
Configured Authorization: sa_role sso_role oper_role replication_role
Locked: NO
Date of Last Password Change: Oct 17 1996 12:02PM
(return status = 0)
```

The **show_role** function displays information about roles enabled in the current login session. The syntax is as follows.

select show_role()

You can use the function **proc_role()** within a stored procedures to check if a particular role is enabled. The next example illustrates one way to use the **proc_role** function.

Example: In this example, the stored procedure **samp_proc** uses the **proc_role** function to check if the user has OPER role. **Proc_role()** returns zero if the user does not have the OPER role, or it returns one if the user has OPER role.

```
create proc samp_proc
as
if (proc_role("oper_role") = 0)
        begin
                print "You don't have the appropriate role"
                return -1
        end
else
        print "You have the OPER role"
return 0
go
```

Managing User Access

SQL Server provides two levels of user access, as Figure 13-1 illustrates. First, you must have access to SQL Server itself, which is done with a login account. Second, you must have access to the databases you need, which is done with user permissions. The sections that follow explain how to log in, add users to a database, and drop users from a database. It also explains what an alias is.

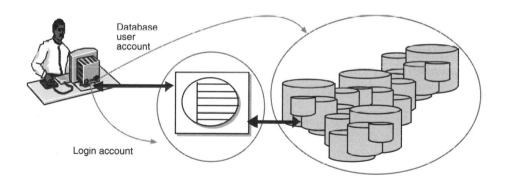

Figure 13-1. *User access is provided via login accounts and database user accounts*

Accessing SQL Server

Because multiple users can access SQL Server simultaneously, every user receives a login account with a unique password. When you log into SQL Server, you must specify your login name and password before you can access any of SQL Server's functionality or data. You can log into SQL Server using **isql**, Client Library, DB Library (introduced in this chapter), or any other application designed for the same purpose. The method you choose depends on the type of work you want to do.

Using isql

Users can log into SQL Server directly from the operating system with the **isql** utility. A commonly-used abbreviated syntax for **isql** follows.

isql -U*username* -P*password*

The *username* and *password* parameters are the user's login name and password. For more information about **isql**, see Chapter 5, Interacting with SQL Server.

Example: A user with login name *rob* logs into SQL Server using the command below.

```
isql -Urob
password:
```

At the password prompt, user *rob* types his password and presses the Return or Enter key. The password is not displayed on the screen while he types it. The following prompt appears on the screen.

```
1>
```

User *Rob* can now interact with SQL Server using Transact-SQL commands. To log out, *Rob* can type **quit** or **exit** at the **isql** prompt.

Using Client Library or DB Library

Both Open Client Client Library and Open Client DB Library provide several routines that handle user authentication and password encryption features between a client and the server. For more information, refer to the *Sybase Open Client Client-Library/C Reference Manual*.

Managing User Logins

The next sections describe many commands for managing user login accounts. Sybase also offers automated administration utilities that you can use to perform these tasks. (SQL Server Manager and Enterprise SQL Server Manager are described in Chapter 15, Database Administration Tools.) The method you choose is a matter of preference in most cases.

Adding Logins

Before users can access the server, their names should be added to a list of valid logins. Logins are added only by a System Security Officer (SSO) using **sp_addlogin**. When executing **sp_addlogin**, SQL Server assigns a unique server user id (*suid*) for the new user and adds a row containing that *suid* to the *syslogins* table in the *master* database. The **sp_addlogin** syntax is provided in Table 13-4.

Table 13-4. *Syntax and parameters for the **sp_addlogin** system procedure*

sp_addlogin *login_name, password*
    [*,defdb*] [*,deflanguage* [, *fullname*]]

login_name	New login name. It must be unique within SQL Server.
password	Password for the new user. Must be at least six characters long.
defdb	Name of the database to which the user is connected immediately after logging in. If not specified, this parameter defaults to the *master* database.
deflanguage	Default language in which the new user's prompts and messages are displayed.
fullname	User's full name.

You can reduce the amount of login name management by using the same SQL Server login name as the user's operating system login name, because many client programs (such as **isql** and Power Builder) use the operating system login name as the default. This simplifies management of both server and operating system login accounts, and makes it easier to correlate usage and audit data generated by SQL Server and the operating system.

Although you can make the *master* database the default database, we recommend that you don't. If you do, users who have necessary permissions to create objects can create tables in the *master* database, which could become full.

Example 1: This command adds a login account for user *lily* and password *goqNrB*. The user's default database is *pubs2*. Because the *deflanguage* parameter is not specified, SQL Server uses the default language to display messages.

```
sp_addlogin lily, goqNrB, pubs2
go
```

Point to Note: All parameters for the **sp_addlogin** command are case sensitive.

Example 2: This example illustrates how you can use a parameter name to pass values to **sp_addlogin**. Here, the user's full name is passed using the *@fullname* variable. The default database and default language are set to their default values. The default database is *master* and the default language is *us_english*.

```
sp_addlogin chris,
    ty125mn, @fullname = "Christopher Alexander"
go
```

Point to Note: A local variable must be declared in the batch, stored procedure, or trigger that will use it.

Denying Users Access to SQL Server

You can deny users access to SQL Server using two different methods. The system procedure **sp_droplogin** completely and permanently drops a user from SQL Server. However, you can neither use this stored procedure if the user is currently in a database, nor can you drop the last SSO or SA login account. If you need to deny access under one of these conditions, use the system procedure **sp_locklogin**. It locks the login and temporarily prevents the user from logging back in. Using **sp_locklogin** without any parameters displays a list of all locked logins. The syntax for **sp_droplogin** and **sp_locklogin** are provided in Tables 13-5 and 13-6, respectively.

Table 13-5. *Syntax and parameters for **sp_droplogin***

sp_droplogin *login_name*	
login_name	User name of the login account to drop

Table 13-6. *Syntax and parameters for **sp_locklogin***

sp_locklogin *login_name* , "{lock | unlock}"	
login_name	Name of the account to be locked or unlocked.
lock | unlock	Specifies whether to lock or unlock the account. You can lock an account that is already logged in, but the user is not locked out of the account until after logging out.

Example 1: This example drops the user with login *andy* from SQL Server.

```
sp_droplogin andy
go
```

Example 2: This example locks *jack's* login account.

```
sp_locklogin jack, "lock"
go
```

Point to Note: Only users with SSO and SA roles can execute **sp_locklogin**.

Modifying Logins

You can modify some of the default login parameters, such as the default database, the default language, and the full name using the system procedure **sp_modifylogin**, which has the syntax provided in Table 13-7.

Table 13-7. *Syntax and parameters for the* **sp_modifylogin** *procedure*

sp_modifylogin *login_name, option, value*		
login_name	Name of the user account to modify.	
option	Tells SQL Server which default to change. It can be one of the following.	
	defdb	Database to which the user is connected after logging in.
	deflanguage	Name of the user's default language. The language options are *us_english*, *french*, *spanish*, *chinese*, *japanese*, and *german*.
	fullname	Full name of the user.

Changes to a user's default database take effect the next time the user logs in. However, simply changing a user's default database will not give the user access to the database if he or she is not registered as a user in that database. Use the **sp_adduser** system procedure (described later in this chapter) to add a user to a database.

Example: Here's the command to change the default database of user *tom* to *sampdb*.

```
sp_modifylogin tom, defdb, sampdb
go
```

Changing Passwords

Users can change their passwords using the **sp_password** system procedure.
You can use the configuration parameter *systemwide password expiration* (also
called *password expiration interval* in previous releases) to force users to modify
their passwords on a regular basis. This parameter sets the number of days that
passwords remain in effect after the passwords have been changed. The default
value, zero, sets no expiration date. If the parameter is set to any number greater
than zero, all passwords expire after the specified number of days. When the
number of days remaining before expiration is less than 25 percent of the value
of system password expiration or seven days (whichever is greater), every time
users log in a message indicates the number of days remaining before their
passwords expire. Users can change their passwords at any time before the old
one expires. Table 13-8 gives the syntax for **sp_password**.

Table 13-8. *Syntax and parameters for the **sp_password** procedure*

sp_password *caller_passwd*, *new_passwd* [, *login_name*]	
caller_passwd	Password of the user currently executing **sp_password**.
new_passwd	New password for the user executing **sp_password**.
login_name	Name of the user whose password is being changed. (This can be used only by an SSO.)

Example 1: This command sets the system-wide password expiration to 100
days. After 75 percent of the interval has elapsed, which in this case is after 75
days, every time the user logs in, SQL Server issue a message indicating the
number of days remaining before the password expires. At the end of the configured interval, the user can still log on, but cannot execute any command
other than **sp_password**.

```
sp_configure "systemwide password expiration", 100
go
```

Example 2: This command changes a user's password from *cefi89* to *ma3ui0*.
The user can execute this command.

```
sp_password "cefi89", "ma3ui0"
go
```

Example 3: This example illustrates how to modify another user's password,
which you can do only if you have SSO role. In this command, the password of

user *jerome* is changed to *8iuy4y*. The password of the SSO executing the command is *3p9iu9*.

```
sp_password "3p9iu9", 8iuy4y, jerome
go
```

Point to Note: A password of *null* is not allowed.

Managing Access to Databases

In a multiuser environment, several users can have permission to log into SQL Server. A database contains database objects such as tables, views, and stored procedures that might hold sensitive data, so it is often important to prevent unauthorized users from accessing a particular database. It is the database owner's responsibility to allow or restrict access to his or her database.

Adding a User to a Database

The DBO or SA can expand a user's access to other databases with the system procedure **sp_adduser**, which adds the user to the database from which it is executed. The DBO or SA can also add a guest user to a database so that even unregistered users can access the database. When you add user name *guest* to a database, guest inherits the privileges of *public*. Then, anyone who has a login account for SQL Server can easily access the database. However, you should keep in mind that this is not a secure database.

This feature is provided as a convenience to accommodate temporary users, but guest users are normally granted very restricted privileges. It is up to the owner of the database to grant or revoke permissions to the guest user. Because *guest* is not a registered user, you should be careful while granting permissions to *public*. Executing an **sp_adduser** command adds a row to the *sysusers* system table in the current database. Table 13-9 shows the syntax.

Table 13-9. *Syntax and parameters for the **sp_adduser** procedure*

sp_adduser *login_name* [, *name_in_db* [, *group_name*]]	
login_name	Login name of the existing user.
name_in_db	Alternate name by which the user is to be known inside the database. If not specified, the user's name inside the database is the same as the *login_name*.

(continued)

Table 13-9. *(continued)*

group_name	Name of an existing group in the database to which the user is added. If not specified, the user is made a member of the default group *public*.

When a login account is established, the user has access only to his or her default database. Suppose there are two users, *Judy Taylor* and *Judy Chang* with login names *judyt* and *judyc*, respectively. If both the users would like to be known as *Judy* inside their default databases, the *name_in_db* parameter allows users to specify a name different from the user's login name by which the user is known inside the database. The next examples illustrate how to add users using defaults, to assign an alias, and to add a guest user.

Example 1: This simple command gives access to user *robh*. Because neither *name_in_db* nor *group name* is specified, user *robh* is added to the *public* group and is known as *robh* within the database.

```
sp_adduser robh
go
```

Example 2: A DBO issues this command to add user *joeh* to group *engg*. Although the login name is *joeh*, this user is known as *joe* inside the database.

```
sp_adduser joeh, joe, engg
go
```

Example 3: This command adds the *guest* user to the database from which the command is executed.

```
sp_adduser guest
go
```

Dropping a User from a Database

The DBO or SA can drop a user from a database with the **sp_dropuser** system procedure. You cannot drop a user who owns database objects, because object ownership cannot be transferred. You must drop objects owned by a user before dropping the user with the **sp_dropuser** command. Use **sp_dropuser**, the syntax for which is provided in Table 13-10, from within the database for which you are dropping the user.

Table 13-10. *Syntax and parameter for the* **sp_dropuser** *procedure*

sp_dropuser *login_name*	
login_name	Login name of the user to drop

Example: This command drops user *John* from the database *sampdb*.

```
use sampdb
go
sp_dropuser john
go
```

Using Database Aliases

If multiple users need the same privileges in a database, you can use *aliases* so that the database sees all of them as a single user. An alias is simply a user name to which any other user name can be mapped. For example, you can add the alias *admin* as a user in a database *empdb*. If you then map all users working in the *admin* group to this alias, all of these users automatically are recognized as the administrator. One advantage of using aliases is that you can map multiple users to the DBO role; another advantage is that you can track the activities of the users in an alias by tracking the activities of the alias.

To create an alias, you must first use the **sp_adduser** procedure to add the alias name as a user to the database. The alias is created for the database from which the command is executed. Then, you can map any number of users to the alias with the **sp_addalias** system procedure. The user to whom you are mapping the alias name must have an account with SQL Server but cannot be a user in the database for which he or she is receiving the alias. Table 13-11 shows the syntax for the **sp_addalias** system procedure.

Table 13-11. *Syntax and parameters for the* **sp_dropuser** *procedure*

sp_addalias *login_name, name_in_db*	
login_name	Name of the user name to map to the alias
name_in_db	Alias name to which *login_name* is mapped

You can drop an alias using the **sp_dropalias** system procedure. If the alias is dropped from a database, all of the users mapped to the alias name lose access to the database. Table 13-12 shows the syntax for **sp_dropalias.**

Table 13-12. *Syntax and parameters for the **sp_dropuser** procedure*

sp_dropalias *login_name*

login_name	Name of the user mapped to the alias name

Example 1: This command adds user *george* to the *admin* alias. The *admin* alias must have been previously added to the database.

```
sp_addalias george, admin
go
```

Example 2: To drop user *george* from the admin alias, use the following command.

```
sp_dropalias george
go
```

What Happens in the Server

When you execute the **sp_addalias** procedure, SQL Server maps the specified login name (*login_name*) to the specified name in the database (*name_in_db*). SQL Server also adds a row to the system table *sysalternates*. When a user attempts to use a database, SQL Server checks for the user's server user id (*suid*) in the *sysusers* system table. If the *suid* is not found, the server checks the *sysalternates* table. If the user's *suid* is found in the *sysalternates* table, the first user is not distinguished from the second user in the database.

Using Groups

Groups let you use a single command to handle permissions for multiple users. Suppose several users need to access a particular table. Instead of granting permission to each user separately, you can create a group for all of the users and grant permission for the entire group. For example, because it is easier to grant and revoke permission for an entire group of engineers than it is to grant and revoke permissions for each engineer separately, you can create a group called *engg* in the *empdb* database, then add all of the engineers to that group. An SSO or DBO can create a group using the system procedure **sp_addgroup** and drop a group using **sp_dropgroup**, as shown in Table 13-13.

Table 13-13. Syntax and parameter for the **sp_addgroup** and **sp_dropgroup** procedures

---

sp_addgroup *group_name*
sp_dropgroup *group_name*

group_name   Name of the group to add or drop

Example 1: This command creates a group called *serverengg*.

```
sp_addgroup serverengg
go
```

Example 2: This command drops the *serverengg* group.

```
sp_dropgroup serverengg
go
```

What Happens in the Server

When you create a group, SQL Server adds a row to the *sysusers* system table in the current database.

Point to Note: A user can be attached to only one group. Identify each user's primary role and attach the user to that group. For example, if you want a user to have the permissions of group A and group B, attach the user to one of the groups and specifically grant the user the permissions associated with the other group.

Managing Permissions

SQL Server provides several commands and features that prevent unauthorized access of database objects and unauthorized use of SQL Server commands. You can grant and revoke permissions to access and update database objects (*database object permissions*) and to execute commands (*command permissions*). You can assign permissions based on individual users, roles, or groups. The next sections describe how to grant and revoke these permissions using the **grant** and **revoke** commands.

Granting and Revoking Database Object Permissions

You can protect database objects by associating permissions with users, roles, or groups for performing **select**, **update**, **delete**, **insert**, **references**, and **execute** commands. Object permissions apply to specific database objects in the database from which you execute the command. Table 13-14 summarizes which objects are affected by the permissions for each command.

Table 13-14. Objects affected by object permissions

Command	Objects permissions affected
select	Table, view, and column
update	Table, view, and column
delete	Table and view
insert	Table and view
references	Table
execute	Stored procedure

Database object owners can grant or revoke permissions to their objects. By default, only SAs and DBOs have permission to use the commands listed in the left column of Table 13-14 on the objects listed in the table's right column. However, SAs and DBOs can use the **grant** command to make database objects accessible to other users. They can also revoke those permissions using the **revoke** command. Table 13-15 gives the syntax for the **grant** and **revoke** commands.

Table 13-15. Syntax and parameters for the **grant** and **revoke** database object permissions commands

grant [grant option for]
{all [privileges] | *permission_list*}
on { *table_name* [(*column_list*)]
   | *view_name* [(*column_list*)]
   | *stored_procedure_name*}
from {public | *name_list* | *role_name*}
[cascade]
revoke [grant option for]
{all [privileges] | *permission_list*}
on { *table_name* [(*column_list*)]
   | *view_name* [(*column_list*)]
   | *stored_procedure_name*}
from {public | *name_list* | *role_name*}
[cascade]

(continued)

Table 13-15. *(continued)*

all	Assigns all permissions (**select, update, delete, insert,** and **references**) applicable to the specified object
permission_list	List of objects that are granted permissions
column_list	List of all columns in the specified table that are granted permissions
public	Used to specify all of the users
name_list	List of users' database names and group names
role_name	Name of the SQL Server role
with grant option	Allows the users specified in *name_list* to grant object access permissions to other users
cascade	Used to revoke access permission for the specified object from all users who were granted permission for the object with the *grant* option

The next four examples show how to grant and revoke command permissions for individual users, for groups of users, and on columns.

Example 1: This command grants **select** permission on the *emp* table to user *robin* and user group *engg*.

```
grant select
  on emp
  to robin, engg
go
```

Example 2: This command revokes the *execute* permission on the stored procedure *emp_proc* from all users who have SSO roles.

```
revoke execute
  on emp_proc
  from sso_role
go
```

Example 3: This command grants **delete** and **update** permission on the *sales* table to user *alvin*. After this command executes, user *alvin* can grant update and delete permissions to other users.

```
grant delete, update
  on sales
  to alvin
  with grant option
go
```

Example 4: This example revokes **select** permissions on columns *title*, *title_id*, and *pub_id* of the *titles* table from all users except for the group *pubs*. First, the **revoke** command revokes all permissions on *titles* table from all users. Then, the **grant** command grants **select** permission for the three columns *title*, *title_id*, and *pub_id* to the group *pubs*.

```
revoke all on titles from public
go
grant select (title, title_id, pub_id)
  to pubs
go
```

Points to Note: Granting and Revoking Database Object Permissions

Bear the following factors in mind when you grant or revoke permissions for database objects.

- If you are granting or revoking permissions on a table or view and you do not specify any columns in the column list, the permissions apply to all columns of the table or view.

- The privilege list can include any combination of **select, insert, delete, update,** and **references**.

- You cannot include **insert** or **delete** commands in the privilege list for columns, because these commands do not apply to columns. Permissions granted to roles override permissions granted to users or user groups.

Granting and Revoking Command Permissions

Command permissions determine which users can execute the SQL Server commands that create databases and the objects within those databases—commands such as **create table**, **create default**, **create rule**, and **create view**. Command permissions are not specific to a particular object; they are specific to a user, role, or group, and apply only to all objects in a particular database. Only SAs and DBOs can grant command permissions.

The **grant** and **revoke** commands manage command permissions. The syntax for these commands is given in Table 13-16.

Table 13-16. *Syntax and parameters for the **grant** and **revoke** command permissions commands*

grant {all [privileges] | *command_list*}
on {public | *name_list* | *role_name*}
revoke{all [privileges] | *command_list*}
on {public | *name_list* | *role_name*}

all	Assigns all permissions: **create database**, **create default**, **create rule**, **create procedure**, **create table**, and **create view**
command_list	List of commands that are granted permissions
public	Specifies all users
name_list	List of users' database names and group names
role_name	Name of a SQL Server role

Example 1: This example revokes command execution permissions for the **create table** and **create index** commands for user *joe*.

```
revoke create table, create view
  from joe
go
```

Example 2: This command grants permissions for all commands to the user group *sa_only*. If you have *sa_role* and are issuing the command from within the *master* database, it means **create database**, **create default**, and **create rule**.

```
grant all
  to sa_only
go
```

What Happens in the Server

When you execute the **grant** or **revoke** permissions command, SQL Server stores the permission information in system table *sysprotects*.

Getting Information About Permissions

Several stored procedures provide information about command and object permissions. These commands are **sp_helprotect**, **sp_column_privileges**, and **sp_table_privileges**. We discuss each of these commands separately in the next three sections.

sp_helprotect

The system procedure **sp_helprotect** reports on permissions by database object or by user. The syntax for this procedure is provided in Table 13-17.

Table 13-17. *Syntax and parameters for the **sp_helprotect** procedure*

sp_helprotect *name* [, *name_in_db* [, "grant"]]	
name	Name of the table, view, stored procedure, user, group, or role in the current database
name_in_db	Name of the user in that database
grant	Displays all permissions provided by the **grant** option

Example: This command displays all permissions of user *ron* on the *emp* table, as in indicated in the output that follows the command.

```
sp_helprotect emp, ron
go

grantor  grantee  type  action  object  column  grantable
-------  -------  ----  ------  ------  ------  ---------
dbo      ron      Grant Select  emp     All     FALSE
```

sp_column_privileges

The **sp_column_privileges** system procedure returns information about permissions on columns in a table. The syntax is provided in Table 13-18.

Table 13-18. *Syntax and parameters for the **sp_column_privileges** procedure*

sp_column_privileges *table_name* [, *table_owner* [, *table_qualifier* [, *column_name*]]]	
table_name	Name of the table
table_owner	Name of the table owner
table_qualifier	Name of the current database
column_name	Name of the column

Example: The following command checks for the permissions on column *emp_name* in table *emp*. The command's output follows the command.

```
sp_column_privileges emp, null, null, emp_name
go
```

| table_qualifier | | table_owner | table_name | column_name |
grantor	grantee	privilege	is_grantable	
-------	-------	---------	------------	
samp		dbo	emp	emp_name
dbo	john	SELECT	NO	
samp		dbo	emp	emp_name
dbo	dbo	INSERT	YES	
samp		dbo	emp	emp_name
dbo	dbo	SELECT	YES	
samp		dbo	emp	emp_name
dbo	dbo	UPDATE	YES	
samp		dbo	emp	emp_name
dbo	dbo	REFERENCE	YES	

sp_table_privileges

The **sp_table_privileges** system procedure reports on permissions associated with a particular table (in contrast to **sp_column_privileges**, which is for column information). The syntax for **sp_table_privileges** is shows in Table 13-19.

Table 13-19. *Syntax and parameters for the **sp_table_privileges** procedure*

---

sp_table_privileges *table_name*
　　[, *table_owner* [, *table_qualifier*]]

table_name	Name of the table
table_owner	Name of the table owner
table_qualifier	Name of the current database

Example: This command retrieves information about the *emp* table. Its output follows the command.

sp_table_privileges emp
go

table_qualifier		table_owner	table_name	
grantor	grantee	privilege	is_grantable	
---------------	-------	---------	----------	
-------	-------	---------	------------	
samp		dbo	emp	
dbo	john	SELECT	NO	
samp		dbo	emp	
dbo	dbo	INSERT	YES	
samp		dbo	emp	
dbo	dbo	DELETE	YES	
samp		dbo	emp	
dbo	dbo	SELECT	YES	
samp		dbo	emp	
dbo	dbo	UPDATE	YES	

User Permissions

SQL Server users can fall into several privilege categories, each of which has a well-defined set of privileges. The categories are *system administrators*, *security officers*, *operators*, *database owners*, and *database object owners*. We've already discussed the roles associated with these user categories. Table 13-20 identifies the permissions associated with them.

Table 13-20. *User permissions for roles*

Role	Permissions
System Administration (SA)	System administrators operate outside the domain of the command and object protection system, and have all of the permissions on commands and objects at all times. They are similar to "super users" in a UNIX operating system. Here are some of the tasks that only SAs can perform. <ul><li>Use the **create database** command. (SAs can grant this permission to other users.)</li><li>Use the disk related commands, such as **disk init**, **disk refit**, **disk reinit**, and **disk mirror**.</li><li>Use SQL Server shutdown commands.</li><li>Use **kill** commands on a SQL Server process.</li><li>Use the **reconfigure** command to change the configuration of SQL Server.</li></ul>
System Security Officer (SSO)	System security officers perform security sensitive tasks such as managing logins and granting roles. Some of the SSO-exclusive privileges are as follows. <ul><li>Change the password of other SQL Server login accounts.</li><li>Set up login accounts, login aliases, and groups.</li></ul>
Operator (OPER)	Operators have authority to backup and restore databases and transaction logs. The following list summarizes the abilities given to those who have OPER privileges. <ul><li>Dump databases and transaction logs of any database without owner role.</li></ul>

(continued)

Table 13-20. *(continued)*

Role	Permissions
	• Load databases and transaction logs from dump devices.
Database Owner (DBO)	Database owners are users who own databases or have database ownerships transferred to them. Only DBOs and SAs can grant command permissions to other users. Some of the major privileges of DBOs are given below. • Can do anything within the databases they own. • Can transfer to other users the permissions to execute such commands as **create table, create default, create rule**, and **create proc. Create view** can be transferred to other users; however, DBOs cannot transfer permission to execute such commands as **checkpoint, dbcc, and setuser.**
Database Object Owner (DBOO)	Database object owners create and, by default, own database objects such as tables, views, and stored procedures. DBOOs are automatically granted all permissions for the objects they own. All other users, including the DBO, are denied permission on the objects owned by the DBOO, unless the DBOO explicitly grants them permission for the object. Other DBOO privileges are as follows. • Permissions to use commands such as **alter table**, **drop table**, **create index**, **create trigger**, **truncate table** and **update statistics** default to the owner of a table and cannot be transferred to other users. • Permission to drop an object (table, view, index, stored procedure, rule, or default) defaults to its owner and cannot be transferred. • Permissions to use **grant** and **revoke** commands can be transferred to other users.

The **setuser** command is used to "impersonate" the owner. Only a DBO or an SA can impersonate a DBOO. (The opposite is not allowed.) For example, a database owner can use the **setuser** command to impersonate the owner of the database object. The following example illustrates this concept.

Example: If user *ram* owns the *empdb* database and user *Krishna* creates a stored procedure called *emp_proc* in that database, *ram* will not have permissions to access *emp_proc*. But *Ram* can impersonate *Krishna* if he uses this command.

```
setuser "Krishna"
go
execute emp_proc
go
```

The Audit System

In a secure system, it is important to monitor and obtain information about the activities of specific users and how specific objects are accessed. For example, the SSO may want to investigate which users have logged in and tried to access a particular table that contains sensitive data. The information of who logged in and when is maintained in the *sysaudits* table (accessible only to the SSO) and is called the *audit trail*. The audit trail is a log of audit records that allows the SSO to reconstruct past system events and evaluate their impact. Events include activities such as login, drop, insert, and delete.

The Sybase audit system consists of the *sybsecurity* database and the *audit queue*. The *sysbsecurity* database has all of the tables required to store the auditing information. The audit queue contains the audit records before they were written to the audit system. The audit queue and its relationship to the audit system are discussed in a later section.

The *sybsecurity* Database

The *sybsecurity* database is created as a part of the auditing installation process. This database has all of the system tables that are in the *model* database and two additional system tables: *sysauditoptions* and *sysaudits*. The *sysaudits* table has information about the audit trail. For example, it contains information about a user who logged in, what time the user logged in, and a record of all the user's activities.

The *sysauditoptions* table contains all the global auditing choices that affect SQL Server as a whole. Some of the options found in this table are presented in Table 13-21. As for all commands, the Transact-SQL Quick Reference in the appendices provides complete syntax.

Table 13-21. *Options for the* **sysauditoptions** *table*

Option	Description
enable auditing	Enables or disables system-wide auditing
logins	Enables or disables auditing of successful, failed or all (successful and failed) login attempts by all users
server boots	Enables or disables generation of an audit record when the server is rebooted

The Audit Queue

When an audited event occurs, the audit record goes first to the in-memory audit queue, where it is held until it is handled by the audit process and added to the audit trail. The SSO can configure the size of the audit queue, which is determined by the amount of auditing required at the specific site. The size is important. If the audit queue size is configured too small, it can result in performance degradation, because the audit record will constantly be written to the audit trail. On the other hand, if the audit queue size is too large, the audit record must wait longer and, if a system crash occurs during this time, the audit record information is lost. We recommend starting with an audit queue size of 100 so that the audit queue can store up to 100 records. However, you will need to optimize the value for most applications.

Figure 13-2 shows the flow of audit data. In step 1, the user tries to insert data into *Table1*. Auditing has been set up. In step 2, permissions are checked, and information about the command and process are recorded in the audit queue in shared memory in a location different from where the data and procedure caches are located. In step 3, rows from the audit queue are copied to disk to the *sysaudits* table in the *sysbsecurity* database. In step 4, auditing saves the information in case it is needed later, so it is necessary to copy *sysaudits* to an archive location. In step 5, data is copied to the storage media using the **dump database** command or the **bcp** utility. Alternatively, you could copy the information directly to tape rather than carry out steps 4 and 5.

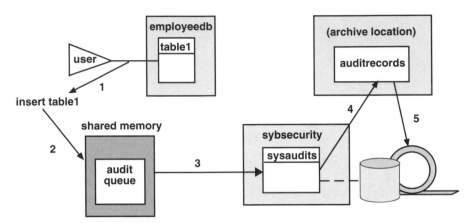

Figure 13-2. *The flow of audit data*

Enabling and Disabling Auditing

When the *sybsecurity* database is installed, no auditing actually occurs until auditing is turned on. The system procedure **sp_auditoption** enables or disables global audit options. Global audit options are those options that affect a server as a whole. Auditing is used for tracing activities of specific logins or users. Table 13-22 shows the four categories of auditable activities.

Table 13-22. *Auditable activities*

Group	Activities
SQL Server level	Logins, logouts, reboots, and fatal errors
Database level	**Grant, revoke, truncate table, use,** and **drop**
Object level	Accessing tables, views, procedures, and triggers
User level	Accessing tables, views, and commands

You enable auditing using the system procedure **sp_auditoption**. Table 13-23 gives the syntax.

Table 13-23. *Syntax and parameters for the **sp_auditoption** procedure*

sp_auditoption *"option"* [, "{on | off}"]	
option	*Option* can be one of the following.

"enable auditing"	Enables or disables system-wide auditing
"all"	Enables or disables all options (except *enable auditing*)
"logins"	Enables or disables successful or failed login attempts of all users
"logouts"	Enables or disables successful or failed logout attempts of all users
"server boots"	Enables or disables auditing whenever a server is rebooted
"roles"	Audits the use of the **set role** command
"{sa | sso | oper}"	Audits the use of privileged commands requiring *sa, sso,* or *oper* roles
"errors"	Audits fatal errors
{on | off}	Enables or disables the specified option

Example: This example illustrates how to enable auditing.

```
sp_auditoption "enable auditing", "on"
go
```

System Procedures for Auditing Events

The following sections discuss these stored procedures, which you can use to audit a variety of events.

- **sp_auditdatabase** For auditing database events

- **sp_auditobject** For auditing object events

- **sp_auditsproc** For auditing stored procedures

- **sp_auditlogin** For auditing users

Auditing Databases

The system procedure **sp_auditdatabase** allows you to establish selective auditing on databases. The events that can be audited include those activities resulting from the use of **drop**, **grant**, **revoke,** and **truncate** commands within a database, and those activities resulting from the use of **drop** database and **use** commands on a database. The syntax for **sp_auditdatabase** appear in Table 13-24.

*Table 13-24. Syntax and parameters for the **sp_auditdatabase** procedure*

sp_auditdatabase [*dbname* [, {"ok | fail | both | off" [, "d u g r t o"}]]	
dbname	Name of the database for which activities are audited
ok	Establishes auditing of successful executions of the commands specified in the third parameter
fail audits access	Attempts that fail due to permission problems
both	Audits both successful and failed executions
off	Disables auditing in the database
d, u, g, r, t, o	Refers to the type of database events that are auditable.
	d Audits execution of the **drop table, drop view, drop proc,** or **drop triggers** command
	u Audits execution of the **use** command (**use**
database_name)	
	g Audits execution of the **grant** command
	r Audits execution of the **revoke** command
	t Audits execution of the **truncate table** command
	o Audits execution of SQL commands within another database

Example: This example sets up auditing in the database *empdb* on the **grant** and **truncate table** commands.

```
sp_auditdatabase empdb,"ok","gt"
go
```

Auditing Objects

The system procedure **sp_auditobject**, the syntax for which appears in Table

13-25, enables auditing of access to specified tables and views. Here, the term *access* is the use of a **select**, **insert**, **update** or **delete** command on a table or view. Auditing can be established on existing tables and views, or you can create default audit settings for newly created tables and views.

Table 13-25. *Syntax and parameters for the **sp_auditdatabase** procedure*

sp_auditobject *objname*, *dbname* [, {"ok | fail | both | off" [, "d i s u "}]]	
objname	Name of the database object whose activities are audited
ok	Establishes auditing of successful executions of the commands specified in the third parameter
fail	Audits access attempts that fail due to permission problems
both	Audits both successful and failed executions
off	Disables auditing of the database object
d	Refers to the auditing delete operation of the database object
i	Refers to the auditing insert operation in the database object
s	Refers to the auditing select operation of database object
u	Refers to the auditing update operation of database object

Example: This example audits all attempts to access the *emp* table and audits update operations on the *emp* table.

```
sp_auditobject emp, empdb, "both", "u"
go
```

Auditing Stored Procedures

The **sp_auditsproc** system procedure sets up auditing on stored procedures and triggers. You can establish auditing of existing stored procedures and triggers, or create default settings for future stored procedures and triggers. The syntax for **sp_auditsproc** is provided in Table 13-26.

Table 13-26. *Syntax and parameters for the **sp_auditsproc** procedure*

sp_auditsproc {*sproc_name* | "all"}, *dbname* [, {"ok" | "fail" | "both" | "off"}]	
sproc_name	Name of the stored procedure or trigger that is audited

(continued)

Table 13-26. *(continued)*

all	Enables auditing of all existing triggers and stored procedures
ok	Audits successful executions of the specified stored procedure or trigger
fail	Audits attempts to execute that fail due to permission problems
both	Audits both successful and failed executions
off	Disables auditing of the stored procedure or trigger

Example: This example audits the successful execution of stored procedure *emp_proc* in the *empdb* database.

```
sp_auditsproc emp_proc, empdb, "ok"
go
```

Auditing Users

The system procedure **sp_auditlogin** is used to audit a SQL Server user's attempts to access tables and views in any database, and the text of commands that the user sends to SQL Server. The syntax of the **sp_auditlogin** procedure is provided in Table 13-27.

Table 13-27. *Syntax and parameters for the* **sp_auditlogin** *procedure*

sp_auditlogin [*login_name* [, "table | view"
  [, "ok | fail | both | off"]]]

login_name	Login name of the SQL Server user
ok	Audits successful access of the specified table or view
fail	Audits failed attempts to access the specified table or view
both	Audits both successful and failed access
off	Disables auditing of the user's attempt to access the specified table or view

Example: This example audits any failed attempts by user *joe* to access table *emp*.

```
sp_auditlogin "joe", "emp", "fail"
go
```

How to Manage Audit Data

Audit data is stored in system table *sysaudits*. Depending on the extent of auditing, this table could fill quickly. If the *sysaudits* table is full, the audit task dies and the records currently in the audit queue are lost. Therefore, it is important to periodically archive *sysaudits* data to a storage medium. You can either archive manually or through a threshold action if *sysaudits* resides in its own segment.

Exercises

13-1.   While adding logins to SQL Server, if the *defdb* parameter is omitted, what will be the user's default database?

13-2.   What command do you use to change the default database to *sampdb*?

13-3.   Execution of **sp_addlogin** requires which of the following permissions?
  a. *sa_role*
  b. *sso_role*
  c. *DBO*
  d. *oper_role*

13-4.   When a user logs in, in which system table does SQL Server look for the user's login and password?

13-5.   What steps does SQL Server perform to verify access to a database?

13-6.   How do you temporarily disable *sa_role* for a session?

13-7.   Your DBA has left on a long vacation and has not left any notes. Assuming no one else has the *sa_role*, how would you execute commands that require *sa_role*?

13-8.   What system table is used to map multiple logins to a single user ID within a database?

13-9.   Specify what permission each of the following commands requires.
  a. alter database
  b. create database
  c. revoke on object

d. create view

e. kill

f. shutdown

13-10. Assume you are the DBO. How would you grant permission to delete certain columns of a table?

13-11. How can you verify if auditing has been installed on a SQL Server?

13-12. What happens to the audited process if the audit queue becomes full?

13-13. How do you disable auditing for an entire SQL Server?

13-14. If you want to audit all of the successful modifications of the *sales* table in the *sampdb* database owned by user *john*, what command would you use?

Answers to Exercises

13-1.   *master* database

13-2.   **sp_modifylogin login_name, defdb, sampdb**

         go

13-3.   b

13-4.   *syslogins*

13-5.   First, SQL Server checks for the user's *suid* in the *sysusers* table of the database and, if an entry exists in the *sysusers* table, it allows the user to access the database. If no entry is found, SQL Server checks for a row in the *sysalternates* table and allows access to the database if it contains an entry for the user's *suid*. If no entry exists even in *sysalternates* table, SQL Server does not allow the user to access the database.

13-6.   **set role sa_role off**

13-7.   Restart SQL Server

13-8.   *sysalternates*

13-9.   (a) SA (b) SA (c) DBOO (d) DBOO (e) SA (f) SA

13-10. Delete permissions do not apply to columns, so they cannot be included in the list.

13-11. Check if the *sybsecuirty* database is installed.

13-12. If the audit queue fills and there is a system crash, the audit record could get lost.

13-13. **sp_auditoption "enable auditing","off"**
        go

13-14. **sp_auditobject john.sales, sampdb, "ok", "uid"**
        go

14

Backup and Recovery

You can use SQL Server's recovery capabilities to protect against data loss that might result from a power outage, hardware failure, or even corruption due to software errors. When you develop and use a good backup and recovery strategy, your system can recover from adverse events without losing data.

The *backup process* is based on variations of the **dump** command. The **dump database** command copies one or more databases to a *dump device*—a disk or tape device. The **dump transaction** command copies a transaction log to a dump device.

The *recovery process* rebuilds by redoing or undoing changes to one or more databases and transaction logs from previously created backups. Recovery can take place automatically or manually using the **load** command.

This chapter explains what's involved with backup and recovery so that you can develop a strategy to protect your system. This chapter covers the following topics.

- A summary of the transaction log and its role in backup and recovery

- An overview of the checkpoint process, which helps you control the frequency of dumps

- The backup process, using the **dump** command for both databases and transaction logs, and for creating and dropping database devices

- The recovery process, including automatic and manual recovery, and using the **load** command for databases and transactions

- Free space thresholds

Backup and Recovery Fundamentals

This section reviews two topics that you must understand to use backup and recovery processes: the transaction log and the checkpoint process.

Transaction Log

The *transaction log* contains the information about each transaction that makes recovery possible. Chapter 10, Transaction Management, introduced the topic of recovery and described the role of the transaction log. To summarize, SQL Server uses transactions to track changes to a database. Each database saves its transaction log in the system table *syslogs*. Recall too that the transaction log uses the write-ahead technique. When a client or user issues a command that modifies a database (**insert**, **update**, or **delete**), the changes are written to the transaction log before they are written to an in-cache copy of the data page. The data page is then written to the disk. SQL Server appends the status of the transaction—either success or failure—at the end of each transaction.

Checkpoint

SQL Server's *checkpoint* process automatically runs in the background and periodically examines each database. It writes log pages and modified data pages from the cache to the disk. During recovery, SQL Server uses each database's transaction log to restore the database to its pre-crash state.

The greater the amount of unwritten transaction information in the log, the longer it takes to restore a database. You can set a limit on the length of time it takes to restore a database from the log by setting the modifiable configuration parameter, *recovery interval*. The checkpoint process ensures that recovery does not take longer than the time in minutes that you set for this parameter.

When a checkpoint is issued, either automatically or through the **checkpoint** command, the checkpoint process performs the following actions.

- Prevents any new transactions from starting in the database for a fraction of a second

- Allows current transactions to continue

- Writes all data and log pages from the cache to the disk

- Writes a checkpoint record in the log

Checkpoints occur due to one of the following circumstances.

- SQL Server automatically does a checkpoint on the basis of the value of recovery interval

- Users can manually force all modified pages in memory to be written to disk through the **checkpoint** command

The *checkpoint process* does a checkpoint for all databases. The **checkpoint** command, by contrast, does a checkpoint only in the database in which you execute the command.

Recovery Interval

The checkpoint process awakens once every minute or so and checks each database on the server to determine how many records have been added to the transaction log since the last checkpoint. This information is used to estimate how long it would take for the server to recover in the case of a failure. If this estimate is longer than the configured recovery interval, the checkpoint process writes the modified pages to the disk. Table 14-1 shows how to set the recovery interval.

Table 14-1. *Syntax and parameter for the **recovery** command*

sp_configure "recovery interval", n	
n	The time interval in minutes that it takes to recover each database

Example: The following command sets the recovery interval to four minutes. SQL Server automatically issues a checkpoint if it estimates that the time it needs to recover is more than four minutes.

```
sp_configure "recovery interval", 4
go
```

Backup and the Dump Command

If a media failure such as a disk crash occurs, databases are only restorable if you have made regular backups. The next sections describe the backup process and how to use the dump command for dumping databases and transaction logs, the types of database devices, and how to add and drop a dump device.

The Backup Process

The **dump database** command makes a physical backup of an entire database, including the data and transaction log. In Figure 14-1, both the data and the transaction log are copied to the backup device (either a tape or a disk). Users can continue working with the databases during a backup performed with SQL Server's **dump database** command.

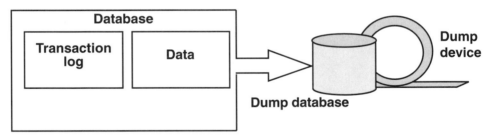

Figure 14-1. *Both transaction log and data are copied with the **dump database** command*

It is also possible to make a physical backup of only the transaction log using the **dump transaction** command. This command is similar to making incremental backups using the operating system. The inactive portion of the transaction log is *truncated* (deleted) as soon as the **dump tran** command completes. Dumping the transaction log is less space- and time-consuming than the dump database process, but it must take place more frequently. Figure 14-2 illustrates the **dump transaction** command in which only the transaction log is copied to the dump device.

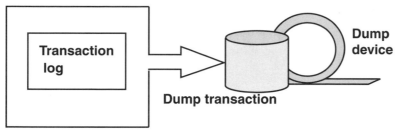

Figure 14-2. *Only the transaction log is copied with the **dump transaction** command*

Dumping Databases

The **dump database** command copies the entire database to the dump device. The process does not truncate the transaction log. SQL Server executes the dump process in three phases and prints informational messages at the end of each phase. Here's what the **dump database** command does.

1. Performs a checkpoint

2. Copies all of the allocated pages for both data and the log to the dump device

3. Copies all of the transactions that occurred while dumping the database

Table 14-2 provides an abbreviated version of the **dump database** command with its most commonly used parameters. The Transact-SQL Quick Reference at the back of this book lists the full syntax for this command.

Table 14-2. *Syntax and parameters for the **dump database** command*

dump database *database_name*
    to stripe_device [at *server_name*]
    [, stripe on *stripe_device*
    [at *server_name*] ...
    [with { dumpvolume = *volume_name*,
    [nounload | unload], ...
    [noinit | init], }]

database_name	Name of the database that is dumped.
stripe on	Writes a single database concurrently across multiple tapes.

(continued)

Table 14-2. *(continued)*

stripe_device	Logical name of the dump device.
server_name	Name of the remote backup server.
dumpvolume	Volume name.
nounload/unload	Used for tape devices, *unload* rewinds the tape and unloads it, while *nonunload* does not rewind and unload after writing.
noinit/init	Used for tape devices, the *init* option overwrites the existing tape contents. The default *noinit* option appends each dump to the tape following the last end-of-tape mark. You can choose to append or not depending on the archive device.

Example 1: The following command dumps a database *sampdb* on a disk as a UNIX operating system file.

```
dump database sampdb
  to "/work/samp_dmp"
go
```

Example 2: On Windows NT, the following command dumps a database *empdb* on a disk.

```
dump database empdb
  to "d:\work\emp_dmp"
go
```

Types of Dump Devices

Dump devices can be either disks or tapes. You can dump only one database to a disk, because the disk is initialized every time a dump occurs. In the case of certain tape devices, multiple databases can be dumped onto the same tape. A database can be dumped across multiple tapes concurrently. This is called *striping*. (See Chapter 6, Database Devices and Fault Tolerance, for information about how to use the **sp_addumpdevice** and **sp_dropdevice** system procedures.)

Examples: Dump Device Types

The following examples show the three possible dump device types: a single database to a single device, multiple databases to a single device, and a single database to multiple devices in the UNIX environment. One example shows a dump in a Windows NT environment.

Example 1: Figure 14-3 illustrates the result of the given command. It shows one database dumped to a single tape.

```
dump database sampdb
  to TAPEDEV1
go
```

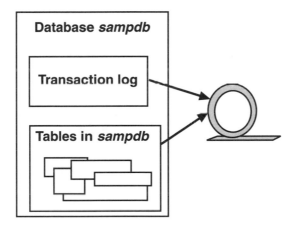

Figure 14-3. Dumping a single database

Example 2: Figure 14-4 illustrates the result of using the given commands to dump several databases to the same tape device.

```
dump database empdb
  to TAPEDEV2
go
dump database salesdb
  to TAPEDEV2
go
dump database mktgdb
  to TAPEDEV2
go
```

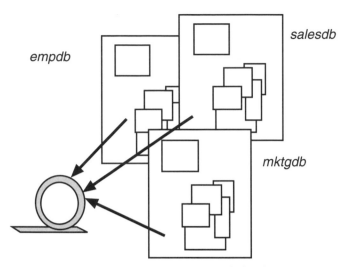

Figure 14-4. *Dumping several databases*

Example 3: Figure 14-5 conceptually illustrates how to dump three different databases to the same tape device.

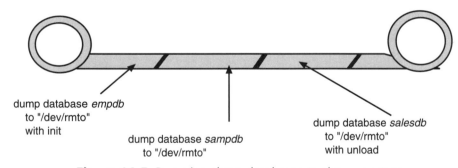

dump database *empdb*
to "/dev/rmto"
with init

dump database *sampdb*
to "/dev/rmto"

dump database *salesdb*
to "/dev/rmto"
with unload

Figure 14-5. *Dumping three databases to the same tape*

Example 4: Figure 14-6 illustrates a striped dump for which a single database is concurrently dumped to three different tape devices, as the following commands do.

```
dump database empdb
 to TAPEDEV1
stripe on TAPEDEV2
stripe on TAPEDEV3
go
```

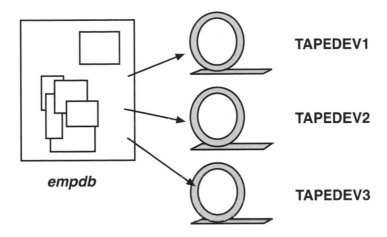

Figure 14-6. *Multivolume dumps*

Example 5: On Windows NT, the following command dumps the database *empdb* to a disk device.

```
dump database empdb
  to "d:\work\emp_dmp"
go
```

Dumping Transaction Logs

You should dump the transaction log often to ensure complete recovery in case of server or media failure. The **dump transaction** command dumps databases for this purpose. The command makes a backup copy of a database's transaction log, then truncates the inactive portion of the log.

Figure 14-7 illustrates what a **dump transaction** command does. The inactive portion represents all committed transactions, which are deleted after a dump of the entire log.

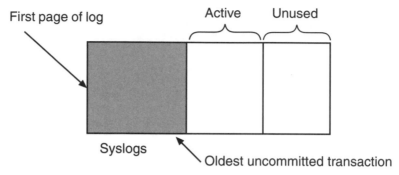

Figure 14-7. Effect of dumping transactions

Table 14-3 shows an abbreviated version of the **dump transaction,** or **dump tran,** command with its most commonly used parameters.

Table 14-3. Syntax and parameters for the **dump transaction** command

dump transaction *database_name*
    to *stripe_device* [at *b_server_name*]
    [, stripe on *stripe_device* [at *b_server_name*]]
    [with { dumpvolume = *volume_name*,
    [nounload | unload],
    [truncate_only | no_log | no_truncate]}]

database_name	Name of the database that is dumped.
volume_name	Volume name.
nounload/unload	Used for tape devices, *unload* rewinds the tape and unloads it, while *nonunload* does not rewind and unload after writing.
truncate_only	Truncates the transaction log without dumping to the dump device. This clears committed transactions.
no_log	Truncates the transaction log without dumping to the dump device and without recording the transaction. Clears inactive transactions.
no_truncate	Dumps the transaction log to the time of the failure and does not truncate the log.

The **dump tran** command has three special options, as follows.

(continued)

Table 14-3. (continued)

- **dump tran with no_truncate** When a data device fails and the database is inaccessible, use the *with no_truncate* option to get a current copy of the log. This option does not truncate the log; instead, it provides a record of transactions up to the time of the failure. Note, though, that you can use the *with no_truncate* option only if the transaction log is on a different segment than the database and the *master* database is accessible.

- **dump tran with truncate_only** This option allows you to truncate the log without making a backup copy. Use this option only if recovering data is less important, for example in young application development environments. Using this option truncates the log, which frees space.

- **dump tran with no_log** Use this option when the log is so full that you cannot even use the *with truncate_only* option. This option truncates the log without logging the dump transaction event.

Example 1: The following example truncates the log in the *sampdb* database.

```
dump tran samp_db with no_log
go
```

Example 2: This command dumps the transaction log to a disk device, which is a UNIX operating system file.

```
dump tran sampdb
 to "/work/samp_tran"
go
```

Recovery and the Load Command

This section discusses the two forms of recovery: *manual recovery* and *automatic recovery*. A system administrator can manually recover one or more databases using the **load** command. SQL Server performs automatic recovery every time it reboots.

Automatic Recovery

When SQL Server reboots, it automatically performs the following set of recovery procedures in each database.

1. Reads the transaction log (*syslogs* table) for each database.

2. Applies all changes since the last checkpoint to the database if it reads a commit in the transaction log. Rolls forward transactions for which the transaction log has more recent information than the database.

3. Rolls back any transactions that were in progress if there is no commit for the transaction. (The data in the database reverts to its state before the transaction started.)

4. Writes a checkpoint record in the log.

5. Logs recovery information in the SQL Server error log.

The two scenarios shown in Figure 14-8 illustrate the automatic recovery process. In the scenario shown in the top part of the figure, the **commit tran** command ensures that the new row is inserted into the table, even if the data is not written to the disk at the time of the server crash. The transaction log has the information about the nature of the transaction (insert), the status of the transaction (commit), and the actual data. When SQL Server reboots, it inserts the row into the table.

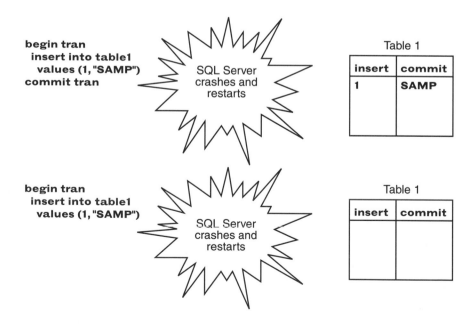

Figure 14-8. Automatic recovery

In the scenario in the bottom of the figure, the transaction was not committed prior to the crash, so the row that was inserted will be deleted from the table to restore the table to its pretransaction state. The transaction log has the necessary information about the transaction, and the changes are applied to the table by rolling back the insert.

Table 14-4 summarizes the effect of rolling back and rolling forward transactions. The table shows the transaction committed, but the row has not been inserted into the table. SQL Server inserts the row using the information in the transaction log (which has the corresponding transaction entries). If the row has already been inserted into the table, SQL Server does not take any action.

If the transaction is not committed and the row has already been inserted, SQL Server rolls back or undoes the transaction by deleting the row from the table. SQL Server does nothing if the row has not been inserted prior to the reboot.

Table 14-4. *The effect of rolling a transaction forward and backward*

If the transaction log has this:	And the database has this:	Then SQL Server does this:
begin tran 　**insert table1...**	Has no rows.	Inserts the row into the table.
commit	Has the new row.	Does nothing.
begin tran 　**insert table1...**	Does not have the new row.	Does nothing.
(no commit)	Has the new row.	Deletes the row.

When SQL Server restarts, database recovery takes place as follows.

1. Recovers *master*

2. Recovers *sybsecurity*

3. Recovers *model*

4. Creates an empty *tempdb*

5. Recovers *sybsystemprocs*

6. Recovers user databases in the ascending order of *sysdatabase..dbid* (*dbid* is the ID of the database)

Manual Recovery

You can use the **load database** command to restore one or more databases by loading the corresponding database backups from the dump device to SQL Server. Figure 14-9 illustrates the **load database** command.

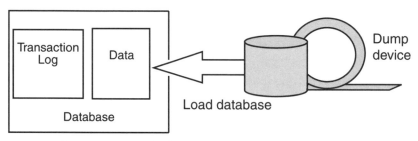

Figure 14-9. *Both the data and log are copied back to SQL Server during manual recovery*

The **load transaction** command applies transactions from the transaction dump device to the database. When a transaction log is loaded, it reconstructs the database by re-executing the changes recorded in the transaction log. Transaction dumps should be loaded in the same order in which they were made. Figure 14-10 illustrates the **load transaction** command.

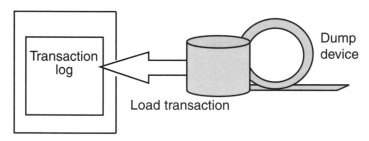

Figure 14-10. *Transaction log changes are applied to a database*

The Restore Process

Restoring is the process of rebuilding one or more databases from database dumps and transaction log dumps. A restore process is different from automatic recovery, which occurs every time SQL Server restarts. A restore process is not automatic; it is initiated by a user.

When a hardware failure such as a disk crash occurs, you can completely restore a database as long as the database and transaction dumps are available. Figure 14-11 represents a backup and restore scenario in which a database device fails after a database dumps to it. Assume that database *sampdb* is dumped to *disk1*. Database sampdb's transaction log dumps to *disk2*. Just after another database dump to *disk3* is complete, the data device fails. Here's how to completely restore the database.

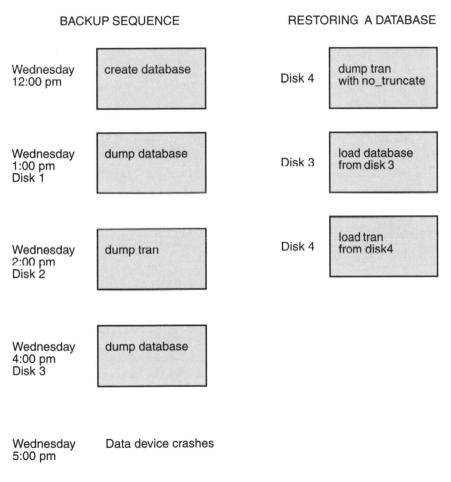

Figure 14-11. *Restoring a database from backup*

Database *sampdb*'s transaction log is dumped to *disk4* with the *no_truncate* option. This ensures that all transactions recorded to the time of failure are dumped to the disk. The database is loaded from *disk3* and the transactions are applied to the database from *disk4*. Here is the command sequence for restoring the database.

```
dump tran sampdb
  to disk4 with no_truncate
go
load database sampdb
  from disk3
go
load tran sampdb
  from disk4
go
online database sampdb
go
```

Loading Databases

By using the **load database** command, you can reload backups created with the **dump database** command. You can load the dump into an existing database or create a new database with the *for load* option. The **load database** command sets the database status to offline. That is, no one can use the database during the database load and subsequent transaction log load. After the database is loaded, SQL Server performs the following tasks.

1. Marks the database as offline

2. Initializes unused pages in the database if the database being loaded into is larger than the dumped database

3. Runs recovery so that any uncommitted transactions at the time of the dump are rolled back

Table 14-5 shows an abbreviated version of the **load database** command with its most commonly used parameters.

Table 14-5. Syntax and parameters for the **load database** command

---

load database *database_name* from
   stripe_device [at *b_server_name*]
   [, stripe on *stripe_device* [[at *b_server_name*]
   [with { [nounload | unload] }]

(continued)

Table 14-5. *(continued)*

database_name	Name of the database that is loaded. *Stripe on* loads a single database across multiple tapes concurrently.
stripe_device	Logical name of the dump device.
b_server_name	Name of the remote backup server.
nounload/unload	Used for tape devices, *unload* rewinds the tape and unloads it, while *nounload* does not rewind and unload after reading.

Example 1: The following command loads database *sampdb* from a tape device.

```
load database sampdb
 from "/dev/rmt0"
go
```

Example 2: The following command loads database *pubs2* from two devices across the network using a remote backup server, *B_RMTS*.

```
load database pubs2
 from "/dev/rmt3" at B_RMTS,
 stripe on "/dev/rmt4" at B_RMTS
go
```

Loading Transaction Logs

After loading a database, use the **load transaction** command to load all transaction dumps in the order in which they were made. Loading the transaction log means applying changes to a database by recreating the changes recorded in the transaction log. Table 14-6 shows the **load tran** command with its most commonly used parameters.

Table 14-6. *Syntax and parameters for the* **load transaction** *command*

load tran *database_name*
    from *stripe_device* [at *b_server_name*]
    [, stripe on *stripe_device* [[at *b_server_name*]
    [with { [nounload | unload] }]	

database_name	Name of the database whose transaction log is loaded. *Stripe on* loads a transaction log across multiple tapes concurrently.
stripe_device	Logical name of the dump device.

(continued)

Table 14-6. *(continued)*

b_server_name	Name of the remote backup server.
nounload/unload	Used for tape devices, *unload* rewinds the tape and unloads it, while *nonunload* does not rewind and unload after reading.

Example: This command loads the table *empdb* transaction log from logical device *DBDEV1*.

```
load tran empdb
  from DBDEV1
go
```

Online Database

When the load sequence is complete, SQL Server takes the database offline so it is unavailable until you use the **online database** command to make the database available to users again. Be sure to load all transaction logs before issuing the **online database** command. The **online database** command is especially useful for upgrading a SQL Server 10.0 single-user database and transaction log to the current SQL Server version. Table 14-7 provides the syntax and parameters for this command.

Table 14-7. *Syntax and parameter for the* **online database** *command*

online database database_name	
database_name	Name of the database that is brought on-line

Example: The following sequence of commands brings database *empdb* created in SQL Server 10.0 on-line and simultaneously upgrades the database to version 11.0.

```
load database empdb
  from "/dev/rmt0"
go
load tran empdb
  from "/dev/rst0"
go
online database empdb
go
  dump database empdb
  to "/dev/rmt1"
go
```

Backup Server

Like SQL Server, Backup Server is an operating system process. Backup Server is dedicated to performing backups and restores for SQL Server. It creates a physical image of an entire database or of a transaction log on an archive device when the **dump** and **load** commands are used. One of Backup Server's greatest benefits is its ability to perform backups at any time while SQL Server continues to run normally.

Backup Server performs all SQL Server backups. You typically install Backup Server at the same time you install SQL Server, and on the same machine. The **startserver** utility installs Backup Server. During backup operations, SQL Server becomes a Backup Server client. Figure 14-12 illustrates how Backup Server dumps a database to a dump device.

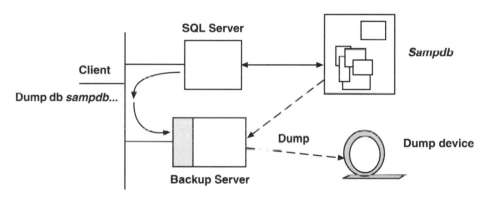

Figure 14-12. *A Backup Server configuration*

Backup and Restore Strategies for User Databases

The most critical factor in developing a sound backup strategy is to determine a proper backup frequency for your system. The next sections focus on scheduling backups of user databases and transaction logs, and restoring the user databases. It is a good idea to run a checkpoint before dumping a database or transaction log to ensure that the data is written to disk.

Scheduling Routine Backups

You should dump each user database immediately after creating it and at regular intervals thereafter. The minimum recommended backup frequency is daily transaction log backups and weekly database backups. In addition to the regular backups, we highly recommend making backups under the following circumstances.

- Make a database backup after you create an index on a table. When a transaction log is loaded into a database, if there is a **create index** log record, the entire index is physically recreated. Therefore, it takes the same amount of time to recreate the index as it took to create the index at run time.

- Make a database backup immediately after performing any unlogged operations, such as fast **bcp** (**bcp** into a table with no indexes or triggers), nonlogged **writetext**, and **select into**.

- Make a database backup after its transaction log has been truncated.

- Make a database backup regularly if the data and the transaction log are on the same device.

- Make complete backups before upgrading to a different version of SQL Server software.

Point to Note: Run **dbcc** checks before performing database backups. See Chapter 15, Database Administration Tools, for more information.

Restoring User Databases

In a typical case of media failure, it is possible to recover a database—provided the database and the transaction log have been backed up periodically. To restore user databases from the backups, follow the procedures listed below.

1. Make a current log dump of the database using **dump tran** <*database_name*> **with no_truncate**.

2. Examine the device allocations of the database on the failed device. You can use the following query to determine device allocations.

```
select segmap, size from sysusages
  where dbid = db_id("database_name")
go
```

3. Drop the database.

4. Drop the failed device using **sp_dropdevice**.

5. Use the **create database** command with the *for load* option to recreate the database.

6. Load the latest database dump to the newly created database.

7. Apply transaction log backups in the order in which they were made. (Load the most current dump last.)

8. Check for the consistency of the database using **dbcc** commands.

9. Bring the database on-line using the **online database** command.

Backup and Restore Strategies for System Databases

This section deals with the backup and restoration of the system databases: *master*, *model*, and *sybsystemprocs*.

Backing Up the *master* Database

Because the *master* database contains critical system tables, back it up as regularly and frequently as possible. The general rule is that you should dump the *master* database whenever you change the *master* database. Back up the *master* database after each command that affects disks, storage, databases, or segments.

We recommended saving the scripts containing all **disk init**, **create database**, and **alter database** commands so that you can use them to generate query output for comparison.

The *master* database has the log and the data on the same device; therefore, you cannot back them up separately. Always use the **dump database** command to back up the *master* database, then use **dump tran with truncate_only** periodically to dump the transaction log.

Restoring the *master* Database

The *master* database contains all of the system tables that control all of SQL Server's functions, databases, and data devices. The procedure to restored *master* database is given next.

1. Keep hard copies of vital system tables needed to restore disks, databases and logins.

2. If other databases on the master device are accessible, back them up with **dump database**.

3. Shut down SQL Server and use **buildmaster** with the -*m* option to build a new *master* database.

4. Use the **startserver** command with the -*m* option to restart the server in *master-recover* mode. This *master-recover* mode allows only one login (SA).

5. Using the hard copy of the *sysusages* table, determine the device allocations for *master*, and recreate them.

6. If your backup server name is not SYB_BACKUP, update the *sysservers* table with your backup server name.

7. Use the **showserver** command to check if your backup server is running.

8. Load the most recent database dump of the *master* database using the **load database** command.

9. Restart SQL Server in master-recover mode and verify the *sysusages*, *sysdatabases*, and *sysdevices* tables in your recovered server against your hard copy.

10. If you have added any new database devices since the last database backup, recreate the devices using **disk init** commands.

11. Check for the consistency of the database using **dbcc** commands.

12. Verify the *syslogins* table if you have added new logins since the last backup of the *master* database.

13. Stop the server and use **startserver** (without any option) to restart the server in multiuser mode.

14. Dump the *master* database.

Backing Up the *model* Database

Because the *model* database has the prototype of the database for the new user database, it is important to make regular backups of *model*. Each time you change the *model* database, make a backup of it. As is true of the *master* database, *model* database stores its transaction log on the same database device as the data. So, you must always use the **dump database** command to back up the database and **dump tran** with the *truncate_only* option to purge the transaction log after each database dump.

Restoring the *model* Database

If you have not made changes to the *model* database, you need to restore the generic model database. The generic model database can be restored using the following command.

buildmaster -d /devname -x

If you have made changes to the *model* database, restore the *model* database by loading the *model* database from backup.

Backing Up the *sysbystemprocs* Database

The *sybsystemprocs* database contains all of the system stored procedures and any new stored procedures that users create. The **installmaster** script only recreates the system stored procedures that Sybase provides. To restore the stored procedures that you've created, you should back up the *sybsystemprocs* database regularly. Like other system databases, *sybsystemprocs* stores its transaction log on the same device as the data. So, use **dump tran with truncate_only**.

Restoring the *sybsystemprocs* Database

If you have not added new stored procedures, you can recreate the original *sysbystemprocs* database by running the **installmaster** script. If you have added system procedures, load the database *sybsystemprocs* from its backup.

Managing Free Space with Thresholds

A transaction log is appended each time a database is modified, which can result in a nearly full transaction log. If the log is full, all future modifications stop. If the log is on its own segment, SQL Server automatically creates a "last-chance" threshold that monitors space usage on that particular segment. Last-chance threshold is the default threshold in SQL Server that suspends or kills user processes if the transaction log becomes full.

Threshold is an estimate of the number of free log pages that would be required to back up the transaction log. When the amount of free space in the log segment falls below the last-chance threshold, SQL Server automatically executes a special stored procedure called **sp_thresholdaction**. Figure 14-13 illustrates how the **sp_thresholdaction** system procedure executes and frees up the log space.

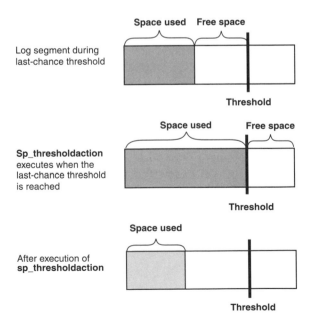

Figure 14-13. Freeing log space

Example: This example is a simple threshold procedure.

```
create proc sp_thresholdaction
 @dbname varchar(30),
 @segmentname varchar(30),
 @free_space int,
 @status int
as
 dump tran @dbname
 to tapedev1
 print "Transaction log dumped: ' %1!' for '%2!' dumped",
 @segmentname, @dbname
return
go
```

When the last-chance threshold is reached, the stored procedure **sp_thresholdaction** is executed, which dumps the transaction log to a tape device.

Points to Note: Backup and Recovery

Keep the following points in mind during backup and restoration operations.

- Only databases at SQL Server version 10.0 or higher can be upgraded using the **online database** command

- The system table *syslogs* should never be directly updated, deleted, or inserted by the user, because doing so can corrupt the *system* tables

- Logical device names cannot be used while dumping to or loading from a remote backup server

- Never change the name of a database that contains primary keys for references from other databases

- While dumping and loading using remote backup server, you should use the same number of devices for both dump and load operations

- Do not use the *no_truncate* option on a database that is currently in use

- A database cannot be partially loaded, because loading data into an existing database overwrites its data

---

Exercises

14-1.   A server is configured with the following command. What is the significance of this command? What is the default value?

```
sp_configure "recovery interval in minutes", 3
go
```

14-2.   The sequence of database dumps and transaction dumps of database *salesdb* is given here. Specify the commands to restore the database from the dumps.

Tape 1   dump database
Tape 2   dump tran
Tape 3   dump tran
Data device fails
Tape 4   dump database

14-3.   What is the command to dump database *empdb* to three tape devices whose logical names are *TAPEDEV1*, *TAPEDEV2*, and *TAPEDEV3*?

14-4.   Describe briefly how would you restore system database *tempdb*.

14-5.   Database *sampdb* has a table *tab1* that has 10 rows. The following operations are performed.

a.   How many rows will table *tab1* have after device */work/SAMPDB* is loaded?

b.   After the transaction log dump is loaded, how many rows will the table have?
A row is inserted
Database *sampdb* is dumped to disk file */work/SAMPDB*
Another row is inserted
The transaction log of *sampdb* is dumped to a tape, whose logical name is TAPEDEV1

14-6.   What are the commands you would use to perform the following actions?

a.   Rebuild the *master* device
b.   Rebuild only the *master* database

Answers to Exercises

14-1.   The maximum time it takes to recover a database is three minutes. The default value for recovery interval is five minutes.

14-2.   The sequence of commands to restore *salesdb* from dumps is given here.

```
dump tran salesdb
  with no_truncate to tape4
go
```

```
load database salesdb
  from tape1
load tran salesdb
  from tape2
go
load tran salesdb
  from tape3
go
load tran salesdb
  from tape4
go
```

14-3.   The commands to dump database *empdb* to three tape devices are given here.

```
dump database empdb
  to TAPEDEV1
  with init
go
dump database empdb
 to TAPEDEV2
go
dump database empdb
  to TAPEDEV3 with unload
go
```

14-4.   System database *tempdb* cannot be recovered, because it is initialized during every reboot.

14-5.   a.   11 rows
        b.   12 rows

14-6.   a.   Use **buildmaster** without the -*m* option
        b.   Use **buildmaster** with the -*m* option

15

Database Administration Tools

Sybase accompanies its SQL Server software with a variety of tools and utility programs that help you administer all aspects of the SQL Server system, from data objects through physical and logical configuration to backups. Many of these tools are complete server products, which you access through sophisticated graphical-user interfaces (GUIs). Also included are command-type utilities that you invoke from the operating-system prompt and from within SQL Server itself. This chapter discusses the tools that we find most useful: **bcp**, **defncopy**, **dbcc**, SQL Server Manger, Enterprise SQL Server Manager, SQL Server Monitor, and **sp_sysmon**.

You'll notice that we discuss the **bcp**, **defncopy**, and **dbcc** utilities in much more detail than the others. The **bcp** and **defncopy** utilities are command-type utilities that you invoke from a UNIX operating-system prompt to copy data and data definitions between operating system files and tables in a database. The **dbcc** utility set is a collection of commands that you invoke from within SQL Server to check the logical and physical consistency of the database. Note that, except for **defncopy**, all of the tools this chapter discusses are available in UNIX and NT environments. **Defncopy** is a UNIX-only tool.

The **sp_sysmon** utility is a command-type tool that complements the other monitor tools. For example, you can use **sp_sysmon** to discover bottlenecks, then use SQL Server Monitor to pinpoint the problem. SQL Server Manager, Enterprise SQL Server Manager, and SQL Server Monitor are server-based GUI tools that are intuitive and don't require much explanation. They greatly simplify database system administration and allow you to monitor the internal workings of a system for debugging and performance purposes. The manager programs automate much of the work that you would otherwise need to perform manually using commands we described in Section II of this book.

bcp

The *bulk copy utility*, **bcp**, copies blocks of data between a table and an operating system file, as Figure 15-1 illustrates. This utility is useful when you want to transfer data from a table among multiple SQL Servers, or among a SQL Server and other data sources that can produce an operating system file. Say that you want to copy data from the *stock_txn* table on SQL Server called *SFO* to the *NYK* SQL Server's *stock_txn* table in the *stock* database. Using the bulk copy utility, you would copy the data from server *SFO* to an operating system file, then use **bcp** to copy the data from the operating system file to the *stock_txn* table of *stock* database on server *NYK*. Similarly, if you want to move data from a table in Oracle to Sybase, you could copy data from the Oracle database to an operating system file using an Oracle utility, then use the **bcp** command to copy the data from the operating system file to a Sybase database.

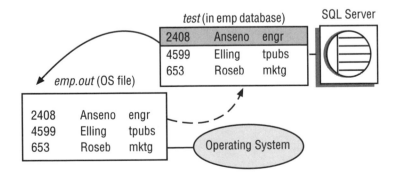

Figure 15.1. *The **bcp** command copies between a file and a table*

The bulk copy utility is also useful for performing backups at a finer granularity than is possible with any other utility. For example, you can back up and then restore just a single table from a database. If you had used the **dump database** command to backup a database, it would not be possible to store just one table; you would have to restore the entire database. (Chapter 14, Backup and Recovery, discusses the **dump database** command.) Table 15-1 gives the most commonly used **bcp** command syntax and parameters.

Table 15-1. *Common syntax and parameters for the **bcp** command*

bcp [[*database_name.*]owner.]*table_name* {in | out} *datafile*
 [-m *maxerrors*] [-f *formatfile*] [-e *errorfile*]
 [-F *firstrow*] [-L *lastrow*] [-b *batchsize*] [-n]
 [-c [-N]] [-t *field_terminator*] [-r *row_terminator*]
 [-U *username*] [-P *password*] [-I *interfaces_file*]
 [-S Server] [-A packet_size]

datafile	The full path name of an operating system file.
maxerrors	The maximum number of nonfatal errors permitted before **bcp** aborts the copy operation.
formatfile	The name of a format file that contains storage type information.
errorfile	The name of the error file in which **bcp** stores any rows that it was unable to transfer from the file to the database.
firstrow	The number of the first row to copy.
lastrow	The number of the last row to copy.
batchsize	The number of rows per serial batch of data copied (default is to copy all rows in one batch). Each batch is a transaction that is committed at the end of the batch. Batching applies only when bulk copying in; it has no effect on bulk copying out.
-n	Performs the copy operation using native (operating system) format. This option does not prompt for each field.
-c	Performs the copy operation with *char* datatype as the default. This uses character format for all columns, providing a new line terminator at the end of each row. Use when sharing data between different platforms or when you want the file to be readable by humans.
field_terminator	Specifies default field terminator.
row_terminator	Specifies default row terminator.
packet_size	Specifies the network packet size to use for this **bcp** session. Use larger packet sizes to improve the performance of large bulk copy operations.

If you do not use either *-n* or *-c* option to specify the format, **bcp** prompts interactively for the storage type, prefix length, and terminator for each column of data to copy. You will see the default value in brackets before the prompt.

Point to Note: The **bcp** command cannot create a table, it can only append the data from a file to an existing table.

Copying from a Table to a File

This section illustrates how to use **bcp** to copy from a table to a file. In the following example, the first line shows the command that the user enters to invoke the **bcp** utility (user input is bold). It tells **bcp** to copy data from a three-column table called *emp* in the *test* database to a file called *emp.out*. The user enters a password, but does not specify a format using either the *-n* or the *-c* option, so **bcp** prompts for storage type, length of the field, and the field terminator for each column. The user responds by requesting character output for all three rows and accepting the default values for field length. If you choose a prefix length of 0, it prompts for the length of the field with length of the column as default length. The user chooses tabs as separators between the columns and specifies a new line at the end of the last column's output. After obtaining the formatting information it needs, **bcp** asks if the user wants to save that format information in a file for later use. The user responds affirmatively and accepts the default file name *bcp.fmt*.

```
bcp test..emp out emp.out -Usa
Enter the file storage type of field no [int]: c
Enter prefix-length of field no [1]: 0
Enter length of field no [12]:
Enter field terminator [none]: \t
Enter the file storage type of field name [char]:
Enter prefix-length of field name [0]:
Enter length of field name [30]:
Enter field terminator [none]: \t
Enter the file storage type of field dept [char]:
Enter prefix-length of field dept [0]:
Enter length of field dept [4]:
Enter field terminator [none]: \n
Do you want to save this format information in a file? [Y/n]
Y
Host filename [bcp.fmt]: emp.fmt
Starting copy...
5 rows copied.
Clock Time (ms.): total = 23    Avg = 2    (434.78 rows per sec.)
```

This session produces the following *emp.out* file. Notice the tabs between columns as specified by the first field terminator and that the output for each entry begins on a new line.

```
1    Guru       MKT
2    James      ADM
3    Joseph     PROD
4    Dick       MKT
5    Charles    ENGG
```

The format file that this session produces, *bcp.fmt*, is shown in Figure 15-2. The first line is the **bcp** software version number. The second line indicates the number of table columns in the format file, and each line after that describes a column in the table.

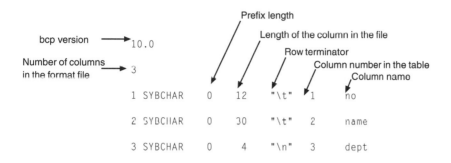

Figure 15-2. A **bcp** format file

Copying from a File to a Table

There are two *bcp modes* for copying data from a file to a table, which are referred to as *fast bcp* and *slow bcp*. Fast bcp is faster because SQL Server logs only page allocations and not the actual insertion of rows, as it does in slow bcp mode. SQL Server decides which mode to use depending on the table definition and database option you specify. It can only use fast bcp for table definitions that do not include indexes or triggers, and the table must reside in a database for which the *select into/bulkcopy* database option is set. If this option is not set and a user tries to load data into a table without indexes or triggers, SQL Server generates an error message.

Example: The following command sets the *select into/bulkcopy* database option for the database *test*.

```
sp_dboption test,
  "select into/bulkcopy", true
go
```

When you copy data to a table that has indexes or triggers, **bcp** automatically uses the slow bcp mode and logs data inserts in the transaction log, whether or not you specify *select into/bulkcopy*. The transaction log can easily become very large during slow bulk copies, so you should use the **dump transaction** command to back it up and ensure that the **bcp** operation does not blow up for want of transaction space. Alternatively, you can set the database option *trunc log on checkpoint* to truncate the growing transaction log.

Point to Note: Use the *trunc log on checkpoint* option with care, because it can disable a transaction dump and load sequence.

Example: Use the following command to set the *trunc log on checkpoint* database option for the *test* database.

```
sp_dboption test,
  " trunc log on checkpoint ", true
go
```

Point to Note: If triggers exist during a *slow bcp* option, they will not fire during the copying.

Achieving Good *bcp* Performance

You can improve **bcp** performance to copy data from a file to a table by partitioning the table and using concurrent bulk copying, which can simultaneously add rows to the end of each part of the table on each partition. Partitioned tables cannot have a clustered index. Chapter 17, Performance Tuning at the Database Level, discusses this System 11 feature in more detail.

The **bcp** utility uses the default network packet size to transfer data between a client program and SQL Server. However, the network packet size is configurable, and you can improve **bcp** performance by specifying a packet size larger than the default. (You need to verify that SQL Server is configured to handle larger network packet sizes before you adjust the parameter.)

Example: The following example uses 4096 as the network packet size.

```
bcp test..emp
  in emp.out -Usa -n -A 4096
```

defncopy

The UNIX command **defncopy** copies the definitions for stored procedures, triggers, views, rules, and defaults within a particular database to an operating system file. You cannot use the **defncopy** utility to get information about table definitions. Notice that you can create a database object from an operating system file using this utility when you are creating a database object from a file. Table 15-2 provides **defncopy** syntax.

Table 15-2. Syntax and parameters for the **defncopy** command

defncopy [-U *username*] [-P *password*] [-S *server*] [-v]
[-I *interfaces_file*]
{ in *filename dbname* | out *filename dbname*
[*owner.*]*objectname* [[*owner.*]*objectname*]...}

username	Login name used by the server
password	Password of above user login
server	Name of the server
interfaces file	Physical location of the interfaces file
filename	Name of the operating system file
dbname	Database name in which the database object exists
objectname	Name of the database object for which you want to extract the definition

Example: This example extracts the definition of the stored procedure *list_emp* from the *pubs2* database to a file named *test*. The *username* parameter indicates a user with an *sa* account.

$defncopy out test pubs2 list_emp -Usa -P

Here is the file *test,* which contains the definition generated by the above command.

$ cat test

```
create proc list_emp
as
select * from emp
/* ### DEFNCOPY: END OF DEFINITION */
```

The dbcc *Utility Set*

The database consistency checker, **dbcc**, is a set of commands that you invoke from within SQL Server to check the logical and physical consistency of the data within a database. The **dbcc** commands are commonly used in the following situations.

- To investigate the extent of damage after database damage or table corruption

- To fix table or index allocation errors

- To perform routine preventive maintenance, ensuring database integrity

The importance of the last point should not be underestimated. The integrity of a database's internal structure depends on executing **dbcc** commands on a regular basis to check allocation structures such as object and page allocation, to check page linkage and data pointers at both page level and row level, and to check consistency among the system catalog tables. You might want to refer to the discussion in the "How SQL Server Manages Storage" section of Chapter 3, The SQL Server Engine, for information about page and object allocation, the OAM page, and linking.

Next, we discuss some important **dbcc** commands. See the *System Administration Guide* on the SyBooks CD for more detailed information about the commands and parameters.

Checking for Problems with Tables and Index Allocations

This section describes how to use **dbcc** commands to check for problems that can affect table and index allocations. These commands check for the following types of consistency. We discuss each of these issues in the following sections.

- Correct linking of a table's index and pages, index sort order, and consistency of pointers

- Index integrity

- Consistency between the system table information about tables and the actual table

- Page and index allocation

Checking for Correct Page-Index Linking

The **dbcc checktable** command checks if a table's index and data pages are correctly linked, the indexes are in the proper sorted order, and the index integrity and pointers are consistent. It also ensures that the data rows on each page have entries in the first OAM page. Table owners can issue the **dbcc checktable** command using the syntax provided in Table 15-3.

Table 15-3. *Syntax and parameters for the **dbcc checktable** command*

dbcc checktable ({*table_name* | *table_id*}[,*skip_ncindex*])

table_name	Name of the table on which you intend to perform **dbcc** check.
table_id	Object ID of the table. You may provide either the table name or the object ID of the table.
skip_ncindex	Allows you to skip the checks for page link, pointers, and sort order on nonclustered indexes.

Example: This example checks the table *emp* to verify that its index and data pages are properly linked. Following the command is its output, which shows that **dbcc** checks the table *emp* and that the table has 10 rows.

```
dbcc checktable (emp)
go
```

```
Checking emp
The total number of data pages in this table is 1.
Table has 10 data rows.

DBCC execution completed. If DBCC printed error messages, contact a user
with System Administrator (SA) role.
```

Checking for Index Integrity

The **dbcc reindex** command checks the integrity of indexes and rebuilds them on the specified table. If you suspect a problem with index integrity, you should use this command to drop and rebuild the index. Table 15-4 shows the syntax for this command.

Table 15-4. *Syntax and parameters for the **dbcc reindex** command*

dbcc reindex ({*table_name* | *table_id*})

table_name	Name of the table for which you intend to perform **dbcc** check.
table_id	Object ID of the table. You may provider either the table name or the object IDof the table.

Example: This example checks the integrity of the table *emp*.

dbcc reindex (emp)
go

```
The indexes for 'emp' are already correct. They will not be rebuilt.
DBCC execution completed. If DBCC printed error messages, contact a user
with System Administrator (SA) role.
```

Checking Data and Index Page Allocation for a Table

The **dbcc tablealloc** command checks that all of the data and index pages for a specified table are correctly allocated, that no unused pages are allocated, and that no page are used but unallocated. Table 15-5 shows the syntax for this command.

Table 15-5. *Syntax and parameters for the **dbcc tablealloc** command*

dbcc tablealloc ([*table_name* |*table_id*] [,fix | nofix])

table_name	Name of the table for which you intend to perform **dbcc** check.
table_id	Object ID of the table. You may provider either the table name or the object ID of the table.
fix	nofix	Use the *fix* option if you intend **dbcc** program to fix the errors that are encountered while running this command. Before you use *fix* option, you must put the database in single-user mode. The default is *nofix*.

Example: This example checks all of the data and index pages of the table *emp*. Figure 15-3 shows the output and points out the types of information.

dbcc tablealloc (emp)
go

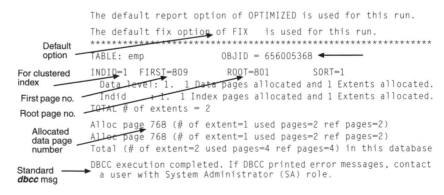

Figure 15-3. *Output from **dbcc tablealloc (emp)***

Checking Page Allocation for an Index

The **dbcc indexalloc** command is used to check for a specified index that all index pages are correctly allocated, that no page is allocated that is not used, and that no page is used that is not allocated. Table 15-6 gives the syntax for this command.

Table 15-6. *Syntax and parameters for the **dbcc indexalloc** command*

dbcc indexalloc ({*table_name* | *table_id*}, *index_id*
  [,{full | optimized | fast | null} [,fix | nofix])

table_name	The name of the table for which you intend to perform **dbcc** check.
table_id	The object ID of the table. You may provider either the table name or the object ID of the table.
index _id	The index number. For example, 1 means clustered index. Index numbers for all nonclustered indexes start from 2.
full | optimized | fast | null	Specifies what method to use while checking. For example:
	The *full* option reports all types of allocation errors.
	The *optimized* option reports allocation pages linked in the object allocation map pages for the table.
	The *fast* option reports pages that are referenced but not allocated in the extent.
fix | nofix	You can also choose to use null for this parameter. The default is *nofix*. Use the option *fix* if you intend for the **dbcc** program to fix the errors that are encountered while running this command. Before you use *fix* option, you must put the database in single-user mode.

Example: This example checks the clustered index of table *emp*. Its output, which follows, is similar to the **tablealloc** output earlier in this chapter, because the *emp* table has only one index.

```
dbcc indexalloc (emp,1,full)
go
```

```
******************************************************************
TABLE: emp        OBJID = 656005368
INDID=1 FIRST=809    ROOT=801    SORT=1
   Data level: 1. 1 Data pages allocated and 1 Extents allocated.
    Indid   : 1. 1 Index pages allocated and 1 Extents allocated.
TOTAL # of extents = 2
Alloc page 768 (# of extent=1 used pages=2 ref pages=2)
Alloc page 768 (# of extent=1 used pages=2 ref pages=2)
Total (# of extent=2 used pages=4 ref pages=4) in this database
DBCC execution completed. If DBCC printed error messages, contact a user
with System Administrator (SA) role.
Checking pubs2
```

Checking System Table Consistency

The **dbcc checkcatalog** command checks for consistency within and among the system tables of a particular database. If you do not specify a database name, the command checks the current database. Here's the syntax.

dbcc checkcatalog ([*database_name*])

Example: This example checks the system catalog tables of the *pubs2* database. Partial output from the command follows. It shows that the command checked the *pubs2* database and the virtual start address of the device on which the database resides. The output shows that the size of the device in 2KB blocks is 1024 and that the segments are *0* for the default segment, *1* for the system segment, and *2* for the log segment.

dbcc checkcatalog (pubs2)
go

```
Checking pubs2
```

The following segments have been defined for database 6 (database name *pubs2*).

```
virtual start   addr   size   segments
--------------  ----   -----  --------
117440514       1024   0
                       1
                       2
DBCC execution completed. If DBCC printed error messages, contact a user
with System Administrator (SA) role.
```

Checking for Database Consistency

The **dbcc checkdb** command runs the same checks as the **dbcc checktable** command does. The difference is that **checktable** runs the checks on a single table, while **checkdb** runs the checks on every table in the database. The **dbcc checkdb** command refers to the sysobjects table to determine all of the table names in the specified database. The syntax of this command is shown in Table 15-7.

Table 15-7. *Syntax and parameters for the **dbcc checkdb** command*

dbcc checkdb ([*database_name*] [,*skip_ncindex*])	
database_name	The name of the database to check using **dbcc**. If you do not specify a database name, the system checks in the current database.
skip_ncindex	Use this option when you do not want to check the index of the database.

Example: This example checks every table in the *pubs2* database. Its partial output that follows gives information about the total number of pages and rows in each table. The *1* in the *Checking 1* phrase is the table's object ID. So, this example checks object IDs 1, 2, 3, and 4.

```
dbcc checkdb (pubs2)
go

Checking pubs2
Checking 1
The total number of data pages in this table is 3.
Table has 50 data rows.
Checking 2
The total number of data pages in this table is 5.
Table has 52 data rows.
Checking 3
The total number of data pages in this table is 7.
Table has 295 data rows.
Checking 4
The total number of data pages in this table is 1.
Table has 30 data rows.
```

Checking Data and Index Page Allocation

The **dbcc checkalloc** command checks that all of the data and index pages of a database are correctly allocated, that no unused pages are allocated, and that no page is used but not allocated. Table 15-8 gives the syntax for this command.

Table 15-8. *Syntax and parameters for the* **dbcc checkalloc** *command*

dbcc checkalloc ([*database_name*] [,fix | nofix])	
database_name	Name of the database that you intend to check.
fix	nofix	Use the *fix* option if you want the **dbcc** program to fix the errors that are encountered while running this command. Before you use *fix* option, you must put the database in single-user mode. The default is *nofix*.

Comparison of *dbcc* Commands

Table 15-9, taken from the *Sybase SQL Server System Administration Guide*, compares the different **dbcc** commands.

Table 15-9. *Comparison of* **dbcc** *commands*

Command and option	Level	Locking and performance	Speed	Thoroughness
checkcatalog	Rows in system tables	Shared page locks on system catalogs. Releases lock after each page is checked. Very few pages cached.	NA	NA
checktable checkdb with skip_ncindex	Page chains, sort order, data rows for tables and clustered indexes	Shared table lock. **Dbcc checkdb** locks one table at a time and releases the lock after it finishes checking that table.	Up to 40 percent faster than without **skip_ncindex** option	Medium
checktable checkdb	Page chains, sort order, data rows for all indexes	Shared table lock. **Dbcc checkdb** locks one table at a time and releases the lock after it finishes checking that table.	Slow	High
tablealloc full indexalloc full	Page chains	Shared table lock. Performs a lot of I/O. Only allocation pages are cached.	Slow	High

(continued)

Table 15-9. *(continued)*

Command and option	Level	Locking and performance	Speed	Thoroughness
checkalloc	Page chains	No locking; performs a lot of I/O and may saturate the I/O calls; only allocation pages are cached.	Slow	High
tablealloc optimized indexalloc optimized	Allocation pages	Shared table lock. Performs a lot of I/O. Only allocation pages are cached.	Moderate	Medium
tablealloc fast indexalloc fast	OAM pages	Shared table lock.	Fastest	Low

Redirecting Server Messages

By default, all **dbcc** messages are sent to the console of the system from which SQL Server was started. You can execute the **dbcc traceon** command to redirect **dbcc output** to the SQL Server error log or to a user's terminal. You can execute the **dbcc traceoff** command to reset output direction to the console.

Here are examples that illustrate how to redirect **dbcc** messages. The code 3604 redirects the output to a user's terminal and 3605 redirects the output to SQL Server's error log file.

Example 1: This example redirects messages to the user's terminal.

```
dbcc traceon (3604)
go
```

Example 2: This example redirects messages to the error log.

```
dbcc traceon (3605)
go
```

Example: This command reverses the display that was previously set with the **dbcc traceon** command.

```
dbcc traceoff (3605)
go
```

SQL Server Manager

Sybase SQL Server Manager lets the administrator perform administration and tuning using a sophisticated GUI-based client interface that greatly simplifies system administration tasks on Windows NT, Windows 95, or Windows 3.1x. SQL Server Manager has many ease-of-use features, including visual representation of object relationships (as Figure 15-4 shows) and drag-and-drop capabilities.

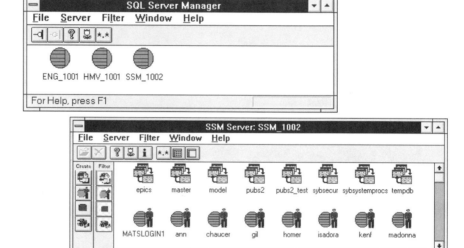

Figure 15-4. *SQL Server Manager windows*

SQL Server Manager handles all the routine system administration tasks, which include the following.

- *Managing SQL Servers* Displaying and terminating SQL Server processes; setting up *sql.ini* file entries for Windows NT; and generating and running SQL Server Data Definition Language (DDL) scripts

- *Managing physical resource* Creating and deleting database devices and dump devices; and creating mirror devices

- *Managing databases* Creating and deleting databases and database objects; setting database options; managing database storage allocation across devices and segments; backing up and restoring databases; issuing database checkpoints; generating and executing database DDL scripts; and running the **dbcc** database checking and repairing utility

Enterprise SQL Server Manager

Enterprise SQL Server Manager (ESSM) handles system administration for multiple SQL Servers. ESSM is an object-oriented product developed using the Tivoli Management Environment (TME), an industry-standard distributed system-management development environment. ESSM architecture is based on the Common Object Broker Architecture (CORBA). It supports SNMP and is accepted by X/Open. Because it is based on Tivoli, other Tivoli-based applications can interact with ESSM. Figure 15-5 shows the ESSM window.

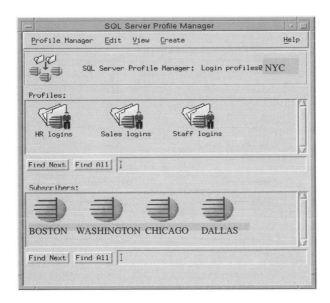

Figure 15-5. *The ESSM window*

ESSM has an Administrator Authentication service that verifies the identity of users and that authenticates local and remote server logins. It also has a Security Auditing service that records system activity in an audit trail to protect against unauthorized entry into the system and misuse of resources. As with SQL Server Manager, ESSM allows administrators to carry out numerous administration tasks from an intuitive GUI interface. These tasks include the following.

- Configure servers
- Monitor server status and performance

- Start and stop servers

- Manage server space utilization

- Administer users and ensure security

- Manage server and database objects such as databases, devices, dump devices, and segments

- Schedule and perform backup and recovery operations

In addition, ESSM allows you to use a command-line interface to perform any task that is available through the GUI interface. This makes ESSM accessible to proprietary applications and third-party products. ESSM can automatically schedule "lights out" operations and other administrative tasks. It can be set to automatically respond to events in the following ways.

- Post a notice on the administrator's notice board

- Notify the administrator by e-mail or beeper

- Log the event to a predefined file

- Execute a scripted program or stored procedure

- Put a visual alert on the system administrator's desktop

SQL Server Monitor

You can use SQL Server Monitor to monitor and improve SQL Server performance and efficiency. It is a UNIX and Windows GUI-based tool that tracks and stores a wide variety of information about SQL Server's database object statistics while SQL Server runs. SQL Server Monitor is an Open Server application. It takes advantage of the fact that SQL Server saves performance data in a shared memory area. In Chapter 16, Performance Tuning at the Query Level, you will see how essential this tool is for performance tuning.

Rather than querying SQL Server directly, which would have a notable impact on performance, SQL Server Monitor can retrieve the statistics from shared memory and only minimally affect performance. Users interact with the GUI-based Monitor Client, which displays the performance data in graphical form. Monitor Client relies on Monitor Server to collect and return the data it requests at user-specified intervals. Figure 15-6 shows the type of output

Monitor Client displays and the client's relationship to Server Monitor and SQL Server.

The Performance Trends window on the user's terminal in Figure 15-6 shows changes in SQL Server statistics over time. The display starts when the user opens the window and it adds data points to the graphs at each sample interval. You can take snapshots of SQL Server performance data before and after you tune, so you can track how your reconfiguration changes performance and to verify that your tuning has the effect you expected. It also helps you determine if opening one bottleneck has created another—a common occurrence in performance and tuning.

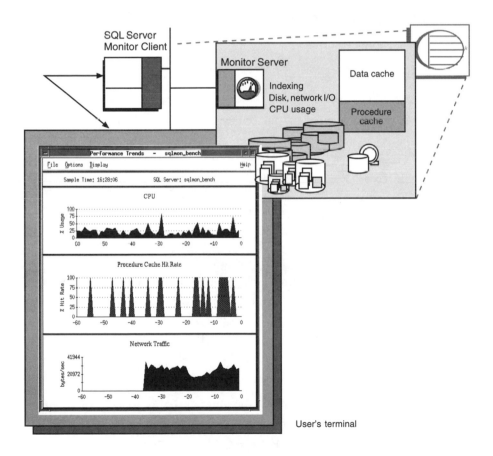

Figure 15-6. *The SQL Server Monitor environment*

You can monitor transaction activity through the Transaction Activity Window of SQL Server Monitor. This information gives a rough measure of how well SQL Server is performing; a high number of transactions per second generally indicates a high performance level. You can also use SQL Server Monitor to help you determine whether a SQL Server configuration is optimal for performance; whether objects are distributed in the most performance-effective way; if there are performance bottle necks and where they are; if and where the application is running into resource contention; and if the procedure cache is the right size. SQL Server Monitor determines this information by tracking the following categories of data.

- Data and procedure cache effectiveness
- Database device activity
- Lock activity
- Memory allocation
- Network traffic
- Disk I/O volume and average completion time by device
- User processes
- Transaction activity

sp_sysmon

The system procedure **sp_sysmon** is a tool that provides a comprehensive overview of system performance. After you identify the area that seems to be responsible for poor performance, you can use SQL Server Monitor to pinpoint contention on a per-object basis. You execute this system procedure using the following command.

sp_sysmon <run_time_minutes>

Run_time_minutes is the length of time in minutes that you want **sp_sysmon** to sample data. This time period is typically one or two minutes. (The default is one minute.) For example, the following command monitors system activities every two minutes.

sp_sysmon 2
go

The **sp_sysmon** command is a quick way to get lots of information about a SQL Server system. The following sample shows **sp_sysmon** output for the Transaction Profile section.

```
Transaction Profile
--------------------
Transaction Summary       per sec   per xact   count   % of total
--------------------      -------   --------   -----   ----------
   Committed Xacts        120.1     n/a        7261    n/a
Transaction Detail        per sec   per xact   count   % of Inserts
--------------------      -------   --------   -----   ----------
   Heap Table             120.1     1.0        7260    10
   Clustered Table          0.0     0.0           0
                          -------   --------   ------  ----------
   Total Rows Inserted    120.1     1.0        7260    2
Updates
   Deferred                 0.0     0.0           0
   Direct In-place        360.2     3.0       21774    10
   Direct Cheap             0.0     0.0           0
   Direct Expensive         0.0     0.0           0
--------------------      -------   --------   ------  ----------
   Total Rows Updated     360.2     3.0       21774    7
Deletes
   Deferred                 0.0     0.0           0
   Direct                   0.0     0.0           0
--------------------      -------   --------   ------  ----------
Total Rows Deleted          0.0     0.0           0
```

Table 15-10 summarizes the SQL Server performance categories on which **sp_sysmon** reports.

Table 15-10. *Monitoring categories on which* **sp_sysmon** *reports*

Category	Description
Kernel utilization	Reports on SQL Server activities. It tells you how busy SQL Server engines were during the time that the CPU was available to SQL Server, how often the CPU yielded to the operating system, the number of times that the engines checked for network and disk I/O, and the average number of I/Os they found waiting at each check.
Task management	Provides information about open connections, task context switches by engine, and task context switches by cause.
Task context switches	Summarizes causes for tasks switching off engines.

(continued)

Table 15-10. *(continued)*

Category	Description
Transaction profile	Reports on transaction-related activities, including the number of data modification transactions, user log cache (ULC) activity, and transaction log activity.
Transaction management	Reports on transaction management activities, including ULC flushes to transaction logs, ULC log records, ULC semaphore requests, log semaphore requests, transaction log writes, and transaction log allocations.
Index management	Reports on index management activity, including nonclustered maintenance, page splits, and index shrinks.
Lock management	Reports on locks, deadlocks, lock promotions, and freelock contention.
Data cache	Reports summary statistics for all caches and statistics for each named cache. It reports spinlock contention; utilization of cache searches, including hits and misses; pool turnover for all configured pools; buffer wash behavior, including buffers passed clean, already in I/O, and washed dirty; prefetch requests performed and denied; and dirty read page requests.
Procedure cache	Reports on the number of times stored procedures and triggers were requested, read from disk, and removed from cache.
Memory	Reports on the number of pages allocated and deallocated during the sample interval.
Recovery	Indicates the number of checkpoints caused by the normal checkpoint process, the number of checkpoints initiated by the housekeeper task, and the average length of time for each type. This information is helpful for correctly setting the recovery and housekeeper parameters.
Disk I/O	This category is useful when checking for I/O contention. It prints an overview of disk I/O activity: maximum outstanding I/Os, I/Os delayed, total requested I/Os, and completed I/Os. A second section includes output for the master device and for other configured devices, reporting reads, writes, and semaphore contention.
Network I/O	Reports on network activities for each SQL Server engine.

Exercises

15-1.   You are copying data into a table using the **bcp** utility. The bcp process aborted after copying 5,000 of 10,000 rows. How many rows will be available in the table?

15-2.   What is the difference between fast and slow bcp?

15-3.   Which utility obtains the definition of a stored procedure?

15-4.   What **dbcc** command checks the consistency of system tables for a database?

15-5.   What command do you use to monitor system activities for two minutes?

Answers to Exercises

15-1.   No rows will be available in the table.

15-2.   Slow bcp generates transaction logs, whereas fast bcp does not generate transaction logs.

15-3.   **defncopy**

15-4.   **dbcc checkcatalog**

15-5.   **sp_sysmon 2**

Optimizing SQL Server for Your System

As the number of queries or connections of a SQL Server installation increases due to an increased number of online transaction processing applications or users, database users and applications can experience two types of performance problems: an increase in contention for shared resources and a higher number of I/O operations. Tasks compete for shared resources such as locks for data access and the transaction log. Activity on the system tables increases, because SQL Server tracks information for the additional queries and connections. Heavily used tables are frequently written into and out of cache; and as we saw in Chapter 2, System 11 Architecture, disk I/O is the most time consuming of all database activities.

It is important to understand the factors over which you have control at each stage in developing and maintaining a SQL Server environment, because you can use this understanding to build in optimization all along the way. Section IV gives you an understanding of the most common types of performance problems at various stages and it describes some of the most effective techniques for solving those problems.

For the sake of a more organized presentation, we have separated tuning topics into three categories—query level, database level, and SQL Server system level. However, factors from these categories can be interdependent, making it difficult to take an approach that focuses solely on a single category. This final section of the book begins with an overview of the performance-tuning process, then discusses tuning at each of the levels that we have mentioned. Chapter 16, Performance Tuning at the Query Level, addresses query-level issues. Chapter 17, Performance Tuning at the Database Level, focuses on issues at the database level. Chapter 18, System-Level Performance Tuning, concludes with system-level concerns.

After this section, you will have a solid understanding of the types of issues involved with performance tuning; however, information in this section is only an introduction to the topic, because database performance tuning is a vast topic. The theory and practice of performance tuning fills volumes, and you can refer to some excellent sources for more information. The *SQL Server Performance and Tuning Guide* on your SyBooks CD is one of the best.

Point to Note: Performance tuning at any level can have serious consequences for system behavior. We recommend that only database administrators with an advanced understanding of how SQL Server works attempt performance tuning.

16

Performance Tuning at the Query Level

SQL Server's mature *cost-based optimizer* determines how to execute queries in the least amount of time in most situations. The optimizer's job is a difficult one. It becomes more difficult as queries become more complicated; for example, because the number of objects increases. In special cases, you might have reasons for wanting to influence or override the optimizer's choices. System 11 lets you do that by providing a set of commands for analyzing how the optimizer executes queries and by giving you control over some of the optimizer's choices.

This chapter introduces the elements of tuning at the query level. Tuning in general is a vast topic that is best performed by someone with a good understanding of SQL Server's internal operation.

This chapter discusses the following topics.

- A foundation for understanding subsequent query-tuning topics by discussing factors that affect query optimization

- Some of the tools you can use to analyze how the optimizer behaves in response to various query constructions

- Advanced techniques you can use in special situations when you want to override the optimizer's choices

Query Processing Fundamentals

SQL Server handles programmatic queries and individual queries in much the same way. Both of these kinds of queries begin with a Transact-SQL statement and end with returned results. Between, SQL Server parses, chooses a query plan, compiles the query plan, and executes the query.

In the *parsing* step, SQL Server analyzes the Transact-SQL syntax for correctness and creates a query plan that represents the query's logical flow.

A *query plan* is a sequence of steps that SQL Server carries out to execute the parsed query. Normally, many alternative query plans can deliver the same results, but some are more efficient than others. SQL Server's cost-based query optimizer attempts to choose the most time-efficient query plan. Among other considerations, the optimizer uses the following information to determine the best data access method or query plan.

- The number of rows and data pages the query accesses.

- Whether the columns the query accesses have one or more indexes; and if so, the density and distribution of key values in the indexes.

- Whether the query requires access to data pages or index pages. If SQL Server will only access index pages, there will be fewer I/Os.

- The size of the data cache, the I/O size the cache supports, and the cache strategy the query uses.

- The estimated cost of physical and logical reads, and the cost of cache access.

- The number of joins or table scans required for each join, and the usefulness of indexes in limiting the scans if the query includes join clauses.

- Whether building a work table with an index would improve performance.

- Whether the pages will be needed repeatedly. If not, the optimizer can choose the faster fetch and discard strategy.

After the optimizer chooses a query plan, it compiles the plan into the executable code that SQL Server runs. If execution is successful, SQL Server delivers the results to the user or client that submitted the query. If execution is unsuccessful, SQL Server returns an error message.

Factors that Affect Query Optimization

Query execution is based on a set of factors that depend both on the physical design of a database and the construction of a query statement.

You can understand that database design plays a very important role in query performance when you consider the effect of some simple variations in design. For example, you might expect that searching a small table takes less time than searching a large table; but if the large table has an index, that might not be so. Therefore, the size and type of objects involved in the query impact its execution time and involve considerations such as: Is there an index? If so, what type of index? Does cache size play a role?

In general, you shouldn't have to think about how you construct a query, because the optimizer analyzes the commands you use and selects the plan that will take the least time to execute from among alternate query plans. Of course, the physical design of the database also affects the structure of each query plan.

The optimizer is only as effective as the quality and accuracy of the statistics with which it has to work. For example, the optimizer could develop a plan for a query with a stored procedure that has a *where* clause value as an input parameter. Though the query can change based on the input parameter, the optimizer will continue to use the original plan. For reasons such as these, the optimizer can't guarantee the fastest execution plan 100 percent of the time. In addition, the number of alternate plans grows with the complexity of the query, and the optimizer cannot always weigh them all against one another before the overhead of weighing alternate plans becomes too great. In these cases, the optimizer statistically weighs the possible gains against the amount of time it would take to investigate every method and makes a decision about what is "optimal enough."

How You Can Affect Query Optimization

Because of the query optimizer's limitations, you might occasionally choose to influence the optimizer's decision when execution time is critical. You can use SQL Server commands, some of which are given in the next section, to investigate how the optimizer is assigning query plans so you can decide if you agree with it.

If time is critical, look for indications such as the following to determine the necessity of your intervention.

- Is the optimizer using an index to access a large portion of a table?

- Is a *where* clause confusing the optimizer?

- Does the actual data distribution match statistical values used by the optimizer, or is it using old statistics?

- Does the particular query lack appropriate indexes?

Getting Information About Optimizer Decisions

When you conduct database administration for performance tuning, it is essential that you understand what's happening internally or your efforts are more likely to degrade performance than to enhance it. Developing this understanding at the query level involves studying how the optimizer "thinks" and responds to queries, and how its response differs when you use alternative semantics for a particular query. The commands in Table 16-1 generate information about the query plans the optimizer is choosing. The commands listed in this table are discussed in following sections.

Table 16-1. Investigating optimizer actions

Command	Information generated
set noexec on	When used with **set showplan on**, displays information about the query without actually executing it.
set showplan on	Displays the execution steps for each query.
set statistics IO on	Displays the number of physical and logical reads and writes that the query requires.
set statistics time on	Displays the time it takes to parse and compile each command, and the execution time of each step.

Using *set statistics*

Because I/O has the greatest impact on performance, one way to measure the effects of query tuning is to look at the I/O statistics before and after making a change in query semantics or influencing optimizer decisions. The **set statistics** commands (**IO on** and **time on**) give you this type of information.

Using *set noexec*

You can use **set noexec** with **set showplan on** to generate an execution plan without actually executing the query. This is useful for studying optimizer responses to variations in semantics for a particular query.

Point to Note: The **set noexec** command should be the last command you issue, because after that SQL Server will not execute any commands until it receives the **set noexec off** command.

Using the *showplan* Command

The **showplan** command issues a number of messages that give complete information about the execution plan that the optimizer chooses. You can use the **showplan** command with or without the **set noexec** command. After you study the showplan output carefully, you will begin to gain insight into how the SQL Server optimizer works. You can use this knowledge to create queries that will use the execution plan that results in best performance.

Table 16-2 lists some of the many showplan messages. The examples that follow illustrate what many of these messages look like for several sample queries.

Table 16-2. Showplan *messages*

Message for	Description
Step	**Showplan** outputs "STEP N" for every query, where N is an integer beginning with 1. Not all queries are executed in one step.
Query type	This message describe the type of query for each step, such as **select**, **insert**, **update**, and **delete**. The query type can also include any Transact-SQL command, such as **create index**.
"FROM TABLE"	This message indicates the table from which the query is reading. In some cases, the table name could be *worktable* if the query uses intermediate steps.
"TO TABLE"	This message displays the name of the target table when a query contains **insert**, **delete**, **update**, or **select into** clauses. Sometimes, SQL Server needs an intermediate step to process the query, and in such situations the table name is *worktable*.

(continued)

Table 16-2. *(continued)*

Message for	Description
Worktable	When you include a *group by* or *distinct* clause in a query, SQL Server stores the intermediate results in a worktable.
Nested iteration	This message indicates one or more loops through a table to return the result rows. Nested iteration is the default method used to join tables and return rows from a single table. For each iteration, the optimizer performs one or more sets of loops to read the table and retrieve a row, to qualify the row based on search condition, to return the results set, and to loop to get the next row until all of the rows are read.
Update modes	SQL Server uses two modes to perform update operations such as **insert**, **delete**, **update**, and **select into**. The modes are direct update mode and deferred update mode.
"GROUP BY"	Queries using a *group by* clause always use at least two steps. The first step writes the qualifying rows into a worktable, and the second step returns the grouped rows.
Grouped	When a query contains aggregates and *group by* or *compute* aggregate *by* clauses, group aggregates message are printed. When a aggregate function is combined with *group by*, the result is called *grouped aggregate* or *vector aggregate*. The query results have one row for each value of the grouping column or columns.
Ungrouped	When an aggregate function is used in a **select** command that aggregate does not include a *group by* clause, it produces a single value and is called *scalar aggregate* or *ungrouped aggregate*.
Worktable	When you include a *distinct* in a query, SQL Server excludes all duplicate rows from the results so that only unique rows are returned. When no useful index is found, SQL Server first creates a worktable to store all of the results including duplicates. It then sorts the rows in the worktable, discarding the duplicate rows, and returns the rows from the worktable.
Sorting	When you submit a query that contains an *order by* clause, the optimizer checks whether it can use an index. When the optimizer cannot use an index to order the results rows, it creates a worktable to sort the results rows.

The output depicted in Figure 16-1 illustrates **showplan**'s various messages. These examples demonstrate various messages that **showplan** generates. In the examples, the output being illustrated is highlighted in bold.

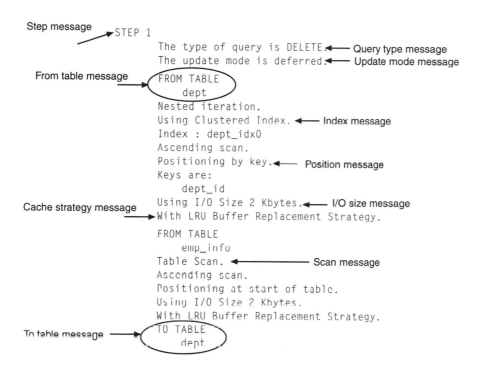

Figure 16-1. *Output from the **showplan** command*

Examples: Showplan Messages

Here's a batch of DDL (data definition language) statements that will generate the tables on which these examples are based. You can use it if you want to verify the **showplan** output for yourself.

```
create table dept(dept_id char(5), dept_name char(30))
create unique clustered index dept_idx0 on dept(dept_id)
go
create table emp_info
(emp_id char(6),
 emp_fname char(30),
 emp_lname char(30),
 emp_dept char(5) references dept(dept_id),
 emp_salary money,
)
```

```
go
create unique clustered index emp_idx on emp_info(emp_id)
go
create nonclustered index emp_name_idx on
  emp_info(emp_lname, emp_fname)
go
```

Example 1. *Query type message*: This example creates a clustered index. The **showplan** output is a query type message that indicates that the index is being created. The output follows the commands.

```
set showplan on
go
create unique clustered index
  emp_idx on emp_info(emp_id)
go
```

```
QUERY PLAN FOR STATEMENT 1 (at line 1).
  STEP 1
    The type of query is CREATE INDEX.
    TO TABLE
      emp_info
```

Example 2. *FROM TABLE message*: This example shows the sequence that the optimizer chooses to access each table. The output shows that the order given in the *from* and *where* clauses of the query can differ from the actual execution order. When you insert or update rows in a table that has a referential integrity constraint, the **showplan** output that follows the commands describes the access methods used to access the referential table.

```
set showplan on
go
select emp_id, emp_lname, emp_fname , dept_name
  from emp_info, dept
  where emp_lname ="James" and dept_id = emp_dept
go
```

```
QUERY PLAN FOR STATEMENT 1 (at line 1).
  STEP 1
    The type of query is SELECT.
    FROM TABLE
      emp_info
    Nested iteration.
    Table Scan.
    Ascending scan.
    Positioning at start of table.
    Using I/O Size 2 Kbytes.
    With LRU Buffer Replacement Strategy.
    FROM TABLE
```

```
      dept
Nested iteration.
Table Scan.
Ascending scan.
Positioning at start of table.
Using I/O Size 2 Kbytes.
With LRU Buffer Replacement Strategy.
```

Example 3. *TO TABLE message*: In this example, the same table is used as both *FROM TABLE* and *TO TABLE*. For update operations, the optimizer needs to read the table that contains the rows to be updated, which results in the **showplan** *FROM TABLE* message. Then it modifies the rows, which results in the **showplan** *TO TABLE* message.

```
set showplan on
go
update emp_info
 set emp_salary=10000
 where emp_id='1000'
go
```

```
QUERY PLAN FOR STATEMENT 1 (at line 1).
  STEP 1
    The type of query is UPDATE.
    The update mode is direct.
    FROM TABLE
      emp_info
    Nested iteration.
    Using Clustered Index.
    Index : emp_idx
    Ascending scan.
    Positioning by key.
    Keys are:
      emp_id
    Using I/O Size 2 Kbytes.
    With LRU Buffer Replacement Strategy.
    TO TABLE
      emp_info
```

Example 4. *Update mode message*: This example deletes an employee from the *master* database that use the index *emp_idx*. This operation involves deleting the *emp* row only. Because it does not have a referential integrity constraint, SQL Server uses direct update mode.

```
set showplan on
go
delete emp_info
 where emp_id='1000'
go
```

```
QUERY PLAN FOR STATEMENT 1 (at line 1).
  STEP 1
    The type of query is DELETE.
    The update mode is direct.
    FROM TABLE
      emp_info
    Nested iteration.
    Using Clustered Index.
    Index : emp_idx
    Ascending scan.
    Positioning by key.
    Keys are:
      emp_id
    Using I/O Size 2 Kbytes.
    With LRU Buffer Replacement Strategy.
    TO TABLE
      emp_info
```

Example 5. *Deferred update mode message*: In this example, SQL Server performs a deferred update, because the **delete** command contains a referential integrity constraint.

```
set showplan on
go
delete dept
  where dept_id='1000'
go
```

```
QUERY PLAN FOR STATEMENT 1 (at line 1).
  STEP 1
    The type of query is DELETE.
    The update mode is deferred.
    FROM TABLE
      dept
    Nested iteration.
    Using Clustered Index.
    Index : dept_idx0
    Ascending scan.
    Positioning by key.
    Keys are:
      dept_id
    Using I/O Size 2 Kbytes.
    With LRU Buffer Replacement Strategy.
    FROM TABLE
      emp_info
    Table Scan.
    Ascending scan.
    Positioning at start of table.
    Using I/O Size 2 Kbytes.
    With LRU Buffer Replacement Strategy.
    TO TABLE
      dept
```

Example 6. *Grouped aggregates message*: This example contains an aggregate function, **avg (emp_salary)**, combined with a *group by* clause. This query must compute the average employee salary for each department. The result set is called *vector aggregate* or *group aggregate*.

```
set showplan on
go
select emp_dept, avg(emp_salary)
 from emp_info
 group by emp_dept
go
```

```
QUERY PLAN FOR STATEMENT 1 (at line 1).
  STEP 1
    The type of query is SELECT (into Worktable1).
    GROUP BY
    Evaluate Grouped COUNT AGGREGATE.
  Evaluate Grouped SUM OR AVERAGE AGGREGATE.
    FROM TABLE
      emp_info
    Nested iteration.
    Table Scan.
    Ascending scan.
    Positioning at start of table.
    Using I/O Size 2 Kbytes.
    With LRU Buffer Replacement Strategy.
    TO TABLE
      Worktable1.
  STEP 2
    The type of query is SELECT.
    FROM TABLE
      Worktable1.
    Nested iteration.
    Table Scan.
    Ascending scan.
    Positioning at start of table.
    Using I/O Size 2 Kbytes.
    With MRU Buffer Replacement Strategy.
```

Example 7. *Ungrouped aggregates message*: This example has only one aggregate function, **avg (emp_salary)**, for the whole table and is referred to as a *scalar* aggregate. It involves using a table scan, and no indexes are involved. It returns only one average employee salary for the whole table.

```
set showplan on
go
select avg(emp_salary)
 from emp_info
go
```

```
QUERY PLAN FOR STATEMENT 1 (at line 1).
  STEP 1
    The type of query is SELECT.
    Evaluate Ungrouped COUNT AGGREGATE.
    Evaluate Ungrouped SUM OR AVERAGE AGGREGATE.
    FROM TABLE
      emp_info
    Nested iteration.
    Table Scan.
    Ascending scan.
    Positioning at start of table.
    Using I/O Size 2 Kbytes.
    With LRU Buffer Replacement Strategy.
  STEP 2
    The type of query is SELECT.
```

Example 8. *Distinct message*: This example uses a *distinct* clause to list departments. Using a *distinct* clause causes SQL Server to create a worktable to store all of the results and any duplicates. It sorts the rows in the worktable, discards the duplicate rows, and returns the results from the worktable.

```
set showplan on
go
select distinct emp_dept
 from emp_info
go
QUERY PLAN FOR STATEMENT 1 (at line 1).

  STEP 1
    The type of query is INSERT.
    The update mode is direct.
    Worktable1 created for DISTINCT.
    FROM TABLE
      emp_info
    Nested iteration.
    Table Scan.
    Ascending scan.
    Positioning at start of table.
    Using I/O Size 2 Kbytes.
    With LRU Buffer Replacement Strategy.
    TO TABLE
      Worktable1.
  STEP 2
    The type of query is SELECT.
    This step involves sorting.
    FROM TABLE
      Worktable1.
    Using GETSORTED
    Table Scan.
    Ascending scan.
```

```
    Positioning at start of table.
    Using I/O Size 2 Kbytes.
    With MRU Buffer Replacement Strategy.
```

Example 9. *Order by message*: The following example shows an *order by* clause that creates a worktable, because there are no indexes on the *emp_dept*, *emp_lname*, and *emp_fname* columns.

set showplan on
go
select emp_dept,emp_lname,emp_fname from emp_info
 order by emp_dept, emp_lname, emp_fname
go

```
QUERY PLAN FOR STATEMENT 1 (at line 1).
  STEP 1
    The type of query is INSERT.
    The update mode is direct.
    Worktable1 created for ORDER BY.
    FROM TABLE
      emp_info
    Nested iteration.
    Table Scan.
    Ascending scan.
    Positioning at start of table.
    Using I/O Size 2 Kbytes.
    With LRU Buffer Replacement Strategy.
    TO TABLE
      Worktable1.
  STEP 2
    The type of query is SELECT.
    This step involves sorting.
    FROM TABLE
      Worktable1.
    Using GETSORTED
    Table Scan.
    Ascending scan.
    Positioning at start of table.
    Using I/O Size 2 Kbytes.
    With MRU Buffer Replacement Strategy.
```

Influencing the Optimizer

This section contains the topics that prompted the words of caution in the introduction, and we'll reiterate them here: Performance tuning at any level can have serious consequences for system behavior.

This section gives an overview of just a sampling of advanced query-optimizing techniques, including specifying the order in which SQL Server accesses tables, specifies I/O size in a query, and influences the treatment of search arguments.

Directing SQL Server Access Order

One way the optimizer minimizes the number of I/O operations is by making judicious decisions about the order in which it accesses tables to perform joins. The order it uses might not be the same as the order you specified when you wrote the query, but it usually is the fastest way to perform the query. However, you might suspect that you can improve query performance by forcing SQL Server to perform the join in the order you specified. SQL Server will let you dictate join order if you use the **forceplan** command before you specify the query.

Point to Note: When you specify **forceplan**, ensure that you do not set this option for all of the queries in a batch. To do so, ensure that you issue the **set forceplan off** command after the query finishes processing.

Performance gains are not in any way guaranteed when you use the **forceplan** command. Always follow up by checking that logical reads and I/O decrease rather than increase. Use **set statistics IO on** before and after comparisons to check.

Large I/O and Prefetch

Virtually the same amount of overhead is associated with all data packets regardless of their size. Most of the time that an I/O operation consumes is spent queuing I/O requests, seeking on disk, and physical positioning. When more data can be sent in fewer packets, it reduces overhead and improves throughput. SQL Server's configurable large I/O feature can greatly improve performance for some types of queries, such as those that scan entire tables or ranges of tables.

The query optimizer evaluates the type of data being accessed and I/O size of the cache. It uses the buffer sizes available in the named cache to which that object is bound, automatically optimizing I/O for each application. (We discussed named caches in Chapter 2, System 11 Architecture.)

When a data cache is configured to allow large I/Os, the optimizer can choose to prefetch data pages if it will be faster. When several pages are read into cache with a single I/O, they are treated as a unit. They age in cache together and, if any page in the unit has been changed, all pages are written to disk as a unit. Because much of the time required to perform I/O operations involves seeking and positioning, reading eight pages in a 16KB I/O performs nearly eight times as fast as eight single-page, 2KB I/Os.

Search Arguments

Sybase uses the term *search argument* to refer to a specific format for the search condition of a *where* clause. The optimizer uses this format to decide which indexes to use to access data. If the *where* clause search condition is not in search argument format, the optimizer will not use the index. The search argument format is *<column> <operator> <expression>*. Example *price <= 12.50* (where the column name is *price*, the operator is <=, and the expression is 12.50). Valid operators are: =, >, <, >=, <=, *like*, and *between*.

Search Argument Equivalents

Sometimes when you submit a query, the SQL construct is turned into a search argument by the optimizer using search argument equivalent. For example, consider the following query.

```
select * from titles
  where price is between 10 and 20
go
```

The optimizer converts it into the following query.

```
select * from titles
  where price is >=10 and price <=20
go
```

Functionally, the two queries are the same; but in the second case, the optimizer has more flexibility in deciding which indexes to use. The optimizer uses the conversions shown in Table 16-1 for the *between* and *like* clauses and expressions. These clauses and expressions are called the search argument equivalents.

Table 16-1. *Optimizer conversions for* between, like, *and expressions*

Clause	Optimizer equivalent
like	The optimizer can convert **like** clauses to *greater than* or *less than* queries if the first character in the pattern is a constant.
between	The **between** clause can be converted to *greater than or equal to* and *less than or equal to* clauses.
expressions	If the expressions on the right side of the *where* clause is an arithmetic expression that can be converted to a constant, the optimizer can use the *density* values, and may use the index. Density is the average fraction of all of the rows in an index that have the same key value.

Search Clauses with Unknown Values

It is common during the execution of stored procedures that the search criteria values are not known until run time, which can confuse the optimizer. For example, when you execute the following query for the first time, the optimizer uses a query plan based on whatever value the **getdate()** function returned at that time. When you execute the same query later, the optimizer will see that it already chose a query plan and use that; but because the value returned by **getdate()** might be different, that plan might no longer be the optimal one.

```
select * from itemlist
  where exp_date < getdate()
go
```

The optimizer can recognize this problem and create a plan based on the average value of the stored procedure, but this might not be good for performance. Therefore, if the query contains a stored procedure for which the value can only be determined at run time, you can use the **recompile** option so that SQL Server will recompile and reoptimize the query every time it executes.

Join Columns and Search Arguments

While coding search arguments in queries, make sure that you avoid using incompatible datatypes. Consider the following stored procedure, which uses a *character* datatype for the employee number and lists all employees above that number. The basic datatype of column *emp_no* is numeric, but it converts the column *emp_no* to the *char* datatype so it can compare the input value. The **showplan** display for the query follows.

```
create proc get_above_emp
   input_value char(5)
   as
   select * from emp
   where convert (char(5), emp_no) >= @input_column.
go
QUERY PLAN FOR STATEMENT 1 (at line 1).
   STEP 1
      The type of query is SELECT.
      FROM TABLE
         emp
      Nested iteration.
      Table Scan.
      Ascending scan.
      Positioning at start of table.
      Using I/O Size 2 Kbytes.
      With LRU Buffer Replacement Strategy.
```

Here's what happens if we modify the preceding stored procedure so that it performs the same function but avoids the data-type conversions.

```
create proc get_above_emp
 input_column char(5)
 as
 declare @emp_test_no int
go
select @emp_test_no = convert(int, @input_column)
go
select * from emp
 where emp_no >= @emp_test_no
go
QUERY PLAN FOR STATEMENT 1 (at line 1).
   STEP 1
      The type of query is DECLARE.
QUERY PLAN FOR STATEMENT 2 (at line 3).
   STEP 1
      The type of query is SELECT.
QUERY PLAN FOR STATEMENT 3 (at line 4).
   STEP 1
      The type of query is SELECT.
QUERY PLAN FOR STATEMENT 4 (at line 5).
   STEP 1
      The type of query is SELECT.
      FROM TABLE
         emp
      Nested iteration.
      Using Clustered Index.
```

```
Index: emp_idx0
Ascending scan.
Positioning by key.
Keys are:
  no
Using I/O Size 2 Kbytes.
With LRU Buffer Replacement Strategy.
```

This preceding **showplan** display indicates that the modified query is more performance efficient than the original query. Also, notice that when the search argument contains the same datatypes, the optimizer uses the clustered index, whereas in the first procedure, the optimizer ignored the index and performed a table scan.

It is best to avoid arithmetic operations, functions, and other expressions on the column side of search clauses. For example, you should not use *where salary * 12 > 100000.* Use as many search arguments as you can so the optimizer has as much information as possible with which to work. Also, you should use the leading column of a composite index. The optimization of secondary keys provides less performance.

Summary

In this chapter, we explored a variety of performance tuning issues at the query level. We looked at factors that affect query optimization and presented some of the tools you can use to analyze how the optimizer behaves in response to various query constructions. Finally, we introduced you to some of the advanced techniques you can use in special situations when you want to override the optimizer's choices. Next, in Chapter 17 we move to a discussion of additional performance tuning matters—those found at the database level.

17

Performance Tuning at the Database Level

This chapter covers the fundamentals of performance tuning in a SQL Server database. These fundamentals include an overview of the tuning process, an analysis of the environment, and a setting of performance goals. This chapter also describes some of the things you can do on the database level to improve performance. It describes the following topics.

- How data distribution can help performance and the types of data that are good candidates for distribution

- How distributing databases across multiple physical devices using segments can help improve performance

- How distributing a specific database object, such as a table, using partitions can help improve performance

- How to create named user caches for critical tables and indexes

Previous chapters discussed the mechanics of using some of the techniques this chapter describes, but here we specifically discuss performance implications. Other areas that can affect performance at the database level are auditing (covered in Chapter 13, SQL Server Security Features) log thresholds, backup, and recovery (covered in Chapter 14, Backup and Recovery.)

Performance Tuning Fundamentals

No RDBMS right out of the box can perform to its maximum potential for all possible applications without some adjustments for the computing environment. That's why a good RDBMS must include a set of performance tuning utilities and monitoring tools. Sybase offers numerous tools and aids for monitoring SQL Server performance. After you've established a running production environment, you can use those tools and utilities to optimize SQL Server for your specific computing environment.

SQL Server Performance Defined

SQL Server system performance is a combination of high scalability, large throughput, and fast response time. Sybase defines these components as follows.

- *Scalability* means that throughput increases linearly with increased resources and increased load

- *Throughput* refers to the volume of transactions that an RDBMS can process in a fixed time period; the higher the volume, the more work your system can perform

- *Response* time is the time it takes for an RDBMS to process a query and return results to a user

Scalability means maintaining consistent performance while supporting an increasing number of users and applications. Scalability is the ability to run on a variety of hardware, from low-end to high-end systems. But it also means taking full advantage of that hardware to deliver high levels of throughput.

The key to attaining the best performance for a SQL Server system is finding and removing hot spots, or *contention points*. Contention points are areas in a system that require concurrent access by multiple users or multiple database servers. Most contention points are found in the areas of cache management, logging, and locking, which can cause transactions to slow each other down. The three chapters in this section of the book provide information that you can use to minimize contention points.

Guidelines for Database and System-Level Tuning

Attempts to improve performance should always begin with careful analysis. As is usually the case, the more you know about a problem, the more likely you'll be able to solve it. The interactions among applications in a SQL Server environment are complex. Furthermore, every environment is different; each involves its own mix of applications, users, and stored procedures, and is characterized by the interdependencies among these entities. Because every SQL Server environment is unique, we really can't say, "If you see X, your problem must be Y, so do Z to improve performance." However, it is possible to give guidelines for a useful progression of steps and to discuss issues commonly related to each step. That is the objective of this section.

The following steps outline the general procedure for tuning at the database level. You can modify these steps as appropriate to use as guidelines for tuning at the query and system levels. Following sections elaborate on these guidelines.

1. Study the SQL Server environment

    - Analyze system behavior and interdependencies by performing benchmark tests to use as a baseline for comparison
    - Think about how to distribute processing in a multiprocessor environment
    - Establish a set of quantifiable performance goals based on the system requirements

2. Understand the effects of using various configuration methods and tools

    - Understand the basic concepts and intricacies of the tuning methods you are considering
    - Understand the implications of using the method—how it will affect the environment in terms of performance gains, losses, and interdependencies

3. Make adjustments to the system using the methods you considered from step 2

4. Analyze the running SQL Server environment after making these adjustments

    - Run the benchmark tests you used in step 1 and compare the results

- If the results are not what you expect, use monitoring tools to gain a deeper understanding of the system
- Investigate dependencies that you might have missed

5. Fine tune the results by repeating steps 3 and 4 as many times as necessary—but know when to stop!

6. Monitor the environment as it evolves

7. Evaluate performance goals and make continual adjustments

Analyze the Environment

The degree to which tuning enhances system performance is a function of the characteristics and the interactions among all factors in a SQL Server environment. These interactions are often complex; consequently, enhancing performance can also be complex. It is essential to study and understand the SQL Server environment in detail so that you can make judicious decisions about how to achieve the performance goals you set.

Performance tuning without first studying the environment and the intricacies of tuning methods and consequences can lead to negative results. For example, in an SMP system, say that you have identified that the system is fully utilizing the combined CPU processing time available, so you add a CPU and a SQL Server engine. This might result in a greater transaction throughput, thus creating lock contention on the last page of the transaction log. Chapter 4, System 11 Features Provide New Solutions, provides an example of how to deal with this by distributing the log across multiple partitions to alleviate last-page contention. However, if you weren't expecting any new bottlenecks, it might take some time to discover and resolve the last-page contention. This could be expensive if you are tuning an on-line production system.

Point to Note: It is best to use a prototype of the production environment for experimentation as you learn the intricacies of your particular system. Until you fully understand the system, you might make changes that affect your system in unexpected and negative ways, because making adjustments to alleviate performance problems in one area can create new bottlenecks in other areas.

Establish a Performance Baseline

Benchmark testing and results analysis are essential for establishing a fully functioning new system. Equally important, they are at the heart of SQL Server's ability to adapt to enterprise requirements and to offer consistently high performance as those requirements change. Perform benchmark tests before tuning so you have a baseline of the results to compare with and quantify improvement. You'll also use this testing to help in initial identification of performance trouble areas.

Monitor utilities let you visualize and record what's going on inside a system. System 11 is equipped with a comprehensive set of tools for monitoring, configuring, and tuning a SQL Server System. Chapter 15, Database Administration Tools, describes several of the tools you can use during benchmarking and to help with configuration. Specifically, the tools we find most useful for the performance-tuning process are SQL Server Monitor and **sp_sysmon**. SQL Server Monitor provides a comprehensive set of performance statistics. It was developed to make it easy to evaluate SQL Server operation for tuning purposes. It offers graphical displays through which you can isolate performance problems. The system procedure **sp_sysmon** monitors system performance for a specified time interval, then prints an ASCII text-based report.

Set Goals

Establish a set of quantifiable performance goals. These goals should be specific numbers based on the benchmark results and your expectations for improving performance. You can use these goals to direct you while you make configuration changes.

Make Adjustments to Improve Performance

A large number of adjustments can improve performance at the query, database, and system levels. The latter half of this chapter, and Chapters 16 and 18, describe several types of performance problems and modifications you can make to solve, or at least alleviate, them. You also can use dozens of performance-related configuration parameters with the **sp_configure** system procedure to help. Chapter 12, Configuring SQL Server, introduced those parameters, and the procedure and concepts involved with using **sp_configure**.

Analyze and Fine-Tune Performance

Here are some suggestion for analyzing a running SQL Server environment after making adjustments for performance.

1. Run the same benchmarks you ran before configuring application priority, then compare the new results to the baseline results

2. Check CPU utilization. Ensure good distribution across all available engines using SQL Server Monitor or **sp_sysmon**

3. If the results are not what you expect, take a closer look at system statistics using monitoring tools

4. Make adjustments to performance attributes

5. Fine tune the results by repeating these steps as many times as necessary

The accomplishment of step 5 is subjective, because in most cases someone with unlimited time and resources could continue to tune and analyze for a long time. Keep your tuning goals in mind, but be aware that the time will come when you should balance performance benefits with tuning resources. In other words, know when to stop.

Monitor the Environment over Time

The behavior of a SQL Server environment generally varies at different times as the workflow changes throughout a 24-hour period, over weeks, and over months. So, it is important to monitor the environment over time to ensure that the system performs well throughout the full cycle of activities and as the system evolves.

Having established the fundamentals, this chapter next describes the major issues for SQL Server database-level performance.

How Distributing Objects Can Help Performance

If an increased number of queries yields slower query results, slower transactions, slower inserts, more activity on system tables, or long access times for mirrored disks, distributing tables and indexes across physical and logical devices are approaches you can take at the database level to improve performance. A simple rule of thumb is to isolate heavily used databases and heavily used tables. This section discusses why distributing data can help improve database performance. Here are databases and tables that often benefit from distribution.

- Performance-critical databases

- User and system databases

- Mirrored data and the mirror

- Heavily used tables

- Frequently joined tables

- Tables and their nonclustered indexes

As we said in Chapter 7, Creating and Managing Databases, you should also store the transaction log and user data on separate disks.

Figure 17-1 illustrates the idea of distributing a database over multiple disks and distributing a table over multiple disks. (A table is distributed over disks C and D.) If a table is large and very heavily used, you can improve performance by distributing it over multiple disks.

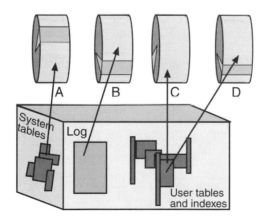

Figure 17-1. Distributed databases and database objects

In general, you use segments to distribute a database's tables and indexes to multiple physical disks, and you use partitions to distribute data across multiple disks. The performance advantage of distributing a single object might not be as obvious as the advantage of distributing objects. The following sections, "Using Segments to Distribute Data" and "Using Partitions to Distribute Data," give more information about these techniques. (Chapter 6, Database Devices and Fault Tolerance, and Chapter 7, Creating and Managing Databases, are prerequisites for understanding how to distribute objects.)

Using Segments to Distribute Data

With a good understanding of the relationships among database devices, databases, and segments, you can effectively distribute a database's objects for performance. We discussed the mechanics of creating and managing database devices, tables, and segments in Chapters 6 and 7. To ensure that you have a solid understanding of the relationships among these entities, we summarize here the process for creating a segment and storing a database or a transaction log on it.

A disk or an operating system file is the basic storage device, which you specially initialize so that SQL Server can store databases and database objects on it. To keep the discussion simple, we'll represent the storage device as a disk, but keep in mind that it could just as well be an operating system file. Figure 17-2 shows a single, unprepared disk.

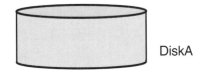

DiskA

Figure 17-2. *A single, uninitialized disk*

To prepare a disk, you initialize it using the **disk init** command, which creates a database device as shown in Figure 17-3. The database device is composed of 256-page allocation units. The **disk init** command lets you specify the number of allocation units with its *size* parameter. Although it is possible to create multiple database devices on the same disk, as a Point to Note in Chapter 7 warned, it is safest not to do so, because some SQL Server commands assume a one-to-one database device to disk relationship. In addition, competition (*contention*) for I/O operations is more likely than in other database device to disk configurations.

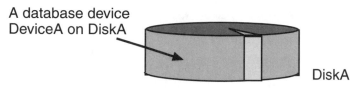

Figure 17-3. *An initialized disk with one database device*

Recall that when you create a database using the **create database** command, you can specify the database device and on which device to store the database's transaction log. If you do not specify a device for either the database or the log, SQL Server puts both of them on the default device. After you create a database device and a database, you can create a segment on the device using the system procedure **sp_addsegment**. During segment creation, you name the segment and associate it with a database and database device.

At this point, if we have created *DatabaseA* on *DeviceA*, we can use the next command to associate one segment with one database device.

```
sp_addsegment segmentA,
  DatabaseA,
  DeviceA
go
```

You don't actually use the segment construct until you create a table or an index. Although you can create more than one segment on a database device, administration is much less complicated if only one segment is associated with the database device. However, to maintain good performance or improve it, it often makes sense to extend the segment to span more than one database device. This allows you to distribute tables and indexes by specifying a segment name when you use the **create table** and **create index** commands.

Figure 17-4 shows a Database 1 that has several objects on the default segment. If the default segment has three busy tables, Disk 1 will have a lot of contention for access. In contrast, if you create each of the three tables depicted in this figure on a different segment and on a different disk, as is the case for Database 2, you reduce contention for any one disk, which improves system performance.

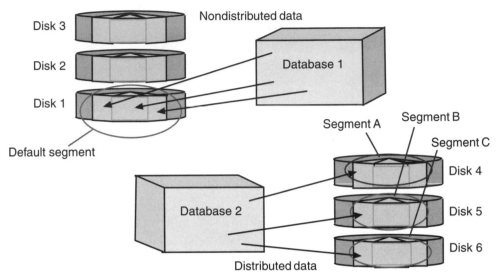

Figure 17-4. *Nondistributed versus distributed databases using segments*

User and System Data

In general, you should separate databases that you know are busy and likely to generate many I/O operations. In a heavily used database environment, it's a given that several system databases will be busy.

Recall from Chapter 3, The SQL Server Engine, that the activity levels for some system databases are directly proportional to actions users take. The *master* database tracks information for the system as a whole. It keeps status for user accounts, remote server accounts, ongoing processes, system messages, active locks, on-line SQL Server engines, and configuration parameters, to name just some of the data for which SQL Server uses the *master* database. If users and applications perform queries that generate temporary data, the *tempdb* database will be busy too. Similarly, the *sybsystemprocs* database is heavily used if numerous queries involve system procedures, and *sybsecurity* will be busy if your system performs auditing.

Mirrored Data and the Mirror

If data is mirrored, the disk on which mirroring is done should be placed on a different device from the device that it mirrors. Keeping the mirror and the mirrored devices on separate disks speeds performance, because SQL Server can perform the disk I/Os in parallel. Even more importantly, though, the point of mirroring is to protect data. If the copy is on the same disk as the original and the disk fails, the mirror isn't really serving its intended purpose. Chapter 6, Database Devices and Fault Tolerances, elaborates on this important point.

Frequently Joined Tables

Joining tables often requires the use of the system database *tempdb*. Therefore, if the system has critical frequently-joined tables, you should put *tempdb* on a separate disk.

Data and Text Chain

A table that has a text or image datatype stores a pointer to the text or image value. The actual data is stored on a separate linked list of pages. Writing or reading a text value requires at least two disk accesses, one to read or write the pointer and the other for the text values. Performance can be improved by separating the table data from the text chain.

Using Partitions to Distribute Data

Heap tables, or tables with nonclustered indexes on which queries frequently perform inserts, can experience bottlenecks if many queries have to wait to obtain a lock on the table so they can make an insert. The reason for the bottleneck is that any new data for these types of tables is inserted on the last page. If the last page becomes full, SQL Server inserts a new page. Figure 17-5 shows a chain of pages that comprise a table. The chain starts with Page 1 and continues to Last page. In the figure, SQL Server Engine 3 has placed a lock on the last page and is inserting a new last page for data that Task 5 needs to insert. SQL Server takes care of setting up the new pointer from the former last page to the new last page. Below the table, several tasks wait in the sleep queue for their turn to insert a page.

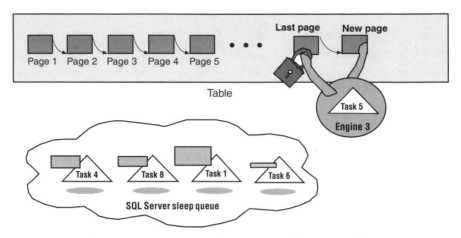

Figure 17-5. *Inserting data into a table's page chain*

How Partitioning Can Help

A technique called *partitioning* splits a table into a set of multiple page chains. Each page chain has a last page, so concurrent inserts are less likely to cause contention. Note that table partitioning won't help much if all of the partitions are on the same physical disk, because contention for disk access can still degrade performance. It is better to put the table partitions on different disks to minimize contention for both disk access and locks on the last page. This involves using segments so that you can extend the table to a database device on another disk.

If you want to create a table with three partitions on three separate disks and you are starting with an uninitialized disk, use the following process to partition the table.

1. Use the **disk init** command to create a database device on three disks. (You probably also want to create a database device for the transaction log on a fourth disk at this point too.)

2. Use the **create database** command on the three data devices (and the log on the log device).

3. Create a segment using the **sp_addsegment** system procedure and map the segment to the first device.

4. Use the **sp_extendsegment** system procedure to include the other two database devices as part of the segment that you will use for the table's three partitions.

5. Use the **create table** or **alter table** command as explained in Chapter 8, Database Objects: Tables and Data Integrity, to create the table's partitions.

Figure 17-6 shows the three disks, the database devices (which occupy the entire disk), the database distributed over the segment, and the table's three partitions. The table is still likely to benefit if you have more than one of its partitions on one physical disk. Either way, SQL Server randomly selects the partition when inserting data.

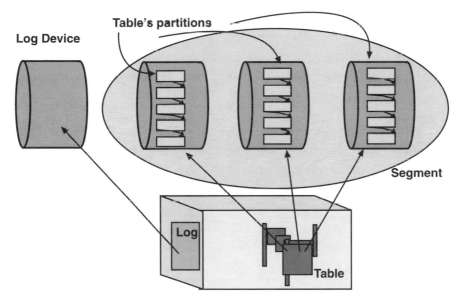

Figure 17-6. *A table with three partitions*

Partitioning Also Helps Read, Write, and Update Performance

Partitioning is a good technique to use for large, heavily used tables because of the way it relieves contention. In general, performance improves when you can distribute a table's data evenly over the available physical devices.

Getting Information About Partitioned Tables

Use the system procedure **sp_helppartition** to obtain information on a table's partitions. The syntax of **sp_helppartition** is as follows, where *table_name* is the name of the partitioned table.

sp_helppartition table_name

Example: The following command displays the information on the partitions of a table *emp*.

```
sp_helppartition emp
go

partitionid       firstpage   controlpage
-----------       ---------   -----------
1                 417         418
2                 425         424
3                 433         432
(3 rows affected, return status = 0)
```

Points to Note: Using Partitions and System Tables

Note the following actions related to partitioning that you *cannot* perform.

- You cannot include the **alter table..partition** command inside a user-defined transaction

- You cannot partition a system table

- You cannot partition tables that have clustered indexes

- You cannot drop a partitioned table

- You cannot truncate a partitioned table

- You cannot create a clustered index on a partitioned table

What Happens in the Server

When a table is partitioned, a row is added to the system table *syspartitions*.

Cache Performance

Cache configuration is another important factor for good performance. Simply having plenty of memory to use for caching goes a long way toward achieving optimum performance, because the more data you can store in cache, the fewer disk I/Os you are likely to need to perform. When a user issues a query, the related data and index pages may be in memory; otherwise, they must be retrieved from disk. The components of memory that affect performance are the following.

- The procedure cache, which is used for stored procedure query plans and triggers

- The data cache, which is used for data, index, and log caches

---

Point to Note: A clustered index is an integral part of its table and must stay on the same segment as the table.

Procedure Cache

Chapter 2, System 11 Architecture, gives the background concepts for how the procedure cache stores query plans for stored procedures. Similarly, the procedure cache stores query plans for triggers. As Chapter 9, Transact-SQL and Its Extensions, explains in the "Stored Procedures" section, the procedure cache ends up with multiple copies of query plans for stored procedures that are simultaneously executed. You need to strike a balance between providing enough memory for all of the copies and using memory space that the data cache could use instead.

Configuring Procedure Cache Size

The default size of the procedure cache is configured as 20 percent of the shared memory that remains after all data structures, overhead, executable, and other SQL Server memory needs are met. This won't always be the best size for every system. You need to determine the correct size based on the applications and the requirements for stored procedure use. You can calculate the optimal size for the procedure cache using the following equation.

procedure cache size = (max concurrent users) * (size of largest plan) * 1.25

Use this next command to determine the size of the stored procedure, view, or trigger.

```
select (count(*)/8) + 1
 from sysprocedures
 where id = object_id ("procedure_name")
go
```

Data Cache

SQL Server uses the data cache to hold data, index, and log pages for current queries. Recently accessed objects are typically system tables such as *sysobjects* and *sysindexes*, active log pages for each database, and parts of frequently used tables.

Chapter 2 addresses the theory of how you can divide the global data cache, called the *default data cache,* into individual named caches, and how that can improve performance. The following sections give the commands and procedures for implementing named caches.

Creating Named Caches

You use the command **sp_cacheconfig** to create named caches. Table 17-1 gives the syntax and parameters for this command.

Table 17-1. *Syntax and parameters for the **sp_cacheconfig** command*

sp_cacheconfig *cache_name*, "*size*[P|K|M|G]"	
cache_name	Name for your named cache.
size	Integer that determines the size of the named cache. It can be in units of pages (P), kilobytes (K)—which is the default—megabytes (M), or gigabytes (G).

Example: The following command creates a 5MB cache called *emp_cache*. You must restart SQL Server to activate the newly created data cache.

```
sp_cacheconfig "emp_cache","5M"
go
```

Binding Caches to Objects

After you create a data cache, you can bind the database or its objects to the cache. Table 17-2 gives the syntax and parameters for binding objects to data caches.

Table 17-2. *Syntax and parameters for the **sp_bindcache** command*

sp_bindcache *cache_name*, *dbname* [,[owner.] *tablename* [, indexname | "text only"]]

(continued)

Table 17-2. *(continued)*

cache_name	Name of the data cache to bind to the database object
tablename	Name of table to bind
indexname	Name of index to bind
"text only"	Used for tables that have text and image columns

Example 1: The following command binds the named cache *emp_cache* to the database *empdb*.

```
sp_bindcache emp_cache, empdb
go
```

Example 2: To bind the index on table *emp*, use the following command.

```
sp_bindcache emp_cache,
  empdb, emp, emp_ind
go
```

Points to Note: Creating and Binding Named Caches

Keep these points in mind while creating and binding data caches.

- You can only bind an existing data cache

- You must be in the *master* database to bind another database to a cache

- Binding operations take effect immediately without the need to restart SQL Server

- You cannot bind an object that has an open cursor on it

- You cannot bind an object when dirty reads are active on it

- You must be the database owner or possess *sa* role to bind an object

Unbinding a Named Cache

You can unbind a named cache from its object bindings using the **sp_unbindcache** command. Table 17-3 gives the syntax.

Table 17-3. *Syntax and parameters for the **sp_unbindcache** command*

sp_unbindcache *dbname* [,owner[, [owner.] *tablename*]
[, *indexname* | "text only"]]

dbname	Name of the database in which the object resides

(continued)

Table 17-3. *(continued)*

tablename	Name of the table to unbind
indexname	Name of the index to unbind
"text only"	Used for tables that have text and image columns

Example: This example unbinds a named data cache from the table *emp* with text columns.

```
sp_unbindcache empdb, emp, "text only"
go
```

To unbind all of the database objects that are bound to a named data cache, use the **sp_unbindcache_all** command, which has the following syntax and where *cache_name* is the name of the data cache.

```
sp_unbindcache_all cache_name
```

Dropping a Named Data Cache

Use the **sp_cacheconfig** command to drop a named cache and reset the value of *size* to zero. For example, to completely remove the data cache *emp_cache*, use the following command.

```
sp_cacheconfig emp_cache, "0"
go
```

Summary

This chapter gave you an overview of the tuning process, of analyzing the environment, and of setting performance goals. It also described some of the things you can do on the database level to improve performance. You can use the performance-tuning concepts that this chapter described to do system-level tuning, which the next chapter introduces.

18

System-Level Performance Tuning

After you've established a running production environment, you can use SQL Server's rich set of tools and utilities to optimize the SQL Server system for your specific computing environment. This chapter discusses the following four important categories of SQL Server system performance, each of which is covered in separate sections that follow. (The syntax and parameters of commands and procedures used in this chapter are more fully detailed in the Transact-SQL Quick Reference appendix in this book.)

- Resource utilization, such as with CPUs, memory, and disk I/O

- Network I/O performance

- Performance of the system database *tempdb*

- Lock-associated performance

Utilization of System Resources

Many performance bottlenecks result from a lack of operating-system resources such as memory and CPU processing power. The good news is that, if the performance limitations are caused by a lack of hardware resources, you can enhance performance by adding, upgrading, or reconfiguring the resources because, in a scalable system like System 11, additional hardware resources yield proportional software improvements. The following sections explore topics related to efficient utilization of these system resources.

CPU Utilization

Understanding how SQL Server utilizes CPUs sometimes requires that you compare the results from two types of monitoring tools. In a UNIX environment, if you use the **ps** command to monitor the operating system and you monitor SQL Server with the **sp_monitor** and **sp_sysmon** procedures, it is possible that the reports might indicate contradictory results. However, that does not necessarily mean that either command is giving inaccurate results. It could be that results are based on differing assumptions built into the analysis part of the commands. You might need to use both sets of results to deduce certain performance characteristics.

For example, if the operating system **ps** command reports high CPU utilization for the SQL Server process and the SQL Server **sp_monitor** procedure indicates that no processes are running, the system procedure **sp_who** could be not listing some process that **sp_lock** lists. In similar situations, you can try restarting SQL Server and rerun the commands to see if restarting fixes the problem. If it does, the command results will show that SQL Server is utilizing operating system resources productively.

Using sp_monitor *to Monitor CPU Utilization*

The **sp_monitor** system procedure is a useful tool for monitoring SQL Server's CPU usage. The following example output is an **sp_monitor** report. In the output, the value 22652 under the *cpu_busy* category indicates that SQL Server was using the CPU for 22,652 seconds. The value 1120 is the number of seconds in CPU time that SQL Server was busy between the two runs (that is, between *last_run* and *current_run*). This report helps you understand how much CPU time SQL Server used. It also reports on I/O and network activities.

```
last_run          current_run    seconds
--------------    -----------    -----------------
Aug 5 1996        9:30AM  Aug 5 1996 10:30AM  3600
cpu_busy          io_busy        idle

22652(1120)-0%   2991(370)-0%  532489(130449)-98%
packets_received  packets_sent  packet_errors

154213(3159)     223242(213803)  4(2)
total_read        total_write    total_errors   connections

861129(401982) 910367(137006)  0(0)    332(61)
```

Using sp_sysmon *to Monitor CPU Utilization*

The **sp_sysmon** category Engine Busy Utilization indicates how busy SQL Server is during **sp_sysmon**'s sample run time. The following report is partial output from running **sp_sysmon** using a sample time of two minutes. The values listed under the Engine Busy Utilization heading are averages over the sample interval. A very high value indicates that SQL Server was very active during the sample period.

```
Kernel Utilization
------------------

Engine Busy Utilization:
  Engine       0         0.0 %
  Engine       1         0.0 %
  Engine       2        34.4 %
  -------    -------   ---------
  Summary:   Total:     34.4 %  Average: 11.5 %
```

The CPU Yields by Engine category reports the number of times each SQL Server yielded to the operating system. A high value of CPU Yield by Engine indicates that SQL Server yielded voluntarily to the operating system. If Engine Busy Utilization is low, you could use CPU Yields by Engine statistics to check whether the data reported by Engine Busy Utilization reflects a truly inactive SQL Server engine.

```
CPU Yields by Engine per sec per xact count % of total
---------- --------- -------- -------- ----------------

Engine 0          0.1      8.0        8        0.2 %
Engine 1          0.1      8.0        8        0.2 %
Engine 2         32.8   3930.0     3930       99.6 %
---------- --------- ------- -------- ----------------
Total CPU Yields:        32.9   3946.0     3946
```

If both operating system and SQL Server utilities report high CPU utilization, it is possible that the value of SQL Server's configurable *housekeeper free write percent* parameter is set too high. You can check this by issuing the command **sp_configure housekeeper free write percent**. A *housekeeper free write percent* value of or near 100 could cause the high CPU utilization, because the housekeeper task works continuously, regardless of the percentage of additional database writes. If the *housekeeper free write percent* value is not so high, it is likely that the system's need for processing power has exceeded available resources. You might be able to improve performance by adding CPUs.

If you do add CPUs, be sure to set the configuration parameter *max online engines* to utilize the new CPUs. While configuring the *max online engines,* we recommend that you set the value to one less than the total number of CPUs. This ensures that, at the least, the operating system has the processing power of one CPU to execute its own functions.

Memory Utilization

SQL Server requires that data needed by a query is in the data cache when the query executes. If the data is not in the cache, SQL Server must fetch it from disk. The less memory you configure for SQL Server, the more frequently it must perform I/O to bring data into cache and to flush it from cache back to disk. The more frequently SQL Server performs I/O, the more performance is degraded. If you want to reduce the time that SQL Server spends performing I/O, you can allocate more memory using the **sp_configure** system procedure with *total memory* as a parameter.

If the machine running SQL Server is strictly a data server—that is, if no processes are running other than SQL Server—you can allocate at least 80 percent of the physical memory to SQL Server. If SQL Server is sharing system resources with other applications, you need to leave enough memory for those applications.

To determine how much memory is currently allocated to SQL Server, you can use **sp_sysmon** or examine the value of the *total memory* **sp_configure** configuration parameter. Check with your operating system utilities to know the physical limitations of memory.

You might also check how much of SQL Server's memory is assigned to database objects in the form of named caches to verify that named caches are using memory optimally. To check this, execute the **sp_helpcache** procedure to list the objects that are bound to a named cache. It is a good idea to make this check often. If you see that the table grows, you should also increase the size of the named cache to accommodate the table's data. If the named cache is not utilized to its full capacity (meaning there is always room available in the named cache), you can reduce the size of the named cache to allocate the unused memory to other named caches.

Procedure Cache Memory

The procedure cache memory is used to compile stored procedures and store the compiled version of stored procedures while executing them. When SQL Server starts, the error log contains information about how much procedure cache is available. The following sample is part of the error log messages pertaining to the procedure cache. The value 705 is the number of objects, and 752 is the size of the procedure cache in pages.

```
96/06/18 16:42:11.04 server Number of proc buffers allocated: 705.
96/06/18 16:42:11.31 server Number of blocks left for proc headers: 752.
```

The number of objects (such as views, rules, defaults, stored procedures, and triggers) represents the maximum number of compiled procedural objects that can reside in the procedure cache at a given time. So in the above example, no more than 705 objects can be stored in the procedure cache. The value for procedure headers in the example is 752. This means that 752 2KB pages have been allocated to the procedure cache. Each object stored in the procedure cache requires at least one page (4KB for Stratus machines and 2KB for others).

When SQL Server is unable to accommodate a compiled object, such as a stored procedure or a trigger, in procedure cache, it could be due to one of several reasons. The cache might have the maximum number of compiled objects, or there might not be enough memory available, in which case SQL Server reports Error 701 and aborts the current query. This is a serious problem, because the same procedure must have been previously executed successfully and produced results. Now, the same procedure is unable to execute for lack of memory resources. If the application does not check for this error and it goes undetected, the results of the associated query could be erroneous.

Tuning the configuration parameter *procedure cache percent* is an iterative process that depends on the computing environment as a whole and can change as the environment changes. For example, while you are building an application, you might need to set this parameter to 50 percent to accommodate the compiling and testing of numerous stored procedures. In addition, in a development environment you might compile and test stored procedures frequently, requiring more memory than for the same application running in a production environment. After you convert your development system to a production system, you might not require such a high value for the *procedure cache percent* parameter.

Although you work with the *procedure cache percent* parameter, it is important to keep in mind that it's actually the total amount of procedure cache that is important. Consider the following example.

If 60MB has been allocated to SQL Server memory, SQL Server has been configured to use the full 60MB. If *the procedure cache percent* is 50 percent, the amount of procedure cache can be 50 percent of 50MB, or 25MB (assuming 10MB is allocated for user connections and other overhead). All applications will share this *procedure cache percent*. If you increase the memory to 100MB, assume that the same 10MB are needed for other purposes, and do not change the *procedure cache percent*, the procedure cache size would be 50 percent of 90MB (100MB minus 10MB), which results in 45MB. This configuration results in more memory allocated to procedure cache. Hence, you need to adjust the *procedure cache percent* to around 25 percent to retain the same amount of procedure cache. This example illustrates that you should only assign a procedure cache percent value after careful evaluation of the environment.

When to Add Memory

If you observe that data is frequently flushed from cache to disk, it is an indication that you could improve SQL Server performance by adding memory. Try using **sp_sysmon** every two minutes during the peak transaction period and study the section of the output called Memory Management.

Here is sample output from **sp_sysmon**'s Memory Management section. In the output, the Pages Allocated row reports the number of times SQL Server allocated a new page in memory. The Pages Released row reports the number of times SQL Server freed a page. If SQL Server allocates and releases pages in increasing numbers, it's an indication that SQL Server could use more memory.

Memory Management	per sec	per xact	count	% of total
Pages Allocated	0.0	0.0	0	n/a
Pages Released	0.0	0.0	0	n/a

If you do add memory to improve performance, be sure to use the system procedure **sp_configure** to configure the system so it recognizes the new memory. In addition to configuring the total memory parameter, reduce the configurable parameter *procedure cache percent* such that the percentage of procedure cache is kept constant. If you don't, the procedure cache might use more memory than it needs, resulting in poor utilization of memory resources.

Disk I/O Management

If you are experiencing a performance problem that you suspect is due to excessive disk I/O during query execution, use **sp_sysmon** every two minutes during the peak transaction period. Check the Disk I/O Management section of the report for values under the Max Outstanding I/Os, I/Os Delayed By, and Device Activity Detail headings. Use the data to determine if there is indeed an I/O bottleneck. The following sample output shows what this part of the **sp_sysmon** report looks like.

```
Disk I/O Management

  Max Outstanding   I/Os per sec per xact count % of total
  ------------------ ------------------ ----------------
  Server            n/a     n/a      0      n/a
  Engine 0          n/a     n/a      1      n/a
  Engine 1          n/a     n/a      1      n/a
  Engine 2          n/a     n/a      1      n/a
  I/Os Delayed by
  Disk I/O Structuresn/a    n/a      0      n/a
  Server Config Limitn/a    n/a      0      n/a
  Engine Config Limitn/a    n/a      0      n/a
  Operating System Limit    n/a   n/a        0      n/a
  Total Requested Disk I/Os    31.6 3788.0  3/88      n/a
  Completed Disk I/Os
  Engine 0      0.1     8.0       8      0.2 %
  Engine 1      0.1     8.0       8      0.2 %
  Engine 2     31.4  3772.0    3772     99.6 %
  ------------ ----------- ------------ ----------- -----
  TotalCompleted I/Os 31.6   3788.0 3788
  Device Activity Detail
  ------------ ----------- ------------ ----------- -----
  /dev/rdata
   data per secper xactcount % of total
  ------------ ----------- ------------ ----------- -----
       0.00.0    0     n/a
  ------------ ----------- ------------ ----------- -----
   Total I/Os   0.0     0.0       0      0.0 %
```

```
/dev/rmaster
 master per secper xactcount % of total
------------- ----------- ------------ ----------- -----
      0.0    0.0    0    n/a
------------- ----------- ------------ ----------- -----
 Total I/Os  0.0    0.0    0    0.0 %
------------- ----------- ------------ ----------- -----


/dev/rsybdata2
 sybdata2per secper xact count % of total
------------- ----------- ------------ ----------- -----
 Reads17.1 2057.0  2057     100.0 %
 Writes     0.0    0.0    0     0.0 %
------------- ----------- ------------ ----------- -----
 Total I/Os  17.1  2057.0  2057    54.3 %
 Device Semaphore Granted
    17.1   2057.0 2057     100.0 %
 Device Semaphore Waited
   0.00.0    0     0.0 %
------------- ----------- ------------ ----------- -----


/dev/rsybdata3
 sybdata3  per sec  per xact  count % of total
------------- ----------- ------------ ----------- -----
 Reads 14.41724.0  1724     100.0 %
 Writes 0.0  0.0    0     0.0 %

 TotalI/Os   14.4  1724.0  1724    45.5 %

 Device Semaphore Granted
    14.4   1724.0  1724    100.0 %
 Device Semaphore Waited
   0.0     0.0    0     0.0 %


------------- ----------- ------------ ----------- -----


/dev/rsybdata4
 sybdata4per secper xact  count% of total
------------- ----------- ------------ ----------- -----
    0.00.0    0    n/a
------------- ----------- ------------ ----------- -----
 Total I/Os  0.0    0.0    0     0.0 %
------------- ----------- ------------ ----------- -----


/dev/rsybdata5
 sybdata5  per sec  per xact  count % of total
------------- ----------- ------------ ----------- -----
 Reads 0.1   7.0    7     100.0 %
 Writes0.0   0.0    0     0.0 %
------------- ----------- ------------ ----------- -----
 Total I/Os  0.1    7.0    7     0.2 %
```

```
Device Semaphore Granted
   0.17.0    7    100.0 %
Device Semaphore Waited
   0.00.0    0      0.0 %

/opt/sybase11/sybprocs.dat
  sysprocsdevper sec per xact count % of total
------------- ----------- ----------- ----------- -----
   0.00.0    0    n/a
------------- ----------- ----------- ----------- -----
Total I/Os  0.0     0.0      0      0.0 %

------------- ----------- ----------- ----------- -----

/opt/sybase11/sybsecurity.dat
  sybsecurity per sec  per xact  count % of total
------------- ----------- ----------- ----------- -----
   0.0     0.0     0    n/a
------------- ----------- ----------- ----------- -----
TotalI/Os          0.0     0.0     0     0.0 %
------------- ----------- ----------- ----------- -----

/opt/sybtemp/temp.dat
  sybtempper sec per xactcount % of total
------------- ----------- ----------- ----------- -----
   0.0     0.0     0    n/a
------------- ----------- ----------- ----------- -----
 TotalI/Os  0.0     0.0     0      0.0 %
```

The comment under the Device Activity Detail section reports disk I/O activity on all logical devices. It is useful for checking that I/O is well balanced across database devices. Examining the report for each device gives you more information about the nature of the problem. If you notice device contention and your system has more available disk controllers, try distributing data over disks and controllers.

Network I/O Management

If performance degrades during execution of queries that return large data rows or when a client process appears to slow all other processes, it could be due to a network I/O bottleneck. If the query result set is not displayed on a client but you see that SQL Server's status for that process is *send sleep*, SQL Server has finished executing the query and is sending the data to a client. If the client is still receiving data, it is probably a network problem.

Execute **sp_sysmon** to report network I/O activities. Under the section called Network I/O Management, **sp_sysmon** reports various network activities such as Number of TDS Packets Received and TDS Packets Sent.

One solution for network I/O problems is to increase the network packet size to a large value. Using a large packet size reduces the number of server reads and writes to the network and the unused space in the network packets. You can also use stored procedures instead of batch queries, wherever possible, to avoid network traffic.

You could also configure the SQL Server parameter *tcp_no_delay* to improve performance. By default, this parameter is set to zero, which means that TCP (transmission control protocol) packets are batched. TCP batches small logical packets into single, larger physical packets to fill physical network frames with as much data as possible. This improves network throughput for a terminal-emulation environment. However, if your application uses small TDS (tabular data stream) packets, you can try setting the *tcp_no_delay* parameter to one so that SQL Server will not batch packets.

tempdb *Performance*

If a system experiences a performance problem while executing queries that use such clauses as *group by* and *order by* but queries that do not use these options perform well, the problem could be the physical placement of the *tempdb* database. When you execute a query that contains a *group by* or *order by* clause, SQL Server creates a temporary table and stores the results in the *tempdb* database. If a relatively large number of such queries run in an environment, many temporary tables are created in *tempdb*, which can lead to a performance problem. Here are some techniques you can use to improve *tempdb* performance.

- Resize *tempdb*
- Place *tempdb* in an operating system file
- Bind *tempdb* to a named cache
- Create *tempdb* database in disk memory, as discussed in the next section

Make sure there is enough room to store intermediate results of queries that contain *group by* or *order by* clauses. Placing *tempdb* on a separate device often leads to performance improvements. We recommend placing *tempdb* in a UNIX operating system file, as Chapter 6, Database Devices and Fault Tolerance, describes.

You can create a named cache and bind the entire *tempdb* database to it. In doing so, all of the objects created in *tempdb* are automatically bound to the named cache. This makes any object within *tempdb* readily available in cache, eliminating disk I/O associated with *tempdb* and, of course, improving performance.

Create *tempdb* Database in Disk Memory

The I/O on memory chips is extremely fast compared to that of a disk drive, but it is expensive. The new solid state disk technology can provide better I/O performance than disk drives. Solid state disks are basically memory chips that can also store data. Although expensive compared to disk drives, solid state disks bring disk technology closer to that of random access memory.

The *tempdb* table is frequently accessed to create and drop temporary tables, which is I/O intensive. By placing *tempdb* on a solid state disk, you can improve SQL Server performance.

Tip! If you execute the system procedure **sp_sysmon** about every two minutes and analyze the results, you'll much better understand how your system works and be able to make performance improvements as they are needed.

Summary

This chapter gave you an overview of the types of tools and methods you can use to tune a SQL Server environment on the system level. We thank you for reading this book and hope that it has helped you gain the SQL Server knowledge you need to move forward with Sybase. We wish you good luck!

Appendix A

System Tables

This appendix provides three compilations of Sybase SQL Server system tables. Table A-1 lists system tables that occur in all SQL Server databases. Table A-2 lists system tables that are SQL Server wide. That is, they exist only in the *master* database. Finally, Table A-3 contains system tables that occur only in the *sybsecurity* database.

Table A-1. *System tables that occur in all databases*

System Table	Contents
sysalternates	One row for each SQL Server user mapped to a database user
sysattributes	One row for each object attribute definition
syscolumns	One row for each column in a table or view, and for each parameter in a procedure
syscomments	One or more rows for each view, rule, default, trigger, or procedure, giving SQL definition statement
sysconstraints	One row for each referential and check constraint associated with a table or column

(continued)

Table A-1. *(continued)*

System Table	Contents
sysdepends	One row for each procedure, view, or table that is referenced by a procedure, view, or trigger
sysindexes	One row for each clustered or nonclustered index, one row for each table with no index, and an additional row for each table containing text or image data
syskeys	One row for each primary, foreign, or common key; set by user (not maintained by SQL Server)
syslogs	Transaction log
sysobjects	One row for each table, view, procedure, rule, trigger default, log, and (in *tempdb* only) temporary object
syspartitions	One row for each partition (or page chain) of a partitioned table
sysprocedures	One row for each view, rule, default, trigger, or procedure, giving internal definition
sysprotects	User permissions information
sysreferences	One row for each referential integrity constraint declared on a table or column
sysroles	Maps server-wide roles to local database groups
syssegments	One row for each segment created in the database
systhresholds	One row for each threshold defined for the database
systypes	One row for each system-supplied and user-defined datatype
sysusermessages	One row for each user-defined message
sysusers	One row for each user allowed in the database

Table A-2. *System tables that occur in the* **master** *database*

System Table	Contents
syscharsets	One row for each character set or sort order
sysconfigures	One row for each user-settable configuration parameter
syscurconfigs	Information about configuration parameters currently being used by SQL Server

(continued)

Table A-2. *(continued)*

System Table	Contents
sysdatabases	One row for each database on SQL Server
sysdevices	One row for each tape dump device, disk dump device, disk for databases, and disk partition for databases
sysengines	One row for each SQL Server engine currently online
syslanguages	One row for each language (except U.S. English) known to the server
syslisteners	One row for each type of network connection used by the current SQL Server
syslocks	Information about active locks
sysloginroles	One row for each server login that possesses a system-defined role
syslogins	One row for each valid SQL Server user account
syslogshold	Information about the oldest active transaction and the Replication Server truncation point for each database
sysmessages	One row for each system error or warning message
sysprocesses	Information about server processes
sysremotelogins	One row for each remote user
syssrvroles	One row for each server-wide role
sysservers	One row for each remote SQL Server
sysusages	One row for each disk piece allocated to a database

Table A-3. *System tables that occur in the* **sybsecurity** *database*

System Table	Contents
sysaudits	One row for each record of audit data
sysauditoptions	One row for each global audit option

Global Variables

This appendix contains a list of global variables, which has been taken from the Sybase *SQL Server Reference Manual*.

Table B-1. *Sybase SQL Server System 11 global variables*

Variable	Description
@@char_convert	Contains 0 if character set conversion is not in effect. Contains 1 if character set conversion is in effect.
@@client_csname	The client's character set name. Is set to NULL if client character set has never been initialized; otherwise, it contains the name of the most recently used character set.
@@client_csid	The client's character set ID. Is set to -1 if client character set has never been initialized; otherwise, it contains the most recently used client character set ID from *syscharsets*.
@@connections	The number of logins or attempted logins since SQL Server was last started.

(continued)

Table B-1. (continued)

Variable	Description
@@cpu_busy	The amount of time, in ticks, that the CPU has spent doing SQL Server work since the last time SQL Server was started.
@@error	Commonly used to check the error status (succeeded or failed) of the most recently executed batch. It contains 0 if the previous transaction succeeded; otherwise, it contains the last error number generated by the system. A statement such as **if @@error != 0 return** causes an exit if an error occurs. Every Transact-SQL statement resets @@error, including **print** statements and *if* tests, so the status check must immediately follow the batch whose success is in question.
@@identity	The last value inserted into an IDENTITY column by an **insert** or **select into** statement. @@identity is reset each time a row is inserted into a table. If a statement inserts multiple rows, @@identity reflects the IDENTITY value for the last row inserted. If the affected table does not contain an IDENTITY column, @@identity is set to 0.
	The value of @@identity is not affected by the failure of an **insert** or **select into** statement, or by the rollback of the transaction that contained it. @@identity retains the last value inserted into an IDENTITY column, even if the statement that inserted it failed to commit.
@@idle	The amount of time, in clock ticks, that SQL Server has been idle since it was last started.
@@io_busy	The amount of time, in clock ticks, that SQL Server has spent doing input and output operations since it was last started.
@@isolation	The current isolation level of the Transact-SQL program. @@isolation takes the value of the active level (0, 1, or 3).
@@langid	The local language ID of the language currently in use (specified in *syslanguages.langid*).

(continued)

Table B-1. *(continued)*

Variable	Description
@@language	The name of the language currently in use (specified in *syslanguages.name*).
@@maxcharlen	The maximum length, in bytes, of a character in SQL Server's default character set.
@@max_connections	The maximum number of simultaneous connections that can be made with SQL Server in this computer environment. The user can configure SQL Server for any number of connections less than or equal to the value of @@max_connections with **sp_configure "number of user connections"**.
@@ncharsize	The average length, in bytes, of a national character.
@@nestlevel	The nesting level of current execution (initially 0). Each time a stored procedure or trigger calls another stored procedure or trigger, the nesting level is incremented. If the maximum of 16 is exceeded, the transaction aborts.
@@pack_received	The number of input packets read by SQL Server since it was last started.
@@pack_sent	The number of output packets written by SQL Server since it was last started.
@@packet_errors	The number of errors that have occurred while SQL Server was sending and receiving packets.
@@procid	The stored procedure ID of the currently executing procedure.
@@rowcount	The number of rows affected by the last command. @@rowcount is set to 0 by any command that does not return rows, such as an *if* statement. With cursors, @@rowcount represents the cumulative number of rows returned from the cursor result set to the client up to the last **fetch** request.
@@servername	The name of the local SQL Server. You must define a server name with **sp_addserver**, then restart SQL Server.
@@spid	The server process ID number of the current process.

(continued)

Table B-1. *(continued)*

Variable	Description
@@sqlstatus	Contains status information resulting from the last **fetch** statement. @@sqlstatus may contain the following values. 0 – The fetch statement completed successfully 1 – The fetch statement resulted in an error 2 – There is no more data in the result set. This warning occurs if the current cursor position is on the last row in the result set and the client submits a **fetch** command for that cursor.
@@textcolid	The ID of the column referenced by @@textptr. The datatype of this variable is *tinyint*.
@@textdbid	The database ID of the database containing an object with the column referenced by @@textptr. The datatype of this variable is *smallint*.
@@textobjid	The ID of the object containing the column referenced by @@textptr. The datatype of this variable is *int*.
@@textptr	The text pointer of the last text or image column inserted or updated by a process. The datatype of this variable is *binary(16)*. (Do not confuse this variable with the **textptr()** function.)
@@textsize	The current value of the *set textsize* option, which specifies the maximum length, in bytes, of text or image data to be returned with a select statement. Defaults to 32KB.
@@textts	The text time stamp of the column referenced by @@textptr. The datatype of this variable is *varbinary(8)*.
@@thresh_hysteresis	The change in free space required to activate a threshold. This amount, also known as the *hysteresis* value, is measured in 2KB database pages. It determines how closely thresholds can be placed on a database segment.
@@timeticks	The number of microseconds per clock tick. The amount of time per tick is machine dependent.
@@total_errors	The number of errors that have occurred while SQL Server was reading or writing.

(continued)

Table B-1. *(continued)*

Variable	Description
@@total_read	The number of disk reads by SQL Server since it was last started.
@@total_write	The number of disk writes by SQL Server since it was last started.
@@tranchained	The current transaction mode of the Transact-SQL program. @@tranchained returns 0 for unchained or 1 for chained.
@@trancount	The nesting level of transactions. Each **begin transaction** in a batch increments the transaction count. When you query @@trancount in chained transaction mode, its value is never zero, because the query automatically initiates a transaction.
@@transtate	The current state of a transaction after a statement executes. @@transtate isn't cleared for each statement. @@transtate may contain the following values. 0 – *Transaction in progress* An explicit or implicit transaction is in effect; the previous statement executed successfully. 1 – *Transaction succeeded* The transaction completed and committed its changes. 2 – *Statement aborted* The previous statement was aborted; no effect on the transaction. 3 – *Transaction aborted* The transaction aborted and rolled back any changes.
@@version	The date of the current version of SQL Server.List:global variablesList:global variables.

Appendix C

Transact-SQL Quick Reference

Sybase has consolidated the syntax for all of the commands, procedures, functions, and datatypes of SQL Server release 11.0 in a handy document titled *Quick Reference Guide for SQL Server Release 11.0*. This document includes all commands and a complete list of parameters for commands and parameters that were not covered in the main part of this book.

We have obtained permission to include the information here for your reference. To arrange additional copies or reproduction rights to disseminate to your entire SQL Server project team, contact Sybase Customer Fulfillment at 800-685-8225 from the United States and Canada, or fax 617-229-9845. Request Document ID: 70202-01-1100-01.

Datatypes	Synonyms	Range
Exact numeric		
tinyint		0 to 255
smallint		-2^{15} (-32,768) to 2^{15} -1 (32,767)
int	integer	-2^{31} (-2,147,483,648) to 2^{31} -1 (2,147,483,647)
numeric (p, s)		-10^{38} to 10^{38} -1
decimal (p, s)	dec	-10^{38} to 10^{38} -1
Approximate numeric		
float (precision)		Machine dependent
double precision		Machine dependent
real		Machine dependent
Money		
smallmoney		-214,748.3648 to 214,748.3647
money		-922,337,203,685,477.5808 to 922,337,203,685,477.5807
Date/time		
smalldatetime		January 1, 1900 to June 6, 2079
datetime		January 1, 1753 to December 31, 9999
Character		
char(n)	*character*	255 characters or fewer
varchar(n)	*char[acter] varying*	255 characters or fewer
nchar(n)	*national char[acter]*	255 characters or fewer
nvarchar(n)	*nchar varying, national char[acter] varying*	255 characters or fewer
Binary		
binary(n)		255 bytes or fewer
varbinary(n)		255 bytes or fewer
Bit		
bit		0 or 1
Text and image		
text		2^{31} -1 (2,147,483,647) bytes or fewer
image		2^{31} -1 (2,147,483,647) bytes or fewer

Transact-SQL Commands

ALTER DATABASE *database_name*
    [ON {**DEFAULT** | *database_device* } [= *size*]
      [, *database_device* [= *size*]]...]
    [**LOG ON** { **DEFAULT** | *database_device* } [= *size*]
      [, *database_device* [= *size*]]...]
    [**WITH OVERRIDE**]
    [**FOR LOAD**]

ALTER TABLE [*database.*[*owner*].]*table_name*
    {**ADD** *column_name datatype*
      [**DEFAULT** {*constant_expression* | **USER** | **NULL**}]
      {[{**IDENTITY** | **NULL**}]
      | [{**CONSTRAINT** *constraint name*]
        {{**UNIQUE** | **PRIMARY KEY**}
        [**CLUSTERED** | **NONCLUSTERED**]
        [**WITH** {**FILLFACTOR** | **MAX_ROWS_PER_PAGE**} = *x*]
          [**ON** *segment_name*]
      | **REFERENCES** [[*database.*]*owner.*]*ref_table*
        [(*ref_column*)]
      | **CHECK** (*search_condition*)}]}...
      {[, *next_column*]}...
    | **ADD** {[{**CONSTRAINT** *constraint_name*]
      {**UNIQUE** | **PRIMARY KEY**}
      [**CLUSTERED** | **NONCLUSTERED**]
      (*column_name* [{, *column_name*}...])
      [**WITH** {**FILLFACTOR** | **MAX_ROWS_PER_PAGE**} = *x*]
        [**ON** *segment_name*]
    | **FOREIGN KEY** (*column_name* [{, *column_name*}...])
      REFERENCES [[*database.*]*owner.*]*ref_table*
      [(*ref_column* [{, *ref_column*}...])]
    | **CHECK** (*search_condition*)}
    | **DROP CONSTRAINT** *constraint_name*
    | **REPLACE** *column_name*
      DEFAULT {*constant_expression* | *user* | *null*}
    | **PARTITION** *number_of_partitions*
    | **UNPARTITION**}

BEGIN
    statement block
    END

BEGIN TRAN[**SACTION**] [*transaction_name*]
    WHILE *logical_expression statement*

BREAK
    statement
    CONTINUE

CHECKPOINT

CLOSE *cursor_name*

COMMIT [**TRAN**[**SACTION**] | **WORK**] [*transaction_name*]

COMPUTE (*see* **SELECT**)

CONTINUE

CREATE DATABASE *database_name*
    [ON {**DEFAULT** | *database_device*} [= *size*]
      [, *database_device* [= *size*]]...]
    [**LOG ON** *database_device* [= *size*]
      [, *database_device* [= *size*]]...]
    [**WITH OVERRIDE**]
    [**FOR LOAD**]

CREATE DEFAULT [*owner.*]*default_name*
    AS *constant_expression*

CREATE [**UNIQUE**] [**CLUSTERED** | **NONCLUSTERED**]
    INDEX *index_name*
    ON [[*database.*]*owner.*]*table_name* (*column_name*
      [, *column_name*]...)
    [**WITH** {{**FILLFACTOR** | **MAX_ROWS_PER_PAGE**} = *x*,
      IGNORE_DUP_KEY, SORTED_DATA,
      [**IGNORE_DUP_ROW** | **ALLOW_DUP_ROW**]}]
    [**ON** *segment_name*]

CREATE PROCEDURE [*owner.*]*procedure_name*[;*number*]
    [[(|]@*parameter_name*
      datatype [(*length*) | (*precision* [, *scale*])]
      [= *default*][**OUTPUT**]
    [, @*parameter_name*
      datatype [(*length*) | (*precision* [, *scale*])]
      [= *default*][**OUTPUT**]]...[)]]
    [**WITH RECOMPILE**]
    AS *SQL_statements*

CREATE RULE [*owner.*]*rule_name*
    AS *condition_expression*

CREATE SCHEMA AUTHORIZATION *authorization_name*
    create_object_statement
    [*create_object_statement* ...]
    [*permission_statement* ...]

```
CREATE TABLE [database.[owner].]table_name (column_name datatype
  [DEFAULT {constant_expression | USER | NULL}]
  {[{IDENTITY | NULL | NOT NULL}]
  | [[CONSTRAINT constraint_name]
    {{UNIQUE | PRIMARY KEY}
      [CLUSTERED | NONCLUSTERED]
      [WITH {FILLFACTOR |MAX_ROWS_PER_PAGE}= x]
        [ON segment_name]
      | REFERENCES [[database.]owner.]ref_table
        [(ref_column)]
      | CHECK (search_condition)}}]...
  | [CONSTRAINT constraint_name]
    {{UNIQUE | PRIMARY KEY}
      [CLUSTERED | NONCLUSTERED]
    (column_name [{, column_name}...])
      [WITH {FILLFACTOR |MAX_ROWS_PER_PAGE}= x]
        [ON segment_name]
      | FOREIGN KEY (column_name [{, column_name}...])
        REFERENCES [[database.]owner.]ref_table
          [(ref_column [{, ref_column}...])]
      | CHECK (search_condition)}
  [{, {next_column | next_constraint}}...])
    [WITH MAX_ROWS_PER_PAGE = x] [ON segment_name]

CREATE TRIGGER [owner.]trigger_name
  ON [owner.]table_name
  FOR {INSERT , UPDATE , DELETE}
  AS SQL_statements
```

Using the IF UPDATE clause:

```
CREATE TRIGGER [owner.]trigger_name
  ON [owner.]table_name
  FOR {INSERT , UPDATE}
  AS
    [IF UPDATE (column_name)
      [{AND | OR} UPDATE (column_name)]...]
      SQL_statements
    [IF UPDATE (column_name)
      [{AND | OR} UPDATE (column_name)]...
      SQL_statements]...

CREATE VIEW [owner.]view_name
  [(column_name [, column_name]...)]
  AS SELECT [DISTINCT] select_statement
  [WITH CHECK OPTION]

DBCC
  {CHECKTABLE({table_name | table_id}[, SKIP_NCINDEX]) |
  CHECKDB [(database_name [, SKIP_NCINDEX])] |
  CHECKALLOC [(database_name [, FIX | NOFIX])] |
```

```
  TABLEALLOC ({table_name | table_id}
  [, {FULL | OPTIMIZED | FAST | NULL}
  [, FIX | NOFIX]]) |
  INDEXALLOC ({table_name | table_id}, index_id
  [, {FULL | OPTIMIZED | FAST | NULL}
    [, FIX | NOFIX]]) |
  CHECKCATALOG [(database_name)] |
  DBREPAIR (database_name, DROPDB) |
  REINDEX ({table_name | table_id}) |
  FIX_TEXT ({table_name | table_id})}

DEALLOCATE CURSOR cursor_name
```

Variable declaration:

```
DECLARE @variable_name datatype
  [, @variable_name datatype]...
```

Variable assignment:

```
SELECT @variable = {expression | select_statement}
  [, @variable = {expression | select_statement} ...]
  [FROM table_list]
  [WHERE search_conditions]
  [GROUP BY group_by_list]
  [HAVING search_conditions]
  [ORDER BY order_by_list]
  [COMPUTE function_list [BY by_list]]

DECLARE cursor_name CURSOR
  FOR select_statement
  [FOR {READ ONLY | UPDATE [OF column_name_list]}]

DELETE [FROM] [[database.]owner.]{view_name | table_name}
  [WHERE search_conditions]

DELETE [[database.]owner.]{table_name | view_name}
  [FROM [[database.]owner.]{view_name | table_name
    [(INDEX index_name [ PREFETCH size ][LRU | MRU])]}
  [, [[database.]owner.]{view_name | table_name
    (INDEX index_name [ PREFETCH size ][LRU | MRU])]} ]...]
  [WHERE search_conditions]

DELETE [FROM] [[database.]owner.]{table_name | view_name}
  WHERE CURRENT OF cursor_name

DISK INIT
  NAME = "device_name" ,
  PHYSNAME = "physicalname" ,
  VDEVNO = virtual_device_number ,
  SIZE = number_of_blocks
```

[, **VSTART** = *virtual_address* ,
CNTRLTYPE = *controller_number*]
[, **CONTIGUOUS**] **(OpenVMS only)**

DISK MIRROR
    NAME = *"device_name"* ,
    MIRROR = *"physicalname"*
    [, **WRITES** = { **SERIAL** | **NOSERIAL** }]
    [, **CONTIGUOUS**] **(OpenVMS only)**

DISK REFIT

DISK REINIT
    NAME = *"device_name"*,
    PHYSNAME = *"physicalname"* ,
    VDEVNO = *virtual_device_number* ,
    SIZE = *number_of_blocks*
    [, **VSTART** = *virtual_address* ,
    CNTRLTYPE = *controller_number*]

DISK REMIRROR
    NAME = *"device_name"*

DISK UNMIRROR
    NAME = *"device_name"*
    [, **SIDE** = { **"PRIMARY"** | **SECONDARY** }]
    [, **MODE** = { **RETAIN** | **REMOVE** }]

DROP DATABASE *database_name* [, *database_name*]...

DROP DEFAULT [*owner.*]*default_name*
    [, [*owner.*]*default_name*]...

DROP INDEX *table_name.index_name*
    [, *table_name.index_name*]...

DROP PROC[EDURE] [*owner.*]*procedure_name*
    [, [*owner.*]*procedure_name*] ...

DROP RULE [*owner.*]*rule_name* [, [*owner.*]*rule_name*]...

DROP TABLE [[*database.*]*owner.*]*table_name*
    [, [[*database.*]*owner.*]*table_name*]...

DROP TRIGGER [*owner.*]*trigger_name*
    [, [*owner.*]*trigger_name*]...

DROP VIEW [*owner.*]*view_name* [, [*owner.*]*view_name*]...

DUMP DATABASE *database_name*
    TO *stripe_device* [**AT** *backup_server_name*]

      [**DENSITY** = *density_value*,
      BLOCKSIZE = *number_bytes*,
      CAPACITY = *number_kilobytes*,
      DUMPVOLUME = *volume_name*,
      FILE = *file_name*]
    [**STRIPE ON** *stripe_device* [**AT** *backup_server_name*]
      [**DENSITY** = *density_value*,
      BLOCKSIZE = *number_bytes*,
      CAPACITY = *number_kilobytes*,
      DUMPVOLUME = *volume_name*,
      FILE = *file_name*]]
    [[**STRIPE ON** *stripe_device* [**AT** *backup_server_name*]
      [**DENSITY** = *density_value*,
      BLOCKSIZE = *number_bytes*,
      CAPACITY = *number_kilobytes*,
      DUMPVOLUME = *volume_name*,
      FILE = *file_name*]]...]
    [**WITH** {
      DENSITY = *density_value*,
      BLOCKSIZE = *number_bytes*,
    CAPACITY = *number_kilobytes*,
    DUMPVOLUME = *volume_name*,
    FILE = *file_name*,
    [**DISMOUNT** | **NODISMOUNT**],
    [nounload | unload],
    RETAINDAYS = *number_days*,
    [**NOINIT** | **INIT**],
    NOTIFY = {**CLIENT** | **OPERATOR_CONSOLE**}}]]

To make a routine log dump:

DUMP TRAN[SACTION] *database_name*
    TO *stripe_device* [**AT** *backup_server_name*]
      [**DENSITY** = *density_value*,
      BLOCKSIZE = *number_bytes*,
      CAPACITY = *number_kilobytes*,
      DUMPVOLUME = *volume_name*,
      FILE = *file_name*]
    [**STRIPE ON** *stripe_device* [**AT** *backup_server_name*]
      [**DENSITY** = *density_value*,
      BLOCKSIZE = *number_bytes*,
      CAPACITY = *number_kilobytes*,
      DUMPVOLUME = *volume_name*,
      FILE = *file_name*]]
    [[**STRIPE ON** *stripe_device* [**AT** *backup_server_name*]
      [**DENSITY** = *density_value*,
      BLOCKSIZE = *number_bytes*,
      CAPACITY = *number_kilobytes*,
      DUMPVOLUME = *volume_name*,
      FILE = *file_name*]]...]
    [**WITH** {

DENSITY = *density_value*,
BLOCKSIZE = *number_bytes*,
CAPACITY = *number_kilobytes*,
DUMPVOLUME = *volume_name*,
FILE = *file_name*,
[**DISMOUNT | NODISMOUNT**],
[**NOUNLOAD | UNLOAD**],
RETAINDAYS = *number_days*,
[**NOINIT | INIT**],
   NOTIFY = {**CLIENT | OPERATOR_CONSOLE**}}]

To truncate the log without making a backup copy:

DUMP TRAN[SACTION] *database_name*
   WITH TRUNCATE_ONLY

To truncate a log that is filled to capacity (use only as a last resort):

DUMP TRAN[SACTION] *database_name*
   WITH NO_LOG

To back up the log after a database device fails:

DUMP TRAN[SACTION] *database_name*
   TO STRIPE_DEVICE [**AT** *backup_server_name*]
      [**DENSITY** = *density_value*,
      BLOCKSIZE = *number_bytes*,
      CAPACITY = *number_kilobytes*,
      DUMPVOLUME = *volume_name*,
      FILE = *file_name*]
   [**STRIPE ON** *stripe_device* [**AT** *backup_server_name*]
      [**DENSITY** = density_value,
      BLOCKSIZE = *number_bytes*,
      CAPACITY = *number_kilobytes*,
      DUMPVOLUME = *volume_name*,
      FILE = *file_name*]]
   [[**STRIPE ON** *stripe_device* [**AT** *backup_server_name*]
      [**DENSITY** = *density_value*,
      BLOCKSIZE = *number_bytes*,
      CAPACITY = *number_kilobytes*,
      DUMPVOLUME = *volume_name*,
      FILE = *file_name*]]...]
   [**WITH** {
      DENSITY = *density_value*,
      BLOCKSIZE = *number_bytes*,
      CAPACITY = *number_kilobytes*,
      DUMPVOLUME = *volume_name*,
      FILE = *file_name*,
      [**DISMOUNT | NODISMOUNT**],
      [**NOUNLOAD | UNLOAD**],

RETAINDAYS = *number_days*,
[**NOINIT | INIT**],
NO_TRUNCATE,
NOTIFY = {**CLIENT | OPERATOR_CONSOLE**}}]

[**EXEC[UTE]**] [*@return_status* =]
   [[[*server*.]*database*.]*owner*.]*procedure_name*[;*number*]
   [[*@parameter_name* =] *value* |
      [*@parameter_name* =] *@variable* [**OUTPUT**]
   [,[*@parameter_name* =] *value* |
      [*@parameter_name* =] *@variable* [**OUTPUT**]...]]
   [**WITH RECOMPILE**]

FETCH *cursor_name* [**INTO** *fetch_target_list*]

label:
   GOTO *label*

GRANT {**ALL** [**PRIVILEGES**]| *permission_list*}
   ON { *table_name* [(*column_list*)]
      | *view_name*[(*column_list*)]
      | *stored_procedure_name*}
   TO {**PUBLIC** | *name_list* | *role_name*}
   [**WITH GRANT OPTION**]

GRANT {**ALL** [**PRIVILEGES**] | *command_list*}
   TO {**PUBLIC** | *name_list* | *role_name*}

IF *logical_expression* statements
   [**ELSE**
[**IF** *logical_expression*] *statement*]

INSERT [**INTO**] [*database*.[*owner*.]]{*table_name* | *view_name*}
   [(*column_list*)]
   {**VALUES** (*expression* [, *expression*]...)
      | *select_statement* }

KILL *spid*

LOAD DATABASE *database_name*
   FROM *stripe_device* [**AT** *backup_server_name*]
      [**DENSITY** = *density_value*,
      BLOCKSIZE = *number_bytes*,
      DUMPVOLUME = *volume_name*,
      FILE = *file_name*]
   [**STRIPE ON** *stripe_device* [**AT** *backup_server_name*]
      [**DENSITY** = *density_value*,
      BLOCKSIZE = *number_bytes*,
      DUMPVOLUME = *volume_name*,
      FILE = *file_name*]
   [[**STRIPE ON** *stripe_device* [**AT** *backup_server_name*]

[**DENSITY** = *density_value*,
BLOCKSIZE = *number_bytes*,
DUMPVOLUME = *volume_name*,
FILE = *file_name*]...]
[**WITH** {
DENSITY = *density_value*,
BLOCKSIZE = *number_bytes*,
DUMPVOLUME = *volume_name*,
FILE = *file_name*,
[**DISMOUNT** | **NODISMOUNT**],
[**NOUNLOAD** | **UNLOAD**],
LISTONLY [= **FULL**],
HEADERONLY,
NOTIFY = {**CLIENT** | **OPERATOR_CONSOLE**}}]

LOAD TRAN[**SACTION**] *database_name*
FROM *stripe_device* [**AT** *backup_server_name*]
[**DENSITY** = *density_value*,
BLOCKSIZE = *number_bytes*,
DUMPVOLUME = *volume_name*,
FILE = *file_name*]
[**STRIPE ON** *stripe_device* [**AT** *backup_server_name*]
[**DENSITY** = *density value*,
BLOCKSIZE = *number_bytes*,
DUMPVOLUME = *volume_name*,
FILE = *file_name*]
[[**STRIPE ON** *stripe_device* [**AT** *backup_server_name*]
[**DENSITY** = *density_value*,
BLOCKSIZE = *number_bytes*,
DUMPVOLUME = *volume_name*,
FILE = *file_name*]]...]
[**WITH** {
DENSITY = *density_value*,
BLOCKSIZE = *number_bytes*,
DUMPVOLUME = *volume_name*,
FILE = *file_name*,
[**DISMOUNT** | **NODISMOUNT**],
[**NOUNLOAD** | **UNLOAD**],
LISTONLY [= **FULL**],
HEADERONLY,
NOTIFY = {**CLIENT** | **OPERATOR_CONSOLE**}}]

ONLINE DATABASE *database_name*

OPEN *cursor_name*

PREPARE TRAN[**SACTION**]

PRINT
{*format_string* | *@local_variable* | *@@global_variable*} [, *arg_list*]

RAISERROR *error_number*
[{*format_string* | *@local_variable*}] [, *arg_list*]
[**WITH ERRORDATA** *restricted_select_list*]

READTEXT [[*database.*]*owner.*]*table_name.column_name*
text_pointer offset size [**HOLDLOCK**]
[**USING** {**BYTES** | **CHARS** | **CHARACTERS**}]
[**AT ISOLATION** {**READ UNCOMMITTED** | **READ COMMITTED**
| **SERIALIZABLE**}]

RETURN [*integer_expression*]

REVOKE [**GRANT OPTION FOR**]
{**ALL** [**PRIVILEGES**] | *permission_list*}
ON { *table_name* [(*column_list*)]
| *view_name* [(*column_list*)]
| *stored_procedure_name*}
FROM {**PUBLIC** | *name_list* | *role_name*}
[**CASCADE**]

REVOKE {**ALL** [**PRIVILEGES**] | *command_list*}
FROM {**PUBLIC** | *name_list* | *role_name*}

ROLLBACK {**TRAN**[**SACTION**] | **WORK**}
[*transaction_name* | *savepoint_name*]

ROLLBACK TRIGGER
[**WITH** *raiserror_statement*]

SAVE TRAN[**SACTION**] *savepoint_name*

SELECT [**ALL** | **DISTINCT**] *select_list*
[**INTO** [[*database.*]*owner.*]*table_name*]
[**FROM** [[*database.*]*owner.*]{*view_name* | *table_name*
[(**INDEX** *index_name* [**PREFETCH** *size*][**LRU** | **MRU**])]}
[**HOLDLOCK** | **NOHOLDLOCK**] [**SHARED**]
[,[[*database.*]*owner.*]{*view_name* | *table_name*
[(**INDEX** *index_name* [**PREFETCH** *size*][**LRU** | **MRU**])]}
[**HOLDLOCK** | **NOHOLDLOCK**] [**SHARED**]]...]
[**WHERE** *search_conditions*]
[**GROUP BY** [**ALL**] *aggregate_free_expression*
[, *aggregate_free_expression*]...]
[**HAVING** *search_conditions*]
[**ORDER BY**
{[[[*database.*]*owner.*]{*table_name.* | *view_name.*}]
column_name | *select_list_number* | *expression*}[**ASC** | **DESC**]
[,{[[[*database.*]*owner.*]{*table_name.* | *view_name.*}]
column_name | *select_list_number* | *expression*} [**ASC** | **DESC**]]...]
[**COMPUTE** *row_aggregate*(*column_name*)
[, *row_aggregate*(*column_name*)]...
[**BY** *column_name* [, *column_name*]...]]

```
[FOR {READ ONLY | UPDATE [OF column_name_list]}]
[AT ISOLATION {READ UNCOMMITTED | READ
    COMMITTED | SERIALIZABLE}]
[FOR BROWSE]

SET ANSINULL {ON | OFF}

SET ANSI_PERMISSIONS {ON | OFF}

SET ARITHABORT [ARITH_OVERFLOW |
    NUMERIC_TRUNCATION]
    {ON | OFF}

SET ARITHIGNORE [ARITH_OVERFLOW] {ON | OFF}

SET {CHAINED, CLOSE ON ENDTRAN, NOCOUNT, NOEXEC,
    PARSEONLY, PROCID, SELF_RECURSION, SHOWPLAN}
    {ON | OFF}

SET CHAR_CONVERT {OFF | ON [WITH {ERROR | NO_ERROR}] |
    CHARSET [WITH {ERROR | NO_ERROR}]}

SET CURSOR ROWS number FOR cursor_name

SET {DATEFIRST number, DATEFORMAT format,
    LANGUAGE language}

SET FIPSFLAGGER {ON | OFF}

SET FLUSHMESSAGE {ON | OFF}

SET IDENTITY_INSERT [database.[owner.]]table_name
    {ON | OFF}

SET OFFSETS {SELECT, FROM, ORDER, COMPUTE, TABLE,
    PROCEDURE, STATEMENT, PARAM, EXECUTE} {ON | OFF}

SET PREFETCH [ON | OFF]

SET QUOTED_IDENTIFIER {ON | OFF}

SET ROLE {"SA_ROLE" | "SSO_ROLE" | "OPER_ROLE"}
    {ON | OFF}

SET {ROWCOUNT number, TEXTSIZE number}

SET STATISTICS {IO, SUBQUERYCACHE, TIME} {ON | OFF}

SET STRING_RTRUNCATION {ON | OFF}

SET TABLE COUNT number
```

```
SET TEXTSIZE {number}

SET TRANSACTION ISOLATION LEVEL {0 | 1 | 3}

SETUSER ["user_name"]

SHUTDOWN [srvname] [WITH {WAIT | NOWAIT}]

TRUNCATE TABLE [[database.]owner.]table_name

    SELECT select_list [INTO clause]
        [FROM clause] [WHERE clause]
        [GROUP BY clause] [HAVING clause]
[UNION [ALL]
    SELECT select_list
    [FROM clause] [WHERE clause]
        [GROUP BY clause] [HAVING clause]]...
    [ORDER BY clause]
    [COMPUTE clause]

UPDATE [[database.]owner.]{table_name | view_name}
    SET [[[database.]owner.]{table_name. | view_name.}]
        column_name1 =
            expression1 | NULL | (select_statement)}
        [, column_name2 =
            {expression2 | NULL | (select_statement)}]...
    [FROM [[database.]owner.]{view_name | table_name
        [(INDEX index_name [ PREFETCH size ][LRU | MRU])]}
    [,[[database.]owner.]{view_name | table_name
        [(INDEX index_name [ PREFETCH size ][LRU | MRU])]}]]...]
    [WHERE search_conditions]

UPDATE [[database.]owner.]{table_name | view_name}
    SET [[[database.]owner.]{table_name. | view_name.}]
        column_name1 =
            {expression1 | NULL | (select_statement)}
        [, column_name2 =
            {expression2 | NULL | (select_statement)}]...
    WHERE CURRENT OF cursor_name

UPDATE STATISTICS table_name [index_name]

USE database_name

WAITFOR { DELAY time | TIME time | ERROREXIT
    | PROCESSEXIT | MIRROREXIT }

WHERE [NOT] expression comparison_operator expression

WHERE [NOT] expression [NOT] LIKE "match_string"
    [ESCAPE "escape_character"]
```

WHERE [NOT] *expression* **IS** [NOT] **NULL**

WHERE [NOT] **EXPRESSION** [NOT] **BETWEEN** *expression*

AND *expression*

WHERE [NOT] *expression* [NOT] **IN** ({*value_list* | *subquery*})

WHERE [NOT] *exists* (*subquery*)

WHERE [NOT] *expression comparison_operator* {**ANY** | **ALL**} (*subquery*)

WHERE [NOT] *column_name join_operator column_name*

WHERE [NOT] *boolean_expression*

WHERE [NOT] *expression* {**AND** | **OR**} [NOT] *expression*

WHILE *logical_expression*
   statement

WRITETEXT [[*database.*]*owner.*]*table_name.column_name*
   text_pointer [**WITH LOG**] *data*

Transact-SQL Functions

Aggregate functions

AVG([**ALL** | **DISTINCT**] *expression*)
COUNT(*)
count([**all** | **distinct**] *expression*)
max(*expression*)
min(*expression*)
sum([**all** | **distinct**] *expression*)

Datatype conversion functions

convert(*datatype* [(*length*) | (*precision*[, *scale*])], *expression*[, *style*])
hextoint(*hexadecimal_string*)
inttohex(*integer_expression*)

Date functions

dateadd(*datepart, numeric_expression, date*)
datediff(*datepart, date1, date2*)
datename(*datepart, date*)
datepart(*datepart, date*)
getdate()

Mathematical functions

abs(*numeric*)
acos(*approx_numeric*)
asin(*approx_numeric*)
atan(*approx_numeric*)
atn2(*approx_numeric1, approx_numeric2*)
ceiling(*numeric*)
cos(*approx_numeric*)

cot(*approx_numeric*)
degrees(*numeric*)
exp(*approx_numeric*)
floor(*numeric*)
log(*approx_numeric*)
log10(*approx_numeric*)
pi()
power(*numeric, power*)
radians(*numeric*)
rand([*integer*])
round(*numeric, integer*)
sign(*numeric*)
sin(*approx_numeric*)
sqrt(*approx_numeric*)
tan(*approx_numeric*)

String functions

ascii(*char_expr*)
char(*integer_expr*)
charindex(*expression1, expression2*)
char_length(*char_expr*)
difference(*char_expr1, char_expr2*)
lower(*char_expr*)
ltrim(*char_expr*)
patindex ("*%pattern%*", *char_expr* [, **using** [**bytes** | **chars** | **characters**]])
replicate(*char_expr, integer_expr*)
reverse(*char_expr*)
right(*char_expr, integer_expr*)
rtrim(*char_expr*)
soundex(*char_expr*)
space(*integer_expr*)
str(*approx_numeric* [, *length* [, *decimal*]])

stuff(*char_expr1, start, length, char_expr2*)

substring(*expression, start, length*)

upper(*char_expr*)

System functions

col_name(*object_id, column_id* [*, database_id*])

col_length(*object_name, column_name*)

curunreservedpgs(*dbid, lstart, unreservedpgs*)

data_pgs(*object_id,* {*doampg | ioampg*})

datalength(*expression*)

db_id([*database_name*])

db_name([*database_id*])

host_id()

host_name()

index_col(*object_name, index_id, key_#* [*, user_id*])

isnull(*expression1, expression2*)

lct_admin({{ "lastchance" | "logfull" | "unsuspend" *, database_id*} | "reserve", *log_pages*})

object_id(*object_name*)

object_name(*object_id*[*, database_id*])

proc_role("sa_role" | "sso_role" | "oper_role")

reserved_pgs(*object_id,* {*doampg | ioampg*})

rowcnt(*doampg*)

show_role()

suser_id([*server_user_name*])

suser_name([*server_user_id*])

tsequal(*timestamp, timestamp2*)

used_pgs(*object_id, doampg, ioampg*)

user

user_id([*user_name*])

user_name([*user_id*])

valid_name(*character_expression*)

valid_user(*server_user_id*)

Text and image functions

patindex("*%pattern%*", *char_expr*[, using {bytes | chars | characters}])

textptr(*text_columnname*)

textvalid("*table_name.col_name*", *textpointer*)

System Procedures

sp_addalias *loginame, name_in_db*

sp_addauditrecord [*text*] [*, db_name*] [*, obj_name*] [*, owner_name*] [*, dbid*] [*, objid*]

sp_addgroup *grpname*

sp_addlanguage *language, alias, months, shortmons, days, datefmt, datefirst*

sp_addlogin *loginame, passwd* [*, defdb* [*, deflanguage* [*, fullname*]]]

sp_addmessage *message_num, message_text* [*, language*]

sp_addremotelogin *remoteserver* [*, loginame* [*, remotename*]]

sp_addsegment *segname, dbname, devname*

sp_addserver *lname* [, {local | NULL} [*, pname*]]

sp_addthreshold *dbname, segname, free_space, proc_name*

sp_addtype *typename, phystype* [(*length*) | (*precision* [*, scale*])] [, "identity" | *nulltype*]

sp_adddumpdevice {"tape" | "disk"}, *logicalname, physicalname* [*, tapesize*]

sp_adduser *loginame* [*, name_in_db* [*, grpname*]]

sp_auditdatabase [*dbname* [, "ok | fail | both | off" [, {"d u g r t o"}]]]

To audit access to tables and views:

sp_auditlogin [*login_name* [, "table" | "view" [, "ok" | "fail" | "both" | "off"]]]

To audit the text of a user's command batches:

sp_auditlogin [*login_name* [, "cmdtext" [, "on" | "off"]]]

To audit existing tables and views:

sp_auditobject *objname, dbname* [, {"ok" | "fail" | "both" | "off"} [, "{d i s u}"]]

To audit newly created tables and views:

sp_auditobject {"default table" | "default view"}, *dbname* [, {"ok" | "fail" | "both" | "off"} [, "{d i s u}"]]

sp_auditoption [{"all" | "enable auditing" | "logouts" | "server boots" | "adhoc records"} [, "on" | "off"]]

sp_auditoption {"logins" | "rpc connections" | "roles"} [, {"ok" | "fail" | "both" | "off"}]

sp_auditoption "errors" [, {"nonfatal" | "fatal" | "both"}]

sp_auditoption "{sa | sso | oper | navigator | replication} commands" [, {"ok" | "fail" | "both" | "off"}]

To establish auditing for existing stored procedures and triggers:

sp_auditsproc [*sproc_name* | "all", *dbname* [, {"ok" | "fail" | "both" | "off"}]]

To establish auditing for future stored procedures and triggers:

sp_auditsproc "default", *dbname* [, {"ok" | "fail" | "both" | "off"}]

sp_bindcache cachename, *dbname* [, [*ownername.*]*tablename*
    [, *indexname* | "text only"]]

sp_bindefault *defname, objname* [, futureonly]

sp_bindmsg *constrname, msgid*

sp_bindrule *rulename, objname* [, futureonly]

sp_cacheconfig [*cachename* [,"*cache_size*[P | K | M | G]"] [, logonly |
    mixed]]

sp_cachestrategy *dbname* [, *ownername.*]*tablename* [, *indexname* | "text
    only" | "table only" [, { prefetch | mru }, {"on" | "off"}]]

sp_changedbowner *loginame* [, true]

sp_changegroup *grpname, username*

sp_checknames

sp_checkreswords [*user_name_param*]

sp_chgattribute *objname, optname, optvalue*

sp_clearstats [*loginame*]

sp_commonkey *tabaname, tabbname, col1a, col1b* [, *col2a, col2b, ...,
    col8a, col8b*]

sp_configure [*configname* [*configvalue*] | *group_name* |
    non_unique_parameter_fragment]

sp_configure "configuration file", 0, {"write" | "read" | "verify" |
    "restore"} "*file_name*"

sp_cursorinfo [{*cursor_level* | NULL}] [, *cursor_name*]

sp_dboption [*dbname, optname,* {true | false}]

sp_dbremap *dbname*

sp_depends *objname*

sp_diskdefault *logicalname,* {defaulton | defaultoff}

sp_displaylevel [*loginame* [, *level*]]

sp_displaylogin [*loginame*]

sp_dropalias *loginame*

sp_dropdevice *logicalname*

sp_dropglockpromote {"database" | "table"}, *objname*

sp_dropgroup *grpname*

sp_dropkey *keytype, tabname* [, *deptabname*]

sp_droplanguage *language* [, dropmessages]

sp_droplogin *loginame*

sp_dropmessage *message_num* [, *language*]

sp_dropremotelogin *remoteserver* [, *loginame* [, *remotename*]]

sp_dropsegment *segname, dbname* [, *device*]

sp_dropserver *server* [, droplogins]

sp_dropthreshold *dbname, segname, free_space*

sp_droptype *typename*

sp_dropuser *name_in_db*

sp_estspace *table_name, no_of_rows* [, *fill_factor* [, *cols_to_max* [,
    textbin_len [, *iosec*]]]]

sp_extendsegment *segname, dbname, devname*

sp_foreignkey *tabname, pktabname, col1* [, *col2*] ... [, *col8*]

sp_getmessage *message_num,* result output [, *language*]

sp_grantlogin {*login_name* | *group_name*} ["*role_list*" | default]

sp_help [*objname*]

sp_helppartition *table_name*

sp_helpcache {*cache_name* | "*cache_size*[P | K | M | G]"}

sp_helpconstraint *objname* [, detail]

sp_helpdb [*dbname*]

sp_helpdevice [*devname*]

sp_helpgroup [*grpname*]

sp_helpindex *objname*

sp_helpjoins *lefttab, righttab*

sp_helpkey [*tabname*]

sp_helplanguage [*language*]

sp_helplog

sp_helpremotelogin [*remoteserver* [, *remotename*]]

sp_helpprotect [*name* [, *username* [, "grant"]]]

sp_helpsegment [*segname*]

sp_helpserver [*server*]

sp_helpsort

sp_helptext *objname*

sp_helpthreshold [*segname*]

sp_helpuser [*name_in_db*]

sp_indsuspect [*tab_name*]

sp_lock [*spid1* [, *spid2*]]

sp_locklogin [*loginame,* "{lock | unlock}"]

sp_logdevice *dbname, devname*

sp_loginconfig ["*parameter_name*"]

sp_logininfo ["*login_name*" | "*group_name*"]

sp_logiosize ["default" | "*size*" | "all"]

sp_modifylogin *account, column, value*

sp_modifythreshold *dbname, segname, free_space*
    [, *new_proc_name*] [, *new_free_space*] [, *new_segname*]

sp_monitor

sp_password *caller_passwd, new_passwd* [, *loginame*]

sp_placeobject *segname, objname*

sp_poolconfig *cache_name* [, "*mem_size*[P | K | M | G]", "*config_poolK*"
    [, "*affected_poolK*"]]

sp_poolconfig *cache_name,* "*io_size*", "wash=size[P | K | M | G]"

sp_primarykey *tabname, col1* [, *col2, col3, ..., col8*]

sp_procqmode [*object_name* [, detail]]

sp_procxmode [*procname* [, *tranmode*]]

sp_recompile *objname*

sp_remap *objname*

sp_remoteoption [*remoteserver, loginame, remotename, optname, optvalue*]

sp_rename *objname, newname*

sp_renamedb *dbname, newname*

sp_reportstats [*loginame*]

sp_revokelogin {*login_name* | *group_name*}

sp_role {"grant" | "revoke"}, {sa_role | sso_role | oper_role}, *loginame*}

sp_serveroption [*server, optname,* {true | false}]

sp_setlangalias *language, alias*

sp_setpglockpromote {"database" | "table"}, *objname, new_lwm,
    new_hwm, new_pct*

sp_setpglockpromote server, NULL, *new_lwm, new_hwm, new_pct*

sp_spaceused [*objname* [, 1]]

sp_syntax *word* [, *mod*][, *language*]

sp_thresholdaction @dbname, @segment_name, @space_left, @status

sp_unbindcache dbname [,[owner.]tablename
    [, indexname | "text only" | "table only"]]

sp_unbindcache_all cache_name

sp_unbindefault objname [, futureonly]

sp_unbindmsg constrname

sp_unbindrule objname [, futureonly]

sp_volchanged session_id, devname, action [, fname [, vname]]

sp_who [loginame | "spid"]

Catalog Stored Procedures

sp_column_privileges table_name [, table_owner [, table_qualifier
    [, column_name]]]

sp_columns table_name [, table_owner] [, table_qualifier]
    [, column_name]

sp_databases

sp_datatype_info [data_type]

sp_fkeys pktable_name [, pktable_owner]
    [, pktable_qualifier] [, fktable_name]
    [, fktable_owner] [, fktable_qualifier]

sp_pkeys table_name [, table_owner] [, table_qualifier]

sp_server_info [attribute_id]

sp_special_columns table_name [, table_owner] [, table_qualifier]
    [, col_type]

sp_sproc_columns procedure_name [, procedure_owner]
    [, procedure_qualifier] [, column_name]

sp_statistics table_name [, table_owner] [, table_qualifier]
    [, index_name] [, is_unique]

sp_stored_procedures [sp_name] [, sp_owner] [, sp_qualifier]

sp_table_privileges table_name [, table_owner [, table_qualifier]]

sp_tables [table_name] [, table_owner] [, table_qualifier][, table_type]

Appendix D

SyBooks
Installation Guide

At the end of this book, you will find a copy of the SyBooks CD-ROM. This CD contains complete sets of the Sybase documentation for SQL Server 11. These collections are fully text searchable. The CD contains five separate collections:

- Sybase SQL Server manuals

- Replication Server manuals

- SQL Server Monitor and SQL Server Manager manuals

- Open Client/Server manuals

- Open Client/Server supplements

You can find all of the manuals referenced throughout *Upgrading and Migrating to Sybase SQL Server 11* in the first collection of the CD-ROM (Sybase SQL Server manuals).

You can view SyBooks on most Microsoft Windows systems (Windows 3.1, Windows NT, and Windows 95) and most popular UNIX systems.

To install SyBooks on a Microsoft Windows-based system, simply go to the \pc\install directory on the CD, select the setup.exe file, and follow the onscreen instructions. To run SyBooks, click on the SyBooks icon.

To install SyBooks on a UNIX system, go to the unix subdirectory on the CD and execute the install.me program. Before you can run SyBooks, you must create a /sybooks/annot directory in your home directory and set two environmental variables. (Note that all users must complete these steps.) The SYBROOT variable points to the SyBooks installation directory, and the EBTRC variable points to the *.ebtrc* configuration file. The *.ebtrc* file is automatically created when you install SyBooks; you find this file in a subdirectory of the SyBooks installation directory. This subdirectory is named after your UNIX platform. To run SyBooks, simply type *sybooks*.

For more information about SyBooks, visit Sybase's web site:

http://www.sybase.com/Products/Sybooks/

Index